Trevor Royle is a highly respected writer on the history of war and empire. His books include *Winds of Change: The End of Empire in Africa, Crimea: The Great Crimean War 1854–1856* and *Civil War: The Wars of the Three Kingdoms.*

THE WARS
OF THE ROSES

England's First Civil War

TREVOR ROYLE

All best wishes,

[signature]

ABACUS

ABACUS

First published in Great Britain in 2009 by Little, Brown
This paperback edition published in 2010 by Abacus

A CIP catalogue record for this book
is available from the British Library.

ISBN 978-0-349-11790-4

Typeset in Garamond by M Rules
Printed and bound in Great Britain
Clays Ltd, St Ives plc

Papers used by Abacus are natural, renewable and
recyclable products sourced from well-managed forests and certified
in accordance with the rules of the Forest Stewardship Council.

Mixed Sources
Product group from well-managed
forests and other controlled sources
www.fsc.org   Cert no. SGS-COC-004081
© 1996 Forest Stewardship Council

Abacus
An imprint of
Little, Brown Book Group
100 Victoria Embankment
London EC4Y 0DY

An Hachette UK Company
www.hachette.co.uk

www.littlebrown.co.uk

Contents

Preface

For the people of the British Isles the dynastic struggle known as the Wars of the Roses is the great defining moment of the late Middle Ages. In common with all civil wars the conflict was a bad business which cast a long shadow over the reigns of six English kings, from Richard II to Richard III, pitting noble families against one another as they struggled to gain the upper hand in the quest for power. For nine decades, from 1399 to 1485, England was in a state of turmoil as successive kings grappled to hold on to power and to keep 'over-mighty' aristocrats in check. Compared with contemporaneous wars in Europe and later conflicts, such as the Wars of the Three Kingdoms two centuries later, the fighting was sporadic and many of the early battles were little more than skirmishes which had little or no wide-spread effect but only impinged on the local civilian population. Apart from the sacking of Stamford in 1461 towns were not besieged and there was little of the human misery that usually attends civil war. There was not much material destruction and almost no disruption of trade and agriculture. Locust-like armies were not in the field for months on end, mainly because neither side could afford the expense, and apart from isolated incidents there was no large-scale collapse of law and order.

That absence of lengthy campaigns and the small size of the subsequent butcher's bill gives the Wars of the Roses a comforting ring but it is not the whole story. While the actual warfare was little more than a series of violent outbursts which interrupted periods of uneasy peace, thousands of ordinary people fell prey to the violence and lawlessness as the nobility perverted justice for their own ends. Battlefield violence and rough justice were also commonplace and stoked up the desire for revenge, not just among the rival factions but even among friends and allies. And, as happens in any civil conflict, the claims of the rival sides were matched by equally intense struggles between their supporters as private feuds escalated into overt violence. More than any other factor the unscrupulous ambition and ruthlessness of the nobility contributed to the brutality of the conflict. For the first time, too, the size and loyalty of the armed forces available to the Crown became critical factors in English politics. In that sense the Wars of the Roses are Janus-like. They look back to the world of the Plantagenets, in which kings and princes repeatedly had to demonstrate resilience and strength to hold on to power, otherwise they could find themselves threatened by powerful magnates who believed that they had superior claims to the throne. At the same time the wars looked forward to a more settled dynastic solution which paved the way for the eventual foundation of the union of the British kingdoms. Ireland, Scotland and Wales also formed part of that equation and events in those countries helped to decide the final outcome.

In writing this book I have made full use of evidence supplied by contemporary or near-contemporary chroniclers. Many of the latter had access to eyewitnesses of the action and, while the subsequent accounts are not always accurate or are biased to one side or the other, they still present vivid and diverse tellings of the events as recorded by the writer in question, be he a cloistered monastic chronicler such as Thomas Walsingham or a visiting Italian humanist such as Dominic Mancini. Their works are listed in the bibliography, together with the principal and most recent studies of the period which have provided the main sustenance during the writing of this book. All quotations from the plays of William Shakespeare have been taken from the Royal Shakespeare Company edition.

One of the vexed questions arising from the conflict was the exact location of the decisive Battle of Bosworth, which brought the Wars of the Roses to a conclusion in August 1485. For years arguments raged about where this so-called 'wandering battle' was actually fought, and the accepted site of Ambion Hill in Leicestershire never gained universal recognition. Even when a modern visitors' centre was constructed doubts remained and it was not until February 2010 that the correct position was finally revealed as being two miles to the south-west, in modern agricultural land. Carried out by the Battlefield

Trust for Leicestershire County Council the research was based on new topographical and archaeological information and a re-reading of contemporary sources and is considered to be the last word on the subject. Its findings have been incorporated in Chapter Twenty-one of this edition.

As ever I am grateful to the National Archives in Kew and the National Library of Scotland in Edinburgh. In both places research is aided, abetted and made more pleasurable by the kindness and helpful ministrations of their thoroughly professional staffs. At Little, Brown, Stephen Guise acted as mentor and saw the book into being with his customary care and skill, but the idea was given to me by Alan Samson, who wanted me to travel further back in time after writing revisionist histories of the Crimean War and the Wars of the Three Kingdoms. Alan's successor, Tim Whiting, helped me greatly in finding a sense of direction. They all have my thanks.

During the writing of the book my youngest son, Patrick, collapsed and died in Oxford after taking part in a charity bicycle run from London on an achingly hot July afternoon. To make matters worse, at the coroner's inquest it emerged that his death could have been avoided had the ambulance service reacted responsibly and with due care and diligence. As a military historian I have written about the deaths of many young people – usually in a clinical and detached way – and this book is littered with examples. The loss of Patrick changed many of my perceptions by underlining just how arbitrary, unfair and unnecessary are so many such deaths, be they intentional or accidental. As with so many things since his unseasonable death in the summer of 2006, this is for Patrick.

Trevor Royle
Edinburgh/Angus
Spring 2010

England during the Wars of the Roses

Introduction: 'This Other Eden, Demi-Paradise'

Imagine a green and heavily wooded land, an island clothed largely by forests and unimproved wastes which has scarcely changed for centuries, and the England of the late Middle Ages starts to come into focus. In some places the forests are orderly and relatively well cultivated: royal preserves where the habitat and the wildlife enjoy a measure of protection and care for the pleasures of the chase. Elsewhere the scrubland and marshland seem to suggest that the countryside has not been touched by man's hand at all. Interspersed are the open fields of sturdy agrarian communities where strips of ridge and furrow mark an age-old system of husbandry, meadowland for the beasts and arable land for the crops. Everywhere there are animals: wild boar and deer, the occasional surviving wolf and semi-wild cattle that roam free in the unenclosed wastes. Sheep abound because they are indispensable to the country's economy. Up to ten million of them produce the wool on which England's wealth is constructed during the span of the fifteenth century, the period from the reign of Richard II to that of Richard III. Wool supplies the looms of the Low Countries with the raw material for making cloth and, although the trade slumps into relative decline by mid-century, English wool is still reckoned to be the best in Europe, as a traditional rhyme has it:

> All nations affirm up to the full
> In all the world there is no better wool.

Exported through Calais, where the English merchant staplers maintain a monopoly, wool is England's main means of raising revenues through the duty paid on each standard sack weighing 364 pounds. As symbol of that wealth the Chancellor sits on a woolsack.

Great flocks are found everywhere, from the dales of the north to the downs and rolling hills of the south and west and the fenland of East Anglia. The wool is graded by quality, the finest clippings coming from Shropshire and the Cotswolds, followed by Lincolnshire and Gloucestershire, Wiltshire and Yorkshire, with Sussex and Suffolk not far behind.

Hundreds of small towns and villages dot the English landscape and there is a road system of sorts – the ancient ridgeways, indifferent cart tracks and the remains of paved Roman road – which allows people to travel, albeit uncomfortably, and with difficulty during the wet seasons of spring, summer and autumn. Most of the towns are middling affairs with populations within their walls that range from a couple of hundred to one or two thousand, but there are also some sizeable cities. London, the capital, is home to around 100,000 people and is very much the focus and main driving force of the country's economy, York has thirteen thousand inhabitants and Norwich and Coventry some ten thousand apiece.

What the people did with their lives was another matter. In the countryside they were largely self-sufficient, growing and producing the food and materials they needed to sustain them in their daily lives and selling the surplus in the nearest market town. In the towns there were trades to be pursued, often under the direction of crafts guilds with their well-ordered harmony of price and wage control but more generally bowing to the conditions of the free market. Already serfdom was on the decline and the labourer was able to put a price on his or her employment. Most people, perhaps as many as nine in ten, worked on the land, where feudal society had all but disappeared largely as a result of the demographic changes caused by the Black Death of the previous century, the great plague which killed off almost half of the population in 1348–9. (Exact figures are difficult to compute but most demographers believe that England's population of five to six million in 1347 had plummeted to three million two years later. Thereafter the figure remained fairly static.)

With the gradual disappearance of serfdom or villeinage (the holding of small-holdings by unfree tenants in return for rent and labour services) the people on the land now enjoyed greater freedom and mobility and some used the benefits to better themselves, becoming in time self-made yeoman farmers paying rents for the right to farm the lord's demesne or estate. In his account of the governance of the country written in 1460 the Chief Justice, Sir John Fortescue, claimed that 'the common people of his land are the best fed and the best clad of any nation'. By the time he was writing things were beginning to get even better: serfdom was becoming a thing of the past and men were being paid for their services, producing a more tolerable existence and better living conditions. At the start of the fifteenth century the peasants' diet was poor and monotonous, based largely on root vegetables, but fifty years later meat and fish were beginning to appear more regularly. Wheat was replacing barley and rye as the main flour for bread and the poet William Langland claimed that the main sustenance of the poor was bread, cheese and curds. Ale, too, was drunk, as much for nutrition as for its alcohol content. Wine from Gascony and Anjou was the preserve of the wealthy.

Clothes were often coarse and verminous but here, too, there were developments which reflected the general sense of greater well-being. Men started wearing tighter-fitting tunics with leggings while women favoured brighter colours and started imitating their social superiors by adorning their dress with buckles and brooches. However, for all the benefits their working day was still long and back-breaking and most peasants lived in a small, basic timber-framed home with wattle-and-daub infills which was little more than a squalid hovel. Each peasant house was surrounded by a small yard known as a toft or croft where vegetables could be grown. Living as people did on the verge of mere subsistence, death was a familiar companion, infant mortality was an accepted fact and life expectancy was fifty for men and thirty for women. Small wonder that there was a preoccupation with the afterlife, the joys of heaven for the virtuous and the everlasting torment of hell for the sinners. A tombstone inscription dating from the fifteenth century (Trinity College, Cambridge MS 366) says it all:

> All ye that passe by thys holy place,
> Both spirituall & temporall of euery degre,
> Remembyr your-selfe well during tyme & space:
> I was as ye are nowe; and as I, ye shalbe.

God's workings were manifest everywhere, not least in the person of the King. Not only was he anointed in God's name but as monarch he enjoyed huge temporal power and was expected to wield it wisely in the best interests of his people. The English royal family was named Plantagenet and its members descended from Henry II, the eldest son of Geoffrey le Bel or Plantagenet, Count of Anjou, and his wife, Matilda, known as empress as a result of her earlier marriage to the Holy Roman Emperor, Henry V. In 1151 Henry Plantagenet had come to the fore when, on the death of his father, he inherited the lands of Anjou and Normandy. In the following year he added to his territorial holdings by marrying Eleanor of Aquitaine, the widow of King Louis VII of France and a woman whose inheritance gave her great wealth and temporal power. The match made the nineteen-year-old Prince Henry the richest ruler in Europe and strengthened his claims to the English throne through his mother, whose cousin was King Stephen. In 1153 Stephen acknowledged Henry as his heir and the young man succeeded him a year later to cement the so-called Angevin Empire, the dominions of England, Anjou, Normandy and Aquitaine, an empire which stretched from the Pennines to the Pyrenees.

In England the name Plantagenet came into use in the fifteenth century and it was associated with the House of York, the successors of Edmund of Langley, the fourth son of King Edward III, who was himself a lineal descendant of Henry II. The name's derivation is not certain, although it is generally believed to have come from the sprig of broom, *Planta genista*, traditionally worn by Geoffrey. Those who bore the name believed that they had a God-given entitlement to rule, a 'divine right', as it was known, that allowed the King to do as he pleased within the constraints of the demands of morality and justice. To his people he was the supreme authority on earth; in time of peace he was responsible for the well-being of the realm and his subjects and in time of war he was the defender and champion of the national spirit. It was an exacting role which demanded the ability to govern effectively and the capacity to retain the throne without attracting rival claims. The King had to command loyalty and respect and he had to be able to keep his subjects under firm control to prevent his authority being challenged by any pretender or usurper.

To help him rule the King had a royal council made up of powerful men from the Church and nobility, many of them magnates who owned most of the country's land and wealth. The term 'magnate' refers primarily to the leading members of the nobility and lesser gentry such as barons and knights with land and influence. At their most powerful magnates were very influential indeed and this power tended to turn them into 'over-mighty' subjects capable of challenging the accepted order.

Beneath the King came the dukes, most of them old Anglo-Norman aristocracy or members of the royal family, wealthy landowners who guarded their authority jealously and were cautious about entering into marriage alliances unless it was to their advantage. Titles were generally associated with specific families – the Percys of Northumberland or the Courtenays of Devon, for example – but they could also go into abeyance or be transferred to other families as a result of the holder dying intestate or being attainted for treason. As dominant personages in their own right, backed by the income from their estates and also from dabbling in trade, the leading magnates retained large private armies, or 'affinities', who were honour-bound to serve their master in the field. These resources meant that the support of the magnate class was of key importance for successive English monarchs throughout the period.

Underpinning the magnates' military contribution to the kingdom's stability was the notion of knighthood. By the fourteenth century this had lost its earlier mystical connections to the Arthurian legends but the concept was still central to the King's ability to raise forces for his own defence and for the good of the country. All knights were landowners but not all landowners were knights. A knight was obliged to arm and equip himself with horse, armour, sword and lance and to do the same for his esquire or closest personal retainer. He also had to raise and equip his retinue, men-at-arms who owed him their allegiance. It was an expensive business, hence the need to own land and derive income from it, but some knights were 'household knights' who gave their services in return for living as a tenant in the household of the King or a great magnate. Because there was no standing army the King had to rely on these men to provide the backbone of his armed forces in time of war or national emergency. Through taxation granted by Parliament great armies could be mobilised for service in the national interest either for the defence of the realm or for service overseas, usually in France. Commissions of array were sent to sheriffs and mayors of towns and this was done by levy, and the raised men had to arm and equip themselves to exacting standards. Training was generally rudimentary except for that of the archers, who provided the English with their main strike force and were professional warriors. These bowmen, drawn from both urban and rural areas, took great pride in their competence and rate of fire, a result of constant practice.

The King also had the services of a representative parliament to raise taxes and pass legislation. Although this was not as powerful as the royal council it had come a long way from its origins in the thirteenth century as an assembly of great men who were summoned by the King to deal with a wide variety of administrative and judicial functions concerning the good running of the country. It was also bicameral, these two chambers being the Lords, or Upper House, which consisted of great landowners, both lay and ecclesiastical; and the Commons, or Lower House, made up of representatives from the boroughs and shires of England. Members of the Commons were summoned by the King to meetings which generally took place twice a year, in the spring and the autumn, or when emergency demanded. They came from the knightly, educated classes and their collective power and authority were not inconsiderable. The main role of the Commons was the provision of consent for taxation by the Crown, but it also dealt with petitions concerning the 'common weal' and in time it developed a legislative role, becoming an important focus for debate about national issues.

The Lords, governed by the hereditary principle, began to play a moderating role in the affairs of the kingdom. There were two great offices of state to direct the country's administrative and financial systems – the Chancery, under the direction of the Chancellor, and the Exchequer, under the Treasurer. Beneath these were the officers of the royal household and a lesser network of judges, sheriffs and customs officers who made sure that the machinery of government was well oiled. The King remained at the apex of everything, his personal direction of his realm being paramount.

Then there was the English Church, *Ecclesia Anglicana*, which was both part of the Catholic Church and integral to the life of the nation at every level. Religious faith was an accepted part of life and spiritual obedience was as important as allegiance to the King. Practically every aspect of life was determined by the Church and the social cohesion of the nation depended on a belief that God ordered society for the good of the people. At its summit was God, below him the King and then, in descending order, the temporal and spiritual princes, the nobility, the lesser nobility such as knights and gentry, the growing professional classes, the merchants and yeomen, and, at the base, the great mass of humanity. This was the accepted order and any disruption of it was both heinous and unnatural. To keep it in good repair, a system of checks and balances was required: while the King's supreme authority gave him superiority over the nobility, in practice he depended on their support and at the same time he had to be strong enough to keep them in check. If the mechanism were ever threatened, either by a weak king unable to command respect or by an overweening nobility determined to challenge a king's sacrality, the common weal would be undermined and disaster would follow.

The Lancastrian kings were great bibliophiles: encouraged by Edward IV, William Caxton introduced the art of printing, a move which helped to cement English as the country's main language. By the fifteenth century English had become the native tongue, French was still spoken and the educated understood Latin, which was still an international language, but throughout the century there was a substantial growth in literacy and English was its medium. Gradually the spell cast by Norman French was broken by the creation of a growing literature in the English tongue, not least by the biblical translations of John Wyclif and the poetry of Geoffrey Chaucer and Thomas Malory. The most engaging and accessible domestic account of the period, the letters penned by the Paston family, is also written in English and there is a wealth of writing from other chroniclers and historians, notably John Rous, Thomas Walsingham, John Hardyng and Robert Fabyan.

Architecture flourished with the introduction of the distinctive English Perpendicular Gothic style and great educational institutions came into being – Winchester and New College, Oxford, in the reign of Richard II, Eton and King's College, Cambridge, under Henry VI – while the Inns of Court in London provided training in law. Trade with the Netherlands and Flanders created the great 'wool churches' of the Cotswolds and East Anglia and the merchants built manor houses which were notable for being less like castles and more like stately homes. In London an upsurge in civic pride saw the introduction of piped fresh water, and throughout England benefactors provided funds for the construction of schools, hospitals and almshouses. At sea navigation aids were improved with the use of the compass and wind-rose or direction card, and scholars finally agreed that the world was a globe ready to be explored.

None of this was taking place in isolation. England occupied a world where her neighbours also influenced events and played a part in the nation's development. The most important of these was France, larger and richer than England but ruled by the erratic Valois dynasty, which controlled only 60 per cent of the French land mass and was in a state of constant conflict with other duchies, notably Burgundy with its holdings in Flanders, Franche-Comté, Artois, Hainault and Brabant (modern Belgium and the southern Netherlands). Once a model of stability under Charles V, France was subjected to the long-running conflict between the Orléanists and the Burgundians which was as vicious and unpredictable as anything experienced in England.

There were also tensions over the Plantagenet holdings in Aquitaine in south-west France, and these had to led to periodic outbreaks of warfare at the end of the thirteenth and the beginning of the fourteenth centuries. In an attempt to settle the issue, in 1340 Edward III formally assumed the title 'King of France' and imposed his will on the Valois dynasty through humiliating victories at Sluys, Crécy and Poitiers. This enabled him to negotiate the Treaty of Brétigny, which in 1360 gave England suzerainty over Aquitaine, Calais, Guînes and Poitou. In return King John II of France, captured and held to ransom at Poitiers, dropped his claims to Aquitaine on condition that Edward relinquish his own claims to the French throne. However, these renunciations were never accepted by either side and during the reign of the forceful King Charles V of France most of Edward's gains were rapidly lost, apart from the bridgehead at Calais with its important trading links to the Low Countries. As a result the scene was set for further warfare.

Scotland, too, was part of the equation. A succession crisis in 1286 following the death of King Alexander III encouraged Edward I of England to intervene in the country's affairs and this led to a series of conflicts known in Scotland as the War of Independence. At the beginning of the fourteenth century the emergence of Robert Bruce,

Earl of Carrick, signalled a fresh willingness in the Scots to defy Edward's attempts to bring the country under his sovereignty and the war entered a new stage. A Scottish victory at Bannockburn in 1314 turned the tide and Bruce was acknowledged as king, a fact confirmed by the signing in 1328 of the Treaty of Edinburgh, which effectively ended the War of Independence. However, skirmishing continued along both sides of the frontier and at varying levels warfare between the two countries was a fact of life for most of the fourteenth century and well into the next.

As in England, the internal situation in Scotland was complicated by the presence of powerful magnates, notably the offspring of the house of Douglas, who frequently challenged the right of successive Scottish kings to rule. A much poorer country than England, Scotland sent soldiers to fight in France as mercenaries in the service of the French Crown in support of a series of treaties known as the 'Auld Alliance' which spanned the reigns of Robert I to Mary Queen of Scots and came into being in 1295. Over the years this alliance was continuously renewed and upgraded, the final agreement being signed in 1558.

The other two Celtic countries, Wales and Ireland, also played crucial roles during the same period. Wales was in effect two political entities: the Marcher lordships established by the Anglo-Norman aristocracy, and the existing native princedoms of Gwynedd, Deheubarth and Powys, which had been recognised by Henry III under the overlordship of Llewellyn ap Gruffudd as Prince of Wales. A Welsh reluctance to accept the feudal overlordship of the Plantagenets led to outbreaks of violence which Edward I attempted to settle through an all-out war of conquest at the end of the thirteenth century. After Llewellyn's death in battle in 1282 the rebellion was continued by his brother Daffydd, but by the beginning of the fourteenth century Edward's hegemony over Wales was complete and he sent a powerful message of his authority by proclaiming his eldest son Prince of Wales in 1301.

The military conquest of Wales was followed by a constitutional settlement which placed the principality under direct English rule, with Welsh land parcelled up and granted to English lords. By the Statute of Rhuddlan of 1284 English-style shires were created in the north and extended into Cardigan and Carmarthen, while the existing

Marcher lordships remained in being on the eastern border with England. Having completed their domination of the principality, the English employed Welsh archers, considered to be the best of their kind, in their campaigns against France.

Ireland, too, was brought under English control. Until the twelfth century it was at the mercy of a number of independent kings who pursued a relentless struggle for ascendancy. In 1166 one of them, Diarmait Mac Murchada, King of Leinster, asked Henry II for help against his opponents and this set in train a sequence of events which led to the Norman conquest of Ireland. England's imposition of control was not an orderly process and took several years. First to arrive was Richard FitzGilbert de Clare, Earl of Pembroke, known as 'Strongbow', and in his wake came English courtiers who grabbed the land and became great landowners, many of them of the absent variety.

Meanwhile the Irish kings were losing power and prestige, and their inability to find common ground or a single, all-powerful leader meant that resistance to the invasion was always fitful and fragmented. However, owing to the absence of any overall English policy, the conquest of Ireland was piecemeal and it took time for a working administration to emerge. In 1297 a parliament was summoned with representatives from the counties of Dublin, Louth, Waterford, Cork, Tipperary, Limerick, Kerry and Connacht and the liberties (lordships) of Meath, Wexford, Carlow, Kildare, Kilkenny and Ulster.

Unlike the Norman invasion of England in 1066, the settlement of Ireland never gained impetus and people did not come in sufficient numbers to complete the process. King John attempted to impose some order in the thirteenth century, but by then the English were preoccupied with France and by the following century the native Irish were able to recover lost ground. Gradually two Irelands came about: the feudalised areas settled by the English colonists, which benefited from the connection, and the surviving enclaves of independent Gaelic-speaking Irish kings, which continued to resist the English presence. Most attempts to create a unified resistance faltered but the successes of the Ó Domhnaill dynasty of Donegal and the Mac Carthaig dynasty of Munster halted English expansionism and managed to consolidate their own independence. Gradually the English presence was confined to the region known as the Pale, a fortified area around Dublin which comprised the medieval counties of Dublin, Meath, Louth and Kildare. Within the Pale language, culture, law and social structures were very similar to those existing in England at that time.

This was the world occupied by the peoples of England, Ireland, Scotland and Wales as the late Middle Ages drew to a close, but already the certainties were on the wane. As the fourteenth century ended the old order was about to change, giving way to events which were about to turn settled society upside down.

Prologue: Shakespeare and the
Wars of the Roses

Seen from the distance of half a millennium, the Wars of the Roses seem inchoate and barely fathomable, and even the antecedents were spread over several lifetimes. At the heart of the conflict was the dynastic dispute which divided the Royal House of Plantagenet. By the time of the reign of King Richard II, who succeeded to the throne in 1377 while still a boy, the Plantagenet succession was in trouble as Richard struggled to keep his nobles in check and he found himself under threat from his cousin, Henry Bolingbroke, eldest son of John of Gaunt, King Edward III's third son. In 1399, having failed to exert himself and thoroughly alarmed the nobles with his weakness and vacillation, Richard was forced to abdicate in favour of Bolingbroke, who became Henry IV and promptly had Richard imprisoned at Pontefract – where he died – to cement the claims of the House of Lancaster.

It was not the first time in history that the English throne had been disputed or that a king had been forced to fight for his crown. Richard's great-grandfather, Edward II, was an inadequate ruler who antagonised the nobility and was deposed by his wife, Isabella, and murdered in 1327; and, further back in time, Henry II's son John plunged the country into an unnecessary war with his barons in 1215. What made the struggle for the Plantagenet succession so awkward and so bruising was its confrontation between the rival factions of two powerful families and their supporters – the House of Lancaster as represented by Henry Bolingbroke's line and the claims of his kinsman Richard, Duke of York. Both lines were descended from King Edward III and by the early part of the fifteenth century, with Bolingbroke's ineffective grandson Henry VI on the throne, the scene was set for a tumultuous power struggle which only one house could win.

From that clash came the name by which the conflict is best known: the Wars of the Roses, the white rose representing the Yorkists and the red rose the Lancastrians. The origin of the term 'Wars of the Roses' has been hotly debated. Purists have protested that there is little evidence to suggest that either side fought under the symbol of a rose and that soldiers in the rival armies tended to wear the badge of their feudal superiors. It is equally clear that the term does not come from the period when the civil war was actually being fought. Even so, the symbolism of red and white roses is still central to the conflict. The House of York had a white rose as one of its many badges (York's personal badge was a falcon and fetter lock) and the red rose frequently appeared on Lancastrian livery (Richard III's badge was a white boar). When William Shakespeare, at the end of the sixteenth century, wrote *Henry VI, Part One* he inserted a crucial scene set in London's Old Temple Gardens in which the plucking of red and white roses by their respective supporters indicates the opposition of Lancaster and York. Although the action is completely fictitious it established the relationship in a dramatic way that would have been understood by contemporary audiences.

Shakespeare returned to the same symbolism in *Richard III*, where the Tudor king Henry VII expresses his desire to 'unite the white rose and the red', while later Tudor imagery made much of the fact that under the rule of their house the red and white roses had been brought together in harmony. Other contemporary or near-contemporary sources also refer to 'the roses' as being central to the conflict. The anonymous chroniclers at Croyland Abbey in Lincolnshire made several references to the rival roses in their account of the war. In the sixteenth century the humanist historian Polydore Vergil claimed that the two sides were represented by different-coloured roses. At the time of the next civil war, a century later, the Royalist diarist Sir John Oglander made mention of 'the quarrel of the warring roses'. David Hume referred to the 'wars between the two Roses' in his *History of England*, published in 1762. Another Scottish writer, the novelist Sir Walter Scott, introduced the concept in the first chapter of his novel *Ivanhoe* (1820), referring to 'the Civil Wars of the Roses'; in a later novel, *Anne of Geierstein* (1829), he returned to the theme, describing the conflict as 'the civil discords so dreadfully prosecuted in the wars of the White and Red Roses'. By the late nineteenth century the term was widely used to describe the dynastic struggle between the two rival lines and it is now too late to change such a well-known and popular title. (The same is true of the Crimean War, which is more accurately the 'Russian War' as it was fought in the Baltic and the Pacific as well as the Crimea.) An alternative would be the 'Wars of Lancaster and York' – the term 'Cousins' Wars' has also been used – but, as several recent historians have argued, the conflict deserves a better fate than to be compared to a cricket match between two rival English counties.

The use of the symbolism of the roses was also prompted by Tudor propaganda. Although the House of York had won back the throne from the Lancastrians with the accession of Edward IV, his brother, Richard III, lost it to Henry Tudor, the Earl of Richmond, who had a shaky claim to the throne by virtue of being the great-grandson of an illegitimate son of a younger son of Edward III. Richard's defeat and his death at the Battle of Bosworth in 1485 effectively ended the Wars of the Roses, although Henry did not feel completely secure until he had quelled unrest in the north and west of England and defeated two pretenders to his throne. After many years of discord the country was in need of harmony and it was in the Tudors' interests to describe the wars as an unbroken conflict, extending from the abdication of Richard II in 1399 to the reign of Richard III (1483–5), which was caused by the disastrous dynastic quarrel between the rival houses.

In fact the conflict known as the Wars of the Roses embraced three major episodes of bellicose activity between 1455 and 1487. The first began during the ineffectual reign of Henry VI and ended in 1461 with the triumph of the Yorkist Edward IV; the second broke out during the latter's reign when his authority was challenged by Lancastrian supporters led by Henry's wife, Margaret of Anjou; the third came into being when Richard III took his nephew's throne, a move which split his Yorkist supporters and led to the Tudor ascendancy. It was only later that the conflict was seen on a larger scale and in a more tragic context, and it was Shakespeare who was most responsible for instilling it in the national consciousness in those terms.

He chronicled the long collapse of Plantagenet power in a cycle of eight history plays extending from *Richard II* through *Henry IV – Parts One and Two, Henry V, Henry VI – Parts One, Two and Three* to

Richard III, and in doing so cemented the concept of the Wars of the Roses as a long and bloody business which blighted English history as the rival houses of York and Lancaster vied for the Crown. As a result of personal weakness or an incapacity to rule wisely and fairly, three kings were deposed, the country was plunged into civil strife and London was seized twice by rampant mobs, and France was lost for ever, leaving a legacy of suspicion and contempt between the two countries which would last for another five centuries (and may still exist to this day). England's first major civil war was tragic in every sense, a time of savage blood-letting which bred a violent habit of mind as rival magnates escalated private quarrels into national civil wars and kings paid with their lives for being weak or unfit to rule. As Henry Tudor, the Earl of Richmond, makes clear in *Richard III*, which concludes Shakespeare's cycle of history plays, for the people of England the transformation had been a time of horror and revulsion:

> England hath long been mad and scarred herself;
> The brother blindly shed the brother's blood,
> The father rashly slaughtered his own son,
> The son, compelled, been butcher to the sire:
> All this divided York and Lancaster.

The conflict was indeed a brutal business. Although the actual fighting amounted to a total of little more than fifteen months of campaigning in the field, the huge death toll among England's ruling classes threatened to bring down the body politic and plunge the country into anarchy as rival families clashed over the royal succession. The wars accounted for the violent deaths of three kings, two Princes of Wales, eight royal dukes and countless more members of the aristocracy and the landed gentry who died fighting in the major set-piece battles or found themselves facing execution on the scaffold as a result of ending up on the losing side. Murder and assassination were commonplace and some noble families were almost exterminated by the blood-letting. During the upheaval old scores were also settled as men jockeyed for position and struggled to maintain their predominance in the ever-changing political climate. Many parts of England were plunged into lawlessness and violence, with thieving, robberies and murder commonplace, especially in the north. Although reports of the criminality were often exaggerated and were tame in comparison with similar wars taking place in Europe at the same time, the events of those years left the survivors with a lasting memory of the dreadfulness of civil conflict, with the result that the period passed into the national consciousness as a byword for calamity.

All this violence forms a major theme in Shakespeare's version of events: a rightful king (Richard II) is usurped by a pretender (Henry IV), a queen (Margaret of Anjou, wife of Henry VI) has her husband's rival (Richard of York) killed, in revenge York's sons dispatch both her son (Prince Edward) and her husband. For those who disturb the rightful order there are ultimate penalties: Henry VI is punished for his grandfather's usurpation of Richard II and Richard III pays with his life for killing his brother (the Duke of Clarence) and his nephews (Princes Edward and Richard, sons of Edward IV) and for being involved in the deaths of other family members and close associates.

For many people Shakespeare's plays form their only knowledge of the period and half-remembered quotations and vividly drawn personalities provide clues to the main events. There is no reason why the plays should not be enjoyed in their own right as powerful pieces of drama, but such was Shakespeare's capacity to recreate the world inhabited by his characters that the histories have often been regarded as a realistic and honest account of what actually happened during that vicious period. As seen by Shakespeare, England is a green and pleasant land – 'this other Eden, demi-paradise' – whose peace and stability is shattered by the violent dismissal of Richard II and his usurpation by the pretender Henry Bolingbroke. This sets the scene for the political turmoil and civil conflict which follows and in that sense the eight plays have as their starting point the prescient warning issued by the Bishop of Carlisle, a relatively minor character in *Richard II*, as the plotters decide the King's fate:

> The blood of English shall manure the ground,
> And future ages groan for this foul act.
> Peace shall go sleep with Turks and infidels,
> And in this seat of peace tumultuous wars
> Shall kin with kin and kind with kind confound.

> Disorder, horror, fear, and mutiny,
> Shall here inhabit, and this land be called
> The field of Golgotha and dead men's skulls.
> O, if you rear this house against this house,
> It will the woefullest division prove
> That ever fell upon this cursed earth.
> Prevent it, resist it, let it not be so,
> Lest child, child's children, cry against you 'Woe!'.

This sends a powerful message about the disruptive effects of regime change and the consequences of unsettling the natural order but the Bishop's words are all poetic effect. Shakespeare was writing as a playwright and was under no obligation to create historical accuracy. While he remained tolerably faithful to his main sources – the chronicles written by Jean Froissart, Edward Hall and Raphael Holinshed – he was happy to depart from historical truth when the moment called for it. Liberties were taken with the timing of events and he was aware of the need to provide a Tudor gloss on what had happened: for much of his life Elizabeth I was on the throne, and chronology always had to play second fiddle to the demands of the stage. The interests of dramatic tension even allowed muddles over the characters. It is unlikely that William de la Pole Duke of Suffolk was Margaret of Anjou's lover and there is no evidence that Richard III proposed marriage to Anne Neville in the presence of the recently slain corpse of Henry VI. Both incidents, though, heighten the drama and add immeasurably to the story.

In common with the chroniclers from whom he took much of his evidence, Shakespeare had a vested interest in presenting the conflict as a bloody internecine struggle between two rival houses which threatened England's common weal and which was healed by the good sense and strong governance introduced by Henry Tudor. Yet there is much in Shakespeare's portrayals that stands the test of historical comparison. For example, Richard II's insistence on the divine right of kings rings true, the concept of Henry V as the hero-king is borne out by his actions in France and few would cavil at the portrayal of Henry VI as a holy fool. Only in the creation of Richard III as a power-crazed and stunted butcher did Shakespeare seriously exaggerate. And even then there was a motive, as we shall see, for he was under an obligation to play up the benefits of the Tudor succession while denigrating the supposed excesses of the House of York.

By the time Shakespeare was composing his history plays the period they portrayed was already fading into the past. In the previous century such had been the mayhem in England that no king had ruled longer than 22 years (Henry VI reigned for a total of 39, but he came to the throne as a nine-month old baby and was severely incapacitated for most of the time), but Henry VII was to provide 24 reasonably pacific years. And the Tudors proved to be solid fixtures: Henry VIII would spend 38 years on the throne while Elizabeth I's reign stretched from 1558 to 1603. In total the Tudors gave England 118 years of settled rule and in that time the foundations for the modern state were laid and a recognisable national identity came into being. What had begun with the usurpation of a Plantagenet king whose reign rested on late-medieval polity ended with the foundation of a line which would give England a previously unimaginable degree of stability and social and political integration which lasted until the middle of the seventeenth century.

Chapter One

WOE TO THE LAND IN WHICH
A BOY IS KING

When considering the great sweep of history sometimes it is impossible to put exact dates on periods which produce substantial change. Events are often too fluid to be granted any coherence at the time; dovetailing can lead to glib generalisations; dates are fixed in the firmament but periods are less certain.

So it is with the Wars of the Roses. To understand why the middle years of the fifteenth century in England witnessed a period of turbulence which threatened the collapse of the English body politic as a succession of rulers failed to deal with an 'over-mighty' aristocracy it is necessary to go back half a century to 1399, the year which saw the forced abdication of the country's anointed king, Richard II, son of Edward of Woodstock, a charismatic figure known as the 'Black Prince', and grandson of the great Plantagenet king Edward III. It was unfortunate that young Richard ever became king in the first place. Not only was he a second son – his elder brother, Prince Edward of Angoulême, had died in 1371 – but his father had predeceased him five years later without succeeding Edward III. As a result of those untimely deaths Prince Richard was propelled to an early throne: on his grandfather's death in 1377 he had the misfortune to be crowned king when he was only ten years old and therefore still a minor, and his reign never recovered from that unhappy start.

Clearly the boy-king needed guidance, but the question of who would be the best mentor was complicated by his grandfather's huge progeny. Edward III had fathered thirteen children and five of the sons had grown to maturity, becoming potent figures in their own right. With their wealth from carefully planned marriages and their noble blood – all had been created dukes – they enjoyed great temporal power and were almost independent of the Crown. Edward the Black Prince had been the eldest and therefore the heir to the throne, but his brothers were equally powerful and as influential magnates they entertained their own ambitions. It was only natural that they could have seen in their young nephew's plight an opportunity to enhance their own standing.

The second surviving son of Edward III was Lionel, Duke of Clarence, who had made a good match by marrying Elizabeth de Burgh, the heiress of William de Burgh, Earl of Ulster. Through her mother she was descended from Henry III, another English king who had succeeded to the throne during his minority, in October 1216. (Elizabeth died in 1363 and Clarence married for a second time, Violante Visconti, daughter of the Duke of Milan.) Although Clarence had died in 1368 and was therefore not a contender at the time of Richard's accession, his daughter Philippa had married into the powerful Mortimer family, who were English Earls of March (there was also a Scottish earldom of March) and would play a considerable role in the dynastic struggles which lay ahead. Descended from Ralph Mortimer, who had crossed over to England with William the Conqueror, the family owned large tracts of land on the Welsh marches and had also acquired property in Ireland.

Third in line was John of Gaunt, who had made an advantageous marriage with Blanche, daughter of Henry of Grosmont, 1st Duke of Lancaster, a distinguished soldier and diplomat who had served Edward III. His family had been founded in the previous century by Edmund Crouchback, the second son of King Henry II. One of the great men of his age, John of Gaunt had been born in Ghent (hence his name) and, like his father-in-law, he was deeply involved in European affairs. Powerful in his own right – Lancaster was a palatinate (a region whose ruler enjoys considerable authority outside royal jurisdiction) and possessed great wealth and authority in England – he gained, on his second marriage, to Constance of Castile in 1371, royal titles as putative King of Castile and Leon and Duke of Aquitaine.

With his acres in England and France, his huge retinue, his castles, his love of soldiering, his skills in diplomacy and his courtly conduct, John of Gaunt would have been the natural choice as regent for the young king, but as one of the most powerful men in England he was suspected by many of wanting the Crown for himself. None of the contemporary records suggest that there was any truth to the rumours but they stuck and it was Gaunt's misfortune to be identified with plots against the throne while loyally doing his utmost to protect his young nephew. It did not help his reputation that he was the main patron of John Wyclif, a radical religious thinker who questioned papal authority and, among other doctrinal cavils, denied the dogma of transubstantiation, the belief that the bread and wine used in the Eucharist are literally replaced by the body and blood of Jesus Christ.

Next to John of Gaunt came Edmund of Langley, Earl of Cambridge and later Duke of York, the founder of the House of York, who was married to Isabella, sister of John of Gaunt's second wife Constance. (Edmund received the Yorkist dukedom from Richard II in 1385 as the reward for participating in an ineffectual invasion of Scotland.) Close to his elder brother the Black Prince, Edmund had fought in France and at the time of Edward III's death he was acting as Governor of Dover. Then there was Edward III's youngest son, Thomas of Woodstock, Earl of Buckingham and, from 1385, Duke of Gloucester. He was perhaps the most feline of the brothers and later emerged as a keen threat to Richard's crown.

Given the clash of family interests and the potential for rivalries to spill over into bloodshed, it was clear that no one brother could claim the title of regent, even though John of Gaunt had the best qualifications for the role. Instead there was a compromise. A 'continual council' of twelve leading magnates was formed to decide policy and to advise the King's ministers, but it proved a mixed blessing. While the arrangement avoided unnecessary splits during Richard's minority and prevented any of the royal uncles from gaining the ascendancy, it also produced paralysis at a time when England's fortunes were going badly, not just at home but in its relations with France.

Since the previous century the two countries had been in on-off conflict over the status of Aquitaine, an independent duchy within the kingdom of France which, together with other holdings, was under the suzerainty of England. In 1137 Eleanor, daughter of the French Duke of Aquitaine, had married King Henry II (having divorced Louis VII of France) and as a result of their marriage alliance successive English kings, as Dukes of Aquitaine, owed homage to the

French throne. However, as Henry II and his lineal descendants were sovereign rulers within their own right, French kings feared, not unreasonably, that their English counterparts would take steps to consolidate their power in France. At the same time the English kings were unhappy with their subordinate position. England had been extending her commercial interests with the weavers and burghers of Flanders, who had become important trading partners. They also considered themselves to be natural allies of the English and their support had encouraged Edward III to claim the French throne and to quarter the French coat of arms with his own.

Another factor in this Anglo-French enmity was the mutually advantageous relationship embodied in the Auld Alliance. While France gave support and assistance to Scotland as a counterweight to English ambitions in France, in return Scottish soldiers fought in French service, often taking part in the fighting against English armies. During this same period Scottish and English forces were in a state of almost constant conflict along the unquiet border between the two countries, with raids and counter-raids commonplace. The Scots' purpose in taking military action was usually to deflect England's involvement in France, while the English embarked on retaliatory operations to dominate the northern marches and, in the longer term, to attempt to bring the Scottish throne under English suzerainty.

The confrontation between England and France lasted more than a hundred years and there were eight periods of all-out warfare between 1337 and 1453. It is generally referred to as the Hundred Years War – a Victorian concept which is still in use even though the timescale is not strictly accurate – and it influenced the contemporaneous dynastic struggles in England. The first period was instigated by Philip IV of France in 1337 after he announced that all English holdings south of the River Loire were forfeit and in response Edward III established bases in Flanders to mount military expeditions into northern and north-eastern France. Following a decisive naval victory at Sluys in 1340 during which 190 French ships were captured in the Zwin Estuary, a truce was declared, only for war to break out again six years later after the French invaded Gascony, the French region lying between the Pyrenees and the River Garonne. Edward III's rejoinder was to invade France with an army of ten thousand archers, three thousand cavalry and four thousand infantry, all of them hardened soldiers with experience of fighting the Scots.

The first major engagement, at Crécy on 26 August 1346, not only left the French badly beaten, with 1542 lords and knights dead and a casualty list of up to twenty thousand foot soldiers and archers, but changed the face of warfare. The decisive strike force in Edward's army was provided by the archers, the force-multipliers of their age. Equipped with a formidable longbow made of yew, each archer had a quiver of 24 iron-tipped arrows which were capable of hitting a target with great accuracy at up to 200 yards. The best archers could fire six arrows a minute and, depending on the angle of flight, these were capable of penetrating plate armour and oak planks up to a depth of four inches. But it was not just the longbows which gave Edward victory. For the first time a superior force of cavalry had been beaten by disciplined and determined foot soldiers who held their ground. It was a watershed in medieval warfare: never before had infantry had the confidence and the ability to take on and beat cavalry in a set-piece battle.

This victory was followed by the English occupation of Calais and the agreement for a further truce which lasted until 1355. During this interlude, between 1348 and 1349, Europe was ravaged by one of the periodic outbreaks of plague, known as the Black Death, which halved England's population and left hardly any country unscathed. Conflict was resumed in 1355 when Scottish forces crossed the border into England to claim an opportunist victory at Nesbit Moor, but this was followed early in the following year by an English riposte led by the Black Prince. Scotland was invaded and so frightful was the carnage in the Lothians – the lowland area around Edinburgh – that the incident was christened 'the Burnt Candlemas'.

The triumph in Scotland was a prelude to further raids in France led by Edward III and his sons and was settled by an English victory at Poitiers on 12 September 1356, where the French were again defeated in a hard-pounding battle. As the French realised that they could not beat the English in set-piece battles the war descended into stalemate and the resulting Treaty of Brétigny settled the territorial arguments: England gave up her claim to Normandy while her holdings in Aquitaine and Calais were recognised by the French. In 1361 once again plague intervened, this time in the form of the epidemic known in

France as *mortalité des enfants*, which killed mainly young people and so affected population growth in both countries.

Desultory warfare continued between 1368 and 1396, during which period the Constable of France Bertrand de Guesclin pursued a war of attrition against English holdings, gradually winning back possessions and extending French authority in Aquitaine. By the time Richard II came to the throne the war against the French was still a live issue but it was an expensive campaign and becoming increasingly difficult to maintain. The Black Prince's victories in France had been extremely popular as they enhanced national prestige but how to pay for them was another matter and it was one of the many problems which Richard would have to confront when he came of age.

Even so, despite the tensions underlying England's relationship with France, the boy-king's reign got off to a good start with a coronation which, by general agreement, was a sumptuous occasion masterminded by John of Gaunt. It lasted two days, the first being taken up with a magnificent formal procession from the Tower of London to Westminster, the participants riding through 'the crowded streets of the city of London, which were so bedecked with cloth of gold and silver, with silken hangings, and with other conceits to entertain the onlookers, that you might suppose you were seeing a triumph of the Caesars or ancient Rome in all its grandeur'. These were the words of the recorder of the event, Thomas Walsingham, Benedictine precentor of St Albans and one of the main chroniclers of the period, who built on the *Chronica Majora* written by Matthew Paris, an earlier chronicler and monk of St Albans.

Walsingham also noted that the coronation was exceptionally well ordered, the procession providing a mirror of English society at the time, with earls, barons, knights and squires riding or walking according to their station. The whole party dressed with white hoods to represent the King's innocence and they were greeted by cheering crowds whose enthusiasm was no doubt helped by the wine which had replaced spring water in the conduits and flowed freely for at least three hours. At Cheapside the throng passed a specially constructed castle where four beautiful girls stood on the battlements and 'as the king approached they wafted down golden leaves before him, then, as he drew nearer they scattered imitation golden florins on him and his horse'. If John of Gaunt had wanted to provide a display of royal pomp and exuberance he could not have done better and the next day pageantry gave way to the sonorous rites of the coronation.

Inside Westminster Abbey Richard was put through the ancient ceremonial which made him an anointed king. Holy oil was poured, the crown was placed on his head, the sceptre was placed in his right hand and the golden rod in his left. The gold coronation crown, one of eleven listed in the King's treasure roll, was so heavy that it had to be supported by the Earl of March after it had been placed on Richard's head. After Richard was enthroned on the coronation chair the *Te Deum* was sung and mass was celebrated. So exhausted was the boy-king by the rigours of the ceremonial that he had to be carried on the shoulders of his tutor and Chamberlain of the Royal Household, Sir Simon Burley, into neighbouring Westminster Hall, where a huge banquet awaited. According to Walsingham, the whole event was designed to emphasise the magnificence of the Crown and to remind those taking part that they had a new ruler who was to be honoured and obeyed: 'If I were to attempt to recount the preparations, the splendour of the tableware and the variety of dishes, the reader, struck as much by the value as the quantity of fine things, would perhaps hesitate to believe me.'

Twenty years later the splendour and purity of the proceedings were commemorated by *The Wilton Diptych*, a hinged devotional portrait which shows the young king kneeling before the Virgin Mary holding the figure of the Christ child with eleven blue-robed angels representing his years on earth. Behind him stand the figures of John the Baptist, together with Edward the Confessor and Edmund the Martyr: the young king is at once sanctified and elevated to the holiest of holies. Richard left no record of his feelings of that day but the proceedings must have left a lasting and profound impression on a boy who, from an early age, was acutely aware of his surroundings and his own position within them. Already solitary and introverted, with no siblings to divert him, he was spoiled by his mother, Joan of Woodstock, known as the 'Fair Maid of Kent', and was considered something of a mother's boy.

Joan was one of the great beauties of her day and had a colourful past: she had married her cousin the Black Prince in 1361 after the death of her second husband, Sir Thomas Holland, and, being a granddaughter of Edward I, she was a powerful figure in her own right. She instilled in Richard the primacy of his position and encouraged him to understand at an early age his unique role as an absolute monarch with limitless powers. Through the efforts of Burley and Sir Guichard d'Angle, Earl of Huntingdon, another strong-minded tutor, the boy was instructed in the absolute sanctity of his office, namely that he enjoyed an unparalleled and mysterious status which from the very outset had been blessed by God. At Richard's birth in Bordeaux in 1367 three kings had been present – those of Spain, Portugal and Navarre – and the symbolism of their presence was so powerful that the young prince developed an intense and lifelong fixation with the feast of the Epiphany, the Adoration of the Magi commemorating the manifestation of Christ, celebrated on 6 January. From the example of his coronation with its regalia, its blessings, anointment and religious symbolism, Richard understood early in his life that his tutors' teachings must be true, that he was indeed God's anointed vessel.

All this mattered. At the time the King was not just a figurehead, he was the embodiment of supreme authority on earth. For the people of England he was the personification of all their hopes and fears, who could intervene decisively in their lives, and he was the ultimate authority in the land. As such he had to maintain the kind of physical presence that announced that he was king as well as the mental agility to keep one step ahead of the requirements of kingship. It was not surprising that Richard believed so strongly in the principle of divine right: everything he experienced as a boy encouraged him to accept that concept. But being king did not mean that he had to act alone. In common with his predecessors Richard enjoyed the advice of a council whose members were drawn from the upper reaches of the nobility or were familiars – men of ability – who helped him form policy and then execute it. There was also a representative parliament to raise taxes and pass laws. This had evolved from medieval beginnings as a 'model' assembly consisting of two knights from each shire and two burgesses from selected boroughs to become an effective council whose members gave consent on taxation and other matters on behalf of those who had sent them. By the time of Richard's reign the term 'Commons' was being used for this body, which met in London and other locations, and the first Speaker was chosen in 1376.

Richard also benefited from the services of his own household of trusted retainers and servants, the costs of which were met by the public purse and were therefore a source of constant financial difficulties. Beyond these, administering the country at local and national level, was an array of judges, sheriffs, justices of the peace, coroners and customs officials. But, at the apex of English society and responsible for its good governance, stood the figure of the King. Not only was it vital that he played the role of supreme arbiter, but he also had to look the part and behave as a true ruler of his kingdom.

On this point Richard scored well. Contemporary portraits show a pleasant-looking young man, tall, fair-skinned and blond, with a clear love of fine clothes. Although his weak chin, thin beard and sly smile betray a less than manly aspect, Richard stares out spiritedly and alert from his state portrait in Westminster Abbey, a man who was keenly aware of his position. At the same time he was a dandy who luxuriated in elegant clothes and had no interest in their cost, an affectation that led to growing discontent about the price of maintaining his court.

Little was recorded about the years of Richard's minority but the fragility of his position was underlined by the Bishop of Rochester, Thomas Brinton, who preached a sermon on the day after the coronation exhorting the nobility to support the new king during the perilous years of his youth and to ensure the kingdom's safety. Inevitably Richard's closest companions and those who exerted most influence over him were his tutors, who largely owed their positions to the earlier patronage of the Black Prince. This led to a belief that a gulf had grown up between the royal household, which was perceived to be all-powerful, and the succession of continual councils responsible for ruling the country.

Matters came to a head at the second Parliament of the young king's reign, held in Gloucester in October 1378, when the Speaker of the Commons, Sir Peter de la Mare, questioned the validity of England's present governance and asked to be informed about the role played by 'the king's councillors and governors of his person', the implication being that the system was not working. A compromise was reached the following month, when two new councillors, Sir Aubrey de Vere and Sir Richard Rous, were appointed to the third council, but this did not dim the growing dissatisfaction with the arrangement. There were concerns, too, about the costs of the royal household and the means of maintaining it. At the time money was raised by a poll tax which was paid at a standard rate of one groat (a silver coin worth four English pennies) by all men and women aged fourteen or more, with graduated rates for richer taxpayers. While the taxation system raised sufficient funds to meet expenditure, it was unpopular and the third council of Richard's reign, held in April 1379, was quick to voice its dissent. Its members felt that the country was getting little in return for the burden of heavy taxation required for England's strategic commitments in France and along the border with Scotland. In an attempt to bring financial matters under control Parliament appointed an assessor, but little seems to have been done and the issue was simply allowed to simmer, to no one's advantage.

Part of the problem was undoubtedly the extravagance of the royal court. From an early age Richard demonstrated that he was not averse to enjoying the fruits of his divine rule. His clothes were well cut and fashionable, made in the style which came to be known as International Gothic. Coats with padded shoulders and high collars were accompanied by tight, two-coloured hose and pointed shoes: men at court dressed for effect and not for comfort or practicality. The King has also been credited with the invention of the handkerchief, although it is not clear if this emerged for health or sartorial reasons. This interest in clothes suggests a strong narcissistic element to Richard's personality which manifested itself not just through his concern for his appearance but through his passion for artistic excellence. A contemporary critic complained that the clothes were 'cut all to pieces', a reference to the fashion for the leaf shapes that were cut into hems and sleeve edges 'full of slashes and devils'. Women joined in the fashion revolution by wearing dresses with longer trains and sporting increasingly elaborate head-dresses which caused a good deal of contemporary comment, much of it unkind. (As the head-dresses became more elaborate and outrageous the resultant confections were thought, wrongly, to be breeding grounds for mice.)

Another cause of the kingdom's financial problems was that its extent made it difficult to maintain. In effect there were a number of regions, all different in substantial ways: the west of England, for example, had very few similarities, cultural or linguistic, with the northern area bordering Scotland. To get from Exeter to Newcastle was a major expedition. Scotland, Ireland and, to a lesser extent,

Wales were separate entities. There were still extensive holdings in France, although there had been a gradual decline in English prestige and the possessions around Calais and Bordeaux and Bayonne in Aquitaine were held only with difficulty. A further source of anxiety was England's coastline: during Richard's minority the French attacked the southern coastal towns of Rye, Plymouth, Exeter and Winchelsea as a prelude to a threatened invasion, and in 1381 a Scottish force attacked the island of Anglesey, off north Wales. The cost of guarding the kingdom from attack ate up much of the national budget and led to unpopular increases in taxation. It was a recipe for disaster. As one of the foremost politicians of the day, William of Wykeham, Bishop of Winchester, put it, 'an over-taxed and leader-less people, at once war-weary and bellicose, was becoming ripe for revolt'.

What eventually sparked a revolt was the decision in 1380 to raise the poll tax per head of population to one shilling (twelve pennies), a move that proved to be unacceptable and led to widespread unrest throughout rural England. Collectors were attacked in the course of their duties and in the most volatile areas, Essex and Kent, anger found expression in a popular uprising as men banded together in common cause against payment of the poll tax. The unrest coincided with a growing dissatisfaction with both the working conditions on the land and the workers' relationship with landowners at a time when serfdom was going into a slow decline as a result of the ravages of the Black Death. A sudden shortage of manpower gave the workforce, composed largely of villeins, or tenant-farmers, an unlooked-for advantage because landowners were unable to fill vacant tenancies and the villeins were now in a position to bargain for better terms. They were also able to travel to seek work elsewhere and this mobility introduced new job opportunities, especially for women in domestic service. After years of paying heed to a social structure in which everyone knew their place and their degree, the world was gradually being turned upside down as the old order gave way to something new and unsettling. Attempts to enforce a maximum wage at pre-plague levels also proved to be difficult, even though it had been backed by a parliamentary statute of 1351. Coming on top of the unpopularity of years of continuous fighting in France which seemed only to benefit the nobility, and dissatisfaction with the expense of maintaining the royal court, this latest tax increase proved to be the final straw.

Later known as the Peasants' Revolt (a more accurate description would be 'English Rising'), the unrest began in June 1381 when a group of disaffected men marched to Rochester Castle in Kent to demand the release of prisoners being held for their refusal to pay taxes. From there the protesters moved on to Maidstone and Canterbury, where they threatened to kill the Archbishop, Simon Sudbury, who was also the King's Chancellor and therefore one of the authors of the tax increases. All the while the mob attracted more people anxious to join their cause and a leader and spokesman emerged in Wat Tyler, a man of radical convictions who for a very short time had England's destiny in his hands. At the same time a similar revolt took place in Essex – at Brentwood an inquiry into non-payment of taxes led to the death of three jurors – and the two groups of protesters converged on Blackheath and Mile End, where, with the help of disaffected citizens, they were able to enter London on 13 June.

Among those who had been set free at Rochester was a religious demagogue called John Ball, who had been a thorn in Sudbury's side as a result of his complaints about greed and corruption among the country's clergy. According to Walsingham, who called him a 'mad priest', Ball's message was simple and dangerous and it entailed a complete reversal of the current social situation. 'Good people,' he would say, 'nothing can go well in England, nor ever will do, until all goods are held in common, until there is neither villein nor nobleman, until we are all one.' Ball also gave his voice to one of the best-known political rhymes of his day when he preached to the crowd at Blackheath on the text:

> When Adam dalf [dug] and Eve span
> Who was then the gentleman?

Tyler and Ball – a third leader, Jack Straw, may have been a later invention – were certain about one thing. Although they demanded social change and wanted to abolish all lordships, they claimed that they were not being disloyal to the person of the King and their quarrel was not with him. On the contrary, they took a common oath of loyalty to Richard, who, they believed, was surrounded by wicked advisers and needed to be saved from them. To their way of thinking that predicament lay at the heart of the matter and they were determined to find a solution, if need be by addressing the King directly and encouraging him to settle their grievances with a stroke of a pen.

But, for the time being, actions had to speak for words and on entering London the rebels set about burning down the buildings of supposed enemies and pillaging their property. Particular animus was reserved for John of Gaunt, whose sumptuous Savoy Palace, on the site of the present-day Embankment, was an early target, but as he was out of London at the time the King's uncle escaped personal harm. For two days London was in a state of anarchy: in addition to the razing of the Savoy Palace the prisons at Fleet and Marshalsea were opened and their inhabitants released, the New Temple was sacked and the Chancery records, held south of the river at Lambeth, were destroyed.

Richard would not have been human had he not been thoroughly alarmed by this rebellion which seemed to be directed against his authority. It was a concerted attempt to bring about far-reaching changes and as it was backed by some ten thousand people the rebels clearly posed a threat and enjoyed widespread popular backing. Prudently, on the first outbreak of trouble the King had moved to the Tower of London from Windsor Castle, which his grandfather had developed as a royal palace. This was a sensible move as the building was both a palace and a fortress which was easily defended, and throughout the experience Richard seems to have remained calm and clear-headed, so much so that he was able to play the leading role in bringing the emergency to a conclusion. He was only fourteen years old but contemporary accounts make it clear that he showed considerable courage and conviction in agreeing to meet the rebel leaders, a risky strategy which could have put his life in danger.

Two suppositions can reasonably be made about Richard's response to the revolt. Perhaps he understood the importance of his own position in the demands being made by Tyler and Ball and he put his faith in the belief that their loyalty to him would be stronger than their grievances. Perhaps, too, there was a wider plan to buy time by negotiating with the protesters and lulling them into a false sense of security, but for the inexperienced boy-king the taming of this revolt was to be a seminal moment in his life.

On 14 June, having announced his intention to meet the rebels, Richard rode from the Tower to Mile End to meet the Essex rebels, accompanied only by Sir William Walworth, the Lord Mayor of London and the first commoner in England to be knighted. As the King approached the rebel camp he showed no fear and in return the leaders treated him with the respect due to their lawful ruler. They assured him that they wished for no other king but him and set out their grievances, which included the abolition of villeinage and its replacement by the right to labour under a free contract, the opening up of the labour market and the creation of fixed rents for agricultural land. It was a tense moment and Richard responded to it by agreeing to all their requests, promising to confirm his decision later with letters carrying the Great Seal and allowing them to return to their homes under a general pardon. 'These words pacified the people there,' recorded Walsingham, 'that is to say, the simple, ignorant folk who had gathered there but did not know what they were asking, and who shouted out, "Well said, well said, that is all we want." And so they were appeased and began to go back into London.'

Whatever their reasons for taking part in the mass protest, this was what the crowd wanted to hear, and Richard's action effectively ended the revolt of the Essex rebels. It was a victory of sorts and as he and his small entourage headed back to the Tower the young king might well have been pleased with what he had achieved. Not only had he persuaded his subjects to call a halt to their attempted uprising but he had displayed the power and authority of the Crown: the rebels had taken him at his word and had bent to his will because he was their liege sovereign. They would not have listened to Sudbury or any other of the King's advisers whose downfall they sought, but the boy-king Richard was another and altogether more serious matter.

It was a good beginning but on his return to the Tower Richard was given the painful lesson that honeyed words and the majesty of the King's person were not always enough to still men's anger. While he was absent there had been further violence in London and Tyler's men had managed to get into the Tower, where they had summarily executed Sudbury and the King's Treasurer, Sir Robert Hales, whom they held accountable for the increase in the poll tax. Also killed was

John of Gaunt's doctor, William Appleton. The victims' heads were paraded through the streets of London before being displayed on London Bridge. To add insult to the offence the mob broke into the royal apartments and smashed to pieces the bed belonging to the King's mother, who was still officially his guardian.

The violence provoked another trial of strength between Richard and the rebels. This time, though, there was to be no subservience on the part of the rebels and Richard was hard pushed to make his position felt. When the two sides met, on 15 June at the cattle market at Smithfield, Tyler was in no mood to kowtow to the King. Instead of bowing or kneeling he stayed on his horse and greeted Richard as an equal, taking him by the hand and addressing him familiarly as his 'brother'. In itself this was hardly heinous behaviour – Tyler did not attempt any violence – but by acting in that way the rebel leader made it clear that he took no account of the King's majesty. In so doing he had committed the crime of treating Richard as an equal. By addressing the monarch as an ordinary man Tyler was not only exposing his radical pretensions but he was also challenging the status quo.

Equally outrageous were his demands. In addition to the ultimatum made by the men of Essex and accepted by Richard, Tyler seems to have insisted on the abolition of all secular and religious titles and the confiscation of Church land. This was going too far but once again Richard appeared willing to make concessions and studiously ignored the rebel leader's increasingly arrogant and impertinent demeanour. As the discussion continued tempers among Richard's retinue became increasingly frayed and, stung by Tyler's behaviour, Walworth decided to act. With his supporters behind him the Lord Mayor rode into the fray, drew his dagger and killed Tyler on the spot, although, according to some accounts, the actual blow may have been made by someone else.

It was a rash move and things could have turned out very badly for the royal party. The leader of the rebels had been killed in front of his followers, Richard and his retinue were outnumbered and lightly armed and could easily have fallen victim to the crowd's revenge, but the King was equal to the challenge. Displaying great personal courage that was all the more praiseworthy given his youth, Richard rode towards the crowd saying, 'I am your leader: follow me.' (The moment was recorded by the contemporary chronicler and Richard's biographer, the Monk of Evesham.) The arrival of militia troops loyal to the King settled the matter and the crowd was gradually and peaceably dispersed.

Even if the outcome was not as dramatic as some contemporary chroniclers suggested in their accounts of the incident, Richard's demeanour had demonstrated to his advisers that he was fast growing into manhood and was emerging as a true ruler. In so far as he had shown his mettle and demonstrated behaviour befitting a king – it helped that the rebels held him in such high regard that they did not react to the slaying of their leader – his confrontation with Wat Tyler was an early milestone in Richard's development. Throughout his minority, with the backing of his council, he had been able to rule as a king in theory; now he had shown that he was able to do so in practice. Furthermore he had demonstrated that he could do so in style.

The incident also underlined the importance of the theory of divine right and gave Richard a valuable insight into the effect he had on his subjects. At Smithfield the rebels had greeted him with loyal words 'We will not have any other king over you' and made it clear that their quarrel was not with him but with his 'evil' advisers. When their leader was cut down and Richard rode towards them they heeded his words and dispersed. All this suggested that the King's majesty was inviolate and that he, Richard, was different from other men, even from his closest family and his advisers, who were the real object of the rebels' ire. That much he would have learned from the confrontation, which took place on the feast of Corpus Christi (the celebration of the Eucharist and a time of religious processions). From a more practical point of view the incident would also have told him that he had to guard against any activity which might threaten his rule. And he was right to be concerned, because the unrest had not been confined to the mutinous move on London. There were outbreaks of trouble in Hertfordshire and Suffolk; in Cambridge the university archives were burned in the Market Square; and in Norfolk a minor insurrection led to the murder of the Bishop of Norwich.

Bearing these events in mind, Richard set about retrieving the situation by making sure that nothing he had promised at Mile End or Smithfield would be put into practice. As the rebels left London they believed that Richard would keep his promises and that they would be granted the charters of freedom which he had pledged at

both meetings. Not for the last time they soon found that Richard
had no intention of keeping his word and they had in fact been
duped. Within a fortnight a deputation seeking confirmation of the
King's promises was told in no uncertain terms, 'Villeins you are, and
villeins you shall remain', and on 2 July Richard issued a formal
revocation of his promises. Some of the ringleaders, including John
Ball, were rounded up and executed, although by the standards of the
day the retribution was not particularly brutal, largely because
Richard was not interested in revenge. It had been enough that his
prerogative had been obeyed. Even so, as a contemporary rhyme in
the possession of St John's College, Oxford (MS.209, f.57.a), made
clear, even moderate people had turned against Richard:

> The axe was sharpe, the stokke [block] was harde,
> In the xiiii [fourteenth] yere of Kynge Richarde.

The Peasants' Revolt had a further bearing on Richard's life: it
suggested to his advisers that the time had come to find him a wife.
Among a number of contenders was the beautiful Caterina, one of the
Duke of Milan's thirty-eight children, who would have brought grace
and a large dowry to the marriage. But the most convenient match
was with Princess Anne of Bohemia, a daughter of the Holy Roman
Emperor, Charles IV, and the sister of King Wenceslas IV of Bohemia.
From the point of view of prestige and winning international
influence the marriage had several advantages. It made Richard the
son-in-law of the Holy Roman Emperor and it would provide a new
scoring point in England's rivalry with France, which had been further
complicated by the events known as the 'Great Schism'.

From 1309 to 1377 the main centre of papal influence had been
Avignon in southern France, but this ended in 1378 when Urban VI
was elected Pope in Rome. Not only was Urban an Italian outsider
but his views were unpopular, and his election was contested largely
as a result of his rigid philosophy, his violent temper and his desire
to reform the Church along ultra-orthodox lines. As a result the
college of cardinals withdrew to Anagni, near Rome, where they
deposed Urban and elected a rival, Clement VII, who reigned as
Pope in Avignon. At the same time Urban remained in Rome,
isolated 'like a sparrow on a housetop', and both Popes were forced

to look for secular support in Europe to further their cause. France and Scotland favoured Clement in Avignon, as did the kingdoms of Aragon and Navarre, while the Holy Roman Emperor and England, being anti-French, supported Urban (who would be succeeded in 1389 by Boniface IX).

The Bohemian connection provided by the marriage of Richard and Anne would cement this support for Urban and, as Urban supported the union, hopes were high that it would increase England's standing in Europe. However, the match was not universally popular in England for the very good reason that it was expensive and seemed to bring few benefits. Instead of producing a dowry, Anne's marriage cost the Exchequer some £16,000, which was given in a loan to King Wenceslas, and she brought with her a Bohemian retinue who were both disliked and expensive to maintain. After the royal marriage, held during the feast of Epiphany in January 1382, Walsingham recorded that a tournament was staged which lasted several days and whose pomp and pageantry was everything that Richard would have desired. Once again it seemed that the court was being aggrandised for no particular advantage to the people of England.

As for the happy couple, they seem to have been just that. Although Richard was only a youngster when they married, and while it was hardly a love match, he grew genuinely fond of his young wife. The death of his mother Joan in 1385 also helped to cement the relationship as she had been a formative and perhaps overbearing influence in his life. Whatever else, Anne's presence stimulated court life. Her Bohemian entourage introduced a feminine ingredient and she encouraged her husband's cultural and sartorial interests, adding to the sophistication which Richard wanted to be the keynote of his reign. From the evidence of her effigy in Westminster Abbey, where, touchingly, she lies hand in hand with her husband, Anne was no beauty, but her grace, dignity and good sense brought much-needed stability to Richard's life as he passed from the shallows of privileged youth into the deeper waters of manhood and kingship.

Chapter Two

CHOSEN BY GOD

In the earliest days of Richard's reign it seemed as if the young man would make a happy start to his role as England's king. There was much residual goodwill for the part he had played in coping with the Peasants' Revolt and in the wake of his marriage to Anne, once the anti-Bohemian sentiments had receded, there was widespread confidence that a settled period would follow and that the royal couple would prosper and produce a family to ensure a smooth succession. As the 1380s got into their stride there was every reason to believe that Richard would emerge as a sensible and stable ruler in the tradition which had been cemented by his grandfather Edward III. Hopes were high, too, that he would add to the achievements of his forebears and his father, not least in the martial field. Much of this confidence came from the fact that Richard's reign marked a new beginning, but there was probably a good deal of self-interest involved as a new king brought with him the possibilities of patronage and advancement for those close to the throne.

As for Richard's style of leadership, it was guided by the conviction that he was not like other men. It was a heady faith, bordering on the reckless, and it encouraged him to think that he alone was responsible for all his actions and that in time of need men would look to him as to the dawning sun. As a theory of personal destiny it was all highly subjective and there were no guarantees that others would follow his reasoning or even pay lip service to it; worse, it was to lead him into deep trouble and mental instability later in his reign.

That Richard was determined to follow his own star became clear when he came to select those advisers and courtiers who would be closest to him. Sensible Simon Burley remained his main confidant and mentor, providing a link with the Black Prince and the comforting past, but two appointments signified a change of direction and demonstrated the new ruler's determination to set a personal seal on his court. When Parliament appointed Michael de la Pole, a wealthy and influential supporter of John of Gaunt, and the Earl of Arundel to 'advise and govern the king' the intention was to provide tutelage and curb Richard's wilder tendencies – he had inherited the Plantagenets' ferociously bad temper and had a short fuse – but the appointments were soon used to the throne's advantage.

Shortly afterwards, in March 1383, the Chancellor, Richard Scrope, criticised the King for awarding lavish grants to his followers but this rap over the knuckles achieved nothing but the sacking of the critic himself. Then Richard intervened to show that he was his own man and would not be hobbled by advisers: de la Pole was appointed in Scrope's place and two years later he was created Earl of Suffolk, a position which increased his authority at court and gave him direct access to the King. This too was a sign of the changing times, for the de la Poles were not aristocrats but had made their way in the world through commerce to gain powerful positions at court. The family's origins were in Hull, where Michael's grandfather, Richard, had come to prominence as a merchant financier and, by lending large amounts of money to Edward III, gained royal patronage. In 1333 Richard de la Pole left Hull for London, where he was appointed chief butler at court, a role which gave him access to customs duty on the sale of wine and, more importantly, brought him to public prominence.

A more pernicious influence on Richard was Robert de Vere, 9th Earl of Oxford, a feckless and widely disliked young man who, in becoming close to the King, soon received royal favours and grants of land and titles. De Vere was created Marquess of Dublin in 1385 and, the following year, Duke of Ireland, an extravagant title which bore no relation to his talents or contribution to public life and was greatly resented by the King's uncles, who, royal dukes themselves, were greatly offended by his rapid advancement. Without producing any hard evidence Walsingham hinted that there might have been other reasons for the elevation:

This action demonstrated the depth of King Richard's affection for this man, whom he cultivated and loved, not without a degree of improper intimacy or so it was rumoured. It also provoked discontent among the other lords and barons who were angry that a man of such mediocrity should receive such promotion, for he was not superior to the rest of them in either nobility of birth or gifts of character.

In fact there is nothing to suggest a homosexual relationship between the two men – de Vere had already caused scandal by seducing Agnes de Launcekrona, one of Queen Anne's Bohemian ladies-in-waiting, and making her his mistress – but the closeness of their friendship, coupled with de Vere's butterfly personality and his capacity for toadying, told against him. It was also an awkward reminder of Edward II's earlier and disastrous infatuation with his favourite, Piers Gaveston, although de Vere did not possess the same degree of personal authority over Richard, being more of a close friend and confidant than a creator of policy. Nevertheless, the establishment of a royal inner circle was not only unpopular but foolhardy. In promoting de la Pole Richard had used his own prerogative and ignored the wishes of Parliament, but in de Vere's case his frivolous presence at court was a constant reminder of the King's recklessness and extravagance. Indeed Richard's repeated promotion of favourites meant that he enjoyed only the briefest of honeymoon periods with those who should have been his closest and most loyal supporters. Among those offended by the King's actions were his royal uncles and his advisers from the days of the Black Prince, who were now pressing for the emergence of a more aggressive foreign policy, particularly towards the French.

Normally a successful war cancelled all moral or social debts even if military campaigns were liable to be expensive and a drain on the Exchequer. Powerful kings were supposed to be good soldiers and from the outset Richard was under pressure from his uncles and advisers to resume hostilities in France at the head of an English army just as his forebears had done. Those campaigns had been waged not only for territorial aggrandisement but to maintain national prestige. It must also be said that a renewal of the conflict would have suited the magnates as they all stood to benefit from any English gains in

France. An opportunity came sooner than Richard might have expected or wanted.

In 1383 a revolt in Ghent was followed by the intervention of a French army in the area and the subsequent disruption halted the wool trade, in which English merchants had substantial financial interests. As the export of wool to Flanders was one of the main sources of England's wealth this was a blow which could not be ignored and the response quickly took on the character of a crusade, literally and metaphorically. Here was an early opportunity to gain military glory and at the same time strike a blow to protect English commercial interests, and it fell to Henry Despenser, Bishop of Norwich, a professional soldier with recent experience of fighting in Italy, to accept the challenge. Using his influence at Rome, the Bishop gained Pope Urban VI's sanction to classify the campaign as a crusade which would be fought with the Church's blessing and would be funded by financial contributions in return for plenary indulgences (unqualified remission of punishment in purgatory, at the time one of the great abuses in the Church).

The intervention in the Low Countries was well intentioned but the result was disastrous. Although Despenser did not lack courage and conviction he was at the head of an army which was little more than a rabble and which lacked those prerequisites of success which might have given him a better chance: experienced commanders, a workable plan and decent weapons and equipment. Having crossed over to Flanders and successfully taken Gravelines and Bourbourg in May 1383, Despenser laid siege to Ypres, only to be forced to withdraw at the approach of superior French forces under the command of Philip, Duke of Burgundy, one of the protectors of the new French boy-king, Charles VI. No sooner had the French arrived than they started offering bribes to the English captains and, as these were promptly accepted, there was no fighting. After sacking Gravelines in a token show of force and defiance Despenser was forced to withdraw his army. It was a shameful episode which did nothing to bring any credit to England and, far from being an honourable undertaking, the entire expedition was considered to be a complete waste of money. On the army's return to England the Bishop was stripped of his temporalities but his disgrace was not the end of the matter.

Quite apart from undermining England's national interest and doing nothing to help the wool trade the continued French presence in Flanders gave rise to fears that an invasion of England was being planned and that, as had happened so often in the past, the Scots would take advantage of the situation to attack from the north. Reports arrived in London that French forces had been dispatched to Scotland under the command of Admiral Jean de Vienne. With a sizeable French army assembling on the other side of the Channel it made tactical sense for the English to deal first with the threat from Scotland.

This time the English army, of some twelve thousand men, was under Richard's personal command, although prudently John of Gaunt accompanied the force and provided the bulk of the archers, the main strike force. By the autumn of 1385 the English had achieved most of their tactical aims but had failed to deliver a decisive blow against the enemy. The towns of Melrose, Edinburgh, Perth and Dundee had been attacked and burned but the Scots refused to offer pitched battle, preferring a scorched-earth policy, much to the scorn of de Vienne's knights, who had to watch helplessly as the Scots burned their crops in the Lothians rather than let them fall into English hands. (The ignominy was compounded when their Scottish hosts billed their French allies for the costs incurred by the loss of the harvest and kept de Vienne as a hostage until the money was paid.) Such as it was, the campaign blooded Richard as a military leader but the operation accomplished little other than to force the Scots to adopt Fabian tactics (a refusal to be drawn into battle) to tie down the English army north of the border. The only outcome of any note was the elevation of two of the King's uncles: Edmund of Langley was made Duke of York and Thomas of Woodstock Duke of Gloucester.

The Scottish adventure also marked a parting of the ways for John of Gaunt, who must have seen which way the wind was blowing. With his nephew emerging as a headstrong ruler unwilling to take advice he decided that his future lay in pursuing his claims to the throne of Castile, where King Juan ruled in place of Gaunt's father-in-law, Pedro the Cruel. Gaunt's allies in the venture were the Portuguese, recently freed from Castilian domination, but he required funds from Parliament, which had earlier blocked his attempts to gain financial support for the adventure. However, at the beginning of 1386 the situation changed and, with the French again threatening to invade England, Parliament reckoned that a military expedition in the south-west of France would alter the strategic balance to England's advantage. Gaunt received his funds and the blessing of his nephew: on 8 March 1386 Richard hailed John of Gaunt as King of Castile. For the young king this had the benefit of keeping his uncle out of the country while he faced the first domestic crisis of his reign.

As for Gaunt, he succeeded in some of his aims by conquering Galicia but he failed to unseat King Juan and in 1388 finally negotiated a settlement through the Treaty of Bayonne, by which he renounced his claim to the throne in return for a payment of £100,000 (an enormous sum worth £37 million today) and an annual pension.

By the time these events had taken place Richard's reign was showing signs that it was starting to unravel. At the sitting of Parliament in October 1386 the Commons faced a demand from the Chancellor for an immediate fourfold increase in taxation to pay for England's neglected sea defences, the strengthening of the border with Scotland and Gaunt's campaign in Castile. Against a background of gathering panic about the possibility of a French invasion this huge rise in taxation was too much for Parliament to bear. It was inevitable that someone had to shoulder the blame and a scapegoat was found in the Earl of Suffolk. Supported by the Duke of Gloucester and the Earl of Arundel, both members of the council, the Commons demanded his removal as Chancellor and the ultimatum plunged the court into crisis. When the news reached Richard at his manor at Eltham, near Greenwich, he refused point-blank to countenance the request for the removal of one of his favourites and sent back a tart rejoinder saying that not even a kitchen scullion would be removed from his household at Parliament's request. The retort was typical of a growing arrogance in the King and it brought a stern response. Accompanied by Thomas Arundel, Bishop of Ely and brother to the Earl, Gloucester rode to Eltham and reminded the King that he had a responsibility to call a Parliament once a year and to attend its deliberations. Unless he did so within forty days Parliament would end its sitting and disperse, with the result that Richard would receive no subsidy. According to the author of the *Eulogium Historiarum*, Richard asked Gloucester whether his companions were willing to take up arms against him, to which the Duke replied: 'we do not rebel or arm ourselves against the king except in order to instruct him.' Once again it was not the person of the King which was threatened, but his policies and those who advised him.

Unwisely, Richard then raised the stakes by petulantly countering that he would seek help from the King of France. It was an idle threat which no one could take seriously but it stung Gloucester into reminding his nephew that a king could be deposed if he neglected his duties and chose to listen to evil advisers, the implication being that it had happened once before in the country's history when Edward II had been forced to abdicate in 1327 in response to an indictment which accused him of being 'incorrigible without hope of amendment'. Richard took the hint and dismissed Suffolk as well as two other officials, the Treasurer and the Lord Keeper of the Privy Seal. Suffolk was impeached and condemned to a period of imprisonment only to be pardoned and allowed to continue to bask in the King's favour. This was another foolish and peevish action which achieved nothing other than to enrage further Richard's enemies but it counted for little as Parliament had already decided on a new strategy to curb the King's spending. A commission was established to review royal finances and to oversee policy and although it would only exist for a year Richard had to undertake to agree to its findings. This he did with little grace, arguing that the imposition of the commission was a violation of his personal prerogative and an affront to his person and the dignity of the Crown. Far from calming the situation, the appointment of the commission and Richard's opposition to it kept the two sides on course for further confrontation.

The King's reaction was to distance himself from what was happening and so began his so-called 'gyration' of 1387, when he took himself and his retinue out of London and began a great peregrination of the country which lasted from February to November. The move kept him out of London at a time when the commission was doing its work but Richard was also looking ahead and planning his next moves. He had been humiliated by his opponents, the inviolability of his royal office had been called into question and he felt threatened by the turn of events. By travelling through his realm he would be able to gauge if he had any support in the shires and to see for himself if he could use the opportunity to rally followers to his cause. While this was happening de Vere used his influence in the north-west to raise an armed force of Welsh archers and Cheshire foot soldiers, ostensibly for service in Ireland but in reality to protect the King's household. At the same time Richard took legal advice from his senior judges, including Sir Robert Tresilian, the Chief Justice, who had been responsible for dealing with the aftermath of the Peasants' Revolt. The intention was to discover how far the King's prerogative had been infringed by Parliament's actions and to get a legal opinion on whether or not the commission had been imposed against Richard's will and, if so, the extent to which those responsible were guilty of treason. The judges found in the King's favour in August and September but he could not use the judicial findings to his own benefit until he returned to London, where he hoped that he would find himself in a stronger position.

The first indications were good. When Richard rode into the city on 10 November he was greeted by enthusiastic crowds but, as Walsingham noted, 'these Londoners were as swallows, found at one time with the lords, at another with the king, never settled and untrustworthy'. When it came to the bit Richard found that the Londoners' expressions of loyalty and support were more for the office of the King – he had been absent from the capital for ten months – and less for the person of the King. Although the Lord Mayor, Nicholas Brembre, rallied support for Richard there was to be no general or widespread backing from the people of London, who clearly had decided to await the outcome of events. By now the weight of the disagreement was swinging in the direction of Gloucester and Arundel, who had been joined by another powerful magnate, Thomas Beauchamp, Earl of Warwick, in gathering support against the King, as much to curb him as to protect their own interests. They were well aware that a judgement had been made against them and had taken their forces north of London, first to Haringey and then to Waltham Cross, where they consolidated their position and sent letters to London setting out their complaints about the King's advisers.

Their next step was to issue a written appeal on 14 November indicting Suffolk, de Vere, Tresilian, Brembre and Alexander Neville the Archbishop of York for treason, giving their reasons to the King in the stark words of a contemporary chronicler, Thomas Favent: 'It is in the interest of the state that any traitors who cluster around you deserve to be thrown out or punished, since it is better for some men to die for their country than for the whole nation to perish.' Three days later the Lords Appellant (as they came to be known on account of their appeal, or accusation) presented themselves in London to make their case in person and to their surprise Richard immediately accepted their appeal. It was agreed that Parliament should reconvene the following year, the date being set for 3 February 1388, but, of course, the King never had any intention of keeping his side of the bargain. He hoped to play for time, while four of the accused went into hiding or exile: Suffolk crossed over to France, Tresilian took refuge in Westminster Abbey, Neville fled north dressed as a priest and Brembre remained in London.

De Vere hurried north to raise his army and to recruit for the King's cause. On hearing the news the Lords Appellant started gathering their own forces and they were joined in their enterprise by two younger men: John of Gaunt's son Henry Bolingbroke, Earl of Derby, and Arundel's son-in-law Thomas Mowbray, Earl of Nottingham. Bolingbroke had an additional score to settle: after seducing Agnes de Launcekrona de Vere had repudiated his wife, Philippa de Courcy, who was Bolingbroke's cousin and a granddaughter of Edward III. Suddenly, after half a century of calm, England found itself on the brink of civil war.

De Vere made the first move at the beginning of December by moving his force of 4250 men south towards London, hoping to impose royal authority on the capital before the Lords Appellant could intervene by offering protection to the royal household. He did this not without hope. His Welsh archers were well trained and battle-hardened, many of them having fought in France, and they were commanded by an experienced soldier, Sir Thomas Molyneux, but de Vere had to move quickly before the opposition blocked his path to London. However, by then it was already too late. Gloucester had moved his forces north of London to take up a defensive position at Northampton, forcing de Vere to take a more southerly route. The original plan had been to head towards Stow-on-the-Wold via the ancient Fosse Way, which ran from Axminster through Bath and Leicester to Lincoln, but when de Vere approached Burford on 20 December he found that Bolingbroke and Thomas Mowbray had cut off the route across the Thames by encamping on the island between Pidnell Bridge and Radcot Bridge on the Berkshire–Oxfordshire border near Faringdon. The trap was then sprung. When de Vere's forces arrived at the two bridges they found

that one had been sabotaged and the other was heavily guarded by
Bolingbroke's men. Unable to cross the Thames, they were further
discommoded by the arrival of Gloucester's force from the north. As
the battle began Gloucester's pikemen advanced and the outnumbered
and surprised Royalists began surrendering in droves or desperately
tried to cross the river to safety. The way was now open for the Lord
Appellants' army to move in triumph towards London, where Richard
had wisely taken refuge in the Tower.

As for de Vere, he thought only of his own safety and was one of
the first to flee by mounting a fresh horse and getting across the
wreckage of Pidnell Bridge. As recounted by Thomas Favent, his
excuse was that he alone was wanted by the Lords Appellant and that
his army could lay down their arms once he had gone: 'Before battle
is joined I shall slip away and save myself, if I can; for they are seeking
me, and me alone; they have no quarrel with you. When I am gone,
you may slip away easily.' But it was a desperate move. The horse
refused to jump and de Vere took it into the river and rode upstream,
lightening his load by removing his armour and sword, which were
found the following day and encouraged the rumour that he had
drowned. In fact, by holding his nerve even when he came under
heavy fire from a company of archers at Radcot Bridge, he managed
to escape in the gathering gloom and after taking shelter in the nearby
woods he made his way westwards and later managed to leave
England for exile in France. Five years later he died in penury, having
been savaged by a wild boar while hunting.

Radcot Bridge does not figure greatly in the list of battles fought
on British soil. It was more of a skirmish than a pitched battle and
without their leader the Royalist army did not offer much opposition.
But it was a turning point: Englishmen had taken up arms against
Englishmen for the first time in over half a century, since Queen
Isabel and Roger de Mortimer had unseated Edward II in 1326, and
for a time it looked as if history would repeat itself with the deposition
of another English king.

Richard was now at the mercy of the Lords Appellant and there is
evidence to suggest that they were minded to depose him there and
then and might have done so had they been able to agree on a
successor. It is possible that Richard lost his crown for three days but
had it restored when it became clear that Gloucester would be the

main claimant, something which Bolingbroke would never accept while his father, John of Gaunt, was still alive. Even so, the outlook was bleak for Richard.

Shortly after Christmas the two sides met to agree terms but, having defeated the Royalist army, the Lords Appellant held all the cards. Backed into a corner and surrounded by an army which had inflicted a decisive defeat on his own forces, Richard had no option but to concede all the demands made to him. Parliament would be summoned, warrants would be issued for the arrest of the five accused and others were added to the list, including Simon Burley and the King's Steward, Sir John Beauchamp. To add salt to the wound warrants were also issued for the arrest of the judges who had found in the King's favour over Parliament's infringement of his prerogative. These were telling blows to the King, who also had to agree to the commissioners purging his own household of extraneous servants and stripping it of unnecessary expenditure. For a ruler who believed absolutely in the singularity of his kingship this was a setback, made worse by the knowledge that he lacked any realisable support in the country.

Parliament duly opened on the agreed date and from the outset it was obvious that the Lords Appellant were in complete control, a point they made tellingly by entering the Palace of Westminster dressed in surcoats of gold and with their arms linked in solidarity. Richard was forced to listen to their lengthy appeal, which was two hours in the reading, and it was upheld, despite a legal challenge from the King's party arguing that it was without known precedent. For the accused there could only be one sentence: the fugitives (Suffolk and de Vere) were sentenced to death *in absentia* but the Archbishop of York escaped death by being outlawed – he was stripped of his honours and possessions – and his case was referred to Rome. Brembre made a spirited defence but he followed Tresilian to the scaffold, the former Chief Justice having been forcibly removed from Westminster Abbey on Gloucester's orders.

This was not the end of the blood-letting. Charges of 'accroaching' the royal power by taking advantage of his youth were raised against Burley and three other courtiers, Sir John Salisbury, Sir James Berners and Sir John Beauchamp, and all were sentenced to death. Queen Anne pleaded desperately to save Burley's life, but in vain: the only concession was a decision to acknowledge his status by beheading him instead of hanging him from the public scaffold. As for the judges, they too were sentenced to death but they were eventually spared and instead sent to exile in Ireland.

It had been a shocking episode and one which brought credit to none of the participants. The Lords Appellant had no legal backing for their actions, the so-called trials were a sham and the death sentences made a mockery of justice, but by acting in this way and by coercing Parliament Gloucester and his fellow rebels had shown that they wielded the real power in the land. It was not surprising that the meeting of Parliament became known later as the Merciless Parliament. A contemporary popular macaronic complaint, written in English and Latin and running to 236 lines (in the possession of the British Library, MS Harley 941) gives some idea of the widespread disaffection with its attack on the mores and fashions at Richard's court and the pressing need for reform:

> Syng I wolde, butt, alas!
> *decendunt prospera grata* [good times are fading away].
> Ynglond sum tyme was
> *regnorum gemma vocata* [once called the jewel of nations],
> Of manhod the flowre,
> *ibi quondam floruit omnis* [where once all flourished];
> Now gone ys that oure [hour] –
> *traduntur talia sompnis* [such things are fading into dreams].
> Lechery, slewthe [sloth] and pryde –
> *hec sunt quibus Anglia paret* [these are the things which England
>   obeys].
> Sethyn trewth [since truth] was set asyde,
> *dic qualiter Anglia staret* [tell how England stands].

And yet, amid the mayhem and the carnage, there was one saving grace. Although Richard had been humbled no attempt had been made to interfere with his personal rule and no one had demanded that he be unseated. It was enough that the court had been cleansed of the King's advisers (like de Vere, Suffolk died in exile), his regal powers had been curbed and his person had been humiliated. The moves by the Lords Appellant had also cleared the air and given the

King a chance to reassert his authority. A year later, on 3 May 1389, at the age of twenty-two and having passed his majority, Richard assumed responsibility for ruling the country, after asking the assembled nobles, 'Why should I be denied a right which is granted to anyone of lower rank?' His first step was to appoint as Chancellor William of Wykeham, an elder statesman who had also served Edward III and risen from a humble background to become one of the great patrons of education, having already founded New College at Oxford and a school for boys at Winchester.

Other appointments to Richard's council also showed the King's independence of mind without offending the Lords Appellant, who had largely withdrawn from public life after getting their way at court. In succession to Wykeham Thomas Brantingham, Bishop of Exeter, became Treasurer and Edmund Stafford, Dean of York, was appointed Lord Keeper of the Privy Seal. Yet despite his claims of maturity Richard still needed a mentor and he found one in the familiar figure of John of Gaunt, who returned from Spain in 1389 without his Castilian throne but boosted by substantial financial rewards. The King's uncle, now approaching fifty, had cast off many of his early ambitions and was thinking of his legacy. Until the end of his life ten years later his loyalty to Richard was unquestioned and he became a constant presence and close adviser. In gratitude Richard gave his uncle one of his own titles, Duke of Aquitaine, although the honour was double-edged as it only served to fuel spiteful and long-held suspicions that Gaunt might use his new authority to claim the Crown.

The next five years of Richard's reign were marked by relative harmony interspersed with episodes which showed that the King had lost none of his impetuosity or his ability to chose the wrong option. The anticipated outbreak of hostilities with France had failed to materialise and thanks to Gaunt's earlier diplomatic interventions in his pursuit of the throne of Castile, a truce held between the two countries. It helped that King Charles VI had suffered the first of the periodic bouts of insanity which would disfigure his reign after declaring himself King of France on coming of age in 1388. The reasons for Charles VI's incapacity are difficult to know – schizophrenia, porphyria and bipolar disorder have all been advanced as causes – but the first outbreak of insanity, in 1392, was recorded.

The attempted assassination of Charles's friend and adviser Oliver de Clisson encouraged him to mount an expedition into Brittany to apprehend the culprits and during the progress the King was unusually on edge. At one point during the journey the royal party was stopped and warned by a stranger that the King was about to be betrayed by unknown assailants. This warning was dismissed but there were terrible consequences. In the midday heat a page dropped the King's lance and as it fell to the ground it made a mighty noise which seems to have unhinged Charles. Drawing his sword and shouting, 'Treason,' he rode through his escorts and started swinging wildly at them. A number were killed before he was overpowered.

In the aftermath Burgundy assumed the regency but it was the beginning of a litany of episodes in which Charles would lose his mind and be incapable of ruling France. On another occasion he was unable to remember his identity and this was followed by periods when he refused to wash or change his clothes. Later he came to believe that he was made of glass and would break if people approached him. The worst incident occurred in 1393, when he was almost burned to death at a ball organised by his wife, Queen Isabeau, for which he and a number of courtiers dressed as wild men, and during their charade their costumes caught fire. Fortunately the King was saved during this incident, which achieved notoriety as 'Le Bal des Ardents' (Dance of the Burning Men), when the Duchess de Berry pulled her skirt over him to extinguish the flames, but he never recovered full sanity.

The French king's incapacity was a boon for English diplomacy as it diverted attention from the possibility of a fresh outbreak of hostilities between the two countries. As a result France's allies the Scots were quiet and that too helped Richard as an earlier period of volatility along the northern border had been unsettling. At the time of the Merciless Parliament the Scots had taken advantage of England's internal problems by sending into Northumberland a strong raiding party which defeated the English defending forces led by Harry Hotspur, the Earl of Northumberland's eldest son and the Warden of the East March. While a diversionary force attacked English positions in Ireland the main thrust was led by the Earl of Fife and the Lord of Galloway Archibald the Grim, who attacked Carlisle and ravaged the valley of the River Eden. At the same time another force under the Earls of March, Moray and Douglas assembled at Jedburgh and swept through Northumberland with fire and sword to lay waste to Durham.

Newcastle was also threatened before the Scots retired northwards with forces led by Hotspur and his brother Ralph in pursuit.

On 5 August (or, according to English sources, 19 August) the English had reached Otterburn in Redesdale to find the Scots camped to the north. Although it was late in the day and his men were exhausted Hotspur decided on a pre-emptive strike and the resultant battle was what the chronicler Froissart described as 'one of the sorest and best foughten without cowardice or faint hearts'. The battle was won for the Scots in the gloaming when Douglas led a ferocious charge into the English flanks only to be axed to the ground. Despite Douglas's death the defeat at Otterburn was a severe embarrassment to Richard not least because Hotspur was captured and subsequently ransomed for a huge sum. One of the countless border battles fought along the Scottish and English marches and one of the infrequent times when the Scots were victorious, Otterburn was the inspiration for 'Chevy Chase', one of the most celebrated and evocative of the border ballads:

> There was slayne upon the English part
> For sooth as I you say,
> Of nine thousand English men
> Five hundred came away.
>
> The others slayne were in the field;
> Christ keep their souls from woe!
> Seeing there was so few friends
> Against so many a foe.
>
> Then on the morn they made them bieres
> Of birch and hazell gray:
> Many a widow with weeping teares
> Their makes they fette [fetched] away.

When news of the defeat at Otterburn reached Richard he was reported to be furious, but it was the last occasion in his reign when he was to be discommoded by the Scots. It was not the last time, though, when the Scots would be involved in the affairs of England.

The relative tranquillity of this period of Richard's life also produced an attractive picture of the creative and artistic aspects of his personality. Court poets were encouraged and patronised and in return they would read their work at the King's table. While there was nothing new in this practice the main development came from the fact that they wrote in English rather than in French, with the consequence that the native tongue gradually became acceptable at court. Richard, too, spoke English as well as French and his positive attitude to the language led to its acceptance at court. Among those literary innovators was Thomas Usk, Under-Sheriff of London, who was executed by the Merciless Parliament and wrote *The Testament of Love* while languishing in prison. In it he argued that people should stick to their own native languages and that the English should use their 'mother's tongue'.

Of those writing in English the most eminent was Geoffrey Chaucer, whose career had begun in the reign of Edward III and who had enjoyed John of Gaunt's patronage. His elegy *The Book of the Duchess* was written in memory of Gaunt's first wife, Blanche, and his own wife, Philippa, was the sister of Katherine Swynford, who became Gaunt's third wife in January 1396 after years as his mistress. One of Richard's first acts on his accession was to confirm Chaucer in his position of Controller of Customs and Subsidy of Wools, Skins and Hides, a lucrative appointment which brought him considerable wealth and political power in London. Chaucer had also been involved in a number of embassies in Europe, most notably in Italy in the winter of 1372–3, when he came under the influence of contemporary Italian writing and may even have met Boccaccio and Petrarch.

Chaucer seems to have suffered at the hands of the Lords Appellant in 1388, when royal appointments came under scrutiny, but a year later he was back in Richard's favour. Appointed Clerk of the King's Works, he was responsible for the Tower and Westminster Palace as well as other royal residences, parks and lodges for just under two years. His last official position was that of Deputy Forester of the Royal Forest of North Petherton in Somerset and the records show that he was in receipt of several gifts and stipends from Richard, including the annual presentation of a hogshead of wine. In return for that patronage he wrote for Queen Anne his long poem *The Legend of Good Women* with its well-known lines from the prologue praising the common daisy which announces the beginning of summer:

That, of al the floures in the mede [meadow],
Thanne love I most thise floures white and rede
Swiche as men callen daysyes in our toun.

During Richard's reign Chaucer wrote *The Canterbury Tales*, the work for which he is best known. Written predominantly in rhyming couplets, it extends to seventeen thousand lines and its prologue describes the meeting of assorted pilgrims in the Tabard Inn at Southwark as they prepare to journey to Canterbury. Detailed portraits are provided of all the pilgrims, who come from all walks of society, and the narrative is driven by the conceit that each should tell a story along the way (the original scheme was for four stories, two on the outward journey and two on the return), with the teller of the best tale receiving a free supper. Although the work is incomplete and there are doubts over the correct order of the stories, *The Canterbury Tales* provides an intimate picture of the various strands of English social life in Chaucer's day, from the courtly Knight with his experience of fighting in Europe to the virtuous Friar and the down-to-earth but lecherous Wife of Bath.

Here is a conspectus of English society in the fourteenth century which covers the main representatives of the different social levels: the soldiery, the learned professional class, the landed gentry, agricultural labourers, the rising middle class, the tradesmen, the monastic orders and people from the provinces. All of the portraits reveal carefully crafted individuals but they are also representatives of a certain type of person who come alive through Chaucer's artful use of physical detail – 'his [the Friar's] neck white was as a fleur-de-lys' – and his ability to create an intimacy between character and reader. Nothing like this series of portraits had ever appeared before in European literature and as a result *The Canterbury Tales* is one of the great ornaments of Richard's reign. Writing three centuries later, in his preface to *Fables, Ancient and Modern* (1700), John Dryden was moved to say of Chaucer: 'He must have been a man of a most wonderful comprehensive nature, because, as it has been truly observed of him, he has taken into the compass of his Canterbury Tales the various manners and humour (as we now call them) of the whole English nation in his age.'

Of the other Ricardian poets – the generic description is now in general use – two stand out. John Gower was a friend of Chaucer and shared with Ralph Strode, a fellow of Merton College, Oxford, the dedication of *Troilus and Criseyde*: he appears as 'moral Gower'. He was fluent in French, Latin and English, his principal work in the latter tongue being his *Confessio Amantis*, written in the 1390s, allegedly at Richard's command after he recognised the poet while sailing on the Thames. Like *The Canterbury Tales*, it is a collection of stories, in this case taking their themes from the Seven Deadly Sins and drawing widely from classical and medieval romantic literature, all related in a narrative style that is plain yet has a metrical sophistication that brings unity to the whole poem. In *Vox Clamantis*, written in Latin, Gower dwelt on the turbulence caused by the Peasants' Revolt and reviewed the foibles of different levels of English society before ending with an admonition to the King. Later in life Gower seems to have fallen out with Chaucer. A compliment in the eulogy was dropped from the poem's final version (1392–3) but this may have had as much to do with politics as a breakdown in a literary friendship. Also absent was the earlier prologue's dedication to Richard II and in its place appeared a similar compliment to Henry Bolingbroke.

The other great poet of the age was the author of *Piers Plowman*, generally ascribed to William Langland, about whom little is known. (Early in the long poem the narrator is revealed as 'Will'.) Written in the South Midlands dialect with a mixture of dialectical colourings, this wondrously imaginative work reveals the ignorance and misery of the lower classes of villeins, whose grievances came to a head in the Peasants' Revolt. The figure of Piers is drawn straight from the Gospels, a Christ-like figure whose pleas for humility, simplicity and honest labour give the work its philosophical direction. Not that the narrator idealises the poor. They are vilified for being shiftless and profligate just as the rich are condemned for their avarice and rapacity, and his message reduces itself to the simple notion that all classes have to reform themselves by modelling their lives on Christ's example. It is no wonder that John Ball invoked the name 'Peres Plouzman' in his address to the peasants of Essex in 1381, for here is a work that is profound while preaching a simple message of redemption as exemplified in the pardon given by Truth to Piers Plowman at the end of the second vision:

Do wel, and haue wel and God shal haue thi sowle;
And do yuel [evil] and haue yuel, hope thow non other
But after thi ded-day Deuel shal haue thi sowle.

In addition to patronising the arts and making his court a place of refinement and grace Richard developed a finely honed sense of himself and the strength of his royal lineage. Of particular interest to him was the figure of Edward the Confessor, with whom he felt he enjoyed a mystical relationship and who had been canonised in 1161. As an outward manifestation of his respect Richard had the royal arms impaled with those of the saint and was responsible for the various manifestations of Edward the Confessor which were used in the rebuilding of Westminster Hall, the magnificent edifice, once the largest in Europe, which had been built in the eleventh century by William Rufus. Its centrepiece was the huge braced hammerbeam roof, designed by Henry Yevele, which dispensed with the need for the supporting arcades of columns, but also worthy of note was Richard's stall. Richly decorated, it was a monument to the King's personal vanity and to the importance he placed on his monarchy, dominated as it was by a huge, full-length portrait. It is the earliest state portrait in English history – today it can be found inside the west door of Westminster Abbey – and as it made rich use of hammered gold the wonder is that it survived at all.

Richard's other infatuation was with Edward II. Given the threats made against him by the Lords Appellant and the warning that he might face the same fate as his doomed forebear it might seem an odd choice, but Richard entertained a devout determination to have his great-grandfather restored to history. After visiting Edward's tomb in Gloucester he arranged for regular devotions to be made in his memory and attempted to persuade the Pope to canonise his murdered ancestor. Nothing came of the submission – a contemporary cult focused on Edward's tomb was short-lived – but the fascination with kings and canonisation was clearly a factor in Richard's view of his role.

Two unfortunate incidents made an impact on this relatively benign phase of Richard's reign. In 1392 he quarrelled with the City of London over the grant of a loan. The City was a wealthy, cosmopolitan place but it had proved to be a fickle partner by supporting the Lords Appellant after it had pledged its loyalty to the

King. This latest refusal to offer the King any financial support led to the imposition of a huge fine and a string of humiliating punishments. Richard decided to suspend the Lord Mayor and the leading magistrates, replacing them with a royal warden, and then he took the unwise decision to remove the law courts and the Chancery to York. As Walsingham noted, 'the innovation did not last long, for these institutions were brought back to London just as easily as they had been taken to York', but the King's rash behaviour cooled his relationship with the City. The matter was papered over with the restoration of the loan and the reconciliation was celebrated with a grand pageant in which the King played a leading role, but lasting damage had been done and he could never again count on London's fullest support.

Two years later Richard suffered a heavier blow when, in June 1394, Anne died suddenly at the age of twenty-seven. The loss unmanned Richard and left him prostrated by grief. Despite the unpromising start to their marriage he had come to love Anne and he seems to have been totally unprepared for her untimely death. A huge state funeral was held for the Queen in Westminster Abbey, where Richard created the joint tomb on which the hands of their effigies are clasped in eternal love. During the service Richard's grief and his capacity for impetuosity resurfaced when he struck the Earl of Arundel with a rod in retaliation for the magnate's rudeness in arriving late and then asking permission to leave early. Arundel was clearly courting trouble by behaving so rudely but the King's response outweighed the slight he had received and is an indication of both the pain he felt at his wife's passing and the inner rage which was never far from the surface when he believed that his person was being affronted.

Further evidence of Richard's disturbed state of mind came when he ordered the destruction of part of the royal manor house at Sheen on the banks of the Thames in Surrey, a favourite residence where he had built a set of private apartments and a chapel. So bitter was his sorrow at the loss of Anne that he could not even bear to look again at the site of a place where they had enjoyed such intense happiness. Both episodes suggest an intemperate personality and there is little doubt that Richard's immoderate response to problems was a worrying behavioural flaw, particularly at a time when he was anxious to set the seal on his personal rule.

Chapter Three

ALL POMP AND MAJESTY
I DO FORSWEAR

After Anne's death Richard went into a period of prolonged mourning but he could not ignore two pressing problems which impinged on his rule and required his urgent attention: France and Ireland. From the evidence of the *Westminster Chronicle* it seems that Richard was fully aware of the need to find some sort of accommodation with France which would end the quarrel or produce an honourable and lasting truce without either side losing too much face. Continuing the struggle or mounting fresh military expeditions against the French meant raising taxes and as that would be an unpopular move it would inevitably harm his own position. He had already witnessed the enforced removal from office of one chancellor (Suffolk in 1386) and it is clear that he understood that 'damaging results' would follow the high costs of any new military campaign.

The French, too, were keen to find a compromise as the constraints on the Flemish wool trade were equally damaging to them at a time when Philip, Duke of Burgundy and uncle to Charles VI, was strengthening his interests in the area, having married Margaret of Flanders in 1383, thereby acquiring further land there as well as in Franche-Comté, Artois, Hainault and Brabant. In 1393 the two countries began negotiations to find a solution to the question of English holdings in Aquitaine, the real bone of contention between them. Richard was eager to settle the issue once and for all, and at one point agreed to the suggestion that he should pay liege homage to the King of France (the practice whereby one sovereign renders feudal allegiance to another) but when that proposal was opposed by the

English Parliament the negotiations came to a standstill. Nonetheless, there was still a desire on both sides to reach a settlement and Richard's freedom to enter into a new marriage produced the solution. In March 1396 he and Charles VI concluded an agreement to work together to end the Great Schism which had divided the Catholic Church and to embark on a crusade at a later date to recover the Holy Land. There would be a truce lasting twenty-eight years and in return Richard consented to marry Isabella of Valois, the six-year-old daughter of the French king and his wife, Isabeau of Bavaria. The marriage took place in October 1396 and, according to Froissart, the girl-queen was entrusted to the care of the Duchesses of Gloucester and Lancaster, who conducted her to Guînes, where the two kings celebrated the union.

> This business accomplished the kings went to their banquet in King Richard's pavilion. King Charles sat on the right-hand side of the hall, and was served in royal fashion, according to the custom of his own country, that is to say, he ate helpings of all the dishes of the first course at once from a single large dish, and likewise the second course. The king of England was served in the manner of his land.
>
> After the feast, the kings kissed each other, then mounted their horses. The king of England set the king of France on his way, and finally they shook hands and parted company.

Despite this kingly amity the union was not popular. Not only was the bride French but she was a child; it would take time before she could produce children to ensure the succession because fourteen was the legal age for sexual intercourse. (More realistically, it was also believed that if a girl child had matured sufficiently to bear children she was ready for marriage.) But for Richard the match was a tempting proposition. As part of the settlement Isabella brought a handsome dowry and in the longer term, with the birth of children, the marriage promised to end once and for all the long and expensive confrontation with France. As Walsingham put it, the new relationship meant that 'both monarchs could live in peace and tranquillity, and could secure a proper state of harmony between their two kingdoms for ever, and no more Christian blood would be shed'.

This was exactly what Richard desired: unlike his forebears, he had no taste for warfare in general and was not in any mood to go to war with France at a time when the confrontation was effectively in stalemate. There was never any likelihood that Richard would emulate his earlier namesake and embark on a crusade in the Holy Land but the agreement with France did put pressure on him to play a part in ending the Great Schism. Under the proposals the French would withdraw support from their candidate Benedict XIII, who had succeeded Clement VII in Avignon, while Richard would take the same course of action against Boniface IX in Rome. (This never happened as Richard dragged his heels over the matter and events overtook the need to do anything.)

Having settled the relationship with France by means of the new period of truce and the marriage agreement, Richard was able to turn his attention to Ireland, another seemingly intractable problem in urgent need of attention. No English king since John in 1210 had taken the trouble to visit the Irish lordship and in that time the country had become almost ungovernable. Parliaments had come into being in the thirteenth century and consisted of county and borough representatives, but real power remained in the hands of the aristocracy. The four main landowning magnates were the great Anglo-Irish earldoms of Desmond, Ormond, Kildare and Ulster (the latter had passed by marriage from the de Burghs to Clarence) and land was also held by absentee English landlords from the English peerage. Warfare with the Gaelic chiefdoms was endemic throughout the century. During Richard's minority Edmund Mortimer, 3rd (English) Earl of March, had been appointed to govern Ireland in 1379 but his period in office lasted barely two years. He was drowned while crossing a ford in County Cork and his title and holdings passed to his seven-year-old-son, Roger.

After becoming king Richard had made the Duke of Gloucester Lord Lieutenant of Ireland but nothing had come of the appointment as his uncle was little interested in Irish matters. Then an expedition to restore control had been planned in 1389 but the exigencies of domestic problems and the possibility of war with France had prevented anything happening. Richard had also hoped that his friend de Vere would take the matter out of his hands in his role as Duke of Ireland but his downfall meant that Ireland was left rudderless with

English authority confined to parts of Ulster and Leinster. Even around the Pale – Dublin, Meath, Louth and Kildare – English rule was liable to attack and disruption by the native Irish.

During this period there had been a revival of Gaelic power as native Irish chieftains started to regain the initiative against the English settlers. Largely this was done through military action against English positions, but the Irish were also helped by English inaction in failing to respond to the attacks. Ireland was divided into two distinct parts which gave recognition to where there was still peace and where fighting was taking place – *terra pacis* (or 'maghery') and *terra guerre* (or 'marches') – and all over the country there were enclaves where independent chieftains held sway beyond reach of the law. It coincided with a revival of Gaelic learning, manifesting itself in works such as the *Yellow Book of Lecan* and the *Book of Ballymote* which helped to record and codify Gaelic knowledge of the day.

So concerned were the English colonists about this revival that in 1366 Ireland's Parliament had flexed its muscles by passing the Statutes of Kilkenny, an ambitious piece of legislation aimed at strengthening the hand of the Anglo-Irish by insisting on the use of the English language and English legislation while halting the renewal of interest in the Gaelic language and culture. The statutes also attempted to prevent further violence by prohibiting the import of weapons and placing restrictions on the use of men-at-arms, but, like most restrictive legislation involving the possession of weapons, it was only successful in the breach. It was also difficult to check the ability to speak Gaelic as many Anglo-Irish families subscribed to the fosterage system. In this popular method of child-rearing, children were sent into the care of Gaelic-speaking families and although there was no intermarriage the practice exposed the Anglo-Irish to the Gaelic language and culture, one reason for the passing of the Kilkenny statutes.

One of the chieftains in the Wicklow Mountains, Art McMurrough, styled himself King of Leinster and 'captain' of his nation and in that role he felt strong enough to attack English-held towns in Leinster and even to threaten Dublin. It was to curb this kind of lawless power that Richard set sail for Ireland in the autumn of 1394 at the head of a large army of eight thousand men and in the company of the Duke of

Gloucester, Roger Mortimer, the now grown-up (English) Earl of March, and the Earls of Rutland, Huntingdon and Nottingham. His tactics were straightforward and turned out to be reasonably successful: to confine McMurrough in the mountains of Wicklow and to restrict his movement as a prelude to pacifying Leinster and colonising it with English settlers. The size of the English army made such an impression on the Irish that they confined their attacks on it to ambushes, which were quickly routed by the English archers.

By the time Richard reached Dublin the Irish were ready to submit to him. Contrary to expectations Richard did not use his overwhelming superiority to punish the chieftains but decided on a policy of appeasement. In return for their oaths of allegiance he promised to arbitrate on their problems with the English landowners and to provide the necessary finance to revitalise local rule. McMurrough even consented to return land he had confiscated and these concessions enabled Richard to count his expedition a great success.

When he eventually left the country the following May he did so in the belief that English rule had been reimposed and that the Gaelic revival had been checked. It did not last: McMurrough reneged on his agreement and the Earl of March failed to make any impact as Lord Lieutenant of Ireland and was soon in conflict with Niall Mhor O'Neill over the terms of this Ulster chieftain's submission to Richard. Even so, the peaceful subjugation of the Irish greatly enhanced Richard's reputation, persuading chroniclers such as Walsingham to believe that a brave new age was at hand:

That year [1397], the kingdom seemed to be on the verge of enjoying a period of great stability, partly because of the Royal marriage and the riches accumulated in aid of that, but also on account of the long truce with France, and the presence of so many noblemen, more numerous and higher in rank than any other realm could produce.

As happened so frequently throughout Richard's reign it was all mirage. He might have scored diplomatic and domestic successes but beneath the glitter there was a good deal of unease. In particular the rapprochement with France was not universally popular because it seemed to place England in a subservient position to the French king. According to the French chronicler Jean Froissart, who was in England at this time and was a pungent observer of the ruling classes, Gloucester was particularly scornful not only because he personally hated the French but because he was suspicious of a clause in the marriage agreement which allowed the French to intervene in English affairs should any of Richard's subjects attempt to harm him. There was also disquiet about the religious and political ramifications associated with Richard's marriage to the French princess. Not only was France a long-standing opponent but it was on the other side of the Great Schism and a marriage agreement would imply a closer union with the House of Valois.

When Parliament assembled in January it quickly quashed a proposal to send an English army to fight in support of Charles VI's territorial ambitions in northern Italy, where the French had a claim on the territory of the Duke of Milan. Once again Richard was seen to be responsible for introducing a reckless policy of appeasement as the offer had been made as the result of a rash promise he had made to his future French father-in-law.

The embarrassment was followed by the presentation of a petition, signed by Thomas Haxey, a clerk in the Court of Common Pleas, complaining about the extravagance of the royal court, owing to the numbers of people in receipt of the King's largesse. This was a sensitive point and, believing it to be a fresh attack on his prerogative, Richard reacted badly. He appealed to the Lords about this 'great offence' against his person and they duly obliged by declaring that the petition was tantamount to treason. As a result Haxey was condemned to death and then reprieved. The wretched man had probably been prompted to act by others, but the incident reflected badly on Richard.

Far from being able to enjoy this unexpected period of relative surface calm, he saw his reign once again in danger of collapse, largely as a result of his increasingly unbridled profligacy. Having prophesied the dawn of a golden age, Walsingham was now obliged to report that 'throughout the realm no prelate, no city nor any individual known to be wealthy could avoid loaning money to the king'. Richard had always been extravagant but his expenditure had generally been kept within bounds; now it was spinning out of control, forcing him to borrow, and, worse, the vainglorious side to his character was being reinforced.

About this time the author of the *Eulogium Historiarum* recorded a worrying new trend at court, where the King 'ordered a throne to be set up in his chamber on which he could sit after dinner until evening, showing himself. He would talk to no one but would look at people and whoever he looked at, whatever his rank, he had to genuflect.' There were even widespread rumours, largely believed, that through his new connection with France Richard was attempting to gain support to have himself elected Holy Roman Emperor. Grandiose behaviour of that kind was unlikely to boost his popularity or his support among the nobility, but in themselves such acts were not the cause of his eventual downfall. Rather, it was the pursuit of a long-held grievance that led to his demise.

For reasons which are neither clear nor logical Richard decided to take revenge on his enemies the Lords Appellant, who had humbled him almost ten years earlier. His main targets were the leaders, Gloucester, Arundel and Warwick, who, he correctly believed, were the main driving force behind the continuing actions against him. At the end of July 1397 all three were summoned to attend a banquet in London but only Warwick accepted the invitation and for his pains he was arrested and imprisoned in the Tower. Arundel was dealt with next, and incarcerated in Carisbrooke Castle, a gloomy stronghold on the Isle of Wight which would be similarly employed as a prison for Charles I 250 years later.

With Gloucester, Richard took no chances: at the head of a powerful force of armed men he rode down to his uncle's residence at Pleshey in Essex and, after arresting him, had him sent over to Calais for safe keeping. Richard had moved quickly and decisively against the three powerful magnates whom he perceived as the deadliest of his enemies, and the pre-emptive move must have been planned carefully. Walsingham referred, with justification, to the 'king's scheming behaviour'. At that stage in his reign Richard would not have taken such a crucial and far-reaching step without weighing up the options. While it is fair to say that he was minded to recover the position he felt he had lost at the time of the Merciless Parliament and the humiliation he had suffered at the hands of the Lords Appellant – Arundel's insistence on Burley's execution still rankled – he could only act against such powerful men, including his uncle, from a position of strength.

What seems to have driven Richard most was the determination to retain and strengthen the royal prerogative, which he felt had been violated in 1388. Now, nearly ten years later, he was in a position to do just that. The truce with France and the settlement of Ireland (chimerical though it was) had strengthened his hand and he had used the intervening years to rebuild his retinue. Among those closest to him were his two half-brothers Thomas and John Holland, respectively Earl of Kent and Earl of Huntingdon (their father Thomas, Earl of Kent, had been married to Joan of Woodstock before she married the Black Prince). Gaunt also continued to support the King, as did John Beaufort, his eldest son from his relationship with Katherine Swynford. (That same year all the royal bastards had been legitimated when Parliament allowed Gaunt to marry his long-term mistress, their children taking the name Beaufort from the castle in Champagne where they were born.)

Also included in the latest royal entourage were Richard's cousin Edward of Norwich, Earl of Rutland and eldest son of the Duke of York, and Thomas Mowbray, Earl of Nottingham. Such was the closeness of relationships at Richard's court that when he decided to act against his enemies to strengthen his position the new affiliations pitched brother against brother (Gaunt and Gloucester), nephew against uncle (Rutland and Gloucester) and son-in-law against father-in-law (Nottingham and Arundel).

When Parliament reassembled on 17 September there was a further show of royal strength with the appearance of Richard's new bodyguard, who were described by Walsingham as 'a savage crowd of Cheshire men, armed with axes, bows and arrows'. In a grim reminder of past events the procedure mirrored the actions taken by the Merciless Parliament, only this time the appellants were on the receiving end of an appeal against them. The first to be tried for treason was Arundel, who answered the indictment read by John of Gaunt with the retort that he had received a charter of pardon at the time of the Merciless Parliament and was also in receipt of the King's personal promise of safety. His protestations were to no avail and Arundel was sentenced to death by the horrible method of being hanged, drawn and quartered. (Reserved for traitors, this involved the victim being hanged until barely conscious, then cut down to have the genitals cut off and stuffed in his mouth, followed by evisceration.) Richard intervened to change the sentence to execution by beheading and without further ado Arundel was led off to the Tower, where, according to witnesses, he met his end with grace and courage.

Arundel's brother, now Archbishop of Canterbury, was also arraigned but his life was spared and he was sent into exile. Gloucester would have been next in line had he been present rather than tried *in absentia*, but when the proceedings began word arrived from Calais that he was dead. This was a fortunate outcome as his execution would have angered Gaunt, for they were royal dukes and brothers. Gloucester had either died from natural causes or, more probably, was murdered by Mowbray on Richard's orders to save him the indignity of facing a trial for treason followed by inevitable execution. In his *Historie of England* Holinshed gives a graphic (and no doubt unreliable) description of a murder in which Gloucester is smothered with towels while asleep in a feather bed.

The last to be tried was Warwick, who immediately pleaded guilty and threw himself on the King's mercy; according to the chronicler Adam of Usk, who was present at the trial, he behaved in an unmanly way, 'wailing and weeping and whining, traitor that he was'. He too was condemned to death but Richard again interceded and he was banished to the Isle of Man, where he faced harsh imprisonment at the hands of the governor, William le Scrope.

Having dispatched his enemies, Richard was able to consolidate his own position and to reward those who had supported him. There were dukedoms for those closest to him in his retinue: his half-brothers John and Thomas Holland were elevated as, respectively, Duke of Exeter and Duke of Surrey, Rutland became Duke of Albemarle, Mowbray Duke of Norfolk and Bolingbroke Duke of Hereford. Richard also made sure that Parliament was packed with his own supporters – the Speaker, Sir John Bussy, had served in his household – but despite successfully eliminating his enemies he was still intent on reinforcing his position. His mind went back to the defeat at Radcot Bridge and those who had supported the Lords Appellant were forced to pay large fines in return for pardons and there were collective fines for London and for those in Herefordshire and Essex who had ridden in Gloucester's armed forces.

As if to rub in the fact that he was the master now, the King ordered Parliament to reassemble early in 1398, not in London but in Shrewsbury, which was close to the centre of his military power in Cheshire and the Welsh marches, where he owned land. During the sitting de la Pole was restored as Earl of Suffolk and it was decided to repeal all of the acts passed by the Merciless Parliament and to reiterate an oath, first sworn the previous September, that these changes would be upheld on penalty of being charged for treason. These were oppressive measures but at the time Richard was able to do as he pleased as there was no opposition and his powers were more or less absolute. As Walsingham put it so graphically, Richard 'began to act the tyrant and oppress the people'.

All seemed to be going the King's way until the third day of the Parliament, when Bolingbroke reported a conversation he had had with Mowbray the previous December while both men were riding from Windsor to London. It seems that Mowbray had warned him that they were 'on the point of being undone' for their participation with the Lords Appellant at Radcot Bridge and that there was a plot to kill them as well as John of Gaunt and the King's two half-brothers with a view to confiscating the Lancastrian lands. Although both men had escaped censure for their role with the Lords Appellant and had received further honours, Richard's vindictiveness was a matter of common knowledge and Bolingbroke was sufficiently alarmed to take advice from his father, who in turn raised the matter with the King.

Because Mowbray was not present to defend his name and was greatly angered that his confidential conversation with Bolingbroke had been reported to Richard the matter was allowed to fester and descended into a quarrel between the two men which quickly spiralled out of control. Mowbray was deprived of some of his offices, including the captaincy of Calais, and for a time was put in prison for his own safety. To safeguard his position each man accused the other of treason and as the quarrel could not be decided by law Richard ordered the matter to be settled by trial of battle at Gosford Green, Coventry, on 16 September 1398. This was a chivalric means of settling a dispute between social equals in which the winner either killed his opponent or disabled him and forced him to surrender by crying, 'Craven!'

If the tournament had taken place it would have been one of the most colourful events of Richard's reign. Both participants were dukes, one of them, Bolingbroke, was the King's cousin, and quite possibly it could have been a battle to the death. Bolingbroke was already practised at jousting and was an experienced soldier: in 1390 he had joined the Teutonic Knights in their crusade against pagan Lithuania, taking part in the siege of Vilnius. For his combat with Mowbray he went into training and ordered special armour to be made for him in Milan. Given his strength and expertise it is probable that he would have gained the upper hand, but dramatically, on the day of the confrontation, Richard, who was arbitrating, threw down his staff and signalled that the contest was over and that there would be no trial by battle. Instead Mowbray was sent into exile for life, while Bolingbroke received the more moderate sentence of ten years' exile. Again there was probably no single reason why Richard acted in this way and his decision dismayed onlookers who had flocked to Coventry in expectation of a notable spectacle. It could hardly have been a desire to stop blood being shed.

Despite his lack of military experience Richard was no coward and knew how to act decisively and, when necessary, brutally. By then, neither of the men involved in the confrontation was particularly close to him and Bolingbroke's lesser sentence was as much due to family ties as to the respect Richard felt for his uncle. (Gaunt was not present at the tournament.) More likely, he realised that neither man's triumph would suit him because at the time people believed that the outcome of a trial by battle revealed the truth of the allegations which had been made. If Mowbray had won, it would have been acknowledged that his claims were just, namely that Richard had intended to punish both men for their roles at Radcot Bridge. If Bolingbroke had won, it would have created equally awkward problems. Not only would it have proved his innocence of the charge of treason, but a triumph in the lists would have made him a popular figure and the King could not afford that at a time when the royal succession had not been settled. In the event the only winner was Richard, who at a stroke had managed to rid himself of two leading supporters of the Lords Appellant who had defied him all those years ago.

Nevertheless, the sentences also carried risks, for although Gaunt was ill he was still alive and the exile of his son was a double punishment for an old and increasingly frail man. Perhaps to soften the blow Richard gave Bolingbroke a cash grant to cover his losses while he was in exile in France – he decided to take up residence in Paris – and more importantly issued him with letters which would allow him, should Gaunt die within the next ten years, to pursue for livery of inheritance. (This term refers to the process by which, in the old feudal tenures, wards, whether of the King or other guardian, on arriving at legal age, could compel a delivery of their estates to them from their guardians.) In fact old John of Gaunt, Shakespeare's 'time-honoured Lancaster', died within six months of his son's exile, meeting his end at Leicester Castle 'by a sudden languor, both for old age and heaviness'. If the chroniclers are to be believed his last act of defiance was to expose his pox-ridden genitals when the King visited him shortly before his death. The story was first recorded by Thomas Gascoigne in his account *Loci et libro seriatim* (Passages from a Book of Truths), in which he alleged that Gaunt 'died of a putrefaction of his genitals and body, caused by the frequenting of women, for he was a great fornicator'.

Gaunt's death presented Richard with a problem and an opportunity. He could have pardoned Bolingbroke or even allowed him to attend his father's funeral but he chose to do neither. Instead he decided to act against him. Knowing that he could not afford to have a wealthy rival and possible claimant to his throne living in France, Richard revoked the letters which would have allowed Bolingbroke to claim his inheritance and, as an added punishment, extended his exile to life. Apart from gaining further revenge in this way, he reasoned that while Bolingbroke was in France his moves would be checked by the French who were keen to keep the truce and would hardly rock the boat by condoning any plotting by an exiled English magnate.

Secure in the belief that he had settled the issue and succeeded in protecting his own position, Richard made plans to return to Ireland. (In so doing he would be the last English or British monarch until Queen Victoria to visit the country more than once during their reign.) He had good reasons to go. The Irish had not lived up to their promises, Art McMurrough had recommenced military activities and the Earl of March had been killed trying to restore order in fighting near Kells. There was a clear need to stop the rot and at the end of

May Richard assembled a new army of some five thousand men and sailed to Ireland, determined to halt the violence and also to avenge the death of the Earl of March, his heir presumptive. (Roger Mortimer's mother, Philippa of Clarence, was Edward III's granddaughter and this relationship gave him a reasonable legal claim to the throne.)

Once again fate intervened and events elsewhere conspired against Richard. In Paris Louis, Duke of Orléans, Charles VI's brother, had come into the ascendancy over the Duke of Burgundy during the period of the regency caused by one of the French king's periodic bouts of insanity. This was to be a source of constant concern throughout the reign: not only did it incapacitate Charles but it led to an increasingly volatile quarrel between Orléans and Burgundy.

The King's madness also affected events on the other side of the Channel. Being pro-war and against rapprochement with England, Orléans used his brother's incapacity to enter into an alliance with Bolingbroke, who had taken up residence at the Hôtel de Clisson and was generally well received by the French court. Under the terms of the agreement with Orléans, which had been facilitated by Burgundy's absence from the French capital, each man pledged to be 'the friend of the other's friends and well-wishers, and the enemy of the other's enemies'. While Richard was dealing with his kingdom in Ireland Bolingbroke decided to take advantage of what seemed to be a God-given opportunity to reclaim his rights. In weighing the odds he might also have been prompted into action by the young Earl of Arundel, who needed little encouragement to avenge the execution of his father, but the most probable reason for his decision to return to England was that he had been given a glorious chance to retrieve his inheritance and in so doing to take his revenge on Richard. The death of his father, to whom he had always been close, would also have been a factor: while John of Gaunt was resident in England Bolingbroke took little part in public life and had supported the Lords Appellant only in 1388, while his father was out of the country.

Four weeks after Richard arrived in Ireland Bolingbroke left Paris and sailed from Boulogne accompanied by a small party of friends and retainers. After making landfall in Sussex the party sailed up the east coast of England and landed at Ravenspur, just north of the Humber Estuary, deep in Lancastrian territory, where they were soon joined by a number of powerful northern lords, including Henry Percy, Earl of Northumberland, his son Henry Hotspur and their cousin Ralph Neville, Earl of Westmorland. All had been discommoded by being sidelined from Richard's court and as they owed the King no favours they decided to join Bolingbroke instead of apprehending him, as was within their power. It is impossible to know if Bolingbroke left France intent on deposing Richard or if he wanted simply to reclaim his inheritance – Henry is said to have made a promise at Doncaster in the presence of an assembly of lords, among them Northumberland, Hotspur, Westmorland and the Archbishop of Canterbury, that his only motive was to retrieve his position in England.

However, the support of the northern magnates and the speed with which other members of the nobility joined Bolingbroke's cause, bringing with them men-at-arms, must have persuaded him that he had the numbers and the capacity to challenge the King. As his slowly burgeoning army made its way south towards Gloucester, Bolingbroke was helped by the hopeless indecision of Edmund, Duke of York, who had been appointed Keeper of the Realm in Richard's absence. It took a week for the news of Bolingbroke's return to reach the Duke and his response was to send a warning to Richard while withdrawing his small forces west towards Bristol, where he hoped to meet up with the Royalist army returning from Ireland.

But it was already too late. Delayed by a lack of ships, Richard was unable to get back to England until 25 July, when he landed at Milford Haven only to find that his cause was collapsing. By now Bolingbroke had taken Berkeley Castle in Gloucestershire and executed three of the King's leading councillors, including John Bussy. Believing his way to be blocked, Richard then headed north to Conwy Castle in north Wales, where he hoped to gather support in Cheshire whose people had always been loyal to his cause. Once more he had been forestalled. Having marched his rebel army quickly north, Bolingbroke was already in Chester, and after his emissaries were arrested the King was left with no option but to attempt to broker an agreement.

At first it seemed as if an understanding could be reached which would keep Richard on the throne and restore Bolingbroke to his rightful position by ending his exile and letting him come into his inheritance. Northumberland conducted the negotiations for Bolingbroke and during the discussions he seems to have done enough to persuade Richard that he would not be harmed and that his position would remain intact and unsullied. During the negotiations Northumberland himself seems to have sworn on the Host that Richard could retain his royal dignity and power if only the family estates and the hereditary stewardship were restored to Bolingbroke. That might have been the intention but the execution was rather different.

Richard was escorted to Flint Castle, where Bolingbroke was waiting, wearing full armour in the office of High Steward of England, as if to show the King that he was now the master and their positions had been reversed. From there they continued south to London, where Richard was locked in the Tower, a prisoner in his own country. By now it was all over for him. His supporters had melted away and Bolingbroke and his backers were clearly in the ascendant. All that remained for the usurpers was to produce a rationalisation for what would happen next: the removal of a crowned king from his legal throne. One option would have been to keep Richard as the nominal king and to appoint a regent, but Bolingbroke had seen with his own eyes the support he had gathered and by then he had been able to gauge the depth of Richard's unpopularity within the country.

What followed next was a mixture of arm-twisting and political fixing. While pressure was put on Richard to stand down, Bolingbroke's party stressed the continuity which he would bring to the throne and the prime importance of rescuing England from the autocratic rule of the King and his self-serving advisers. In particular, according to Adam of Usk, when Richard's record was investigated by Bolingbroke's followers they found that it provided sufficient grounds to depose him on the evidence of his 'perjuries, sodomitical acts, dispossession of his subjects, reduction of his people to servitude, lack of reason and incapacity to rule'. A total of thirty-nine accusations was made against him, based on the understanding that he had broken the terms of his coronation oath and that he preferred to rule 'according to his own arbitrary will' instead of upholding the laws of the country.

There was also the precedent of Edward II to take into account and when Parliament was summoned on 30 September there was only one item for it to consider. On the day before it convened Richard had succumbed to pressure from a visiting deputation which included Bolingbroke and had agreed to resign as king. According to one contemporary record, he did so 'with a cheerful expression' and gave Bolingbroke his signet ring as an earnest of his wishes, but it is difficult to believe this version. Shakespeare probably came closer to the truth when he described an angry and frustrated Richard washing away his balm with his own tears: a reference to the oil with which he had been anointed during the coronation ceremony. For Richard, giving up his crown would have been a painful business and he was not the kind of man who would have made it any easier for either himself or his usurpers.

After attending mass Bolingbroke rode to Westminster Hall and told the assembled members that he was making a challenge for the Crown based on his blood rights through descent from Henry III and that with the help of his kinsmen and followers he meant to recover his rightful inheritance, adding that the 'realm was in point of being undone for default of governance and the undoing of good laws'. As there was no one to speak for Richard the assembly joined in acclaiming Bolingbroke the new king and declaring that Richard was deposed. They had no standing to do this as Parliament had no authority without the King's presence but the time for political niceties had passed, and a fortnight later Bolingbroke was crowned King Henry IV.

From the outset Bolingbroke had proclaimed his willingness to forget the past and forge a new beginning and in pursuit of that ideal only Richard's closest supporters were stripped of their titles. It was as if the new king were intent on making good the promise given on his accession, that he was not minded to 'disinherit any man of his heritage, franchise or any other rights that he ought to have, nor put him out of that that he has had by the good laws and custom of the Realm, except those persons that have been against the good purpose and the common profit of the Realm'.

In fact Henry was as good as his word and proved to be surprisingly lenient, perhaps remembering the sentence of exile which he had received and the refusal to allow him to claim his inheritance. There was, though, the question of what should be done with the anointed king, who was imprisoned first at Leeds Castle in Kent and then at

Pontefract Castle in Yorkshire after an intervening short stay at Knaresborough. For everyone it was a difficult position. Richard had been usurped and his crown had been taken from him but he was still alive. As long as he lived he would be a focus for those who either wanted to see him restored to the throne or intended to use him as a pawn against Henry for their own ends. It did not take long for events to conspire against the new king.

Shortly after the beginning of 1400 a plot was uncovered to kill Henry and his sons, the so-called Epiphany Uprising, led by the Earls of Salisbury, Gloucester, Exeter and Surrey, all of them Richard's reprieved supporters, but it came to nothing. The ringleaders were killed without trial before any mischief was done and a number of lesser supporters were tried and executed. In the middle of February it was announced that Richard was dead, either deliberately or by his own hand. The official version was that he starved to death although it is impossible to know if this was done with intent or if he decided to end it all by refusing to eat. Walsingham claimed that the King killed himself by voluntary starvation, while Adam of Usk argued that his death was caused by a deliberate policy of starvation 'as he lay in chains in the castle of Pontefract'.

Richard's body was taken to London, where he had expressed a wish to be buried alongside Anne in Westminster Abbey. In a final act of pique Henry paid no attention to his last will and testament and had him buried in the priory at King's Langley in Hertfordshire and his body remained there until December 1413, when in an act of piety and reconciliation Henry's son Henry V had him reburied in Westminster Abbey.

Although Richard had not been popular and his last years had aroused a good deal of acrimony within the country, his passing was followed by persistent rumours that he had not died but was in hiding and would return at some future and unspecified date to reclaim the throne. In 1407 Walsingham recorded that documents existed in London 'which claimed that King Richard was still alive and would return in glory and splendour to recover his kingdom', but the most common gossip was that he was being sheltered by the Scots. In fact there was some substance to the story. For reasons which were almost certainly bound up with the long-standing friction between the two countries the Scots awarded an annual pension to a man who claimed to be Richard and they kept up the pretence throughout Henry's reign. The impostor, known as the 'Mummet', was found wandering around the Hebridean island of Islay two years after Richard's death and was recognised by a local woman who claimed to have seen the King while she was visiting Ireland.

At the time Scotland was ruled by the elderly King Robert III, who was unable to prevent his relatives plotting against him and had such low self-esteem that he condemned himself in his own words as 'the worst of kings and most wretched of men in the kingdom'. In 1402 his eldest son died in suspicious circumstances while under the protection of the Duke of Albany, and to prevent a similar fate befalling his second son, James, he was sent to the safety of the French court. However, James's ship was intercepted by English pirates in the North Sea, with the result that the young Scottish prince fell into Henry's hands and became a hostage in England for the next eighteen years. In the circumstances it is perhaps easy to understand the Scots' willingness to believe that Richard was alive and a puppet in their hands. It was a useful ploy but it was not believed by the English, who later identified the 'Mummet' as Thomas Warde of Trumpington in Cambridgeshire. Nevertheless, the rumours about Richard's survival refused to die down and remained potent issues for most of Henry's reign.

Richard's fate cast a long shadow over the fifteenth century. Whatever else he had been, he was a usurped king and it proved difficult for Henry IV and his successors to gloss over the fact that they had come to the throne not through inheritance but by deposing and perhaps killing one of their close relatives. In time the feebleness and many blunders of Richard's reign were forgotten or ignored, as were his vanities and his extravagance, and he was remembered as the king who had lost his crown unnaturally and almost certainly illegally. Instead of living out his life and reign in tranquillity, with the comforting knowledge that he might have fathered an heir to confirm the succession, he had died under suspicious circumstances, shorn of his crown and his honour. It was a harsh fate for a man who believed that his existence was a divine mission and that he enjoyed powers denied to lesser men. To the very end Richard II seems to have clung on to his belief in the absolute monarchy and although he eventually gave ground to Bolingbroke his decision to abdicate was forced on him at a time when he was enfeebled and had no room to manoeuvre.

Inevitably the pathos of Richard's position has coloured history's verdict of a king who was brought down by his bad judgement and by his refusal to trim his beliefs or to cultivate working relationships with the powerful magnates who wielded such power in his kingdom. Over the centuries his personality and psychological make-up have also been subject to investigation and conjecture. The findings have ranged from a belief that he might have been clinically insane to a more sober contention that he was rash and weak-willed and was liable to base his decisions on what he wanted to believe rather than on any rational conviction that he was doing the right thing.

There is also a case to be made for blaming Richard's failings on his narcissism and his inability to keep his actions grounded in reality. Certainly, during the last two years of his life, when he alienated so many people who could have been useful to him, Richard frequently behaved in an irrational and intemperate fashion. Instead of showing the coolness and firm judgement that he brought to his affairs in Ireland or as a young man when he boldly confronted the rebellious peasants in London, he allowed himself to be seduced by the delusion of his own omnipotence. In particular, the decision to proceed aggressively against Gloucester, Arundel and Warwick in 1397 left him vulnerable to attack and showed a lack of political judgement. As happened so often in his life, he had nothing much to gain by taking his revenge but a great deal to lose by acting against them when he did.

Against that, like any other human being, Richard possessed attractive qualities, and in no other incident did he show his emotional side more clearly than in his grief at the death of his wife Anne. In light of her moderating influence and good sense, it is tempting to wonder if his life would have turned out differently had she survived. Richard's comportment during the Peasants' Revolt, when little more than a boy, demonstrated that if the occasion demanded he was capable of showing good sense and moral courage. As a soldier and the son of the Black Prince his conduct was blameless and in Scotland and Ireland he showed that he could be a leader of men, although his uncles would have preferred him to have demonstrated his bellicosity by leading his armies against the French. On that score his great achievement in terms of foreign policy was his steadfast refusal to reignite the war in France, although latterly this was helped by the rapprochement brought about by his marriage to Isabella. Richard's patronage of the arts also puts him in a good light, especially his support for the use of English, even though he often used the expenditure to glorify his court at the expense of his people.

His long, fatherless childhood in preparation for assuming the crown must have affected him adversely and indeed the charges brought against him by Parliament at the time of his abdication suggest that he had never grown up mentally or accepted his responsibilities as king. But, compared with many other rulers before or after him, Richard was not a particularly evil man. Unscrupulous and duplicitous, wrong-headed and convinced of his own infallibility: those charges can be laid against him as evidence of his vanity and his irrationality, but he was very much a product of his background and upbringing. He made the mistake of alienating the very people who should have supported him; worse and all too often, he befriended those who only led him into deeper trouble.

In the final analysis Richard was doomed not by any particular aberration in his mental make-up but by his steadfast belief in his own supremacy as king and by his incapacity, or refusal, to produce good governance when it was most needed. More than any other factor, this failing helped to seal his fate.

Chapter Four

THE USURPER KING

From the very moment Bolingbroke became King Henry IV his reign was clouded with dark suspicions about his right to the throne and as a result there were always lingering misgivings that in the long term his authority might become untenable. In front of Parliament he had claimed the Crown as his by right of hereditary title, because he was descended 'by right line of the blood coming from the good lord Henry the Third', but it was a statement dripping with insincerity and laden with half-truths. Not only had he seized the Crown after declaring that he was justly pursuing his rights as Duke of Lancaster but his statement to Parliament was based on the spurious assumption that Edward of Lancaster and not Edward I was the eldest son of Henry III and therefore he was the rightful heir through his mother, Blanche of Lancaster. As this was little more than an idle legend his claim did nothing to mask the fact that he was a usurper king.

Not even his coronation eased those doubts. The ceremony took place on St Edward's Day, 13 October, but although it was replete with religious trappings it failed to reinforce his right to the Crown. Even before he entered Westminster Abbey to sit on the throne – which was rumoured to contain the Stone of Scone, Scotland's traditional coronation stool – there were problems about the key points of the ceremony.

So that the mystique of the divinely appointed king could be maintained, anointment was central to the proceedings. Richard had made much of that conceit when he was crowned and matters were

helped for Henry by the miraculous discovery of the fabulous golden-
eagle ampulla of sacred ointment which had been missing for many
years – the symbolism of its unexpected reappearance in time for
Henry's coronation is obvious. This sacred oil was supposed to have
been presented by the Virgin Mary, who appeared in a vision before
the martyred Archbishop of Canterbury Thomas Becket in the
twelfth century. Thereafter the ampulla had been lost for many years
and its sudden recovery should have been a good portent but, on the
contrary, its reappearance only made matters worse. When the
Archbishop of Canterbury began the anointment it was discovered
that Henry's head was crawling with lice. And another bad sign
followed when the newly crowned king's traditional gold coin fell
from his hand at the offertory and, despite strenuous efforts, could
not be recovered.

All this was recorded by Adam of Usk and to the superstitious the
incidents were signs of ill omen which did not bode well for the reign
of Henry IV. Later, at the traditional banquet in Westminster Hall,
there was another awkward moment when the official champion
challenged anyone to gainsay Henry's title: the new king simply said
that he was prepared to defend it himself.

Nevertheless, for all that Henry had seized the Crown and his
coronation seemed to suggest that his kingship might be built on
unsound foundations, his reign got off to a reasonably good start. His
accession and the deposition of Richard had been relatively popular –
it helped that the former king was decidedly out of favour – and
Henry showed that he was anxious to restore prestige to the throne
and to reward those who had been loyal to him. The chronicler John
Capgrave went so far as to compare the new king to Solomon,
choosing 'not wealth or honours but the succouring wisdom of God',
and there were high hopes that his reign would usher in an age of
achievement and blessings.

On a more temporal level one of Henry's first acts was to create a
new order of chivalry, the Order of the Bath (this soon died out and
was not restored until 1725), and two days after his coronation he
proclaimed his eldest son Henry heir to the throne and created him
Prince of Wales, a title first conferred on the Black Prince in 1343. In
order to create an atmosphere of confidence Henry repeated over and
over again that he had no intention of being any different from his

predecessors and that there would be no slackening of the traditional discretionary rights and privileges of the Crown, the so-called royal prerogatives.

He also took steps to ensure the future of his position in 1406, when his title to the Crown was cemented by Act of Parliament, and a year later he introduced legislation to exclude his father's Beaufort children and their descendants from the succession. Cleverly, he avoided offence and potential family strife by confirming their legitimacy by letters patent, but by adding the words 'excepting the royal dignity' he made sure that they would never succeed to the throne. This did not stop Henry from relying on his half-brothers John and Henry Beaufort, both of whom served on his council of advisers, but the step did provide a legal check on any ambitions they might have entertained as the offspring of John of Gaunt. Henry had good reason to be touchy about his position: King Charles VI of France refused to recognise him – after all, Henry had usurped Charles's son-in-law – and took to treating English envoys with more than usual contempt.

At the same time, during that honeymoon period in office, Henry chose to reward the loyalty of his supporters and to keep the allegiance of those who had been in Richard's employment. This meant giving grants of land and expensive annuities, the costs of which inevitably fell on the Royal Exchequer, and just as inevitably this profligacy was bound to lead to problems with Parliament. In his own right Henry was a wealthy man who enjoyed the income from his Lancastrian lands and properties as well as those of his wife, Mary Bohun, younger daughter of the Earl of Hereford, whom he had married in 1380 and whose elder sister, Eleanor, was married to Henry's uncle, Thomas of Woodstock, Duke of Gloucester. (In an attempt to keep the wealth to himself Thomas of Woodstock had tried to persuade Mary Bohun to enter a nunnery.)

From an early stage in his life Bolingbroke had come to rely on the large subventions made to him by John of Gaunt and was used to the trappings of wealth and power. On becoming king he continued to regard his family wealth as his private income to be used at his pleasure and discretion; but while this gave him the kind of affluence which had been denied to Richard it did not solve the perennial problems of paying for the upkeep of the court.

At the time a king was supposed 'to live of his own', that is, he was supposed to use his own revenues for his personal expenditure while using taxes to pay for the defence of the realm. But in Henry's case there was a misunderstanding from the very beginning. His Lancastrian wealth could not be ignored and it proved difficult to separate his private needs from his public position as head of state. In an attempt to resolve the matter Henry argued that the cost of his household was a public expense which should be met from Crown revenues but that he would 'put the household in good and moderate governance'. But, despite his well-intentioned efforts, the finances of the royal household remained a sensitive subject for much of Henry's reign.

His first Parliament showed a reluctance to grant taxes, offering the new king nothing more than the income from customs duties, which were themselves reduced as a result of the slump in the wool trade, and a year into his reign appeals to the Church and the aristocracy for funds fell on deaf ears. Although the nobility and the Church's princes were largely minded to support Henry, finding the money was another matter, and an indication of the problems he faced can be found in the fact that he employed six treasurers during the first five years of his reign. Nor did it help matters that there was confusion over Henry's own position on what should be done about taxation. While making his move to claim the throne, he had promised to reduce taxation but his comments were taken to mean that he would not be raising taxes at all, and among many of his subjects this assumption came to be believed.

The fact that Henry had huge personal wealth must also have reinforced the idea that as far as finance was concerned his reign would be a golden age and that there would be no repetition of Richard's profligacy and the abuse of the prerogative to obtain funds. John Gower thought as much when he wrote his welcoming poem to the new king and he went further, emphasising his belief that Henry's claim to the throne came not only from royal descent but from the Almighty. As Gower had already changed the dedication to his *Confessio Amantis* to suit the different circumstances of the new reign – the reference to Richard II was quietly dropped – this may have had as much to do with the pragmatics of patronage as anything else, but the prologue to the long poem was clearly rewritten to underline the fact that Henry enjoyed the support of the English people:

On worthi noble kyng, Henry the ferthe,
In whom the glad fortune is befalle
The people to governe upon this erthe,
God hath the chose in comfort of ous alle:
The worschipe of this lond, which was doun falle,
Now stant upriht thurgh grace of thi goodnesses,
Which every man is holde forto blesse.

The highe god of his justice alone
The right which longeth to thi regalie
Declared hath to stonde in thi persone,
And more than god may no man justefie.
Thi title is know upon thin ancestrie,
The londes folk hath ek thy riht affirmed;
So stant thi regne of god and man confermed.

Gower also enjoined the new king to court the pleasures of peace
and to avoid the pain of war, but from early in his reign it became
clear that Henry had an embarrassing lack of experience of
administration and good governance. He was not short of courage or
self-confidence and possessed a willingness to learn, but he had no
training for the actual business of kingship. As a young man he had
travelled extensively in Europe and had won renown as a soldier – as
well as serving in the crusades in Lithuania he had made the
pilgrimage to Jerusalem – but now he had to learn new administrative
skills.

Not surprisingly, Henry relied heavily on the support of trusted
Lancastrian retainers but although experienced administrators such as
Sir Hugh Waterton and Sir Thomas Erpingham served him well, any
king who leans on his own people to the exclusion of others creates
suspicions among those who are outside what appears to be a charmed
circle. That being said, in Henry's case securing his family's patronage
was an astute move as throughout his reign the support of his
Lancastrian retinue did much to shore up his position, especially
when he faced the inevitable challenges to his authority. As he was
soon to discover it was one thing to claim and win the throne but
quite another to hold on to it. Not only would he face a seemingly
never-ending battle with Parliament over money but there would be

far too many occasions when he had to struggle with others to retain his own authority. Throughout his reign the threat of a descent into civil war was never far away.

The first challenge came on Twelfth Night in 1400: the 'Epiphany Uprising', when a group of Richard's supporters led by the Earls of Salisbury, Gloucester, Exeter and Surrey attempted to assassinate Henry and his sons but were betrayed by Henry's cousin the Earl of Rutland. Previously in Richard's camp, Rutland and his father the Duke of York had transferred their loyalties to the new king on his accession. The switch had brought them the contempt of the plotters, who paid with their lives for their disloyalty, while the House of York prospered as a result of supporting the King. On hearing of the plot Henry rode from Windsor to the safety of London but he had no need to fear for his safety. There was no public support for the would-be rebels, who were quickly hunted down and subjected to mob justice.

The captured leaders were lynched by angry crowds who showed no sign of the devotion to Richard which a successful rebellion demanded and the attempt on Henry's life was crushed even before it began. Six days later the other leading figures faced trial at Oxford, where twenty-two of their number were executed. Among them was a charlatan called Richard Maudelyn, an impostor who had been paid to impersonate Richard in one of the many attempts to prove that he was alive and remained a threat to Henry's rule. Unhappily for the recently deposed king, this last-ditch attempt by his supporters probably sealed Richard's fate and the uprising, such as it was, played into Henry's hands by ridding him of the potentially troublesome presence of his predecessor. A month later Richard's death was announced.

The plotters had clearly misjudged the mood of the country and by staying within the bounds of the law – the lesser nobles were tried before a court of law before being executed – Henry had acted sensibly. Equally prudently he also spoke out against the peremptory executions of the ringleaders and stated that it was wrong to kill accused men without trial, but despite his sensible response this was not the last effort to usurp his authority. As had happened before and as would happen again for many more centuries, an English king had to face a fresh challenge from the country's northern neighbours. In theory Henry stated that his intention was to live in harmony with the Scots but he had to face the reality that Robert III and the council backing him refused to acknowledge his position as King of England. Such a state of affairs could not persist and in November 1399, at the very outset of his reign, Henry decided to go to war against the Scots.

It was not a difficult decision to take. Scotland was in a state of disarray as a result of its king's weakness and real authority lay in the hands of Robert's brother, the Duke of Albany, who had just seized power on behalf of the Crown Prince, David, Duke of Rothesay. Appointed Lieutenant of the Kingdom, Rothesay was supposed to work through a council, but Albany was the real power in the land and with Robert little more than a cipher Scotland had become, in the words of Walter Bower's *Scotichronicon*, 'a den of thieves': 'In those days there was not law in Scotland but whoever was more powerful oppressed the lesser and made the entire realm one robbery; homicides, plunderings and fire-raisings and therefore the other evils remained unpunished, and outlawed justice lived in exile beyond the boundaries of the kingdom.'

So shocking was the situation that another of Robert III's brothers, Alexander, had earned himself the nickname of the 'Wolf of Badenoch' for his depredations, which included the infamous destruction of Elgin Cathedral. Henry's hand was also strengthened by the disaffection of George Dunbar, the (Scottish) Earl of March. This was a serious blow to the Scots as March was an experienced soldier and the incident could have been avoided. Rothesay had promised to marry one of the Earl's daughters but had reneged on the agreement at the last minute, preferring a match with the Douglas family, and had added to the insult by refusing to return the dowry. As his king was too feeble to intercede in the quarrel March took matters into his own hands and transferred his allegiance to Henry.

By the middle of the month the English forces had reached Edinburgh. Faced by this display of strength – there were over two thousand feared archers in Henry's army – Rothesay took the line of least resistance. The Scots produced a vague suggestion that the issue should be settled by a fight between a limited number of knights but this was rejected out of hand and eventually Rothesay issued an equally ambiguous promise to recognise Henry as King of England. At the end of August the English army started pulling out of the

Scottish lowlands with nothing achieved other than the avoidance of unnecessary bloodshed. It was Henry's only visit to Scotland and it was also the last time that an English king invaded Scotland at the head of an army, but it was not the end of his troubles with the Celtic nations.

While returning from Scotland Henry received the disquieting news that an obscure Welsh landowner named Owen Glendower (properly Owain Glyn Dŵr) was causing trouble on the Welsh marches following a quarrel with his English neighbour, the Lord Grey of Ruthin, and on 16 September 1400 he had been proclaimed Prince of Wales by his supporters, a title the Welshman was happy to assume. The local squabble quickly became a more general revolt to liberate the Welsh from English overlordship and it was clear that Henry had a major problem on his hands. The English response was to quell the trouble before it could spread and gain wider support. Glendower was condemned as an outlaw and traitor and instead of returning to London Henry led an expedition into Wales in a major show of strength to overawe the inhabitants of the north of the country, including those living in the fortified towns of Harlech and Caernarfon. It succeeded in its purpose in that Glendower's supporters melted away and refused battle, but as had happened in Scotland the lack of an outcome was not the end of the problem.

Within a year, in the spring of 1401, rebellion had broken out again throughout Wales and Glendower had emerged as a serious contender to make good his promise that he was the country's new ruler. On Good Friday 1401 Conwy Castle was seized and Henry was forced to reconsider and take stock of the extent of the problem facing him. Not only was fighting a low-intensity war a difficult and time-consuming business, but it was expensive and a drain on an already overstretched Exchequer. Besides, Henry was a major landowner in Wales and suppression of the uprising would create unpopularity and lose him revenues in the disaffected areas. The following year he mounted two further punitive expeditions into the country but neither succeeded in bringing Glendower to heel.

Worse, they encouraged the Welsh to support Glendower's rebellion in greater numbers and the rebel leader started looking for friends outside Wales. In Scotland he won the moral support of Robert III and his council and by 1406 had entered into an alliance with Charles VI of France through a treaty known as the Pennal Policy which also contained proposals to recognise the Avignon papacy in return for the establishment of a Welsh Church free from Canterbury's control. These moves were backed by the creation of a Welsh Parliament, which met at Machynlleth and Dolgellau and, more importantly, by a major military victory over English forces led by Sir Edmund Mortimer at Pilleth in Radnorshire in June 1402. By then Glendower had emerged as a leader who inspired pride and loyalty in his supporters and fear and hatred in his enemies. His name took on almost mythical proportions and he was held to possess mystical powers – not for nothing did Shakespeare emphasise the supernatural in his fictional creation who declares: 'At my nativity/The front of heaven was full of fiery shapes . . . I am not in the roll of common men.'

The victory at Pilleth also gave Glendower a remarkable pawn in the shape of Edmund Mortimer, who was an uncle of the English Earl of March and was to play a leading role as the drama in Wales unfolded. Henry's response to the defeat was a late-summer military operation in Wales mounted by a huge army – some said 100,000 strong – which assembled in Chester, Shrewsbury and Hereford. Unseasonable weather hindered its progress and as it turned out no military gains were made because, like the Scots, the Welsh showed an unwillingness to take part in pitched battles. The campaign was a setback but it could have been worse: during one fierce summer's storm Henry's tent collapsed and he narrowly missed being hurt by his own lance, being saved by the fact that he was wearing armour at the time. Although the revolt posed a huge problem for Henry it could have been kept in check but for the fact that Glendower was holding Edmund Mortimer to ransom.

Mortimer, as a member of a leading family close to the throne and one which had supported the succession – an important fact as the English Earl of March had previously been named as Richard's heir presumptive – was not without influence. Even so, Henry remained unwilling to enter into negotiations and this refusal led to difficulties with the formidable Earl of Northumberland and his son Henry Hotspur, who was married to Mortimer's sister, Elizabeth. There was another sticking point. The Percys had supported Bolingbroke when he began the journey which ended with his deposing Richard in 1399, but they entertained suspicions that he had overstepped his authority by making himself king. Equally, they suspected that they had not been treated with due respect by Henry in the period since he came to the throne. As a result of these smouldering concerns the family felt that it had a grievance against the King and Glendower gave them the means to make something of it.

Once again the Scots provided a flashpoint. Shortly before Glendower's victory at Pilleth a Scottish army under Archibald, Earl of Douglas, and the Earls of Angus and Moray mounted a large-scale raid into the north of England to pillage and lay waste the country as far south as Durham. While returning to Scotland with their plunder the Scots were intercepted by an army under Northumberland to the north-west of the English border town of Wooler. Acting in support of the English force was the Scottish Earl of March and his expertise was to be a crucial feature in the resultant battle. He also had a score to settle with Douglas, who had been granted most of his lands after deserting to Henry IV.

Douglas faced a difficult predicament. The opposition blocked his route back into Scotland and, knowing that he had no option but to give battle, he deployed his slightly larger army on the steep slopes of nearby Homilton Hill. With their densely packed schiltrons of bristling spears the Scots seemed to have the advantage and, indeed, had Northumberland heeded the urgings of his son, who recommended an immediate frontal attack, they might have won the day. Instead, taking March's advice, Northumberland placed the bulk of his archers on Harehope Hill, to the north-west, while the rest of his army faced the Scots from the north. Because Harehope was at the same elevation as Homilton it allowed the English archers to shoot their much-feared weapons with some hope of hitting their targets while preventing any counter-attack by the Scottish cavalry.

In the end it was the weight and accuracy of fire of the English archers that won the battle. As March had forecast, the English bowmen caused havoc as they poured their fire into the dense ranks of the enemy. Not only did the barrage kill hundreds of Scots but it encouraged the survivors to try to end their misery by rushing down the hill to attack their tormentors. In the *Scotichronicon* there is a bitter response to the English arrow storm when the Scottish knight Sir John Swinton angrily berates his fellow Scots for meekly accepting their fate like fallow deer instead of attacking their enemies 'in the Lord's name, either to save our own lives in so doing or at least to fall as knights with honour'. Swinton's words prompted a band of his fellow knights to join him in a suicidal attack; among them was his great rival Adam de Gordon, who knelt before Swinton and declared him to be the bravest knight in the Scottish army. Douglas, too, joined the fray, seizing a lance and leading a troop of horsemen into the attack. For a short time it seemed that the English bowmen had been unnerved by the assault but, as Walsingham pointed out, Douglas's outdated armour was no protection against a weapon which was the battle-winner of its day:

> Despite his elaborate armour the earl of Douglas received five deep wounds. The rest of the Scots, who had not come down the hill, turned tail and fled from the arrows. But flight did not avail them, for our archers followed them, so that the Scots were forced to give themselves up for fear of the deadly arrows. The earl of Douglas was captured, as were many of those who fled, but many were drowned in the River Tweed because they did not know the fording places. It was said that the waters devoured five hundred men. In this battle no lord or knight dealt a blow to the enemy; but God gave a miraculous victory to the English archers alone, and the magnates and men-at-arms remained idle spectators of the battle.

Walsingham's praise of the archers is well meant and deserved, but at the time Homildon Hill was hailed as a Percy victory and a fitting revenge for the earlier defeat at Otterburn (Chevy Chase) in 1388. It also compared badly with Henry's lack of success in Wales, but instead of using the victory to gain some kudos the King made matters worse by demanding that the prisoners, including Douglas, be sent to London, where they would be ransomed. This proved to be a terrible mistake. In the first place it was an insult to Hotspur, who had been captured and ransomed at Otterburn and would not have been human had he not wanted to exact revenge from the Scots for that earlier insult. There was also a question of unpaid salaries and expenses to the Percys, which would have been ameliorated by the Scottish ransoms. In the second place the demand to ransom the

Scots, plus the sums that would be raised, was in direct contrast to Henry's refusal to treat with Glendower over the release of Mortimer, who was, after all, a kinsman of the Percys. If Henry had been looking for a quarrel with this proud and powerful northern family he could not have a found a better way to provoke one.

Hotspur owes his fiery reputation to Shakespeare, who took the name from Holinshed, who had dubbed him a 'captain of high courage', but on this occasion his decision to stand up to authority was justified. The Percys had been snubbed by Henry and, added to their reservations about the legality of his right to the kingship, they clearly believed that their honour had been impugned over a matter – control of the Scottish marches – which they considered to be in their own bailiwick. Now, from Wales, there was an unexpected chance to do something positive to retrieve the situation. In December Mortimer threw in his lot with Glendower by marrying his daughter Katherine and announced his intention to support the struggle for the freedom of Wales. Furthermore, he decided to back his nephew the Earl of March in his own claims for the English throne and asked the Percys to provide the necessary military assistance. This was granted, not least because a fresh grievance had emerged over payment of money for the protection of the Scottish border. In an attempt to placate the Percys Henry had granted the family a tract of land on the other side of the Scottish border, but this would have required additional financial and military support if it were ever to be taken over.

That summer Hotspur was back in Scotland at Cocklaws, a fortified tower near Hawick, and he and his father made an immediate appeal to Henry for the necessary funds and support to complete the operation to grab the local land. The letter was written by Northumberland in respectful tones and on receiving it Henry was minded to offer help by marching north with an army of five thousand soldiers, but before the King could make good his promise Hotspur had decided to offer his support to Glendower. As he marched north Henry was greatly discommoded to hear news of this betrayal. He also discovered that Hotspur had not tarried but had acted immediately by quitting Scotland for the area around the old Royalist stronghold of Chester, where he had joined forces with his uncle Thomas Percy, Earl of Worcester, and was busy proclaiming that

Richard was alive and with him in his army. The rebels' intentions were to combine Glendower's and Hotspur's armies and then to defeat Henry before putting Mortimer's nephew on the throne.

To forestall them Henry moved his army south and picked up more support in his Lancastrian heartlands. By the third week of July he was in Shrewsbury and the two armies met three miles to the north of the city at Albright Hussey, on the road to Whitchurch. The rebels lined up to the north – fighting with them was the Earl of Douglas, having switched his allegiance to his erstwhile Percy captors – while the Royalists were divided, with the King's men on the right and those of Henry, Prince of Wales, on the left. This was the first battle to be fought on English soil in which the opposing armies were evenly matched in terms of the numbers and efficiency of their archers, and in the opening rounds dreadful damage was done to both sides by those deadly weapons. If anything, the Cheshire bowmen under Hotspur were the more lethal and before too long men in the King's forces were falling 'as fast as leaves fall in autumn under the hoar-frost'. Men waiting under the arrow shower – knights, squires and men-at-arms – could only stand and take what cover they could until the order was given to begin the charge. Then they moved forward with swords and axes to start the next and equally bloody phase of the battle as men fought hand to hand in the killing zone. During this phase Hotspur advanced rapidly with a small force of thirty hand-picked men to attack the royal standard but although they killed the standard-bearer, Sir Thomas Blount, the King was unscathed.

Soon the shout was being heard that Henry Hotspur was dead – later it emerged that he had indeed been killed – and despite the vociferous denials his supporters started fleeing from the field. Some made good their escape but many more 'struggled with such obstinacy that when night came on they did not know which side had won; and they sank down in all directions a chance-medley of weary, wounded, bruised and bleeding men'. Among those who survived was Prince Henry, who was wounded in the face. However, the day belonged to the King, who took immediate revenge by having Worcester executed. As for Hotspur, his body was found on the battlefield and was buried, but to prevent rumours of his survival it was dug up again and covered in salt and put on display in nearby Shrewsbury. Then it was beheaded and quartered, the relevant body parts being sent for display in London, York, Bristol, Chester and Newcastle. Legends grew up that Hotspur had been killed during the battle by young Prince Henry, but there is no evidence that this was the case. Shakespeare played on that conceit in *Henry IV, Part One*, but this was a dramatic device to highlight the alleged differences between the two men – the courageous but hot-headed Hotspur and the dissolute and irresponsible Prince Hal. In reality the two men were not the same age, Henry Percy being twenty-two years older than the Prince of Wales, who was only seventeen at the time of the battle. Even so, it is difficult to disagree with Shakespeare's final assessment of the man through the words of Prince Henry:

> For worms brave Percy. Farewell great heart!
> Ill weaved ambition, how much art thou shrunk?
> When that this body did contain a spirit,
> A kingdom for it was too small a bound,
> But now two paces of the vilest earth
> Is room enough. This earth, that bears thee dead,
> Bears not alive so stout a gentleman.

Because Northumberland arrived late and took no part in the fighting he was pardoned after being tried for the lesser crime of trespass. But the victory at Shrewsbury was not the end of Henry's troubles. France once again became an irritant, thanks to the machinations of the Duke of Orléans, who was so outraged by Henry's accession that he attempted to end it by proposing a duel to the death between the two men. The days were long over when Orléans had promised to be a friend of Henry: far from supporting him in his rivalry with Richard, as he had done in 1399, he now regarded him as a usurper and a potentially dangerous opponent who might one day threaten France. However, nothing came of the offer: Henry refused to accept the challenge because it had been issued by a lesser mortal, a mere duke, but that social nicety did nothing to quell French fretfulness to strike a blow against England. Charles VI was still subject to fits of insanity and he seems to have developed a real hatred of Henry not just for seizing the English throne but for taking the life of his son-in-law and the sentiment was fanned by Orléans.

On that score there was also a degree of French animus about the treatment of Queen Isabella, who remained in England after her husband's downfall and was a drain on Henry's Exchequer at a time when he was under pressure to reduce his household expenditure. An ill-advised attempt to have her married to the Prince of Wales was brushed aside in Paris and thereafter English diplomacy centred on having her returned to France as soon as possible. In normal circumstances this would have been the ideal solution. At eleven years of age she was still a girl and if she was not to be married to Prince Henry she was of little use to the English court. But she was a queen of England and a princess of France and she could hardly be sent back to the land of her birth as if she were a nobody. There was also the question of her dowry, which the French wanted to be returned, but as those funds had been spent long ago there was no expectation that Henry would make good the loss.

Agreement was eventually reached to allow her to return to France in the summer of 1401, but the absence of the dowry and the feeling that they had been belittled continued to rankle with the French. Orléans was the prime mover in stirring up rancour, not least because he saw opportunities to retrieve land in Aquitaine. The first steps in the confrontation were taken shortly after Isabella's return: an outbreak of French naval attacks on English vessels in the Channel. To put further pressure on Henry France entered into a new alliance with the Scots, and to strengthen the Celtic connection it was decided to send 2500 French soldiers to help Glendower in Wales.

At the same time English possessions in Aquitaine were attacked and Calais had to be reinforced, all of which added to Henry's financial problems with Parliament and led to complaints of a repetition of Richard's extravagance. One positive upshot of the confrontation with France was Henry's marriage to Joan, the daughter of Charles II of Navarre and the widow of John de Montfort, Duke of Brittany. Henry had been a widower since 1394, when Mary de Bohun had died, and the new alliance brought with it the promise of the Bretons' support against France and the possibility of using their ports to put a stop to the piracy in the Channel. However, nothing came of those hoped-for benefits: the English were unpopular in Brittany owing to the maritime problems and Joan was forced to give up her rights as Regent of Brittany. One consequence was that she was

forced to surrender her son to the safe keeping of Philip, Duke of
Burgundy. Despite the absence of any benefits from the alliance the
marriage seems to have been a happy one, even though the actual
process proved to be a prolonged business: the couple were married
by proxy in April 1402 but the final ceremony did not take place until
the following year in Winchester Cathedral.

None of this activity did anything to halt Henry's continuing
problems with Parliament over taxation. On the contrary the
confrontation with France and the threat of more to come hinted at
the necessity for even greater expenditure and when Parliament met
in January 1404 there were complaints both about the cost of
maintaining Henry's court and the mismanagement of French
depredations in the Channel. A second Parliament held that same
year, in Coventry in October, failed to resolve the financial difficulties
and Henry was left in the awkward position of having to meet his
obligations as king – putting down rebellions, dealing with the
French, the Scots and the Welsh – while coping with a body which
was seemingly indifferent to his financial inconveniences.

Fortunately, at a personal level Henry enjoyed a reasonable
relationship with Parliament, most of whose members were loyal to
him or were recipients of his annuities, and there was little of the
squabbling which had clouded the previous reign. At the very least the
deliberations at Coventry provided a grant for the continuation of the
war against Glendower and a new offensive was planned for the
following year. The Speaker, Sir Arnold Savage, was close to the royal
household and Henry was careful to make requests for money only
when his own resources had dried up, but for all the absence of direct
confrontation between the King and Parliament over funding, worries
over finance remained the biggest bugbear of Henry's reign. It was a
far from easy position and it was not without reason that Adam of
Usk recorded his bleak assessment of the events of 1404, which had
seen continuing French aggression and two unhappy meetings of
Parliament: 'When the Duke of Lancaster seized the Crown he can
have had little notion of the financial burden which was to weigh
upon him for the rest of his life.'

The next year proved to be no better for Henry, with a fresh
outbreak of rebellion, once again involving the Percy family, whose
grievances against him continued to fester. Even though Hotspur had

been killed and his father humbled at Shrewsbury, the King had been unable to curb Northumberland power in the north of England, where the castles of Alnwick and Warkworth were occupied by Percy forces and kept effectively outside the royal writ. At the same time Glendower had control of the Welsh fortresses at Harlech and Llanbadran and showed every sign of continuing his rebellion against royal authority, with the intention of gaining independence for his country.

From a military point of view, if Henry wanted to regain his authority he would have to fight a war on two fronts. This fearful prospect became a reality in February 1405, when Glendower, Northumberland and March entered into a new compact, the Tripartite Indenture, which proposed dividing England and Wales into three new areas of control. Glendower would be given Wales and most of the west of England, Northumberland would receive Norfolk, Leicestershire, Northamptonshire, Warwickshire and all areas to the north, while the Mortimers would be given control of the rest of southern England.

Now that Parliament had provided the necessary funds Henry's first inclination was to crush the rebellion in Wales once and for all. Before Easter he summoned a general muster of his forces and, after the Garter ceremony at Windsor on 23 April, he set out for Hereford, on the Welsh marches. While he was there he received information from his council that Thomas, Lord Bardolph, an important military supporter, had headed north to join Northumberland and that as a result a new northern revolt was a distinct possibility.

Henry took his forces to Worcester before moving his army north and sent a party ahead to discover what was happening. When he reached Derby his worst suspicions were confirmed. Bardolph had indeed thrown in his lot with the Percys and they had been joined by Thomas Mowbray, the Earl Marshal (son of Thomas Mowbray, the banished Duke of Norfolk) and by Richard Scrope, Archbishop of York, who had been a member of the delegation which accepted Richard's renunciation of his throne in the Tower of London. At the time the Archbishop had supported Henry but had later come to believe that Henry was in breach of the promise made at Doncaster that he would not make a claim to the throne of England and was therefore guilty of a major perjury. Scrope's support for the rebellion carried weight: he was a senior churchman who had read aloud to Parliament Richard's statement of abdication and had assisted the Archbishop of Canterbury during the coronation. Not only was Scrope's defection an embarrassment to the King, but he and Mowbray had raised a force of several thousand local men, including a number of knights.

For the second time in his reign Henry was facing the possibility of a civil war and this time he would be fighting on two fronts: against Glendower in Wales and against the Northumberland faction in the north of England. On his side he had the support of Westmorland and it was this other important northern magnate who saved the day. With Henry's son Prince John he rode ahead with a small force and caught up with Scrope at Shipton Moor, near York. Following a short parley Westmorland agreed that Scrope's grievances would be considered and redressed. Among those were requests for an end to undue taxation and restoration of peace in Wales, though it is unclear if the agreement included the allegation that Henry had broken his oath and should therefore stand aside in favour of Richard's heir, the Earl of March. In return Scrope agreed to disband his army but in so doing he fell into a trap; he and Mowbray were immediately arrested as traitors and taken back to York to await Henry's arrival. If the action smacked of sharp practice it has to be remembered that Henry was fighting for his survival and could not afford to let Northumberland's revolt get out of hand: arresting the Archbishop was a pragmatic way to neutralise a sizeable force and its influential leader.

What followed next was equally brusque and to the point. On 8 June, the feast of St William the Confessor, Scrope, Mowbray and one of the knights in their force, Sir William Plumpton, were tried for treason at the Archbishop's palace, Bishopthorpe, and all three were condemned to death. In Scrope's case the sentence was read by Sir William Fulthorp, a knight, because the Chief Justice, William Gascoigne, declined to act after telling the King: 'According to the laws of the kingdom, neither you, my Lord King, nor any of your subjects acting in your name, can legally condemn any bishop to death.'

Scrope met his death by beheading with great dignity, excusing the executioner Thomas Alman and asking him to strike five blows, 'for I long to bear them for the love of my Lord Jesus Christ, who, obedient to his Father even unto death, bore the first five wounds for our sake'. The treatment Henry meted out to Scrope was unusual by his standards, for he was not a particularly vengeful man and the execution of a prelate was held to be a sin for which he could have faced excommunication. Clearly the King felt deeply betrayed, because he chose to ignore the attempts at intercession made by Archbishop Thomas Arundel, who had rushed north in an unsuccessful attempt to change his mind.

Some good did come out of the affair. On hearing of Scrope's fate Northumberland and Bardolph fled north into Scotland and abandoned their attempted rebellion. Henry's pursuit was hampered by a sudden illness which struck him near Ripon and he had to halt for a week in the village of Hamerton, where he was reported to be afflicted with 'horrible torments'. This could have been occasioned by stress or by feelings of guilt about the execution, but some contemporary documents allege that he was struck down with 'large leprous pustules' as a divine punishment for his actions. Scrope's death came back to haunt him in other ways. The Archbishop had been popular in York and soon there were reports of miracles taking place at his tomb and in the field where he was executed:

In the place where the Archbishop was beheaded there were five strips of plough land sown with barley which were totally ruined on the day of his execution by the feet of those trampling through the field. But in the autumn, without any human effort at all, God in His grace caused such a remarkable growth above the normal amount that some stalks bore five heads of grain and others four, and even the stalks which produced less still bore at least two heads of grain.

More unhappiness followed as the summer drew to a close. Although Northumberland's revolt had been nipped in the bud and the castles at Alnwick and Warkworth were soon back in royal hands, the campaign in Wales faltered for the fourth year running. Carmarthen was retaken, as was the fortress at Coety in Glamorgan, but the campaign ended with Glendower still free and able to continue his rebellion. To cap it all, Henry's baggage train was lost in sudden floods and most of it fell into Welsh hands. It was a dispiriting end to a disappointing year.

Chapter Five

Uneasy Lies the Head

Henry cut a sorry figure when he returned to London at the end of 1405. The defeat of the northern rebels and the reimposition of his authority should have given him fresh confidence for the new year but he was in poor physical shape after his collapse at Hamerton. While the allegations of leprosy were probably untrue and were spread by mischievous rumours, most likely in retaliation for Scrope's execution, Henry was suffering from some kind of skin complaint as well as a leg injury – Capgrave also noted that 'the King lost the beauty of his face' at this time of his life – and also there seem to have been problems with his heart and circulation. All these physical concerns added to the strains of the later stages of his reign and caused procedural difficulties when the sixth Parliament of his reign opened at Westminster on 1 March.

The 'Long Parliament', so called because of the intermittent nature of its business, sat until 22 December with breaks for Easter and in late summer for the harvest and, like its predecessors, its agenda was dominated by finance. There was also an urgent need to address the question of procedures. As the conduct of parliamentary business was hampered by interruptions caused by breakdowns in Henry's health, it was decided to create a small governing council to advise him and to oversee royal expenditure. Its members included Prince Henry, Archbishop Arundel, the Bishops of Winchester and London, Edward, Duke of York, and John Beaufort, Earl of Somerset, and its main aim was to reduce the costs of maintaining the royal household. One measure was the expulsion of members of Queen Joan's Breton household who were considered an unnecessary expense who had brought nothing in return for their keep. New regulations were also introduced to control defence expenditure by careful auditing and taxation was extended 'to be levied on chantry priests and mendicant friars and other religious men who celebrated anniversary masses'. The council's creation did much to improve the governance of the country, not least in terms of the timeless question of royal finances.

When Parliament met the following year at Gloucester its members were able to ease some of the restrictions on royal expenditure as well as taking measures to keep taxation within agreed levels. One reason for this new and unexpected development was the efficiency of the smaller council; another was the reduction in the costs of defence. Northumberland's rebellion had been effectively crushed, thereby lessening the need to garrison the northern counties, and although Wales continued to present problems it was by no means the drain on the Exchequer that it had been in the earlier years at the height of Glendower's revolt.

In the wake of Northumberland's and Bardolph's flight into Scotland, and the confiscation of the former's estates, the grandiose plans for the dismemberment of the kingdom had lapsed and Glendower was left out on a limb. With Edmund Mortimer, he retired into the fastness of Harlech Castle and although the French offered further intervention, with attacks from the sea on Kidwelly and Caernarfon, the high-water mark of his revolt had already passed. Even so, armed resistance continued to be a problem in the principality until 1409, when Harlech fell to Royalist forces commanded by Prince Henry. Mortimer was killed during the action and the loss of Glendower's most important ally was a crushing blow from which the Welsh leader never recovered. Although he was able to continue a guerrilla war until 1410, Glendower's claim to be the rightful Prince of Wales died with the failure of his rebellion to make any headway against the English. Its collapse marked the end of his dreams and he simply disappeared from sight, to live on in people's minds as a folk hero, an Arthurian figure who might one day reappear to help his country in its next hour of need.

By 1413 the Welsh rebellion had petered out and Glendower went to ground, never to be seen again. He may have died three years later, probably in the manor house of one of his daughters in Herefordshire. A chronicle (Peniarth MS 135) written by the bard Gruffudd Hiraethog simply records the following bald and ambiguous comment: 'Owain went into hiding on St Matthew's Day in Harvest, and thereafter his hiding-place was unknown. Very many say that he died; the seers maintain that he did not.'

Much of the credit for the success of the Royalist cause was due to the legitimate Prince of Wales. By then, with his father ill and incapacitated, Prince Henry had assumed overall command of the Royalist forces in Wales and the experience left its mark on him. He learned about soldiering and about the need to create an effective system of command and control, he gained an understanding of the problems of organising and administering a campaign and during his time in the field he forged friendships which would last a lifetime. And, just as important, he came to understand the relevance of taking decisions and operating in isolation, far removed from his home base and unable to seek advice from his superiors. All those lessons would stand him in good stead in the years ahead.

As for Northumberland, in 1408 he mounted one last desperate attempt to overthrow the King by fomenting revolt in the Percy heartlands in the north but nothing came of his efforts. On 19 February, in driving snow, his small and unprepared army was defeated by Royalist forces under the command of the Sheriff of Yorkshire, Sir Thomas Rokeby, at Bramham Moor, near Haslewood Castle, to the south-west of Tadcaster. Northumberland was killed in the battle and his death and Mortimer's earlier disappearance from the scene meant that, for the first time in his reign, the King could live without fear of civil war.

It was also the last time that Henry involved himself in any military action. While he did not ride with Rokeby or take part in the fighting at Bramham Moor he followed on behind with the Royalist army and in the palace at Selby he meted out justice to those who had taken part in the revolt. Among those executed was the Abbot of Halesowen, who was discovered on the battlefield wearing armour, thereby demonstrating his culpability and his support for Northumberland, while the Bishop of Bangor was pardoned, having been captured after the battle wearing his clerical dress. It was Henry's last hurrah as a soldier. According to a contemporary record he purged the north of any further hopes of rebellion during his sitting at Selby, where 'many were condemned, and diverse put to great fines, and the country brought to quietness'.

Scotland, too, was proving to be less of a problem than it had been in the past, owing to the renewal of a number of truces and, more importantly, the continuing presence at Henry's court of James, the heir to the throne of Scotland. Even though the regent, Albany, showed little desire to bring about the Prince's release – his own son Murdoch Stewart, Duke of Fife, had been captured after Homildon Hill – James proved to be an important bargaining counter. As long as he was in English hands the Scots held their peace and in their relations with France James was a useful ally in English attempts to stop Scottish mercenaries fighting in French service. There were benefits for the young Scottish prince as he used his eighteen years in English confinement to improve himself and to complete his education at Henry's court. An intelligent youth, he showed an interest in English political institutions, especially Parliament, and Henry also offered to help in his instruction, telling his council: 'If the Scots were truly grateful they would have sent this young man to me to be educated, for I too know French.'

There was also better news from France, where the hapless Charles VI continued to inhabit a twilit world of mental chaos with ever fewer periods of lucidity. The power struggle between Burgundy and Orléans had dominated his reign and continued without remission into the new century. In 1404 Philip, Duke of Burgundy, died and was succeeded by his son, John Sanspeur ('the Fearless'), and this first cousin of the French king showed no sign of relaxing his family's ambitions to dominate the royal court. Then, three years later, Louis of Orléans was killed in a street brawl in Paris and the assassination was blamed on the Burgundians, a claim they did not deny. (According to Walsingham, Orléans had simply received his just deserts as he had been 'taking his pleasure with whores, harlots, incest' and had committed adultery with the wife of an unnamed knight who had taken his revenge by killing him. The avenging knight was then supported by the Duke of Burgundy.)

After the murder of Orléans the Duke was succeeded by his son Charles, who had recently married Richard II's widow, Isabella. Her untimely death during childbirth in 1409 led Charles into a second marriage to Bonne, a daughter of Bertrand, Count of Armagnac, one of France's great noble houses and a major power-broker in its own right. The marriage created an alliance which was notably anti-English in character, although that did not stop Charles from seeking an alliance with Henry IV, and in time the Armagnacs, in alliance with the Orléanists, came to represent most of the aristocracy in the south and the west of the country.

The continuing friction in France was greatly beneficial to Henry, who had hoped that the return of Isabella would reduce tensions between the two countries and put a stop to the debilitating piracy in the Channel. To his pleasure he now found that he was being courted assiduously by both French parties. From his holdings in Flanders the Duke of Burgundy offered Henry possession of the towns of Gravelines, Dunkirk, Dixmude and Sluys, which would be important acquisitions for providing additional links for the lucrative wool trade. In return Burgundy requested military help to expel the Armagnac faction from Paris. This was given, and in the summer of 1411 a small English force under the command of the Earl of Arundel sailed to France and made for the French capital to join the Burgundians in this task. Walsingham's chronicle suggests that the operation was a resounding success and those who took part in it were well rewarded by the Duke of Burgundy for their services:

The English soldiers sent out to forage decided to enter Saint-Cloud [a suburb of Paris and residence of the Duke of Orléans] but found the bridge across the River Seine had been broken by their opponents. The enemy had spread over it some planks, which were narrow, but long enough to enable the townspeople to come out of the gates. They could then fend off the English, or according to what sort of encounter it was, retreat from the enemy if necessary.

A battle took place in which the French were put to flight. In their terror they slipped on the narrow planks and were drowned in the river. One thousand and three hundred were reported dead; the others fled into the town and told the weeping duke of the disaster. He saved his own life only by fleeing from a different part of the town. The English then looted Saint-Cloud, took many prisoners and returned with them to Paris.

The victory was welcomed in England, especially by the Prince of Wales, who favoured the Burgundian faction because Duke John was effectively the master of France and as such retained control of strategically important Flanders. Ideally, King Henry would have liked to secure a French match for his son but nothing came of the proposals to marry the Prince of Wales to one of the Burgundian princesses.

However, any arrangement would have probably foundered because the following year the Duke of Orléans played his hand by sending an embassy to England offering a much bigger opportunity for the King. Under the terms of a secret treaty agreed at Bourges he offered to make available territory in Aquitaine – Guyenne, Poitou and Angoulême – in return for military assistance against the Burgundians. Orléans had seen the English soldiers in action at Saint-Cloud and clearly felt that they would be a notable asset. Henry was captivated by the idea, flimsy though it was, for not only would it restore English prestige in France but it might produce a much-needed military triumph to bolster his reign at a time when he had been sidelined from national and international affairs. An agreement was signed and an English army was dispatched to Normandy under the command of Henry's younger son Prince Thomas, Duke of Clarence. At one point the King announced his intention of leading the army himself but with his broken health and lack of energy the idea was stillborn. By now he was in a pitiful condition, unable to ride and a poor shadow of the gallant young man who had gone crusading in eastern Europe and had been known throughout Europe for his skill on the jousting field.

It was perhaps as well that Henry did not undertake the operation, for, unlike the previous year's canter, Clarence's campaign achieved very little. Having landed at Vaast-la-Hogue intending to raid suspected centres of piracy on the Normandy coast, the English forces remained somewhat aimlessly in the Cotentin Peninsula until they were unexpectedly recalled to England. The decision was taken by Orléans, who had suddenly found himself in a state of new military confrontation with the Burgundians. On hearing about the secret Treaty of Bourges John the Fearless denounced the Armagnacs as traitors and prepared an army to drive them out of the south. Facing the possibility of civil war, Charles VI, happily in a lucid state, ordered Orléans to renounce the agreement and peace of a kind was restored. Under an accord signed at Auxerre that summer the two sides were reconciled and agreed to pay off Clarence's army, which was preparing to march into Anjou. The whole incident was immensely embarrassing to the English, not least because the Prince of Wales had opposed the adventure from the outset as it compromised his preferred policy of dealing with the Burgundians.

This was a sensitive point. By the end of the decade relations between the King and his eldest son were tense and provided the potential for even greater disagreements. By that time Prince Henry was well into his twenties and, having gained considerable experience of soldiering in Wales, he was keen to add to his knowledge and political skills. Since becoming a member of his father's council he had emerged as a thoughtful and energetic young man who clearly wanted to have a greater involvement in the governance of the realm. With him on the council he had the support of his father's half-brothers Henry and Thomas Beaufort and close allies such as Thomas Langley, Bishop of Durham, Richard Beauchamp, who had served with him in Wales, and Henry Chichele, a future Archbishop of Canterbury. Their task was to govern England efficiently and responsibly at a time when the King's physical condition prevented him from accepting the full responsibilities of his Crown.

Poor health made Henry's last years unpleasant and while it is difficult to understand the exact nature of his illness – leprosy, plague (which erupted again in 1408) and venereal diseases have all been suggested – it was clearly painful and debilitating: Adam of Usk described the ailment as 'a rotting of the flesh, a drying up of the eyes and a rupture of the intestines'. Rumours abounded about his condition: the French believed that his toes had dropped off, while the Scots were adamant that he had shrunk in size and was no bigger than a child. One thing is certain: the visible tumours, rashes and suppurating flesh were dreadful to behold and tested even the strongest stomach. It did not help matters that Henry's illnesses were strangely spasmodic. One day he would be so weak that he appeared to be on the verge of death and would lie comatose on his bed; the next he would have recovered his powers and would be able to resume his royal duties. Unfortunately for everyone concerned, when Henry was in control of his mind and body he became increasingly fretful and dictatorial, especially in his dealings with his eldest son.

Matters came to a head in the autumn of 1411 when Henry Beaufort suggested that the time might have come for the King to stand down from his throne in favour of the Prince of Wales. It was a serious point which was made to address a well-known problem – the King's physical condition could not be ignored – but coming on top of the recent disagreement over which faction should be supported in France it was also a direct challenge to Henry's throne and, like an old war-horse, he rose to meet it. In common with any other ruler who had supplanted his predecessor, Henry was intensely aware of the fragility of his position and understood only too well the uncomfortable truth that usurpers could themselves be usurped. Unwilling to stand aside and fearful perhaps that if he did not do so his son might act against him by using force to claim the throne, Henry decided on pre-emptive action.

When Parliament opened on 3 November Henry was unable to attend, but two days later he rallied to tell the new speaker, Sir Thomas Chaucer, son of the poet, that he wanted 'no novelties' but preferred to preserve his own prerogatives. The Beauforts were thanked for their services – a sure sign that they had been dismissed – and Henry packed the council with men who would be loyal to him, such as Archbishop Arundel as Chancellor and Prince Thomas in place of the Prince of Wales. The decision caused an open breach between Henry and Prince Thomas, who responded the following year by parading his men-at-arms in London in a show of force. Nothing came of the confrontation but there is little doubt that in 1411 and 1412 the relationship between Henry and his brother was at rock bottom.

Following Holinshed's account of what happened, Shakespeare took the disagreement between the two men and turned it into a dramatic device to compare Prince Hal's alleged debauchery with the courage and mettle shown by Harry Hotspur. In *Henry IV, Part One* this conceit leads King Henry to make offensive comparisons between the two young men:

> O that it could be proved
> That some night-tripping fairy had exchanged
> In cradle-clothes our children where they lay,
> And called mine Percy, his Plantagenet:
> Then would I have his Harry, and he mine,

Shakespeare's version of the father–son relationship in *Henry IV, Parts One and Two* inconveniently ignores the fact that, although there is contemporary evidence to suggest that the Prince of Wales sowed his wild oats while he was a young man, most of his earlier years had been spent campaigning as a soldier in Wales. He might have been a natural roisterer but he was also intensely aware of his princely duties and obligations. That being said, one scene in *Henry IV, Part Two* (Act 4, scene 2) does have historical resonance, quite apart from being a key to understanding the troubled relationship between the King and his son. As Henry lies ill in his chamber the Prince enters and, thinking that his father is already dead, removes the crown from his father's pillow and places it on his own head. At that point the King wakes and calls for help and his son is forced to explain his motives. When the Prince replies that he never thought to hear his father speak again he is chided for his presumption:

> Thy wish was father, Harry, to that thought:
> I stay too long by thee, I weary thee.
> Dost thou so hunger for my empty chair
> That thou wilt needs invest thee with mine honours
> Before thy hour be ripe? O foolish youth!
> Thou seek'st the greatness that will o'erwhelm thee.

It is a significant moment in the play and, according to several contemporaries, including the Earl of Ormond and the later Burgundian chronicler Enguerrand de Monstrelet, it was founded in an incident that actually happened before the King's death. Given the parlous state of Henry's health and the intermittent nature of his disease it could well have been true. De Monstrelet writes:

It was the custom in England, whenever the king was ill, to place the royal crown on a cushion beside his bed, and for his successor to take it on his death. The Prince of Wales, being informed by the attendants that his father was dead, had carried away the crown. Shortly after, however, the King uttered a groan and his face was uncovered. Looking then for the crown, he asked what had become of it. His attendants replied that 'my lord the prince has taken it away'. He bade them send for the prince and, on his entrance, asked him why he had carried away the crown. 'My lord,' answered the prince, 'your attendants, here present, affirmed to me that you were dead and, as your crown and kingdom belong to me as your eldest son after your decease, I had it taken away.' The king gave a deep sigh and said, 'My fair son, what right have you to it, for you know well I had none.' 'My lord,' replied the prince, 'as you have held it by right of your sword, it is my intention to hold and defend it in similar manner during my life.'

The chronicler might have been using his own fancy to interpret a story that had wide currency at the time – some later historians have poured cold water on the account – but the event as he narrates it sums up many of the main concerns of Henry's life. It underlines the tense volatility of the relationship between father and son and more than anything else it reveals the King's lasting unease about the legality of his own position. There is even a suggestion that just as Henry had no right to the Crown, neither did his son, a painful position for any father to be forced to admit so soon before his death. More than any other factors the legality of his own rule and the security of the succession were concerns that obviously weighed heavily on Henry's mind in these latter stages of his life.

During this period the King's closest associate and adviser was Thomas Arundel, brother of the Earl of Arundel and one of Henry's firmest supporters when he made his bid for the throne in 1399. Thanks to his influence as Archbishop of Canterbury, any opposition to the King from the senior Church figures was quickly stilled. The only major objector was Thomas Merks, Bishop of Carlisle, who made a spirited protest about the usurpation and into whose mouth Shakespeare put the famous words about the act spawning future civil wars in which 'the blood of English shall manure the ground'. It helped that Arundel had no love for the previous regime – his brother Richard had been executed on the orders of Richard II and he himself had been sent into exile – but there seems to have been a genuine and lasting friendship between him and Bolingbroke. In his correspondence Henry referred to Arundel as his 'true friend' and restored him to the See of Canterbury after he came to the throne, as well as appointing him Chancellor.

The King also supported Arundel in his lengthy and vigorous campaign to extirpate the heresy of Lollardy, the name given to those who espoused the teachings of John Wyclif, who had died in 1384 but still attracted a powerful following. The son of a Yorkshire landowner, Wyclif had attended Balliol College, Oxford, where he had propagated revolutionary doctrinal ideas which denied the theory of transubstantiation and argued that right of property depended on attaining a state of grace. As he argued that the Church was not in that happy position it should be disendowed and transformed into a state of purity and poverty. Wyclif's ideas were published in two books, *De Dominio Divino* and *De Civile Dominio*, and their appearance led to his expulsion from Oxford and his withdrawal to Lutterworth in Leicestershire. Here he spent his last years translating the Bible, which he believed to be 'the one perfect word preceding from the mouth of God'.

By the time Henry came to the throne Lollardy enjoyed some support within the political establishment – John of Gaunt had been one of Wyclif's patrons and the 'Knights of the Lollards' represented a substantial following among the upper classes – but it had also become a catch-all phrase to describe any kind of behaviour which seemed to go against the grain. As the historian Miri Rubin splendidly puts it in her social history of the period, Lollardy was 'a label attached to people who failed a number of tests of social acceptability through sexual incontinence, clerical wanderings, an outspoken manner in criticism of the clergy, suspicious puritanical yearnings, attachment to vernacular books, or distaste for ostentatious religious expression'. In other words anyone who was 'different' or 'strange' was looking for trouble and would promptly be written off as a 'Lollard'.

Lollardy was a heresy which attracted a wide variety of vaguely anti-establishment manifestations and in all those different guises it was a potential source of political and social unrest. As such it seemed to be a suitable case for treatment, especially in those difficult years after Richard had been usurped, when there was a good deal of incontinent talk about his still being alive and perhaps even returning to claim his rightful throne. Given also the physical assaults on Henry's own right to rule – from the Epiphany Revolt in the first days of his reign to the more serious confrontation mounted by the Percys and Glendower – he had a vested interest in making sure that any heresy, real or imagined, was contained or crushed. Under those circumstances it was all too easy to assume that anyone suspected of any kind of deviation was a potential traitor who had to be punished.

The result was the production of the statute *De Haeretico Comburendo* (On Burning Heretics), passed by Parliament in 1401 to punish 'divers false and perverse persons of a certain sect' who were suspected of preaching and teaching heretical doctrines. 'They hold and exercise schools, they make and write books, they do wickedly instruct and inform people and . . . stir them to sedition and insurrections and make great strife and division among the people'. The statute was aimed at Wyclif's followers as one of the main tenets of the Lollards' belief was the importance of the Bible and religious tracts to propagate the Christian religion. Instead of using the established Church and its priests as a conduit, the Lollards believed that the word of God could be distributed directly to the people or through unlicensed preachers. For the King and his bishops, though, this was not freedom but licence and because the propagation of unorthodox knowledge could lead to dissent and perhaps even rebellion it had to be brought under control.

Until the passing of the statute ecclesiastical courts had dealt with the phenomenon of blasphemy (which had never been a widespread problem in England), but they could not inflict punishments which took life or shed blood. Henry's laws changed all that by producing a procedure by which convicted heretics would be turned over to the local sheriff or mayor, who 'caused them to be burnt before the people in a conspicuous place, that such punishment may strike fear into the minds of others'. It was hoped that this legislation would concentrate the minds of those who caused trouble by demanding change or simply kicking against the established order.

For the first time Church and state were brought together to punish those who might be guilty of spreading unorthodox opinions. In fact the dangers posed by Lollardy were not only exaggerated at the time but the passing of the statute led to a good deal of witch-hunting as the authorities went about the business of making people see the error of their ways or took their revenge on suspected troublemakers. All too often this enthusiasm developed into the persecution of people for no other reason than to destroy their reputation and the denunciation of people whose only fault was to be on the wrong side of those who accused them of heresy. However, the extreme penalty was only rarely used and the main import of the statute was to deter potential malcontents and to strike fear into anyone who might be troublesome in the early years of the new king's reign. For example, in Leicester an Augustinian canon named Philip Repton was accused of heresy but recanted and went on to become Abbot of St Mary's in the same town and was later created Bishop of Lincoln. Others were less fortunate, but even so, in the ten years after the statute was passed only two heretics were actually burned, and between 1423 and 1522 only thirty-four Lollards suffered the extreme penalty while over four hundred abjured their beliefs rather than face the flames. The two Lollards who were executed during Henry's reign were William Sawtry (or Sawtre), a priest from St Margaret's Lynn in Norfolk, and John Badby, a tailor from Evesham, both of whom were burned at the stake for refusing to abandon their beliefs.

The first to die was Sawtry, who was cross-questioned by Arundel in St Paul's Cathedral on 23 February 1401 before being taken to Smithfield by the civic authorities, who had paid for the costs of his execution and provided the necessary combustible materials. Sawtry's 'crime' was disputing transubstantiation and arguing that money spent on pilgrimages would be better spent on helping the poor at home. Arundel spent three hours attempting to persuade him to change his mind but to no avail and Sawtry was duly burned to death.

Nine years later Badby met a similar fate after facing the same process but the manner of his death was vile even by the standards of the day. Once again Arundel gave the accused every opportunity to recant, as did the Prince of Wales, who was present at the trial and interested himself in such matters, but Badby refused to go back on his belief that transubstantiation was a wicked heresy. Like Sawtry, he was taken to the open tournament ground at Smithfield, but as the fire was lit he started screaming. Thinking that the awful noise was the sound of Badby repenting, the Prince of Wales ordered the execution to stop and the man was dragged from the flames. Badby was offered three pence a day as a pension for the rest of his life provided that he recanted, but that proved to be no incentive and, as Walsingham reported the incident, the execution was restarted: 'The wretched man, rekindling his breath, spat on this generous offer, doubtless because he was possessed of an evil spirit. So Prince Henry ordered him to be put back on the flames and to receive no more mercy. This trouble-maker died for his own sins, pitifully burned in the fire.'

The presence of the Prince of Wales and his involvement in Badby's trial and execution were powerful reminders that the state would not tolerate Lollardy or any other kind of dissent. Heretics continued to be punished in this way throughout the century and the last to be burned was Joan Boughton in 1494, an 'old cankered heretic' who was punished for claiming that Wyclif was a saint.

It helped that Henry was a devout man who was anxious to maintain good relations with the Church, hence the importance of his close friendship with Arundel. In return he received subventions which helped to ease the constant financial burden, and in time he managed to survive the scandal caused by the execution of Archbishop Scrope. Although those involved in the execution were excommunicated by Pope Innocent VII, the continuation of the Great Schism meant that the edict could be safely ignored and in effect it lasted only until 1409, when the Council of Pisa deposed the Avignon and Rome popes and elected a successor to both, thereby bringing to a temporary closure the long-lasting split in the Church by creating a third papal line at Pisa. An English embassy sent by Henry attended the council and this was to be one of his more successful foreign policy initiatives.

The alliance of Crown and Church, as exemplified by the friendship between Henry and the Archbishop of Canterbury, had other consequences. It meant that nothing came of several Lollard proposals in Parliament to sequester the Church's riches, especially the immense wealth of the ecclesiastical sees, and it would be another century before religious endowments were diminished through the dissolution of the monasteries. Arundel also received the King's support when he insisted on making a 'visitation' to Oxford as part of his campaign to extirpate Lollardy. Although the Archbishop's attempted interference was resisted by the university, which produced an earlier papal bull of exemption in a last-ditch attempt to protect its own interests, Henry backed the procedure and anyone who had supported Wyclif in any way at Oxford was forced to recant. In the last years of the reign Arundel was forced to concede his position as Chancellor of the Exchequer to the Beaufort faction, but it was a measure of his importance that he returned to influence during the brief emergence of Prince Thomas at court in 1412.

With a sad inevitability the last years of Henry's life were clouded by both his dreadful illness and his tense relationship with Prince

Henry. Equally inevitably, perhaps, his physical afflictions gave contemporaries and some later commentators the opportunity to see them as divine punishments for his act of usurpation and then for his illegal murder of an archbishop. What more could he have expected following his act of unseating a lawfully anointed king and then misusing his power and authority to execute a senior churchman? Such meanderings about cause and effect are not uncommon throughout history and although they usually have no basis in fact, in this case they are irresistible.

As a young man King Henry represented the flower of chivalry. Powerfully built and possessing a commanding presence, he had all the kingly attributes that were lacking in Richard. He was courageous and dignified and much admired for his military skills, he was fêted in European courts and was a wealthy and powerful man in his own right even before he became king. The son of a distinguished family, descendants of Edward III, who enjoyed great temporal and political power in England and throughout Europe, Henry had influential friends and supporters and in his youth he even enjoyed the encouragement and backing of his kinsman the King. But for Richard's foolhardy decision to exact revenge by sending him into exile and then to double-cross him by denying him his inheritance, Henry, as Bolingbroke, could have led a very different kind of life as a loyal supporter of the status quo and a true friend of the royal house.

His troubles began when he seized the throne and continued after he put himself on it. From the very outset of his reign he was beggared by the need to produce adequate funds and then to balance them; he was also hamstrung by the necessity to use armed force to protect what he held. At a time when the country's finances were parlous he found himself fighting a potentially disastrous and immensely expensive civil war on two fronts, confronting the Percys, who had once supported him, and being forced into fighting a bitterly contested counter-insurgency war in Wales. For any king this unwanted exercise in crisis management would have been a trying beginning to a reign; for Henry it proved to be a fight for outright survival, for if he had failed all would have been lost.

And yet, at the very moment that he had overcome his worst difficulties, tragedy struck him down. Having crushed the last vestiges of the revolts against him in the north and in Wales, he was assailed by a wasting illness and this meant that his last years were spent in a kind of limbo in which he struggled to keep his dignity and to maintain his prerogatives while others were forced into action to make sure that the country was governed. It must have seemed dreadfully unfair. By now the Scots were no longer the problem they had been at the beginning of his reign, the Welsh had been brought under control, England was once again reasonably quiet and there was no immediate danger of a fresh conflict with France. Against that settled background it does not take much imagination to read the final years of Henry's life as a tragedy and to agree with the words Shakespeare, in *Henry IV, Part Two*, gives the dying usurper king in the last exchanges with his son:

> Heaven knows, my son,
> By what by-paths and indirect crooked ways
> I met this crown, and I myself know well
> How troublesome it sat upon my head.
> To thee it shall descend with better quiet,
> Better opinion, better confirmation,
> For all the soil of the achievement goes
> With me into the earth.

Henry collapsed on 20 March 1413 while he was praying at the shrine of Edward the Confessor in Westminster Abbey and he was carried into the chambers of the nearby abbot's house to die. For a man who had longed to go on crusade to the Holy Land and in his wildest dreams still planned to put those plans into effect, it was fitting, as Fabyan noted, that the rooms should have had a suitably resonant name:

At length when he [Henry] had come to himself, not knowing where he was, he asked of such as were about him, what place that was. They said to him that it belonged to the abbot of Westminster. As he felt himself so sick, he asked if that chamber had any special name: they answered that it was called Jerusalem. Then said the king, 'Praise be to the father of Heaven, for now I know that I shall die in this chamber, according to the prophecy made about me before that I should die in Jerusalem.'

The dead king was carried by water to his palace at Faversham in Kent and from there he was taken for burial in Canterbury Cathedral, where he lies near the tomb of his uncle the Black Prince. After Henry's death his executors discovered that the king who had begun his reign as one of the wealthiest men in England was virtually bankrupt. In his will he asked that his affairs be put in order but the harsh reality was that King Henry was so much in debt that it was impossible to pay back everything that he owed.

At the time of his death Henry had finally come to terms with the Prince of Wales and they seem to have reached a quietus which suited them both and appears to have been constructed on something approaching affection.

It would be easy to regard Henry as the author of many of his misfortunes. He seized the throne in a manner which suggested sleight of hand – as he showed after his arrival at Ravenspur in 1399, he was no stranger to deviousness – and while he proved to be a master of his own destiny in carrying out the act of usurpation he was less successful in the business of actually ruling the country. As has often been said of Henry's reign, it had been easy enough for him to win the crown but he found that it was much more difficult to wear it and then to accept its many responsibilities. Lack of money proved to be a perennial problem and strained his relations with Parliament, forcing him to accept compromises and only to make requests for funding through taxation when no other means of support were available.

This did not make him a constitutional monarch in the modern sense but it is true that he tried to rule with the assent of Parliament and did not seek any confrontation with it, preferring wherever possible to find consensus. It helped that the body was packed with Lancastrian appointees or supporters and many of the speakers owed their positions to royal patronage. In the latter days of his reign the ruling council proved to be an effective instrument, even if it never overcame the anomaly of its position, the King still being alive and in his senses while it carried out the great business of the governance of England.

One fact was indisputable. At the time of Henry IV's death his kingdom was at peace and his son faced no challengers to his throne. It was a solid foundation for the reign which followed.

Chapter Six

No Tongue Can Tell of his Renown

Prince Henry came to the throne of England blessed with a wide-ranging political intelligence and a sound knowledge of how the country should be governed. (The exact date of his birth and therefore his age at the time of his accession are uncertain, both 9 August and 16 September 1386 or 1387 having been mooted. It was probably not recorded because he was never expected to become King of England.) He had waited long for the moment and had spent the intervening period fruitfully and sensibly, quietly learning the realities of kingship. For two years he had served on the country's governing council and had reached a fine understanding of the mechanics of good government; he had also come to appreciate the need to surround himself with loyal advisers.

As a soldier he had proved himself fighting against the Welsh and in his boyhood he had been taken to Ireland as part of Richard II's military entourage. An astute young man, he had witnessed at first hand the effects of his father's frailties: his exile and dispossession, followed by the seizure of the throne and the long fight to retain it. As he himself had lusted after his father's crown he knew only too well what could happen to the unwary: after quarrelling with Henry IV he had been marginalized by his brother Clarence in the last years of their father's reign. One of his first steps as king was to ensure the solidity of his father's main Lancastrian supporters, namely his Beaufort relations and the Earls of Warwick, Arundel and Westmorland.

Henry was wise to watch his back as his reign was less than a year old when a group of Lollards hatched a plot in January 1414 to take him and his brothers prisoner while they were in residence at Eltham Palace. Nothing came of the attempt, which was ill-conceived and badly planned, and most of the ringleaders were rounded up and promptly executed – a sure sign that the new king was determined to clamp down on any move which might threaten his position. Among the plotters was Sir Roger Acton, a Shropshire knight who had once served Henry when he was Prince of Wales. In the event Acton was not burned as a Lollard but hanged as a traitor, but the ringleader, Sir John Oldcastle, a veteran soldier from the wars in Wales and France, managed to escape. One of the first acts of Henry's first Parliament, held in Leicester, was to enact further legislation against the Lollards, whom he believed to be heretics and beyond the law.

Although there is now some doubt about the extent of the Lollards' influence and the real danger posed by that attempt on Henry's life it did allow him to portray the incident as proof that the anointed king enjoyed God's favour and his divine protection. It also forced him to deal with Oldcastle, who, as the Lollards' main leader in Parliament, had supported Wyclif's proposals for the confiscation of the principal monastic houses. Henry admired the man as a soldier – he had served with him in the Welsh wars – but he could not stand by while Oldcastle denounced the authority of the Pope, as he had done when arrested on charges of heresy in September 1413.

The hearing took place in the chapter house of St Paul's and was heard before a number of clerics, including Archbishop Arundel and the Bishops of London and Winchester, but despite facing the full panoply of the Church's learning Oldcastle was obdurate. While he conceded his belief in the Eucharists he denied the theory of transubstantiation: in his opinion the bread remained bread and the Church was wrong to claim its transformation into Christ's body. Then he refused to concede that confession was a necessary prelude to salvation and to the horror of those present he called the Pope the Anti-Christ and his cardinals and followers his tail. This was heresy and Oldcastle cannot have been surprised when Arundel handed him over to the legal authorities to be punished. He was sent to the Tower of London and given forty days to reconsider his opinion.

For Henry the incident was thoroughly embarrassing. He liked Oldcastle but at the same time he could not agree with any of his views. The King had vowed to crush the Lollards yet here was a prominent leader of the sect making a public stand on a contentious religious matter and in so doing defying royal authority. It seems that Henry genuinely wanted Oldcastle to recant and hoped that the period of grace would enable him to change his mind, but on the night of 19 October Oldcastle mysteriously disappeared from the Tower and vanished into thin air. Rumours persisted that the King had arranged the escape or that it had been engineered by a member of the court but this is unlikely. Subterfuge of that kind was not in Henry's character and it is difficult to believe that he would permit such a potentially dangerous personality to escape and propagate his heresies. That might explain why Henry acted so ferociously against the Lollards the following January.

In the official indictment Oldcastle was named as the ringleader of the plot to kill the King and become regent in his stead. If that was the intention the plan failed miserably, although, as has been said, Oldcastle was not among those hunted down, tried and executed in the immediate aftermath. He remained at large until the end of 1417, when he was captured near the Welsh border and brought to London for trial. This time the authorities were taking no chances with a man who had become such a bugbear and a focus for further discontent. On 14 December Oldcastle was tried as a traitor and heretic, found guilty and executed by being 'hung and burnt hanging', a savage sentence.

Henry's coronation, on 9 April 1413 in Westminster Abbey, seems to have had a profound effect on him. Like Richard II, he believed implicitly in the sanctity of his position and had already concluded that he had been divinely ordained to carry out God's great work. Later, as his reign progressed, this conviction was extended to embrace a more profound belief that England had been chosen by God to be a favoured nation to humble the pride of France. On the day of the coronation it snowed and this was taken as a sign that change was in the air and that better days lay ahead, although others regarded the snow not as a sign of purification but as a bad omen which boded ill for the country. Whatever the portents, the symbolism of the snow might have had some meaning for the new king and those who witnessed the ceremony. Not only was it an unexpected change in the weather but its appearance coincided with a transformation in the young king's attitudes.

During his youth Henry had enjoyed life to the full and even if his experiences had not been as riotous as Shakespeare suggested in his portrayal of Prince Hal's antics with Falstaff and his crew, there is Thomas Elmham's evidence that Henry 'found leisure for the excesses common to ungoverned age'. His biographer Tito Livio dei Frulovisi, an Italian humanist who completed his account in 1437, confirmed that Henry became a reformed character on acceding to the throne and that after the death of his father 'his life was free from every taint of lustfulness'. The Italian also left an attractive portrait of the new king and his attributes:

> Let me describe the prince; he was taller than most men, his face fair and set on a longish neck, his body graceful, his limbs slender but marvellously strong. Indeed, he was miraculously fleet of foot, faster than any dog or arrow. Often he would run with two of his companions in pursuit of the swiftest does – he himself would always be the one to catch the creature. He had a great liking for music and found enjoyment in hunting, military pursuits and other pleasures that are customarily allowed to young knights.

Unlike his father, Henry V did not pursue the art of jousting but he more than made up for this through his military abilities. A great lover of music with a fine singing voice, he also possessed an extensive library and encouraged writers such as Thomas Hoccleve, who worked as a clerk in the office of the Privy Seal. His major work is *The Regement of Princes* (1411–12), a moralistic study of kingship which Henry was urged to study, and for Henry's coronation he wrote verses in which the new king was compared to the Emperor Constantine. Also patronised was the poet John Lydgate. Although he was later dismissed as 'a drivelling monk' who was not the equal of his greater and better-known contemporary Chaucer, Lydgate responded to Henry's encouragement to write poetry in English and in due course he became a court poet.

Henry's cultural interests make him an appealing personality and, like the high moral tone which he adopted for his reign, give the impression that he was a king of whom great things could be expected. Most contemporary descriptions of his life and reign deal only in superlatives but, of course, there was another, less agreeable side to the man. He could appear cold and aloof and his well-advertised piety was often mistaken for excessive sanctimony. On occasion he could appear high-handed and he had a cruel streak which manifested itself in the brutal treatment of anyone who opposed him or stood in his way. On the credit side, this harsher aspect to his character also gave him a single-mindedness of purpose and a common sense which stood him in good stead in the great business of ruling his country.

Shortly after becoming king Henry was advised by Henry Beaufort to provide 'bon gouvernance' and that became the watchword for the early years of his reign. In place of the endless profligacy of his father's period royal finances were brought under strict control and household expenses were reduced while revenues from land were increased. The stability of the realm was also addressed through a mixture of firmness and hard-nosed pragmatism. As Tito Livio put it, he 'appointed men whom he considered to be honest and fair to be judges throughout the kingdom' and on occasion proved that he was no mean law-giver himself. When two northern landowners failed to find a solution to a long-running quarrel Henry called them into his presence as he was about to dine and told them that unless they settled their differences before he had finished his plate of oysters they would be hanged.

A firm hand, common sense and conciliation were also applied to his relationship with those nobles who had been close to Richard II or had opposed his father. The young English Earl of March was released from house arrest and created a Knight of the Bath even though his claim to the throne was well known. At the same time Harry Hotspur's son was restored to the earldom of Northumberland. Henry clearly believed that it was better to keep potential enemies in sight and grateful to him, although in this case there was an ulterior motive in that he needed the Percy family to guard England's border with Scotland, their traditional duty and one which gave them great temporal power in the north. After his father's death at Shrewsbury the young earl had lived in exile in Scotland, effectively a hostage, and Henry secured his release by exchanging him with Murdoch Stewart, Earl of Fife, who had been in English hands since the Battle of Homildon Hill in 1402. No comparable steps were taken to release James Stewart, the rightful heir to the Scottish throne, and for the time being Scotland remained obdurately in the hands of the Albany faction.

As for Wales, Henry introduced a policy of reconciliation: corruption by officials in the north of the country was investigated and punished and Welshmen were encouraged to serve in England as soldiers, notably and successfully as archers.

As for England itself, Henry's long-term aim was to unite the country and to provide the people with a sense of purpose that had been lacking in his father's reign. And he succeeded. He restored gravitas as well as popularity to the kingship, his well-attested piety was much admired (the French thought he looked more like a priest than a soldier), he was a conservative in religious matters and he proved to be a great supporter and patron of the Catholic Church. Two religious houses were built close to the River Thames, one for the Carthusian order at Sheen and a second, for the nuns of St Brigit at Twickenham, which was given the name Syon. The idea was that Henry was to be prayed for perpetually, while bells would be rung at the end of prayers to start a new round of devotion. Certainly he was religious-minded and set in his beliefs, but, as we have seen, that adherence to a strict religious orthodoxy revealed another side in his dislike of Lollardy and the vehemence he brought to its extirpation. Walsingham praised Henry for being 'pious in soul' but the King could also be ruthless in dealing with those who challenged his authority. Enguerrand de Monstrelet, admittedly as a Burgundian not an objective witness, found Henry autocratic and unfeeling and not given to leniency or acts of charity when faced by disobedience or rebellion:

> He was so feared by his nobles and captains there was no one, however close or dear to him, who was not afraid to go against his orders, especially those of his own kingdom of England. Everyone under his rule, in France and England alike, whatever his rank, was reduced to this same state of obedience. The chief reason for this was that anyone who thwarted his orders was most cruelly punished and received no mercy.

Twice in his reign Henry was forced into a position where he had to act condignly to preserve his position and on neither occasion did he flinch from doing what was expected of him. He had already demonstrated his ruthlessness in putting down the attempted rebellion by Lollards in the new year of 1414. The second attempt was much more serious as it involved magnates who should have owed him their loyalty. Worse, it happened in the summer of 1415, when Henry was on the point of invading France to press his claims to the French throne. As his armed forces began assembling at Southampton he received the astonishing news from the English Earl of March that a well-organised plot to kill him was about to be put into effect by men who were thought to be loyal to the Crown. March was party to the plans but at the last minute thought twice about his involvement and confessed everything to Henry while he was staying at Porchester Castle on the night of 31 July.

What made the revelation so shocking was that the main instigators were all Lancastrians close to the King whose loyalty should have been taken for granted. At the heart of the conspiracy was Henry, Lord Scrope of Masham, the nephew of the Archbishop of Canterbury who had risen against Henry IV and a man described by Tito Livio as a 'an ornament of chivalry'. The treatment meted out to his uncle might have given him a motive for revenge but he himself had played no part in his kinsman's revolt and had risen in the King's service, becoming his Lord Treasurer of the Household. However, he did enjoy close family connections with the other main conspirators: the Earl of Cambridge and Sir Thomas Grey of Heton, both noblemen with influential positions at court. All were connected in one way or another and through their relationship with March may have believed that they had a legitimate claim to usurp the Crown.

Richard, Earl of Cambridge, came from an impeccable background. He was the King's cousin, being the second son of Edmund of Langley, Duke of York, and a godson of Richard II. He was also the brother-in-law of the English Earl of March, having married his sister Anne Mortimer in 1408; after his wife's death in childbirth three years later he married Matilda Clifford, the sister of Hotspur's brother-in-law John Clifford. To complete the circle, his son Richard by Anne Mortimer had been named as March's heir, the Earl being childless.

However, for all that Cambridge enjoyed powerful family connections he was a man with a grudge against the King. On being created Earl of Cambridge he found that he was in financial difficulties and could not meet all his obligations. An endowment from the King would have eased his problems but this was not forthcoming and personal unhappiness with his lot seems to have turned into enmity towards Henry. His first ally was Sir Thomas Grey of Heton, a powerful northern magnate who enjoyed family links with the Percys and therefore needed little encouragement to throw in his lot with the conspirators. The idea was to bring March into the plot and to make him king in place of Henry, thereby confirming his position as Richard II's heir presumptive and putting an end to Henry IV's usurpation. If March failed to produce an heir there would be the happy result that Cambridge's son Richard, later Duke of York, would succeed to the throne – later, during the Wars of the Roses, he would be one of the main contenders for the crown worn by Henry V's son.

Having secured Grey's support, Cambridge rode south from his seat, Conisburgh Castle in Northumberland, and made contact with Scrope at Southampton. March was then admitted to the plot but from the outset he seemed to be an unwilling participant even though his residence at Cranbury, near Winchester, was used for much of the preparation. Like the earlier conspiracies to get rid of Henry IV, it was planned as a nationwide uprising even though it was doubtful that all the participants would play their expected roles or had even been contacted. Northumberland would seize the north of England, March would be entrusted with raising the revolt in the west, where he would make contact with Oldcastle (still at large) and even with Glendower to secure Wales. There were plans, too, for the Scots to join in and at one stage Cambridge even thought of enlisting the support of the Mummet, the wretched impostor who was supposed to be Richard II. It was all fantasy and ended messily.

The first day of August was fixed for the King's assassination and thereafter March would be speedily enthroned as King Edmund I. However, March's nerve failed him and he decided to turn coat. Memories of the earlier attempts to oust his father led Henry to take this plot seriously and after listening to March's revelations he acted swiftly and savagely. The three traitors were arrested and imprisoned. Grey was tried in Southampton the following day and after making a full confession was beheaded. Scrope and Cambridge exercised their right to be tried by their peers in front of twenty noblemen but they too were found guilty and sentenced to death. Henry commuted Cambridge's sentence to beheading but no such good fortune awaited

Scrope, who was judged to be the most guilty and forced to face the traitor's fate of being hanged, drawn and quartered, and as a warning to others his head was put on public display at his home city of York.

Towards the others implicated or named in the plot Henry showed mercy. March was forgiven and remained loyal and Northumberland, having already been pardoned, returned to the royal fold. It had been an unsettling experience. Not only were the main plotters powerful magnates in their own right whose loyalties clearly lay not with the King but with their own interests but the conspiracy had been hatched at the very moment when Henry was about to launch a military expedition against France. That was one reason why he acted so quickly and so decisively in trying and executing the leaders: time was not on his side, for he had on his mind the great business of leading a major cross-Channel offensive against England's old enemies. On 11 August, a week after the sentences had been carried out, Henry set sail with his army for France to pursue the most audacious foreign policy initiative of his reign: to break the truce brokered by Richard II in 1396 and stake his entitlement to be the rightful King of France as originally claimed by Edward III.

His thinking was guided by several factors. As a result of his father's seizure of the throne in 1399 Henry had received the title Duke of Aquitaine and he maintained a seigneurial interest in those lands. He also believed strongly that the French had reneged on the conditions of the Treaty of Brétigny of 1360 and that the failure to execute its main points had created a *casus belli*. This agreement had come about as a result of the capture of King John II of France at the Battle of Poitiers in 1356, an incident which produced an exceptionally strong bargaining position for the English negotiators when they met at Brétigny, near Chartres. During the talks the principals were the Black Prince and the French Dauphin and the main points agreed by them were supposed to bring the conflict to a mutually satisfactory conclusion. In return for renouncing the French Crown and claims on Brittany and Flanders, Edward III would be given full suzerainty over Aquitaine, Montreuil, Ponthieu and the Calais Pale (Calais, Guînes and Marck). To cement the decision John II would be ransomed for three million gold crowns, to be paid in instalments, and the French Crown would drop its claim to the new English possessions. In the event the renunciations were never carried out and

the whole of the ransom was not paid, a state of affairs which led
Henry V to believe that he had a valid reason to go to war with France
over half a century later. A victorious campaign would have had two
advantages: it would have brought about the restitution of the English
claims and of the unpaid ransom.

Henry's French policy was also driven by a desire to enter into an
alliance with the Burgundians at a time when the country's central
government had been enfeebled by civil strife. As we have seen, from
the outset of his reign Henry had reckoned that the Burgundians were
the better bet, not least because they were the dominant force in the
country and held the key to the security of Calais and its Pale. Also
to be taken into account was the aggravation caused by French piracy
and associated warlike naval activities in the Channel which were
injurious to English trade. The port of Harfleur at the mouth of the
River Seine was a particular bugbear as it was the main French naval
base in the area. Personality also influenced Henry's thinking. Unlike
Richard II, he was a soldierly individual, more like Edward III or the
Black Prince, who believed that it was a king's duty to lead his armies
to victory in battle. A campaign in France would test that concept to
the full.

It was a bold plan and the time seemed to be right to execute it.
Although, as the son of a usurper, Henry's claims were weak – any
rightful English claimant would have to be March as Richard II's heir
presumptive – he could see that the muddled political conditions
inside France had presented him with his best chance of success.
While the French court was fractured and in disarray, he ruled a
settled country. With Charles VI still enfeebled, the split between the
Orléanists and the Burgundians was as pronounced as ever it had been
and Henry could sense opportunities by exploiting the two factions.
Although the earlier détente at Auxerre had reconciled them it was
only a temporary agreement and Duke John of Burgundy had been
banished from Paris, making an alliance with England more attractive.

Initially, in the first year of his reign, Henry had tried diplomacy
and opened his account by making territorial demands in Aquitaine
and asking for the hand of Princess Katherine of Valois, the French
king's daughter. The demands were not disagreeable to the Orléanists,
who would have welcomed a truce or a treaty based on marriage, but
they were unwilling to discuss any move involving the sovereignty of

France. Their intransigence on this point was revealed and made manifest during the final discussions, held at Winchester at the end of June 1415, when one of the French envoys, the Archbishop of Bourges, responded to Henry's claims for the French throne with the retort that he was not even the rightful King of England.

While these discussions continued Henry was also in contact with Duke John of Burgundy, who was keen to wrest control of France away from Charles VI and regain his influence in Paris. At the same time he continued to be wary about entering into any alliance with the English. When the demand for support was pressed Burgundy backed away and decided to throw in his lot with the Orléanists rather than support an English monarch in his attempt to seize the French throne.

Throughout the discussions Henry had been preparing for war, almost as if he knew it was his manifest destiny to fight for what he believed were his legal rights. Weapons, especially bows and arrows, were stockpiled in the Tower of London and siege machines – scaling ladders, battering rams and artillery pieces – were prepared for the capture of French towns. Ships were constructed or bought or hired in the Low Countries to form an armada to cross the Channel. When the force was finally brought together in the summer of 1415 it consisted of 10,500 fighting soldiers, who were transported with their horses and equipment on a total of fifteen hundred ships. The make-up of the force revealed its purpose and Henry's determination to make a lasting impression on his enemies. In addition to archers and men-at-arms, both mounted and dismounted, the English army included crossbowmen and a variety of support troops: labourers, armourers, cooks, fletchers, carpenters and 120 miners from the Forest of Dean for the siege operations.

Under the terms of Henry's compact (or indenture) with the nobility, barons and knights who served as his captains brought their own retinues of men and these could range in number from fifty to five hundred, depending on the wealth and standing of those raising the force. Lesser captains had to recruit their men, while big landowners would find the men from their own estates. Local sheriffs also acted as commissioners for the King to raise men for service in France.

If the size of the fleet seems unlikely it should be remembered that the ships had to carry, as well as men, sufficient provisions and equipment for a long campaign, fifteen thousand horses, various siege guns and hundreds of thousands of arrows. Some of the ships would have been minor coastal vessels with small capacities. In the first seven years of his reign Henry spent £20,000 on naval construction and Southampton became the navy's principal base with ships constructed and anchored on the River Hamble, with the entire dockyard area protected by a military garrison. By the time of the invasion Henry had under his command thirty royal ships armed with cannon, as well as men-at-arms equipped with bows, arrows and spears. Henry's flagship was the 540-ton *Trinity Royal*, which carried him to France on 11 August in the company of seven other royal ships. As they passed down Southampton Water swans accompanied the armada and this was taken to be a good omen.

Instead of pursuing the traditional English war-fighting policy of *chevauchées* (rapid, long-distance raids deep into French territory) Henry had decided to embark on a war of conquest and was determined to prepare the ground well by creating a secure base before engaging in more mobile operations. Another consideration was that he could not afford to have extended lines of communication and his invasion force would have to engage numerically superior French forces once they had landed. This limited his options and meant that he had to chose Normandy or the Pas de Calais as his point of entry, through either Cherbourg or Calais. A similar choice had to be made by the planners of the D-Day operations in 1944, five centuries later, and, like them, Henry decided to plump for the longer crossing. However, his route took his forces not into Artois or Normandy but into the mouth of the River Seine, which would allow them to threaten Paris.

Three days after setting sail, on 14 August, the English armada made landfall at Chef de Caux and although the landing was unopposed Henry had to lay siege to the huge and imposing fortress of Harfleur, which was generally held to be unassailable by besieging forces. It was a prize worth winning. If the port and its fortress could be captured, the way to Paris, one hundred miles away, would be open and Henry would have secured a firm foothold on French soil.

However, from a military standpoint, the siege of Harfleur was not to be undertaken lightly. The fortifications were solid and on the seaward side they stretched for over two miles. The Seine offered protection on the south, the River Lézarde to the north and the eastern approaches were covered by a belt of marshes. It took three days for the siege to begin and for three heavy guns to be dragged into position to start their bombardment of the defences. An attempt was made to mine the moat but the French defenders fought this off with the creation of counter-mines, the standard defensive counter-measure to any assault from beneath the ground (the French desperately tried to dig into the English mines before any charges were exploded). As a result stalemate ensued and the English settled down to what would clearly be a lengthy affair.

It also proved to be an unhealthy business. The marshes were home to millions of flies and mosquitoes and in the summer heat men quickly succumbed to illness. Dysentery was rife and inadequate food supplies added to the English army's woes. By the time the siege came to a successful end, on 22 September, over two thousand of Henry's men had become casualties, including the Earl of Suffolk and the Earl of Arundel, both of whom died of dysentery, and many more had to be repatriated as a result of sickness. Among them was the Earl of March, who returned to England to manage the country's naval defences.

The siege ended when the English artillery breached the walls. Not only was this a crushing blow which damaged morale within the fortress, but it was compounded by the failure of the French to send a relieving army, which convinced Harfleur's commander, Raoul de Gaucourt, that further resistance was useless. The English invasion had given the French a rude surprise and it had taken time for them to assemble an army at Rouen, where, in the absence of Charles VI, the Dauphin gathered his senior commanders to discuss tactics.

The next stage of the English operation should have been an immediate assault on Paris, followed by a further attack south, deep into French territory towards Bordeaux, but the protracted battle for Harfleur made an ambitious move of that kind impossible. Henry had lost a third of his fighting men either to sickness or in battle and he was reduced to leading a force which consisted of fewer than a thousand men-at-arms and around five thousand archers. Given the approach of the autumn rains his best option might have been to return to England and leave Harfleur strongly garrisoned by English forces, but that would have been a pyrrhic victory. More than anything else he wanted to engage the French in the set-piece battle which had been avoided during the recent protracted siege. It was a high-risk strategy as the French forces would soon be superior in number but at a council of war held on 5 October Henry came up with a compromise plan which would satisfy English honour and, so he hoped, also keep his army safe.

Instead of seeking an immediate engagement with the French in the vicinity of Harfleur his army would march north-east across French soil towards Calais, a move that would bring it back to England and safety without giving any hint of retreat. Four days later the English began pulling out of Harfleur to begin a march of 120 miles which would take them across the great river barriers of Picardy, including the Somme, towards the Channel.

It was an epic undertaking. Henry's soldiers were traversing hostile territory and the whereabouts of the French army was initially unknown, but they made good progress in the first week, crossing the obstacles of the Rivers Bresle and Béthune, near Eu, and making eighty miles in five days. As they approached the Somme Estuary on 13 October the first intelligence was received about the position of the enemy and it also became clear that the chosen crossing at Blanche-Taque was impassable as it was heavily defended. Undaunted, Henry led his army south-east along the southern bank of the Somme, passing Amiens and Abbeville, until they came across two undefended causeways at Béthencourt and Voyennes. By now, 19 October, the English had been on the march for ten days and were not only exhausted but uneasily aware that they were being shadowed by a huge French force on their right flank.

The arrival of French heralds on 21 October with a challenge to fight provided confirmation that battle could not be avoided, but it was not until three days later, after further forced marches along a route to the south of Arras between Bapaume and Albert, that the two armies came into contact near the villages of Tramecourt and Agincourt on the road to Calais. On one side were the English, exhausted and hungry and outnumbered at least three to one; vastly superior in numbers and defending their homeland, the French were not only confident but well fed. All that united the soldiers on both sides was the need to shelter from the incessant rain. As night fell on

24 October it was obvious that the French held the upper hand and that it would take either a miracle or superior military judgement for the small and worn-out English force to survive whatever the next twenty-four hours would bring. According to Tito Livio, there was nothing for them to do except take what refuge they could and pray to a higher authority for their salvation:

> On 25 October, at dawn, the most Christian of kings, Henry V, led forth his army in battle array, after his priests had duly said prayers and supplications and sung matins and masses. He gave instructions that many horses and a large quantity of equipment should be left in the charge of a small garrison, in the hamlet where he and his men had spent the night, and led forth only arms and men. The king trusted to divine guidance, God and justice, and behold, fortune favoured him a safe position and a field protected in the rear by the hamlet where the army had passed the night and to the sides by thorny hedges. These shielded the king's army from the enemy's ambush or attack.

At dawn the French army was in position to the north of the English. Owing to the lack of space in the open ground between the woods which surrounded Tramecourt and Agincourt, it was drawn up in three battles, or columns, the first two composed of dismounted men-at-arms flanked by crossbow men and the third composed of cavalry, the right flank commanded by the Count of Vendôme, the smaller left flank by Clignet de Brébant and Guillaume de Saveuse. Mounted troops also flanked the front battle. Against them the English had also lined up in three battles but their smaller numbers allowed them to deploy line abreast, with the archers defending the flanks. Henry commanded the centre, Edward, Duke of York, led the right and on the left was the experienced knight Lord Camoys, who had fought against the Scots and under John of Gaunt in Castile.

The ground was little more than one thousand yards wide and as it had been freshly ploughed for winter wheat it produced heavy going, especially as the recent torrential rains had turned parts of it into a quagmire. For three hours after sunrise both sides held their ground in the cold, damp air. It must have been a nerve-racking experience, especially for the tired and hungry English. The French contemporary chronicler Jean de Waurin described the front ranks sitting down to eat and drink or to jostle for the best position but that was on the French side. On short rations – the archers had managed to find some nuts and berries – the English could only watch and wait, alone with their fears about what lay ahead.

At around eleven o'clock the first move was made when Henry ordered his army to move slowly forward across the sodden ground to take up a new position within three hundred yards or 'extreme bowshot' of the French lines. When they came to a halt the English line stretched over nine hundred yards and the archers, the main strike force, took up position in echelons in front of the men-at-arms. This ensured that although the men were drawn up in lines parallel to one another, none were on the same alignment. Pointed stakes were hammered into the ground to form palisades to defend the archers' positions against cavalry attack. Their task was to fire into the French lines both to kill and to provoke the enemy into retaliation, and this they did by concentrating their fusillades in groups on particular targets. Arrows were placed in the ground in front of each archer, bows were strung and had already been checked by Sir Thomas Erpingham, Steward of the Royal Household; now they had to wait for the order to begin firing off their missiles.

When they did go into action, in de Waurin's words the 'air was darkened by an intolerable number of piercing arrows flying across the sky to pour upon the enemy like a cloud laden with rain'. It looked impressive but at that stage in the battle the arrow shower did little immediate damage as the mounted men-at-arms wore steel armour and were reasonably protected; only their horses would have fallen victim.

Yet it was enough to provoke the French commander, Charles d'Albret, the Constable of France, to give the order for an advance across the front. As the dismounted men-at-arms began their ponderous move forward the cavalry charged the English lines with the intention of sweeping the archers from the field. Another round of arrows was fired at them but then, just before the point of impact, the English archers moved away to reveal their stakes. For the advancing cavalry, moving at around fifteen miles an hour on their big, caparisoned hunter horses, the momentum they had gained was too great. Some crashed on to the defences and were impaled, others fell to the ground to be bludgeoned to death by archers who had exchanged their bows for mallets and axes, while the lucky ones managed to rein in their horses and turn around towards their own lines. Some French cavalry got in among the English archers but in this second phase of the battle they had been badly mauled and most retreated in disarray.

Worse, as the frenzied horses made their way back across the field they collided with the dismounted men-at-arms as they went into the attack. The interruption allowed the English archers to reopen fire on the advancing French lines, this time lowering the trajectory and using heavier arrow points, and the French began to fall in numbers. Although most wore steel armour there were weak points, so that as the range closed many arrows were able to penetrate lighter steel. The heavy fire also channelled the French attack into a narrower front, but although this gave the attackers an initial advantage as the English moved back a spear's length to receive the charge, it was also the cause of their undoing. As the two fronts clashed and the French started falling to the ground the speed and strength of the English attack pushed the French men-at-arms into close and deadly contact with their opponents. This must have been a horrible phase. Despite wearing steel armour, when men fell to the ground they were easy prey for the close-quarter weapons – the maces, bills and battle-axes – to finish them off. As men stumbled around in their death throes the rump following on from behind fell over them and added to the slaughter.

At this point the English archers rejoined the battle, once more exchanging their bows for hand-held weapons to stand by their comrades in the killing zone. A further attack by the French second line under the command of the Duke of Alençon fared little better. Seeing what had happened to their comrades in front of them, the third line of cavalry held their ground and did not make the charge which could have done serious damage to the undefended and temporarily confused English lines. Men exhausted by the butchery would have been hard pushed to withstand a determined cavalry attack and by that stage in the battle the English archers were desperately short of arrows. Within an hour, around midday, the English had gained the upper hand and had control of the battle:

No one thought of spoils, only of victory. No captives were taken and many met their deaths. In short, countless French warriors found they had been led – by fate and their own pride – not to battle but slaughter. However, when many of the French had gone to their deaths and an English victory seemed assured, the English stopped killing their enemy and took them captive instead.

Unfortunately Tito Livio's account does not tell the whole story and the comforting words of that last sentence are not altogether true. Towards the end of the battle Henry received intelligence that the French were about to mount a counter-attack on his rear, where he had left his baggage train and where the French prisoners were assembled. Mounted men were seen in the vicinity of the baggage park and there was renewed activity in the French third line which suggested that mounted men-at-arms were being marshalled for a renewed assault under the command of the Counts of Masle and Fauquemberghe. An attack of that kind could have had serious consequences for the English king, not only because he would be facing a new assault from the rear but because a successful assault would have encouraged the rest of the French third line to join the battle and they would have made short work of his weary forces.

Later it emerged that the only tangible threat had been posed by a mob of local peasants led by three knights under the command of the Lord of Agincourt who had overwhelmed the rear area and made off with their plunder. However, at the time the threat seemed real enough and for reasons that were clear from a strictly military point of view Henry ordered the French prisoners to be slaughtered. His decision went against all the rules of war but he believed that an uncertain victory was about to be snatched from him and he could not protect the prisoners or prevent them from rejoining the battle while defending his own flanks. Many men in the English army refused to obey the order either because they found it a repulsive task which betrayed the chivalric code or they did not want to lose ransoms – the real reasons remain unclear – and so the task of execution was given to the archers, who numbered two hundred.

Even though these were battle-hardened and professional soldiers for whom an order was an order, it would have been a beastly task. Many of the French men-at-arms would still have been in armour, which would have meant dispatching them at close quarters with hand weapons including axes and hammers and it is difficult to believe that those proud men would have stood by while their social inferiors clubbed them to death. With good reason Henry has been criticised by later commentators for giving the order to kill the prisoners but by any standards it is difficult to know how the executions would have been carried out. The archers stood outside the chivalric order and were accustomed to killing but the French prisoners who had surrendered outnumbered them ten to one. From contemporary evidence it seems that some of the higher-ranking prisoners were set aside for the more lucrative possibility of ransom and that the dead may have numbered little more than a hundred. When it became clear that the French third line was not going to attack Henry gave the order for the killing to stop, but, of course, the fact that he gave the order in the first place leaves a stain on his standing as a military commander. In his favour it should be pointed out that before the battle he had ordered the unfurling of a red war banner known as the Oriflamme which signalled that no quarter would be granted.

By three o'clock in the afternoon, with dusk fast approaching, the fighting petered out and peace of a kind returned to the battlefield. As was the custom of the period, the French heralds approached Henry to inform him that he had won the day and that the battle should be known as Agincourt. The grim task of counting the dead and tending to the wounded then began. English casualties were relatively light – estimates range from four hundred to sixteen hundred (killed and wounded) – but among them were the Duke of York and the Earl of Suffolk, whose father had died at Harfleur. For the French it had been a disaster. Of the Constable's army of twenty thousand which had lined up earlier in the day around a third were dead, most from dreadful blows to the body or from arrow wounds, and many more would die later of septicaemia, or blood poisoning, or from fractures.

Many notable names were among the dead – the Constable, the Duke of Brabant and Count of Nevers, both brothers to Burgundy, and the Duke of Alençon. Among the French nobles who survived the battle but found themselves in English captivity were the Duke of Orléans, the Duke of Bourbon and the Counts of Vendôme,

Richemont, Eu and Boucicaut. By any standards, the battle fought on the feast day of Saints Crispin and Crispinian was a glorious victory for the English and a personal triumph for Henry, who had directed the forces. (The saints in question lived in Soissons in the third century and had been martyred for their Christian beliefs.)

A superior French army had been defeated and once again the skill and killing capacity of the English archers had sent a powerful message across Europe. Four days later Henry's little army reached Calais, where it had to wait for shipment across the Channel and it was not until 23 November that the soldiers returned to London as heroes. It was typical of Henry that he refused to accept any personal credit and preferred to offer thanks to God for his support in making the victory possible: the Archbishop of Canterbury ruled that henceforth the feast day of Crispin and Crispinian was to be celebrated with due reverence, a move that underlined both the scale of the victory over the French and God's role in making it happen.

From that moment onwards the names of King Henry V and Agincourt were to be linked for good or for ill. The battle defined Henry's reign and seemed to reinforce its legitimacy by putting a seal on the right of the Lancastrians to occupy the throne of England. Not only had the King displayed great leadership on the field, demonstrating no little personal bravery by leading from the front, where he was often in the thick of the action, but his ascription of the victory to God made it seem that England had been granted divine protection and assistance. On a temporal level Henry had shown that he was a true leader of men and a worthy successor to Edward III; on a spiritual level he had been revealed as a man doubly blessed. How else could so few have defeated so many unless they had received divine protection?

All this mattered: in the heady days following the return of the hero king and his victorious army perception became more important than reality. No one could doubt Henry's right to wear the crown of England and just as importantly there were no longer any qualms about his entitlement to claim the throne of France. The courage and steadfastness of around six thousand Englishmen on a muddy autumn field in Picardy had seen to that.

Chapter Seven

THE MIGHTY AND PUISSANT CONQUEROR

At Agincourt Henry had won a stupendous victory, there was no doubt about that, and his name resounded through Europe as a great leader; but the military reality of his situation was rather different. He had launched the campaign to further his territorial ambitions in France but, apart from winning a single battle and crushing the opposition's army, he had done nothing to encourage the French to make any concessions and neither had he made any tangible gains in pursuit of his policy of conquest. All that he had in his possession was a town in France at the mouth of the Seine and it was obvious that his opponents would soon take advantage of the garrison's precarious position and attempt to win it back.

The Orléanist faction, now led by the new Constable of France, Bertrand, Count of Armagnac, had refused to enter into fresh negotiations with Henry, while the Burgundians stayed aloof, preferring to push their own claims when and if the opportunity arose. Armagnac had an especial hatred for Burgundy and believed implicitly that the English should be driven out of France. He did not have long to wait. Shortly after Charles VI returned to Paris at the end of November 1415, Burgundy tried to capitalise on the situation by forcing Armagnac out of the capital but his bid failed and fizzled out altogether when the sickly and ailing Dauphin suddenly died in mid-December.

The French king's son and heir was succeeded by his younger brother, John, and this subtle change in relationships encouraged Burgundy to remove his forces from the Paris area and take them back into Flanders. Not only did this strengthen his position militarily but it made him less likely to seek any compact with the English at a time when his main aim was to oust Armagnac from Paris. From the point of view of diplomacy none of this helped Henry and he had further cause to be discommoded when the French took steps to besiege Harfleur early in the following year.

Before the French intervened in earnest to win back their possession the garrison had been reinforced and placed under the command of the Earl of Dorset, but its safety was by no means guaranteed. That much became clear in March when an English foraging party narrowly avoided defeat at the hands of the French investing army, led by the Count of Armagnac. In an attempt to bring the issue to a speedier conclusion Armagnac started hiring warships from Genoa and Castile and employed them to blockade the approaches to the Seine to prevent supplies getting through to Harfleur. Among the naval force were eight huge carracks, heavily fortified, two-masted warships weighing up to six hundred tons, as well as a number of galleys under the command of Giovanni de Grimaldi, a noted Genoese sailor. The new tactics worked – Harfleur was now under siege by land and sea – and it provoked the English into a response. Preparations were made for a new expedition and on 15 August a naval force led by the King's brother John, Duke of Bedford, arrived off Harfleur to engage the French fleet.

The subsequent action lasted six hours and ended in Bedford's favour. According to the Italian chronicler Antonio Morosini, it was one of the most vicious and hard-fought naval battles in history. Bedford had superior numbers but his ships, mainly barge-like ballingers, were smaller, more adaptable and less heavily armed than their opponents and the outcome of the battle depended on superior seamanship. The English cause was also helped by the fact that many of the Castilian ships fled when they saw the size of the English fleet ranged against them. During the engagement three carracks were sunk and another was run aground and destroyed.

Control of the Channel was returned to the English fleet, allowing the blockade of Harfleur to be lifted. Bedford's triumph came just in time because the garrison was on the verge of starvation and surrender would have been the only option. It was a good outcome for the English. Harfleur was saved and English sailors had shown that their smaller and lighter ballingers were capable of taking on and destroying the high-sided and more heavily armed carracks. (In common with his predecessors Henry depended on the royal prerogative to order ship owners to hand over their vessels in time of war. These were then adapted for fighting purposes, mainly by reinforcement with wooden castles fore and aft.)

Although it was a welcome victory the lifting of the siege of Harfleur does raise questions about Henry's policy in 1416. Having defeated the French, he seemed to lose his nerve about what to do next. Finance was one reason: the previous year's expedition had been costly and although Parliament was minded to provide further subsidies it would take at least a further year before Henry could raise another army to launch a fresh attack on French soil. It is also possible that he had been unnerved by the circumstances of his victory at Agincourt. While he took it as a sign of God's grace and a reminder that his claim over France was a just one, he would not have been human had he not realised that it had been a close-run thing and that the battle could have been lost but for French pride, intransigence and bad leadership.

International diplomacy had also been brought into play. In that same year, 1416, Henry's attention had been diverted by the arrival of Sigismund, King of Hungary and since 1411 Holy Roman Emperor, the titular ruler of large swaths of eastern and central Europe. Founded in 800 with the coronation of Charlemagne, this curious confederation of states had lost much of its power and authority by the fifteenth century largely because of its inability to raise taxation, but the Emperor remained a potent European figure. In this role Sigismund was no exception. A complicated man whose authority had been eroded by internecine fighting in Bohemia, he regarded himself as a European peace-maker and his greatest diplomatic ambition was to bring to an end the Great Schism which had plunged the Catholic Church into chaos. To that end he had summoned a General Council of the Church at Constance in November 1414 and in the intervening period he used his best endeavours to convince the princes of the Church to return to a single universally recognised papacy.

Part of that effort took Sigismund to Paris in March 1416, his aim being to persuade the French to withdraw support from

Benedict XIII, the Avignon Pope, and from there he continued across the Channel and reached Dover on 1 May. He arrived with the intention of acting as a peace-broker between the two countries, not just because they were in a state of conflict but because French and English clerics continued the national rivalry at Constance. Voting at the General Council was in the hands of 'nations' (English, French, German and Italian) and because England and France were on separate sides of the schism, there was great scope for carrying on the war by other means, using the papal discussions as a proxy for the wider political disagreements of the day. Sigismund saw his visits to France and England as an opportunity to bring the council's work to fruition – he was keen to find a compliant pope who would validate his claims in Germany and Bohemia, where he was intent on suppressing the Hussites, followers of John Hus, who had much in common with Wyclif – and at the same time he wanted to stop the cross-Channel confrontation. With him he brought a French embassy headed by the Archbishop of Reims and a large retinue which included the Duke of Berry. As described by Tito Livio, the visit started well, with Henry keen to make a favourable impression on his guest:

> When King Sigismund came into the outskirts of London, the most victorious King Henry came forth to meet him with all regal pomp, attended by his brothers, their highnesses the dukes of Clarence, Bedford and Gloucester, and other members of the Royal family. The two kings greeted one another with the utmost gentility, each exemplary in his graciousness. They then progressed to the city where a vast crowd of people was gathered, eager to see the foreign king. Indeed, those most invincible kings and the other Royal princes who attended them were scarcely able to make their way even through the broadest squares, so great was the throng of onlookers.

Henry had high hopes that Sigismund would back his territorial claims in France, while the Emperor hoped to add to his reputation as a peace-maker and diplomat, but neither side gained much from the discussions, which lasted until late summer. On 15 August a treaty of mutual support was signed at Canterbury, on the same day that the

Duke of Bedford had destroyed the French fleet at the Battle of the Seine. The treaty was couched in such general terms that there was uncertainty over whether or not Sigismund would have provided military assistance to Henry as the alliance demanded, but the new relationship and the great naval victory gave considerable encouragement to the English king.

Three weeks later Henry followed Sigismund to Calais for fresh talks with the French ambassadors and a series of secret meetings with the Duke of Burgundy, whom he hoped to cajole into an alliance. Each side wanted something from the covert talks. Henry was keen to get Burgundy's support for his claim on the French crown; Sigismund desired the same outcome but for the different reason of making the Council of Constance work; while Burgundy simply wanted to understand how the Canterbury alliance would affect his own position in France. Of the three he had most to put on the table but, apart from offering vague assurances about his own neutrality – the records of the meeting are unclear about the outcome – he made sure that no one knew what his position really was. In the words of Henry's chronicler, Burgundy behaved with 'evasions and ambiguities' and appeared as 'a double dealer, one person in public and another in private'.

Nonetheless, the meetings in Calais did help to point Henry in the right direction. He had tried diplomacy and it had achieved nothing other than to buy time, and this impasse persuaded him that he had to regain the initiative by renewing hostilities with France. On his return to England he informed Parliament that he intended to restart military operations in France the following summer and that he would require a double subsidy to fund these. This time Henry decided to invade Normandy and to protect what he conquered by firstly pacifying the area and then bringing it under English control. Because he was planning for events in the longer term he needed to create secure lines of communication for supply and resupply, and for that to happen he had to retain control of the Channel. At the end of June 1417 an English naval force under the Earl of Huntingdon and Lord Castelhon destroyed four Genoese carracks in the mouth of the Seine, effectively giving England naval supremacy along the French coast.

When Henry landed at Toques, west of Honfleur, on 1 August he knew that he would now be able to maintain the logistic tail to keep his army of some ten thousand men (one in three of them archers) in the field for the rest of the year and perhaps even longer. His cause was helped by a fresh outbreak of hostilities between the Burgundians and the Armagnacs which resulted in Duke John's army surrounding Paris, a move which made it difficult for Armagnac to respond to the English invasion.

A month after the English landing, and as a result of a gruelling siege undertaken by forces under Clarence's command, Caen fell. There followed the capture of a number of smaller towns along the eastern Normandy border, including Argentan and Falaise, and these provided Henry's forces with winter quarters and a springboard for the invasion of the Cotentin Peninsula. As a warning to the other main towns in Normandy Henry ordered the expulsion of those of Caen's population who refused to accept his rule. Their property was then confiscated after they had been driven out of the city. As an exercise in compliance it worked. Norman towns under siege by English forces knew what was in store for them if they failed to surrender and subject themselves to English rule; while those who refused to acknowledge English rule were replaced by those followers whom Henry wished to reward.

Cherbourg was besieged the following spring – it fell in September – and at the beginning of July 1418 the strategically important town of Pont-de-l'Arche fell into English hands. This had the significant outcome of cutting off Rouen, the capital of Normandy, from any support that may have been coming from Paris. In fact the chance of receiving any military assistance had already crumbled. In May Burgundy's armies had taken control of Paris and during the fighting Armagnac and many of his supporters were slaughtered. At the same time King Charles VI became a prisoner of Burgundy, who emerged from the bloody incident as the virtual ruler of France.

The political pendulum had swung once more and created a new set of alliances. The Dauphin John had died and was succeeded by his younger brother Charles, the third son of Charles VI, who was of the Armagnac faction, but, because of his mother Isabeau's sexual incontinence in having taken a succession of lovers, his legitimacy was widely doubted. Not surprisingly, the new dauphin fled Paris when, on 14 July, Burgundy arrived in the city, bringing with him Queen

Isabeau, who had been proclaimed regent to rule in place of her incapacitated husband while the Duke rejoiced in the new title of Governor of France. With the Burgundians in the ascendancy in Paris the Dauphin joined the Armagnacs at Melun, where he assumed leadership of their party. In the wake of these dramatic changes this faction, described as Armagnacs or Orléanists, came also to be known as Dauphinists. While all this was happening Henry was encamped in Lower Normandy, where he was able to tighten his grip on his new holdings. As he had shown, his operations in 1417 and 1418 were no *chevauchée* but a full-blooded invasion in which the English were determined to hold on to everything they had won.

As for the people of Rouen, they were left with no hope of help from the outside and settled down for a long siege in their seemingly impregnable fortified city. Matters were complicated by the fact that Rouen was a Burgundian stronghold. Enmeshed as he was in civil strife with the Dauphinists, the Duke of Burgundy found himself in a quandary. He was obliged to defend Paris against English attack yet it was an affront to his dignity that Henry had put one of his key cities under siege at a time when he lacked the military capacity to come to its rescue.

For Burgundy the only way out of the impasse was a reordering of his priorities and he took that route by entering into peace talks with the Dauphin with the eventual aim of forging an alliance to attack the English. Given the internal situation in France the move reeked of pragmatism but when the two sides met at St-Maur-des Fossés that autumn nothing came of the talks other than an outbreak of fresh diplomatic initiatives. Having failed to reach any agreement with his fellow countrymen, the Dauphin made contact with Henry and held out the prospect of a fresh alliance against the Burgundians in return for meeting some of the English king's demands. For the Dauphin, anxious to reinforce his position and to maintain his claim to his father's throne, this made sense, but once again the talks failed to achieve anything as the French were unwilling to entertain Henry's territorial demands in France.

Everything now turned on the siege of Rouen. This became a trial of strength between the defenders, who soon realised that no help would be coming their way, and the English, who were determined to bring the siege to a successful conclusion. To ram home the point that the inhabitants of Rouen were on their own and could not expect to be relieved, Henry arranged for some of his army to be dressed in Burgundian uniforms and as they approached his knights chased them away in full view of the city's walls. Rouen was one of the most bitterly contested confrontations of Henry's second expedition in France and it became a test of endurance for both sides. The siege had opened on 31 July 1418 and in the early stages the defenders were confident that they would be able to hold out and break the will of the English army. Although heavily fortified, the city had not been strengthened to withstand attack by siege engines and cannon, but shortly before the arrival of the English the surrounding countryside had been razed to deny the attackers access to foodstuffs. This meant that everything needed by Henry's army – food, fuel and reinforcements – could not be foraged locally but had to be brought in from England, the main reason why naval control of the Channel was so important.

But Henry decided to be patient. Rouen was surrounded and the Seine was closed to traffic with chain booms and block-ships to prevent it being used as a passage. Having encircled the city and cut it off from the outside world, Henry simply waited, secure in the knowledge that neither the Burgundians nor the Dauphinists would make any move to come to the rescue of their beleaguered fellow countrymen.

It took five months before there was any action. That winter turned out to be one of the worst in living memory and for the 400,000 inhabitants conditions inside Rouen became unbearable. Food, water and fuel ran low and with the population beginning to starve the commander of the garrison, Guy le Bouteiller, decided to release all the non-military personnel, including many refugees from the surrounding countryside, who were unable to play any part in manning the defences. Around twelve thousand people were simply thrown out of the city and left to their own devices in a wintry wasteland. All that stood between them and a slow death was the mercy of the English army, but Henry decided to prevent them from escaping and the hapless refugees were left to starve or freeze to death along the marshlands of the Seine, their fate immediately apparent to the city's defenders.

Like the expulsion of the population of Caen, this decision left a question mark over Henry's ethics as a military commander, but in the hard arithmetic of siege warfare he had no option. Feeding such a large number of people would inevitably have weakened his own army and he must have reckoned that the fate of the starving refugees within sight of Rouen's walls would send an unforgiving message to those on the inside. Writing long after the event, but basing his account on the evidence of those who had taken part in the siege, Tito Livio wrote an imaginary, though no doubt grimly accurate, description of the fate awaiting the people of Rouen as the siege entered its last days:

Daily the famine in the town grew worse. First the inhabitants shared out and consumed the flesh of their horses. They ate dogs, cat, mice, shrews and whatever else they thought edible in their famished state. Eventually there was nothing left to eat at all. As a result of the famine, the city was invaded by the plague. People fell victim to it in their houses, in the streets, in churches and in the market-place. Sons expired before their parents and infants watched as their mothers died.

As things finally fell apart and it became evident that further resistance was futile, le Bouteiller surrendered the keys of the city on 19 January 1419 and Rouen, a huge prize, was in Henry's hands. He entered the city the following day and after a mass of thanksgiving set about establishing an administration for his new duchy of Normandy. The idea was to run it as an efficient English bailiwick – taxes would be raised, there would be a sound system of government based on the former estates and land would be granted to English colonists and to Normans thought to be loyal to the new ruler. In short, Henry intended to win Norman hearts and minds as a prelude to renewing his claims on the French throne.

The next step was to decide whether or not to attack Paris. In the longer term that must have been Henry's ambition but at the beginning of the new year, following a long and gruelling campaign to subdue Normandy, he lacked the military means to make a successful attack on the French capital. Instead he turned once more to diplomacy. An attempt was made to convene a meeting with the Dauphin at Évreux in March but this came to nothing when the

French side did not turn up on the appointed day. That failure drove Henry once more towards the Burgundian camp and after the establishment of a two-month truce the three sides met near Meulan at the end of May, the main protagonists being Henry, Burgundy, Queen Isabeau, her daughter Katherine of Valois and her son the Dauphin. In all, eight meetings were held over five weeks and the negotiations came tantalisingly close to reaching an agreement.

Henry's demands came straight to the point. For the first time he agreed to put aside his claims to the French throne, at least for the time being, but in return he wanted major territorial concessions to match his military successes. Everything he had captured since landing in France would remain in English hands and in addition he laid claim to the territories which had been ceded to King Edward III as a result of the Treaty of Brétigny in 1360. Finally he gave notice that he was serious in his intention to marry the Princess Katherine. The marriage had been considered an ideal possibility since 1408, when Henry was twenty-one and she just eight, and it had also been central to the negotiations in 1414, but, having met her for the first time at Meulan, Henry seems to have been sufficiently attracted by her to press the suit with considerably more firmness.

All the sides had much to gain from reaching a workable agreement. The Burgundians would enter into a powerful new alliance with England and Henry would achieve most of his territorial goals. The French also wanted a solution but there was the huge stumbling block that it would be dishonourable and potentially fatal to cede so much land to an English king at a time when Henry had only postponed and not dropped his claim to the French throne. There was also disagreement over Katherine's dowry. Henry wanted 800,000 crowns but the French family wanted to deduct 600,000 crowns from the dowry they had already paid for Queen Isabelle, Richard II's widow.

As it was the French who were being asked to make most of the concessions it is hardly surprising that the talks foundered and eventually broke down. A meeting fixed for 3 July failed to take place and, just as inevitably, Duke John responded to the setback by making contact with the Dauphin and asking for a fresh reconciliation. Given Henry's demands, it was always possible that the Burgundians and the Dauphinists would combine in common cause and, although their subsequent agreement was limited to a promise that neither side would enter into a treaty with him, it did put a stop to the cycle of negotiations. The English response was rapid and effective.

On 29 July, the day after a local truce with the Burgundians ended, an English force seized Pontoise, a strategically important town lying between Rouen and Paris, and by the middle of August Henry's army was threatening the French capital, forcing the court to move to Troyes. Everywhere there was panic and, to add to the confusion, Duke John was suddenly and shockingly murdered by a follower of the Dauphin when the two men met at Montereau-faut-Yonne, south-east of Paris, in the second week of September. To the horror of those present Duke John was killed as he knelt in front of the Dauphin when they met on the bridge over the River Yonne. Apologists for the Dauphin later claimed that Duke John had been struck down because he was reaching for his sword, but it seems a far-fetched excuse for the attack, which plunged the country into confusion. Whatever else, one thing was clear: the most powerful man in France had been killed and his death was blamed on his greatest rival.

The murder at Montereau changed everything. Burgundy was succeeded by his son Philip 'the Good', an inexperienced young man who had had thrust upon him the weight of ensuring his own family's position as well as protecting the French throne. The Dauphin had weakened his faction's position by being associated with John's murder and Queen Isabeau had to decide if it was in her interests to continue as regent under Burgundian protection. Only Henry emerged from the shameful events with his position enhanced. Suddenly he seemed to be the one person who could bring some order to the chaos and by so doing strengthen his own position within France. Henry began negotiations with the new Duke Philip at the end of September and he did so from a position of considerable strength. His opening gambit made it clear that he intended to press his own claim to the French throne by emerging as Charles VI's heir, with the Dauphin being disinherited, and that his position would be strengthened immeasurably by his marriage to Katherine. Both England and France would be ruled by him and his successors, although the two countries would be administratively independent of each other and French laws and institutions would be respected. As a sweetener, Henry agreed to accept Katherine without dowry.

These were radical and far-reaching proposals and it was to the credit of Duke Philip that he did not cave in immediately. However, he could only play for time because not only were conditions in Paris worsening as a result of the English blockade but there was the very strong possibility that if nothing were decided Henry might decide to reopen negotiations with the Dauphin. No doubt Duke Philip also recognised the harsh reality that Henry was now in a position to seize the French throne by force of arms and that he was unable to offer much resistance. The talks dragged on until Christmas Eve, when agreement was reached on Henry's terms, and a general truce was signed between the two parties in Rouen. Under its provisions Henry entered into an alliance with the Burgundians, each party agreed to lend assistance to the other, the blockade of Paris was lifted and arrangements were set in train for Henry's marriage to Katherine.

A few months later, on 20 May 1420, the agreement was ratified by the Treaty of Troyes, which made the French royal family party to the agreement. As Charles was not well enough to sign the deed of ratification this was done on his behalf by Queen Isabeau and Duke Philip. The diplomatic niceties completed, Henry married Katherine in the Church of St John in Troyes in a simple ceremony held on 2 June and from the outset it was clear that the nineteen-year-old French princess was to be an English queen first and foremost. 'No French person remained in her entourage,' noted Walsingham, 'except for three noblewomen and two maids who were personal servants of their mistress.'

For Henry the Treaty of Troyes was a personal triumph and the diplomatic high-water mark of his reign, one which equalled the earlier Treaty of Brétigny brokered by Edward III. Through a mixture of warfare and diplomacy, plus some good fortune, he had achieved a dynastic settlement which gave him most of what he wanted. He and his heirs would rule France, peace had been restored, both England and France would retain their integrity and all this had been achieved reasonably amicably. He had also succeeded in his aims while spending almost four years out of England, where his absence had been regretted but had not led to any local difficulties or scheming among the nobility. Given England's turbulent recent history it was quite an achievement to leave the country and not face a challenge from any potential rival.

As for the people of France, they appeared to accept the new dispensation largely because it brought peace after years of internecine warfare and also because those who supported the Burgundians, especially the Parisians, had come to believe that it was the only possible way forward. In return for that support, important and lucrative benefices were returned to them. The only opponents were those whose opinion had not been asked – those who supported the Dauphin who had been disinherited by the treaty. However, the Dauphin and his party still controlled much of the south and the area to the south-east of Paris, where three fortified towns, Melun, Montereau and Sens, were still loyal to him. Under the terms of the treaty Henry was obliged to bring the towns under control to protect Paris and each was subjected to siege.

Sens fell first, on 10 June, followed by Montereau, the scene of Duke John's murder, but Melun held out until November. Having battered them into submission, Henry formally entered Paris on 1 December 1420 in the company of Charles VI and Duke Philip of Burgundy and a large English retinue. Mass was said in Notre Dame and, according to a contemporary journal written anonymously by 'A Bourgeois of Paris', 'no princes were ever welcomed more joyfully than these; in every street they met processions of priests in copes and surplices carrying reliquaries and singing *Te Deum Laudamus* [We praise you, O God] and *Benedictus Qui Venit* [Blessed is he who comes]'.

For the defeated French the words of the *Benedictus* would have been especially poignant. The successful conclusion to the campaign allowed Henry to think about returning home to have his new wife crowned Queen of England and to cement the new marital relationship. After spending the new year at Rouen the royal couple made their way back to England, reaching Dover on 1 February 1421 to be greeted by a joyous and enthusiastic reception. Three weeks later Katherine was crowned in Westminster Abbey in a service conducted by the Archbishop of Canterbury, but there is no record of Henry attending any part of the ceremonial or the following banquet. That done, the King set off on a peregrination of England to revisit places he had not seen for many years and, just as importantly, to allow himself to be viewed by his subjects following his long absence in France. Important shrines were visited and Easter was celebrated with his wife, now pregnant, in Leicester, the burial place of his mother.

Next on his itinerary was Beverley in Yorkshire, the site of the shrine of St John, who had been canonised in 1037 and whom Henry revered for his intercession to give him victory at Agincourt, the battle having taken place on his feast day, which is shared with Saints Crispin and Crispinian. Henry's Eastertide celebrations were conducted with all solemnity – Maundy money was handed to the poor on Palm Sunday – but the pilgrimage ended in calamity.

Soon after leaving Beverley Henry received distressing news from France. Just before Easter his brother and Lieutenant General of the English Army in France, the Duke of Clarence, had received intelligence that a large Dauphinist force was assembling at the village of Baugé, near Angers, and, to make the matter more serious, it had been reinforced by large numbers of soldiers from Scotland under the command of the Earl of Buchan. Clarence was courageous and an experienced soldier but he was also hot-headed. As he was not far from Baugé he decided on a pre-emptive strike and without delay set out to take the Franco-Scottish army by surprise. With him he took a small force of mounted men-at-arms while the rest of his men followed on behind. There was no reconnaissance of enemy dispositions or the lie of the land and, fatally, Clarence pushed ahead without his archers.

Cannily, Buchan had kept the bulk of his force out of sight of the village and did not commit them to battle until later, timing his charge to perfection. Although the smaller English force fought well when they engaged the opposition and believed that they were encountering only light resistance in the initial stages of the battle, soon they were heavily outnumbered and quickly overcome by a force which was three times stronger. In the mêlée Clarence was killed and a number of notable English nobles were taken prisoner before the English force was extricated from the battlefield through the skilful handling of the reinforcements led by the Earl of Salisbury.

The defeat was a serious setback – until there was any issue to the royal marriage Clarence was Henry's heir – and although the Dauphinists did not capitalise on their unexpected victory by marching on Paris, as might have seemed sensible, it did encourage them to think that the English were not invincible. Henry, too, seemed to realise that his authority had been checked, or at least called into question, and set about creating a new army to bring his French kingdom under control. Money suddenly became a problem, as it had been in father's reign, but Parliament voted him funds and the rest he raised as loans or gifts from friends and supporters.

By the beginning of June the necessary forces were in place and Henry landed in France with a retinue which included the Duke of Gloucester and James Stewart of Scotland, still in English captivity, who, Henry hoped, might be useful in persuading his fellow Scots to withdraw their support for the Dauphin. This latter plan was by no means certain of success: at Montereau the previous year the Scottish soldiers in the Dauphinist garrison had ignored their rightful king's call to surrender and had remained in French employment.

By now Albany was dead: in 1420 he was succeeded as regent by his son Murdoch Stewart, who saw the advantage of discomforting Henry by sending more Scottish mercenaries to France to serve in the Dauphin's army. At the same time he continued to refuse to haggle over James's ransom and that refusal gave the future Scottish king a clear indication of where the loyalties of his fellow countrymen lay. Under Murdoch's increasingly feeble stewardship Scotland remained in a state of civil strife, with the main magnates dictating their own local policies and settling disputes by arbitration or force of arms, Parliament being unable to sit without the authority of a crowned king. This unhappy state of affairs made France a welcome and lucrative distraction and around five thousand Scots served in the Dauphinist army during Henry's reign, a not insignificant contribution to French military capacity. A total of twenty-five Scottish captains of men-at-arms were listed in Charles VI's personal retinue during this period and as a result of the victory at Baugé the Earl of Buchan was created a marshal of France.

Henry headed for Paris to make plain to the inhabitants that he was intent on avenging the setback at Baugé and meant to punish the Dauphinists for their presumption. He also had discussions with Duke Philip, who agreed to put down an unexpected upsurge of support for the Dauphin in Picardy while the English forces dealt with the Dauphinists south of the River Loire. It was to no avail. The Dauphin refused to engage in a set-piece battle and although Henry got as far as Orléans he was forced to return to Paris in September with his army weakened by illness. Frustrated by the lack of action he turned his attention to besieging the fortified town of Meaux, which lay to the east of Paris and guarded the lower reaches of the River Marne. Meaux stood on the Marne before the river debouched into the Seine, so once the town fell into his hands it would complete his attempts to control the larger river.

Once again Henry decided to use tactics which had served him so well in the past. Instead of attempting to bludgeon Meaux into submission his forces surrounded the town and set about starving the garrison by cutting off all access to the outside world. This time, though, it proved to be a more difficult task. Henry's besieging army came under attack from marauding Dauphinist cavalry forces and, because the winter was unusually wet, foraging became a problem, with the result that supplies were soon running low. The garrison also proved to be more obdurate than expected, not least because it included a number of Scots who knew that they could expect no mercy if the town fell into English hands. It was turning into a protracted and time-consuming affair and the only good news came from London on 6 December, when it was announced that Katherine had given birth to a baby boy, to be christened Henry.

Eventually, in May 1422, Meaux fell. English cannon were used to blast the weary garrison into submission but it had been a hard-won victory which had taken up a good deal of energy and resources. So it was not surprising that the terms were equally tough. The four main leaders were executed, as was a trumpeter who had been foolish enough to dance provocatively on the walls and mock Henry by blowing his trumpet in imitation of a fart. Around a hundred Dauphinist prisoners were dispatched to England for imprisonment and many more were expelled from the town and sent south to rejoin their leader.

In the longer term the fall of Meaux raised as many questions as it answered. While a sizeable asset had been prised out of the Dauphin's hands the siege had created huge problems for Henry's army in France. It was also an unpleasant reminder of the fact that while Henry and his heirs were titular kings of France their writ did not extend over the whole country, large swaths of which remained loyal to the Dauphin. Was that what lay ahead in the future: a succession of long and expensive campaigns to wear down the Dauphinists before Henry could call himself the rightful ruler of the whole of France? And before that came about could he rely implicitly on the loyalty of the French people? The answers were probably yes and no, respectively. The Treaty of Troyes must have seemed like a distant triumph as Henry took stock of his position after Meaux had capitulated. Something else he took away from the siege was illness, probably dysentery, from the unsanitary conditions inside camp in the middle of winter. The heat of the summer also exacerbated his dehydration and the attempts to slake his thirst with wine and beer only made matters worse.

Shortly after the end of the siege Katherine arrived from England with her brother-in-law the Duke of Bedford, having left her six-month-old son in the care of the Duke of Gloucester. She joined her husband in Paris at Whitsun and then they moved on to Senlis, a small town to the north-east, where it became clear that Henry was ailing. Even so, he seemed to be fit enough to answer a request for military assistance from Duke Philip, who was engaged with Dauphinist forces near Bourges.

Ever the soldier, Henry set off with Bedford and Warwick in attendance, but during the journey his condition worsened so much that he had to change his horse for a litter. His condition was now critical and he was moved to Vincennes, where no one, least of all he himself, could doubt the seriousness of his position. As his physical condition worsened he remained sufficiently lucid to put his affairs in order but already he was in a steep decline. He revised his will and placed his son in the protection of his brother Gloucester, who would be appointed warden of England while the regency of France would be given to Duke Philip or, failing him, to Bedford. His old friend Thomas Beaufort was entrusted with Prince Henry's education. It was all very neat and orderly and to the end Henry managed to keep his mind fixed on the actualities of what would happen once he had died.

The end came on 31 August, Henry's last spoken thoughts being a regret that he had never fulfilled his wish to visit the Holy Land to rebuild the walls of Jerusalem. He was the first English king to die in a foreign country since 1199, when Richard I had died at Châlus, near Limoges, attempting to regain his French properties.

Despite his illness and its wasting nature, which left him gaunt and sunken-eyed, Henry was able to gather his thoughts and left precise instructions on the form of his funeral, including the number and size of candles. After his death his sadly wasted body was embalmed – the intestines were removed and buried in the church of St-Maur-des-Fossés – and he was taken by river to Rouen, where the funeral obsequies lasted several days, before he was moved to London for burial in Westminster Abbey on 7 November. Requiem mass was celebrated 'with great solemnity', recorded Walsingham, and the entire commemoration was notable for the genuine sense of loss which accompanied the mourning. The coffin was covered in black velvet, five black-draped horses pulled the hearse and a huge number of black-clad mourners followed in its wake. Most of these were men who had served Henry in life and accompanied him in death to his last resting place.

Walsingham's tribute was couched in conventional terms of piety but across the centuries it still manages to reflect the great sense of loss and grief in England at the King's untimely passing while he was still only in his mid-thirties:

King Henry V left no one like him among Christian kings or princes: his death, not only by his subjects in England and France, but in the whole of Christendom, was deservedly mourned. He was pious in soul, taciturn and discreet in his speech, far-seeing in counsel, prudent in judgement, modest in appearance, magnanimous in his actions, firm in business, persistent in pilgrimages and generous in alms; devoted to God and supportive and respectful of the prelates and ministers of the Church; warlike, distinguished and fortunate, he had won victories in all his military engagements. He was generous in constructing buildings and founding monasteries, munificent in his gifts, and above all pursued and attacked enemies of the faith and the Church.

All that was true and in a personal sense the encomiums were not misplaced, but Henry was more complicated than the simple hero-king remembered by history and recreated in Shakespeare's patriotic play (not least the film version of 1944 starring Laurence Olivier, which magnified the King's valiant character). Of Henry's abilities as a soldier there can be no doubt. He learned the art of war the hard way by fighting as a young man in the counter-insurgency campaign against Owen Glendower and in the campaigns in France he emerged as a natural leader, a soldier who could encourage others to rise above themselves and do more than they thought themselves capable of achieving.

At Agincourt Henry held his nerve and rode his luck, fighting in the thick of the action, while in the later campaigns in Normandy he demonstrated patience and a dogged determination which stood him and his army well in the lengthy sieges, most notably at Rouen. Never a faint-heart, he knew when and how to be ruthless and although some of his actions bordered on the callous he understood the necessity of firm and decisive action in warfare. Having made up his mind about what needed to be done to win the day, he moved his army forward and pushed home any advantage as soon as it appeared. That ability to stand apart and to view events disinterestedly helped him as a commander and at Agincourt it gave him the edge over his opponents.

On a more spiritual level Henry's piety and his devotion to his duty as a king cannot be doubted. Some contemporaries thought that he appeared and behaved more like a priest than a monarch and much of his personal life was guided by prayer, the *Gesta Henrici Qunti* recording that his sole desire in life was 'to promote the honour of God, the extension of the Church, the deliverance of his country and the peace and tranquillity of kingdoms'. The deeply religious nature of his personality manifested itself in other ways, notably his opposition to the Lollards and in his foundation of major religious houses in London. Even the way he ordered his personal matters in advance of his death indicates a mind which believed that there was more to a man's life than its earthly manifestation. When Henry put his trust in God in prayer he was not mouthing platitudes but enunciating a deeply held belief in the spiritual nature of the relationship between man and his maker. And that orderliness of thought was matched by the stability and good sense he brought to his kingdom throughout his reign.

Unlike his father, who was hamstrung by the belief that he had usurped a rightful king and was somehow dishonoured by the action, Henry V came to the throne secure in his position and by personal example reinforced the family and tribal loyalties that supported him. In contrast to what happened in his father's day, Henry V's domestic reign was not unsettled or threatened by civil strife – other than the quickly quelled plot on the eve of the Harfleur expedition – and he provided an effective form of governance which unified his kingdom.

In short, he deserves his reputation as one of England's greatest kings, above all perhaps for the victory he won against all the odds at Agincourt.

And yet Henry was not just a simple paragon. For all that he waged a successful war against France and for all that he exacted from his defeated enemy a peace treaty which gave him most of what he wanted, Henry's campaigns in France created as many problems as they solved. Imposing the conditions at Troyes was a diplomatic triumph but it is impossible to know if the dual-monarchy arrangement would ever have worked, even if Henry had not died so young. Large parts of France remained under the Dauphin's control and it is doubtful that King Charles VI's son, having been dispossessed, would have accepted his inferior and debased position. The siege at Meaux demonstrated the difficulties which would have lain ahead for the English ground forces and in the ever-changing world of French political alliances the support of the Burgundians was not guaranteed to last for ever.

There was also the question of national pride. Henry was admired by many French people and his death was widely mourned – the commemorations in Rouen were particularly sincere and sonorous – but there was also resentment. This was, after all, a relationship which had been imposed on the French people by force of arms. It would only have been natural for them to kick against it at some point in the future.

As for the war itself and the reasons for waging it, whatever problems it created for future generations, the conflict can be justified in the realpolitik of Henry's day. Although Henry based his French policy on the premise that possession of the country would secure England's future happiness and prosperity, he also believed that it was a legal war in that he had a rightful claim to rule France following the French refusal to honour obligations made to his great-grandfather in 1360. When events played into his hands at Agincourt and, later, through the death of Duke John of Burgundy, he had no option but to follow his destiny. In so doing he came tantalisingly close to achieving his objectives before his unseasonable and, for England at least, tragic death.

Chapter Eight

A Sceptre in a Child's Hand

On Henry's death his son Prince Henry was proclaimed King of England and France at the age of nine months. For everyone connected to the English court it was a testing moment as once again the country had a child-king. Without a monarch the country needed to be governed and steps had to be taken to forestall any outbreak of internecine fighting among those who might have believed that they had a better claim to the throne – notably the King's uncles, Bedford and Gloucester – or who thought to take their chances during a period of transition.

Before his death Henry had made known his wishes for the protection and guidance of his realm during his son's minority, but those good intentions depended on the good will of those chosen by him to carry out his plans. Fortunately there were enough bricks in place to ensure the safety of the edifice that Henry had created. Although there was by no means a sense of complete common cause among all the magnates, and there were times when hidden enmities almost rose to the surface to threaten the country's stability, the governance of England did not collapse and by and large the arrangements made by Henry survived the new king's minority.

It was a tribute to the loyalty expressed by those who followed Henry V, and to the maturity which had been the benchmark of the warrior king's reign, that England and most of France remained calm. In the days and months that followed the King's death there was none of the turmoil that might have arisen had the arrangements been weak or ineffective. Of course there were tensions. Not all of the personalities were on mutually friendly terms and there was a sense that some of the younger magnates, such as Humphrey Stafford, the wealthy Duke of Buckingham, were marking time until Henry VI came into his own, but the years of the royal infancy proved to be surprisingly tranquil and well ordered.

One of the beneficiaries of this new order was James I of Scotland, who had been in English captivity since 1406. Thinking that his release would guarantee Scottish neutrality at a time when Scots were still fighting in France, the council decided that in return for the payment of a ransom he should be set free and sent back to Scotland.

During his years in English hands James Stewart had become thoroughly Anglicised and had developed into an intelligent young man with strong literary and cultural tastes. He had also put his time to good use by writing *The Kingis Quair* (King's Book), a long poem in 197 stanzas which is at once a spiritual autobiography and a reflection on his experiences in English captivity. Written in 'rhyme-royal' (so called because of its use by James but also employed earlier by Chaucer), the poem reveals the captive poet's reliance on the Boethian philosophy that even the noblest of men can be wronged by fortune but that comfort can be found in resignation and patience in order to control the urges of the will. Heavily influenced by Lydgate and Chaucer, *The Kingis Quair* is also a dream-vision which traces the story of a young man's love for a beautiful woman – seen walking in the garden below his room – and ends with a hymn of thanksgiving celebrating James's own happiness in love:

> Unworthy, lo, bot only of her grace
> In luves yoke, that easy is and sure,
> In guerdon [recompense] of all my luves space
> She hath me tak, her humble creature.
> And thus befell my blissful aventure,
> In youth, of luve, that now from day to day
> Flourith ay new

Here the Scottish king was speaking from experience. He had met and fallen in love with Lady Joan Beaufort, whom he married on 2 February 1424, shortly before he returned to Scotland. She was a daughter of John Beaufort, Duke of Somerset, and a cousin of

Henry V, and the English council had high hopes that the marriage to a leading member of such an important family with royal connections would produce a lasting period of peace with Scotland – in addition to agreeing to pay a ransom to cover the costs of his upkeep and education James signed a seven-year truce – and for a while the policy worked.

On retrieving the Scottish throne two months after the marriage James I imposed a centralist form of government and re-established his authority by executing Murdoch Stewart, Duke of Albany, and his two sons and confiscating their lands. Elsewhere he pursued an equally ruthless policy to cement his position by checking the power of magnates such as the Earl of Strathearn, who, like James, was descended from Robert II. The restored king also made inroads into the Highlands by arresting troublesome chiefs, including the Earl of Ross and the Lord of the Isles (leader of the loosely federated Macdonald clans occupying much of Argyll and the Hebrides). As expressed in his first statute, James I's aim was to keep 'firm and sure peace throughout the realm', but his heavy-handed policies inevitably caused trouble among the nobility, who resented the additional taxation which had to be raised to help pay off the English ransom.

Under the terms of his final will Henry V had made specific arrangements for his son's inheritance. As we have seen, the three most important personages trusted with looking after his infant son and the realm were the dead king's two surviving brothers, Humphrey, Duke of Gloucester, and John, Duke of Bedford, and his uncle Thomas Beaufort, Duke of Exeter, the youngest of John of Gaunt's three sons by his mistress Katherine Swynford. Surprisingly perhaps, the younger of the two brothers, Gloucester, had been appointed guardian of the future king and Warden of England, but that was probably due to the fact that he was acting in that role at the time of Henry's death. Bedford, a more stable and upright character, was to take charge of France as regent until Prince Henry came of age. It was a task he accepted gladly as a sacred duty and he proved to be both a wise administrator and a doughty protector of his country's interests – no easy matter considering that France had been ravaged by the long years of confrontation and warfare.

Exeter was also a good choice, as Henry had trusted his Beaufort cousins, but he was an older man and he was overshadowed by his brother Henry Beaufort, Bishop of Winchester, who had also been given a role as a conciliar in the new king's upbringing. The Bishop was one of the most influential men in England: not only was he created Chancellor for the third time in 1424 but he was immensely wealthy. After making a huge fortune from the wool trade he had helped Henry V with extensive loans and, according to the chronicler Edward Hall, he was 'rich above measure of all men'.

There was one other important and constant factor in the infant king's life: his mother, Queen Katherine. Through her husband's will she had been denied any role in the regency but she was entrusted with the upbringing of her son in his infancy. As his mother she was responsible for looking after the boy while they were in residence at Windsor and she proved to be an admirable queen dowager. She was still in early life, had retained her looks and it was always possible that she might wish to remarry. If that happened it would complicate matters as an ambitious new husband might want to exert his authority by making a claim to the throne.

However, when Katherine did fall in love she proved to be remarkably discreet. While her son was still an infant she entered into a relationship with a member of the Welsh gentry named Owen Tudor (properly Owen ap Maredudd ap Tewdwr) whose family had been involved in the Glendower rebellion against Henry IV. Next to nothing is known about their relationship: they may have married in secret and they certainly had children, the eldest being Edmund Tudor, who later became the Earl of Richmond. As Tudor belonged to the minor landed gentry and occupied a modest position at court – he was Keeper of the Wardrobe – he was a social inferior and any relationship with the Queen Dowager was ill advised. Surprisingly, no scandal attached to the affair, although the council seems to have accepted the fact that it existed.

Against all the odds this secret relationship survived until Katherine's death in 1437. She was interred in the Lady Chapel of Westminster Abbey but when it was demolished in 1509 during the building of the Henry VII Chapel her coffin was removed and her remains were put on public display. It was not until 1878 that they were reburied. As for her lover Owen Tudor, on Gloucester's order he was briefly imprisoned in Newgate before returning to Wales, while their sons, Edmund and Jasper, were placed in the care of Katherine de la Pole, Abbess of Barking and sister of the Earl of Suffolk.

Given that Prince Henry's three principal advisers were all powerful and wealthy men in their own right there was bound to be rivalry, and the wonder is that any jealousy did not break out into something more serious. Each man was different from the others. Bedford was a soldier's soldier, an upright and loyal leader of men who had the complete trust of the men under his command. He was also the right man to represent England's interests in France and it helped that he was married to Anne, the sister of Philip of Burgundy. In return Bedford carried out his duties with a light hand, keeping French administrators in their positions and maintaining an enlightened view of French institutions by ruling through a grand council in Paris. When his authority was challenged he also knew when to use military force and revealed his strengths as a battlefield commander by inflicting a serious defeat on Scottish–Orléanist forces at Verneuil on a baking-hot day in August 1424.

Among the dead were the Earls of Buchan and Douglas, who led a large Scottish contingent in support of the French forces; these two were already in France and were not a party to James I's agreement made in the previous year to end the attacks on the English. The Scottish commander was the same Earl of Douglas who had been in charge of the Scottish army crushed at Homildon Hill twenty years earlier and in view of his fate perhaps he deserves the unkind nickname given to him by his countrymen of 'Tineman', or loser.

In some respects the battle was a rerun of Agincourt with the French cavalry over-extending their lines as they attempted to break the English archers' positions. However, unlike in the earlier battle, the English archers were unable, owing to the hardness of the ground, to drive in their stakes to protect themselves from the cavalry and at one stage the French were able to break into their positions. However, when the English knights attacked the French centre it collapsed and on the right the Scottish force of six thousand was soon isolated. After re-forming his forces Bedford continued the battle and the Scots were massacred almost to the last man, having decided not to surrender. Also killed were a number of leading French noblemen, including the Duke of Aumale and the Count of Narbonne.

As recounted by the anonymous chronicler of *The Brut*, Verneuil was a crushing defeat: 'Bright was the crescent moon when they [the Scots] set forth; homewards they came at its baleful setting.' Having defeated an Orléanist–Scottish force at Cravant the previous year, Bedford was now able to overrun Maine and Anjou, but he failed to take Bourges, a move that would have weakened the Dauphin's power. The nature of the defeat at Verneuil also put paid to further large-scale Scottish involvement in French military affairs but, given the nature of the Auld Alliance, it did not stop completely and companies of Scottish soldiers continued to serve the French throne throughout the fifteenth century and beyond.

Bedford's brother Gloucester was altogether different, although he was no less prone to bellicosity. Known to history as 'the good Duke Humphrey', he had a personality that belied this enviable description. His sudden and unexpected marriage to Jacqueline of Hainault and Holland had given him territorial claims in the Netherlands which he intended to pursue to prevent his wife's former husband, the Duke of Brabant, naming Philip of Burgundy as his heir. At one point, in 1424, the year of Verneuil, Gloucester rashly led an armed force into Hainault, a move which threatened the Burgundian alliance and enraged Bedford at a time when he was attempting to consolidate English authority in France. There was even talk of a duel to the death between Gloucester and Burgundy but nothing came of it after the English Parliament refused to finance any such adventure.

Although Gloucester had his good points – he was highly educated, widely read, intelligent and a serious patron of the arts who encouraged several writers and helped to endow the Bodleian Library in Oxford – he was also irresponsible, self-serving and extremely ambitious. While Henry V lived, his younger brother could be kept under control but when Duke Humphrey was unsupervised he was a menace. It did not help matters that he was jealous of Bedford's soldierly qualities and position in France or that he developed a dislike of his Beaufort relatives, particularly Henry, who became a cardinal in 1426. Their rivalry, intense and bitter, was to last a lifetime.

The three men nominated by Henry as advisers were also involved in the governance of the realm, which during the King's minority was in the hands of the seventeen members of a regency council. Their task was to continue the policies laid down by Henry V and, by directing the national finances and controlling foreign policy, to make sure that England remained unified and peaceful while the King was still a minor. One possible font of dissent was removed in January 1425 when the English Earl of March died of the plague at Trim Castle in Ireland, where he was fulfilling his duties as Lord Lieutenant. He was the last of the male line of the Mortimers and with his passing his claim to the throne as heir general to Richard II died with him but, as we shall see, it did not disappear completely.

March died without an heir, so his lands devolved to his sister's son, the fourteen-year-old Richard of Cambridge, Duke of York, whose father had been executed after plotting against Henry V on the eve of the Agincourt campaign. However, he was not allowed to inherit immediately and the Mortimer lands were held for the Crown by Gloucester until York came of age. As there was no single, all-powerful regent all of the council's decisions had to be taken in front of the baby king to maintain the belief that the person and office of majesty were inseparable. The Great Seal was placed in his possession and to all intents and purposes the illusion was kept up that the infant king was the supreme authority while decisions were being taken. Anything less would have damaged the legitimacy of the Lancastrian succession and had either of Henry V's brothers made any attempt to usurp the Crown it would have had disastrous consequences not just in England but also in France. This pretence had a unifying effect on the council, which was responsible for all executive action, but Gloucester found it difficult to operate without hankering for the title and authority of regent, ruling in the place of the King. Not only was he sufficiently ambitious to want the position for his own purposes but he believed that Henry V's wishes, as expressed in his will, gave him the authority to fulfil that role.

From the outset of the new arrangements Gloucester promoted his interests with a persistence which angered the other councillors, so much so that they were forced to declare that they were collectively responsible for the good governance of England until the King came of age. While this avoided an immediate confrontation with one of the most powerful conciliars it did not dampen Gloucester's aspirations and gradually a split did appear in the council between him and Henry Beaufort. More than any other matter, one subject divided the two men: what to do in France. Gloucester wanted to continue military operations and to defeat the Orléanists in order to cement the Treaty of Troyes, whereas Beaufort worried about the costs of waging war and preferred brokering an honourable peace. Inevitably, perhaps, France was to be the first great crisis of the infant king's reign.

Within six weeks of Henry V's death, Charles VI was also dead, a state of affairs which meant that all at once the agreement reached at Troyes would have to be put to the test. Throughout his life the French king had been tormented by mental illness and his supporters claimed that his condition had been exacerbated by his wife Isabeau's sexual licence and riotous living. That he survived so long and was not deposed owed everything to the power of the Burgundians and to his wife's machinations, including the final détente with Henry V at Troyes. Under the treaty's terms Charles's heir was now an eight-month-old English boy, the son of the man who had all but deposed him. However, that agreement only held good in Burgundian France. South of the Loire, the old Orléanist or Armagnac faction acknowledged the claims of the son of Charles VI, the Dauphin Charles, who had finally convinced his supporters that he had a legitimate claim on the French throne in spite of lingering doubts about his paternity. (His mother, Isabeau, had repudiated him as being illegitimate, the result of one of her numerous affairs.)

It was one of the ironies of Henry V's life that, had he survived the illness which killed him, he would have been able to claim the throne of the country he had tried so hard to bring under English control. As a king still in his prime he would have been well placed to turn his succession into a lasting reality. Instead those two deaths, one early and unforeseen, the other predictable and largely unlamented, were to have a huge influence on the sons who followed them. One was King of France by right of treaty; the other believed himself to be King of France by rightful succession.

After Henry V's untimely death his infant son had been proclaimed King of England and France in succession to his father, but he was not crowned until 6 November 1429, shortly before his eighth birthday. Young Henry's care during his early years had been entrusted to his mother and her largely female retinue, and it was not until shortly before his second birthday he made his first public appearance, at the opening of Parliament. As any child of that age might do, he played up, refusing to continue the journey from Windsor after a halt at Kingston, where he 'shrieked and cried and sprang and would not be carried further'. A night's rest did the trick and to the delight of the crowds in London the infant king arrived in the capital with 'merry cheer'.

Arrangements were also made for young Henry to have the company of boys of his own age and shortly after his fifth birthday he was taken out of the care of women so that his education could begin in earnest. By now his tutor and 'master' was Richard Beauchamp, Earl of Warwick, one of the country's leading soldiers and a prominent diplomat who had served Henry IV during the lengthy negotiations to solve the papal schism at the Council of Constance. Warwick's role was to school his charge in the basics of kingship, to provide him with a rounded education and to instruct him in the art of war: attributes which every contemporary king needed if he were to survive and prosper. In those respects, even down to his provision of a miniature suit of armour and appropriate weapons, Warwick proved himself to be the ideal mentor. Earlier Henry's governess, Dame Alice Butler, had begun his education along similar lines and by the time of his coronation the young prince would have had a good enough concept of the responsibilities that lay ahead of him.

If he did not, then the solemnity of the coronation rituals would have reminded him that he was of the blood royal and an anointed theocratic king under God's protection and guidance. Like his grandfather, Henry IV, he was anointed with Thomas Becket's miraculous oil from the golden-eagle ampulla which was carried into Westminster Abbey with great reverence. According to Adam of Usk, the boy's head and upper body were anointed and it was not until eight days later that the oil was washed off, with lukewarm white wine. The whole service underlined the sanctity and regality of his office; it was a lengthy and, for a child, a time-consuming ceremony, but young Henry appears to have borne it with solemnity and good grace. Contrary to normal custom, no wine flowed, but the crowds were large and appreciative and later people remembered two things about him: the young king's pious aspect as he gazed on those attending his coronation and the fact that he was too small to wear the heavy crown with comfort.

One other fact intruded: the words of the ceremonial insisted that he was 'born by descent and title of right justly to reign in England and in France' and, to underline that fact, the next stage would be his coronation in his other kingdom. In fact recent events made this need all the more pressing.

By the time Henry arrived in France the following year, 1430 – fittingly on St George's Day (23 April) – his possessions in northern France consisted of Normandy, Gascony and the Île de France, including Paris, while his Burgundian allies brought the security of Picardy and Flanders. Bedford promised his young nephew that English policy 'prospered' in France but the reality was slightly different. For all that the regent had worked wonders in maintaining English authority and prestige, things were already in danger of falling apart, largely because of the need to deal with the ever-present threat of the Dauphin's supporters. Bedford had already inflicted heavy defeats on Orléanist–Scottish armies at Cravant and Verneuil but he had been out of the country from 1426 and during that time the faction loyal to the Dauphin had regrouped.

In the summer of 1428 Bedford summoned his main commanders, the Earls of Salisbury, Suffolk and Warwick and Sir John Talbot (later Earl of Shrewsbury), to a war council in Paris, where it was decided to take immediate steps to crush the Orléanists in their seat of power south of the Loire. After a rapid campaign Salisbury laid siege to Orléans with a joint English and Burgundian field army while the Dauphin was at nearby Chinon. The operations got off to a poor start when Salisbury was mortally wounded by a cannon ball four days into the siege and command passed to Suffolk, a shrewd and competent soldier but lacking his predecessor's flair. Suffolk's plan was to continue the siege and starve the city into submission, the tactics which had worked so well in the past, but the army available to him needed reinforcements from England, which were not forthcoming because of the costs and the increasing unpopularity of waging war in France.

As the winter dragged on the garrison in Orléans showed no sign of surrendering, but, in an evening of the odds for those under siege, an English relief convoy was ambushed in February 1429 near Rouvray, five miles north of Janville, by a joint French and Scottish force (contrary to James I's wishes, Scottish forces remained in France). Although the attack was beaten off after the English commander, Sir John Fastolf, ordered his wagons to form a laager, the

English convoy lost most of its provisions to cannon fire. Their casks contained salted fish which were scattered everywhere, earning the encounter the nickname of the 'Battle of the Herrings'. This was followed by a proposal from inside the city that the English should surrender to the Duke of Burgundy, a request which was angrily dismissed by Bedford with the thought that 'it was not honourable nor yet consonant to reason, that the King of England should beat the bush and the Duke of Burgoyne [sic] should have the birds'. In disgust Burgundy withdrew his troops from the investing force. A few weeks later, in May, Suffolk was forced to raise the siege and disperse his forces. It was not a good move: on 12 June he would be defeated at Jargeau, a village close to the city, and fall into the hands of the Dauphin's forces.

By now there was a new aspect for Bedford to consider, a factor that had been central to the raising of the siege of Orléans: the sudden appearance in the Dauphin's camp of a young peasant girl known as Joan of Arc (Jeanne d'Arc), who was rallying the French cause. One French courtier described her as 'a girl who came from no one knows where and has been God knows what', but in fact quite a lot is known about this enigmatic figure who helped to change the course of French history.

Joan was born in January 1412 in Domrémy, near Vaucouleurs in Champagne, the daughter of a peasant farmer, and in her early teens she came to believe that she had been put on earth to do God's great work. This was not simply an inner belief but one that was inspired by the voices of St Catherine, St Margaret and St Michael, who had appeared to her in visions exhorting her to go to the aid of the Dauphin in Chinon and help him in his struggle against the suzerainty of the English. So persistent were these manifestations that Joan was convinced that she had to act. An initial overture to Sir Robert de Baudricourt, the garrison commander at Vaucouleurs, was rebuffed but when she foretold the events of the 'Battle of the Herrings' he was sufficiently convinced of her sincerity to send her with an escort to Chinon. It was at this point, early in 1429, that this short, stocky girl started wearing men's clothes, as much to disguise her identity as to convince others of her martial abilities. Not surprisingly, her arrival at Chinon did not immediately inspire the Dauphin or his closest advisers, as de Waurin makes clear:

At court, they thought she was a deluded lunatic, because she boasted of being able to accomplish tasks so difficult that the great princes thought them impossible, even if they combined all their forces in order to attempt them. Her words were mocked and ridiculed, for the princes thought that it was dangerous to believe blasphemy coming from the mouths of the people, and it is a great fault for a wise man to be deceived by believing too readily in dangerous things.

However, after listening to what Joan had to say, the Dauphin was sufficiently convinced by her argument to have her interrogated at Poitiers by a committee of clerics and theologians, who pronounced that her mission was genuine and that she was spiritually sound. This was a time when the Dauphin's fortunes were at their lowest ebb. It was by no means certain that Orléans would survive the siege and if it succumbed the entire Loire Valley would fall into English hands. The Dauphin's court was short of money and morale was low, so it is not difficult to see why the Dauphinists came to put their trust in this strange peasant girl with her determination and her inner belief that she enjoyed divine approval. A further benefit was that Joan's intervention settled any lingering doubts about the Dauphin's legitimacy: if she enjoyed God's favour this could only be possible if Charles was the rightful heir to the throne of France.

Having persuaded the Dauphin and his court that she was engaged on a godly mission, Joan was put in command of an army to relieve Orléans. Wearing a suit of armour, she managed to persuade the French soldiers under her command to take solemn vows to eschew robbery and fornication and to follow behind her as she marched along the Loire to meet their destiny.

Although she became known as 'La Pucelle' (the Virgin or Maiden) and was fully supported throughout the operations by the experienced Duke of Alençon, Joan proved to be a remarkably forceful and prescient military commander. Under her direction the French attacked and captured the English blockading fort at St Loup on 4 May and within a week the siege of Orléans was lifted, forcing the English army to disperse. A month later Suffolk had been defeated at Jargeau and this was followed by a further victory over Talbot's army at Patay. Suddenly, within eight weeks, everything foreseen by Joan had come true and the Dauphin readily fell in with her proposal that without further ado he should be crowned King of France.

From Tours the triumphant pair marched their forces to Reims, the traditional coronation place of French kings, and it was there on 17 July 1429 that the Dauphin was crowned King Charles VII. At one stroke the conditions of the Treaty of Troyes had been shattered and the English position in France was under substantial threat. More than any other factor, the French coronation and Charles VII's subsequent proclamation promising to restore all French property persuaded the English to crown Henry VI before the year had come to an end. Now that events had moved so rapidly in France they had to act equally quickly to reassert their authority before the new king and 'La Pucelle' used their new-found strength and self-belief to attack and capture Paris.

This was a golden opportunity for the House of Valois to reassert its claim on the French throne by retaking the French capital, but jealousies within Charles VII's camp prevented Joan of Arc from retaining the initiative. Bedford responded resolutely to the challenge that suddenly confronted him. While arrangements were being made for young Prince Henry to be crowned and to travel to France the following year, he moved forces to Compiègne in preparation for an attack on Reims and at the same time Henry Beaufort (now Cardinal Beaufort) was charged with raising fresh forces for service in France.

By acting firmly and by bringing the newly crowned Henry VI to France for his French coronation, Bedford hoped to convince the Burgundians that their best option still lay in the Troyes agreement and that Charles VII and his supporters represented a false dawn. For that reason it was vital to demonise Joan of Arc, who was dismissed as 'a creature in the form of a woman' or, as Bedford described her, 'a disciple and limb of the fiend called the *Pucelle* that used false enchantments and sorcery'. Unable to bear the thought that a French army led by a woman had chased them out of the Loire, the English encouraged rumours that Joan was at best a man and at worst, as Bedford hinted, an agent of the Devil.

By now it was obvious that the French coronation was going to be a protracted business for the English. Reims was now out of the question and even Paris was becoming unsafe, yet it was vital that the ceremony should proceed if English prestige was to be maintained.

Henry and his retinue had arrived in Calais in April 1430 to find that the situation was still too unsafe to allow them to travel to Paris and he had to stay put in the Channel port until the beginning of the summer, when he was moved to Rouen.

While this was happening Joan of Arc fell into the hands of John of Luxembourg, an ally of the Duke of Burgundy, on 24 May, after she had rashly attacked Burgundian forces outside Compiègne on the River Oise. Outnumbered and attacked in the rear by an English force commanded by Sir John Montgomery, she and her entourage were quickly overwhelmed. As recorded in *The Brut*, it was a key moment for the beleaguered English forces, who had the satisfaction of seeing the defeat of French and Scottish forces, including the deaths of 'eight hundred first-class troops' as well as the capture of their nemesis:

> In this battle the witch of France, known as '*la Pucelle*', was also captured, dressed in full armour. Her followers, and all the French, were confident that her cunning sorcery would overcome the English army. But God was lord and master of our victory and her downfall, so she was taken and held captive by the king and his council for ever, at his will.

Joan's fate was quickly sealed. Her captors haggled over her and she was eventually sold to the English and sent in chains to Rouen, although there is no evidence to support the legend that she met Henry VI during that time. Warwick, the King's protector and governor of the castle, would hardly have allowed his young charge to come into contact with a person whom the English considered to be a witch. Joan was put on trial for heresy and witchcraft in February 1431 and appeared before a panel of inquisitors led by Pierre Couchon, Bishop of Beauvais, but the proceedings were a travesty. Although she remained constant in her defence, her claim to have enjoyed direct communication with God through the saints – 'it is for God to make revelations to whom He pleases' – told against her. She also stood condemned for wearing men's clothes as the practice hinted at loose morals. At one point towards the end of the trial Joan recanted and promised to dress as a woman in return for receiving communion and accepting a life sentence, but that decision was quickly and predictably repudiated when the 'voices' suddenly returned to chide her. 'I have done nothing except by revelations,' she told the court, 'I have done nothing but by God's command.' This time there could be no mercy. She was condemned as 'an heretic, idolater, apostate and relapsed; a liar, a pernicious miscreant; a blasphemer, cruel and dissolute'.

On 30 May 1431 Joan was burned at the stake in the marketplace in Rouen, an act which smacked of political expediency on both sides. The man she had put on the French throne did nothing to try to help her and it was not until 1456, at Charles VII's instigation, that a papal court reversed the decision of the court at Rouen on the grounds that it had come under undue English pressure and ignored key pieces of evidence. By then Joan of Arc was long dead and her memory as France's saviour was more useful to the French king than she would have been had she lived.

Hers is the story of a meteoric intervention which had the desired effect of restoring the fortunes of the Orléanists for all that it was prompted by a mixture of intense yet simplistic patriotism and a single-minded, almost fanatical belief in the workings of the supernatural. (In 1920 Joan was canonised.) Through her intervention France had its own king again in Charles VII, national pride had been restored during the miraculous summer campaign of 1429 and the dual monarchy had been put under immediate and unwanted pressure. The unrest generated by her crusade meant that it had also become impossible for the English to carry through their plan to crown Henry at Reims, a move that would have been a direct challenge to the Dauphinists, and instead Bedford had to make do with Notre Dame in Paris. Even then he had to secure the route to the French capital and it was not until after Louviers had been recaptured that Henry's party was able to make its way into Paris.

The boy was crowned king on 16 December 1431 in a ceremony which started badly and ended up making a poor impression on the French, who had already objected to the mass being taken by the Bishop of Winchester. To them the whole thing was considered to be alien and too English and great offence was taken when a large silver wine goblet was removed by the King's officers instead of being returned to the canons, as was customary. Worse followed at the coronation feast, which quickly degenerated into farce. While the

Palais had been sumptuously decorated the food was badly cooked –
a result of using English cooks, according to the contemporary
account by the anonymous 'Bourgeois of Paris' – and, away from the
high table, there were no place settings for the lesser guests. (This was
denied by the chronicler of *The Brut*, who claimed that 'the
coronation was carried out in a fitting manner, with all possible ritual
and ceremony'.) In return Henry had been expected to grant favours
such as lifting taxes and releasing prisoners, but that aspect of the
ceremonial was also botched, leaving the people of Paris feeling that
they had spent a great deal of money on an increasingly unpopular
king and received nothing in return.

This belief was exacerbated when Henry and his court hurriedly
left the city on St Stephen's Day, the day after Christmas, and returned
to England, where, in contrast to his experiences in France, he was
welcomed back by cheering crowds. It was destined to be Henry VI's
only visit to his French kingdom. In planning the expedition and the
coronation Bedford had hoped to cement the Burgundian alliance
and to emphasise the importance of the Treaty of Troyes, but the
whole thing had been a fiasco. Not only had the coronation been
postponed by the failure to take Reims and the interminable delays
in Paris, but the event itself had been badly stage-managed, a curious
failing on Bedford's part. Worse, it had done nothing to reassure the
Duke of Burgundy, who was a notable absentee in Notre Dame and
did not bother to seek an audience with the young king. Shortly after
Henry's departure Burgundy signed a local truce with Charles VII.
Slowly but perceptibly he was easing himself out of the English
alliance and his instincts were matched by a new national mood
which supported the House of Valois. Fifteen years had passed since
the defeat at Agincourt and people were tiring of English rule and
wanted a new arrangement which would protect and enhance French
interests. Henry's coronation was supposed to cement his French
kingdom; instead it marked the beginning of the end of his father's
peace settlement.

The need to continue the war in France, given also the costs of the
King's coronation, proved to be a heavy financial commitment which
had to be borne by funds raised in England and Normandy. An
additional burden was the need to garrison the country to protect
English interests and it soon became clear that Bedford's forces were

overstretched, with never more than four thousand troops available to him. Disaffection with the English presence prompted outbreaks of violence and, while much of Normandy remained quiescent in the aftermath of Henry's departure, in Avranches and Caen there was unrest which escalated into attacks on English possessions.

Once again Bedford mounted operations against Valois holdings, mainly in Picardy and Maine, but it was becoming clear to him that Philip of Burgundy was uninterested in making the alliance work. Having signed a new truce with Charles VII, Burgundy pulled out of the following year's offensive on the Somme. The campaign was purely of concern to the English and they paid heavily as a result of this lack of support. In the fighting at Gerneroi the Earl of Arundel was killed and the towns of Étaples and Le Crotoy fell into Valois hands. Only poor generalship and a lack of commitment prevented the forces of Charles VII from making greater gains, and it was clear that the balance of power was swinging away from Bedford.

Slowly but with grim inevitability Henry V's power-sharing agreement was collapsing under the weight of renewed Valois authority and the inability of the English to counter it in the field. A further blow had been struck in 1432 when Bedford's wife, Anne, died, thereby cutting his family alliance with the Duke of Burgundy. The matter was exacerbated when Bedford remarried Jacquetta of Luxembourg: although her family were Burgundian allies it seems that Duke Philip had not been consulted and took offence at the new liaison.

There is also evidence to suggest that Burgundy feared that one day Henry VI would make peace with Charles VII and leave him isolated. At the time such a move would have been impossible as both sides were unwilling to compromise at all. A Burgundian embassy sent to London was able to report that Henry would only enter into negotiations with Charles provided that he renounce the French Crown, but the concern clearly preyed on Burgundy's mind. He was also under pressure from the Pope to patch up the constant bickering with the House of Valois and to repudiate the terms of the Troyes agreement.

Eventually the demands on Burgundy led to a peace conference, held in Arras in August 1435, where the three sides – English, Burgundian and Valois – were represented by delegations who took part in what today would be called proximity talks. None of the delegates met in direct negotiation but instead were represented by papal mediators. With each delegation consisting of up to eight hundred representatives, it was one of the biggest diplomatic summits ever to be held in Europe, and its findings destroyed the Treaty of Troyes. Despite furious English protests and the withdrawal of their delegation, led by Archbishop Kemp of Canterbury, the papal mediators found that the agreement was flawed and that the Duke of Burgundy could be released from its terms. In return Charles VII promised to make atonement for the murder of Duke John of Burgundy and to punish those responsible for committing the outrage. Burgundy's decision was confirmed in letters which were delivered in London in late September.

It was a bad moment for the young Henry VI: when he read their contents he found that he had not been addressed as Burgundy's sovereign but merely as King of England. Tears welled in his eyes as he faced the inescapable conclusion that his cause in France was as good as lost and he contemplated the treachery of a man he considered to be a loyal kinsman bound by treaty to carry out an agreed policy. The English king was only thirteen years old but he never forgot nor forgave what he considered to be a great betrayal by a man, Burgundy, whom he considered to be his 'good uncle'.

Besides, he was already beginning to discover the full implications of kingship. Following his coronation, relations between Gloucester and Beaufort had reached a new nadir when the former failed to come to terms with the fact that he was no longer in the powerful conciliar position he had occupied during Henry's infancy. In an attempt to regain his position and to weaken Beaufort, Gloucester produced evidence in November 1431 claiming that on becoming a cardinal Beaufort should have surrendered the See of Winchester, along with its substantial revenues. Far from embarrassing Beaufort into quitting his office as Gloucester intended, the charges stung him into action and he fought back and made a successful appeal to Parliament to maintain his rights. The decision was made conditional on the payment of loans to the King's Exchequer, but at least Beaufort had not seen his position fatally weakened, or his cardinal's hat removed, and he retained his precedence in council.

Gloucester also quarrelled with his brother Bedford, who returned from France at the end of 1433, for only the second time in ten years, to defend his record and to try to raise more money for military operations in France. Bedford found that he also had to protect his position in council from his brother's troublemaking and on one occasion the young king had to intercede to stop his uncles' incessant squabbling.

Now an adolescent, Henry was a robust, large-boned and fine-looking young man with interests in hunting, and, according to the Duke of Burgundy's ambassador, 'a very gracious and clever child'. He had clearly received a good education under Warwick's direction and showed an enthusiasm for reading and learning which lasted a lifetime. History remembers him for the austerity and piety of his later years, when he was given to wearing a hair shirt next to his skin, but as a youth he demonstrated a surprising interest in elegant clothes and fine hats. He was also capable of showing precocity. In a note to the council Warwick said that Henry had 'grown in years, in stature of his person, and also in conceit [learning] and knowledge of his Royal estate, the which cause him to grudge with chastising'. As the young king's mentor Warwick had already been given the right to punish Henry physically and on more than one occasion had exercised it by administering a sound thrashing.

In Henry's teenage years that need to keep him in check became more apparent. There were rumours that he was being badly influenced by his uncle Gloucester and in the winter of 1433–4 he was secluded at Bury St Edmunds Abbey, where he was admitted into the fraternity of the foundation, an experience which left a lasting influence on him. It also helped him to understand more fully his position as king – how could it have been otherwise given the symbolism and ceremonial of his coronations with their insistence on his divine right? – and by the early 1430s he was anxious to embrace his majority. This must have made life uncomfortable for his mentor Warwick and at one meeting of the council in November 1434 Henry had to be reminded that he was not yet ready to accept his full responsibilities. At this stage in his life he was developing into an intelligent and potentially forceful young man but, as Warwick hinted to the council, he lacked subtlety and seemed to be easily influenced.

Shortly after the congress at Arras, in September 1435, the young king had more to weep over when he received news that Bedford, his uncle and most powerful supporter, had suddenly died at Rouen, a broken and disappointed man. A few weeks later, on 1 October, Henry attended the council for the first time in a role that was not simply ceremonial: the day was fast approaching when he would come into his own.

Chapter Nine

A Man of Mild and Plain-dealing Disposition

On 12 November 1437 Henry brought his minority to an end when he received the full panoply of power of personal kingship. He was not long past his sixteenth birthday, still an adolescent, but he had been well schooled for the task that lay ahead: over the past two years he had been initiated in the workings of the council and had a reasonable understanding of his duties and responsibilities. The new order meant that the role of the council had to change to reflect the King's majority. Henceforth its task would be advisory and it is to the great credit of those who had served on the body during Henry's minority that the transition was a smooth one. Although they had enjoyed fifteen years of virtually autonomous rule and were not always in full agreement they had kept to the letter and spirit of Henry V's wishes as expressed in his will. To reflect the new beginning four new councillors were appointed: Sir John Stourton, Thomas Rodbury, Bishop of St David's, Richard, Earl of Salisbury, and Robert Rolleston, Keeper of the Great Wardrobe.

However, differences remained, especially over the great matter of France, where Bedford's death in 1435 had changed the complexion of the English presence in the country. While Bedford lived he stood at the apex of English power in France, controlling a system of patronage which gave military authority to a tightly knit Lancastrian circle of lords and captains in return for grants of land. Although this system remained in place the defences of Normandy were gradually coming under pressure from forces loyal to Charles VII, who reoccupied Paris in 1437, and there were worrying signs of local disaffection among some sectors of the population. Garrisoning Normandy was also hugely expensive, requiring subsidies from England, and doubts about its continuing viability refused to go away.

To address this difficulty the Duke of York had been appointed Lieutenant in France in the year before Henry's accession – his wealth and temporal power made him an obvious candidate – and during his short time in charge of England's affairs in that country he had managed to stabilise the position with the assistance of Suffolk and Talbot. He was succeeded for a short time by Warwick, who had been retired as the King's tutor and was not replaced, a sure sign that the task of educating the young man was complete. Warwick received the French post not because he was particularly suited to it but because he was being rewarded for his period of service in the royal household.

Scotland, too, was causing a problem once more and, given the nature of its alliances with the French king, this had an impact on English rule in France. With Bedford no longer a factor in English affairs in France, James I was persuaded to pursue a more aggressively Francophile policy. In 1428 a marriage had been arranged between James's eldest daughter, Margaret, and the new Dauphin (later Louis XI); at the same time the military alliance with France was renewed and Scotland was promised the possession of French territory, namely the county of Saintonge and the Seigneurie of Rochfort. (The promises were never made good, although Scotland continued to press her claims until 1517.) In return James sent small companies of Scottish soldiers to serve in France in the campaign led by Joan of Arc, fighting at Rouvray and taking part in the defence of Orléans under their countryman, Bishop Carmichael of Orléans. (As a result of the losses sustained at Verneuil their numbers were never large but they brought with them military experience and provided the French king with an important ally.) From their ranks Charles VII formed the Garde Écossaise, a bodyguard of 120 men, and in time this became an élite formation manned by generations of Scottish soldiers of fortune. James also considered the possibility of taking advantage of England's difficulties with France by recovering Roxburgh in 1436, but the garrison had been strengthened and when his army arrived outside the castle walls it was forced to retire. That same year also saw the marriage of Margaret to the Dauphin at Tours but, as became all too depressingly clear, James's own position at home was not unassailable.

At the end of the year James celebrated Christmas in the Dominican friary at Perth and it was there, outside the city's walls, that he was murdered on the night of 20 February 1437. His assailants were led by Sir Robert Graham and Sir Robert Stewart, who hoped to advance the claims of their kinsman the Earl of Atholl, Robert II's youngest son. James tried to escape through the undercroft but the assassins pursued him and stabbed him to death. Even so, the plot failed in that those involved were rapidly hunted down and savagely executed. James's son, the future James II, was only six years old at the time and Archibald, 5th Earl of Douglas, was appointed his guardian with the title Lieutenant of the Realm. During the boy-king's minority the alliance with France was strengthened by his betrothal to Mary of Gueldres, a niece of Philip of Burgundy through his sister Isabella's marriage to Duke Francis of Brittany.

However, despite the slaying of James I and the potentially destabilising effects of rule through a regency, a fragile truce with England held and the main problem facing Henry continued to be France. Although the terms of the Treaty of Troyes had been effectively negated at Arras, he still considered himself to be King of France and was anxious to retain his claim to the throne. In an attempt to find a way out of the impasse produced by the Arras concord another diplomatic initiative was pursued, in the form of a peace conference held in Calais on 10 July 1439. Leading the English delegation was Cardinal Beaufort, who had been empowered to offer compromises on Henry VI's claim to the French throne in return for guarantees about the sovereignty of England's French possessions, but it soon became clear that the French were not interested in brokering a deal along those lines. Beaufort thought that he possessed powerful cards in the persons of the Dukes of Orléans and Angoulême, who had been captured at Agincourt and were still being held hostage in England, but he was mistaken.

During the talks Charles VII's advisers insisted that the English could hold land in France only as vassals of the French Crown and that they would agree to the extension of the truce only if the English agreed to restore land in Normandy and surrendered the Duke of Orléans without a ransom. An attempt at finding a compromise by instituting another round of truces also failed and Beaufort was left with little option but to return to England to allow the council to discuss what had been placed on the table.

The French terms were rejected out of hand and a fresh military campaign opened in 1440, with several Norman towns being restored to English control, including Harfleur and Pontoise. However, this succession of sieges and counter-sieges did not improve matters for the English: nothing short of a complete victory over Charles VII would restore them to the position they had achieved under Henry V. The English situation had also been weakened by the sudden death of Warwick in April 1439, less than two years into his occupation of the post of the King's representative in France, and this was followed by a delay in reappointing York as his successor. York was already beginning to demonstrate the headstrong stubbornness and purposefulness that would mark his later career. Before accepting the post he insisted on being given the same powers as Bedford and also demanded adequate funding for the task in hand.

He was still relatively young at twenty-nine and his position in public life had been strengthened by his marriage to Cecily Neville, the daughter of the Earl of Westmorland and Joan Beaufort, daughter of John of Gaunt and Katherine Swynford. It was a fruitful union during which thirteen children were born to them: four sons (Henry, William, John and Thomas) and two daughters (Joan and Ursula) died in infancy, while four sons (Edward, Edmund, George and Richard) and three daughters (Anne, Elizabeth and Margaret) survived into adult life. In stark contrast to the Lancastrian succession, where the only surviving offspring of Henry IV consisted of Gloucester and Henry VI, York's fecundity would only help to strengthen his own position should he ever decide to make a claim to the throne.

In the midst of these confusions the king showed a precocious willingness to become involved in French policy, but it soon became apparent that his interference was not always helpful as it led to unforced changes of plan, the creation of policies on a whim and undue meddling by members of his council. The situation was summed up in a highly emotional letter written by the council in Normandy complaining about a lack of positive action which left them 'as a ship tossed about on the sea by many winds, without captain, without steersman, without rudder, without sail, tossed, staggering and driving among the stormy waves, filled with the storms of sharp fortune and all adversity, far from the haven of safety and human help'.

At this unsettled time Gloucester should have come into his own. He was the surviving brother of Henry V – a powerful factor – and his counsel should have been valued, not least because he was vastly experienced in French affairs. But already his star was waning and it showed. He opposed the release of the Duke of Orléans as a means of showing good faith to Charles VII during the peace negotiations in Calais, but this was approved by Henry VI, who argued that everything possible should be done to achieve 'good peace' between the two countries. In fact the King took the final decision on the advice of Suffolk, who had acted as Orléans' keeper and become a firm friend of the French nobleman as a result of their close association.

Even so, the gesture did not help matters. On his return to France in 1440 Orléans was hailed everywhere but in the court of Charles VII, who refused to receive him. This was a double disaster as Orléans had been an important diplomatic pawn and had only been granted his freedom in a bid to further the peace talks with the French king. Now he had been released to no avail and, worse, he quickly became involved in a new series of internal plottings involving the Burgundian camp. One such move occurred when, to Gloucester's ire, Orléans unexpectedly married Mary of Cleves, Burgundy's fourteen-year-old niece, and promptly withdrew to his estates, where he was of no use to either side. Gloucester had also reignited his feud with Cardinal Beaufort by accusing him of treachery for allowing the release of Orléans, but the heaviest damage to his reputation was done by his second wife, Eleanor of Cobham. To general astonishment, in the summer of 1441 she stood accused of practising sorcery against the King's person by indulging in necromancy and the black arts, a serious business at a time when witchcraft was associated with the powers of the Devil.

The charges were thoroughly scandalous. In conjunction with other accomplices, among them Roger Bolingbroke, a well-known astrologer, and Margery Jourdemain, a self-confessed witch, Eleanor had attempted to use a horoscope to predict if she would ever become queen in the event of the young king's death. Given her husband's position as heir presumptive this was a possibility if Henry died unmarried and childless, but the necromancers went a step further by making a wax image of the King and burning it. The allusion was obvious and the discovery of the sorcery aimed against the King could have led to charges of treason in respect of which none of the conspirators could have expected mercy. For Gloucester their reckless behaviour was a tremendous blow to his position and prestige at court. Bolingbroke had been a member of his household and another member of the plot, John Home, had acted as his secretary. In July 1441 Eleanor and her accomplices were tried before an ecclesiastical court containing Gloucester's great enemy Cardinal Beaufort. For Bolingbroke and Jourdemain, also known as the Witch of Eyre, there could be no mercy: the former was sentenced to the traitor's death of being hanged, drawn and quartered, while the alleged witch was burned at the stake.

For Eleanor there was a different fate. In November she was forced to carry out three days of public penance by walking through the streets of London with a lighted taper as if she were a common prostitute and not the wife of one of England's most powerful magnates. Thereafter she was sentenced to a lifetime's imprisonment in various isolated castles in England, including Kenilworth, Peel on the Isle of Man and Beaumaris on the island of Anglesey. She was never released and died in 1452. During her ordeal, upon which Henry insisted, Gloucester was forced to divorce her and was unable to help her in any way. Even if Gloucester had not been involved in his wife's foolish activities – and he seems not to have been – that public display of political and personal impotence was telling confirmation of his fall from grace.

It was not the end of the matter. After Eleanor's incarceration Gloucester was denied access to the court as Henry himself became increasingly apprehensive that his uncle was trying to engineer his downfall. Given what had happened this was not an unnatural suspicion, but Henry seems to have allowed himself to be infatuated with the idea that his uncle posed a threat. He became so convinced that Gloucester was plotting to have Eleanor released as a first step to taking over the throne from him that in February 1447 he had him and his retinue arrested during a session of the Parliament held at Bury St Edmunds. It was a thoroughly disagreeable and disreputable

King Richard II as he wanted to be remembered. In *The Wilton Diptych* he is presented to the Virgin and Child by his patron Saint John the Baptist and saints Edward the Confessor and Edmund the Martyr. (NPG, London)

The Peasants' Revolt led by Wat Tyler was the defining moment of the early years of King Richard II's reign. Aged only fifteen, he confronted the rebels who were demanding an end to the feudal system. During the incident Tyler was stabbed to death by William Walworth, Lord Mayor of London (bottom left). (Mary Evans Picture Library)

Old John of Gaunt, time-honoured Lancaster. The most powerful of Edward III's sons and the most fecund. With his three wives he fathered ten children, including Henry IV.
(Bridgeman Art Library)

Henry Bolingbroke, the usurper king. After taking the crown from his cousin Richard II he ruled as King Henry IV until his death on 20 March 1413. (NPG, London)

So little is known about the mythical Welsh leader Owen Glendower that even his likeness is a mystery. Following the failure of his rebellion against Henry IV in 1413, he went to ground and was never seen again.
(Bridgeman Art Library)

The French thought that Henry V looked more like a priest than a soldier but his great victory at Agincourt in 1415 re-established English military prestige in France.
(NPG, London)

The English victory over the French at Agincourt was one of the greatest military feats of all times. Although the English were outnumbered and exhausted, their superior tactics and the skilful deployment of their archers won the day for King Henry V.

(Lambeth Palace / Bridgeman Art Library)

The wooden funeral effigy does little justice to Katherine of Valois, Henry V's queen. Although the match was part of the political settlement with France, Henry was genuinely smitten by her. Widowed at the age of twenty-one, she entered into a secret marriage with an obscure Welsh squire, Owen Tudor. (Getty Images)

King Charles VI of France suffered his first period of insanity after attacking his followers in the mistaken belief that they were committing treason. Later he came to believe that he was made of glass and would break if people approached him. (AKG Images)

A claimant for the French throne. Duke John the Fearless of Burgundy was the main rival of Louis of Orléans, brother of the mad King Charles VI. Following a détente with the Dauphin, the future Charles VII, he was ruthlessly murdered during peace talks on the bridge at Montereau. (Corbis)

She helped to win back the kingdom of France but was burned at the stake as a witch. Joan of Arc, also known as 'La Pucelle', was the inspiration behind the military victories which returned King Charles VII to the French throne.

(Bridgeman Art Library)

The son of John the Fearless, Duke Philip the Good of Burgundy pursued a policy of friendship with Henry V of England. He handed Joan of Arc over to the English to be executed as a heretic but in 1435 he changed sides to support King Charles VII of France.

(Bridgeman Art Library)

In his youth Henry VI was described as a robust, large-boned and fine-looking young man, but mental disorders took their toll and towards the end of his life he cut a sorry figure 'not worshipfully arrayed as a prince and not so cleanly kept as should seem such a prince'. (NPG, London)

The description of Queen Margaret of Anjou as 'a Great and Strong-laboured Woman' was probably unfair but she was the power behind the throne of her husband Henry VI. (MEPL)

Held captive in the English court for most of his boyhood and young manhood, James Stewart came to the Scottish throne as King James I. An accomplished poet, he checked the power of the Scottish nobility, including the Lordship of the Isles, the federation of Macdonald clans.

(Scottish National Portrait Gallery)

The most serious of several uprisings during the reign of King Henry VI was the revolt of 1450 when Kentish rebels marched on London. Led by Jack Cade (or Mortimer), they managed to enter London, where the rebellion was ended with the promise of free pardons. Later Cade and his followers were hunted down and killed.

business. After arriving in the town on 18 February Gloucester was denied access to the King and was promptly detained, along with the leading members of his entourage, who were then rapidly dispatched to places of imprisonment throughout England.

For reasons which are impossible to verify but are perhaps all too understandable, this sudden and unexpected turn of events so shocked Gloucester that he dropped dead five days later. There were no signs of any violence on his body, which was placed on pubic view to allay suspicions – a contemporary French account alleged that he had been murdered by the singularly unpleasant method of driving a hot poker into his anus, and the rumour was accompanied by an implication that the murder had been carried out on Henry's orders. After the distress caused to him by his wife's incarceration and his realisation that he could no longer influence policy, it is probable that Gloucester died of a stroke brought on by the despair of knowing that he had little left to live for. He was the last Lancastrian prince of the blood royal and with his death a link with John of Gaunt and the great days of Henry V's rule had been lost.

Although Gloucester had been a pest as a politician with his scheming and his many vacillations, he was remembered as a patron of the arts and the contemporary *Gregory's Chronicle* lamented the loss of 'a man of letters, and a true enthusiast for learning, the faith, the church, the clergy and the realm'. It was not the end of the affair: Gloucester's bastard son Arthur and eight other members of his household were tried for treason that same year and all received traitors' sentences, which were to be carried out at Tyburn on 14 July. This, too, was a nasty little business. Each man was hanged and then cut down alive for the process of evisceration, but as the knives were made ready the Earl of Suffolk suddenly appeared carrying the King's pardon and each man was spared the next stage of the terrible execution. It sent an unmistakable warning to anyone else who might have considered taking any action against Henry VI.

By then, as part of the wider diplomatic game with France, the young king had taken a wife. He was of age and the Eleanor of Cobham affair had reinforced the need to produce an heir sooner rather than later, but the match was also dictated by realpolitik. Ideally a marriage to one of Charles VII's many daughters would have created a strong alliance but they were either betrothed or died young (a common Valois failing). There was also the case of consanguinity: any daughter of the French king would be Henry VI's cousin and the Valois family had an unfortunate history of mental disorders, most notably in the case of Charles VI. Instead, in 1444, the choice fell on Margaret of Anjou, the second daughter of René of Anjou, brother of Charles VII's queen, Marie of Anjou. Described by a contemporary chronicler as a great beauty renowned for her 'wit and her lofty spirit of courage', Margaret was a strong-willed young woman well versed in the ways of court life and, importantly for the succession, she came from a fecund family.

The embassy sent to France to arrange the match was directed by the Earl of Suffolk, who had been rising in the King's favour since returning from France. While serving there he had become friendly with the Earl of Salisbury, one of the better English commanders in France, and the relationship had brought him into the Beaufort faction. This alliance had then been strengthened in 1430 by his marriage to Salisbury's widow, Alice Chaucer, granddaughter of the poet. (Salisbury had been killed during the siege of Orléans two years earlier.) Suffolk's star had risen as a result of this alliance and the King's burgeoning friendship – Henry warmed to the man, making him the head of his household and paying attention to his advice – but his rise to power had brought him into conflict with Gloucester. With good reason Suffolk was lukewarm about accepting the commission to arrange the King's marriage as he did not want to be associated with any peace agreement which might affect Henry's claims to the French throne. However, Henry insisted that Suffolk should lead the delegation and in return provided him with a written indemnity for his actions.

With a small group of advisers Suffolk sailed to France in March 1444 and received a surprisingly warm welcome from both Charles and Duke René. The marriage negotiation was concluded by the Treaty of Tours on 22 May but its terms were remarkably one-sided. Margaret agreed to surrender all claims to her father's possessions and there would be no dowry as René was virtually penniless despite his many grand (though empty) titles, among them King of Jerusalem. A two-year truce was also concluded at this time as well as a secret agreement by which Henry was prepared to cede to René the provinces of Anjou and Maine. This latter indulgence had to be kept confidential as its exposure would have confirmed all of Gloucester's fears about the dangers of making peace with France by making concessions. Unlike Suffolk and Beaufort, he believed that negotiations were a sign of weakness.

Two days later, in the church of St Martin, Margaret was betrothed to Henry in a magnificent ceremony attended by the King and Queen of France, with Suffolk standing proxy for the English king. It was not until the following year that arrangements were made for Margaret to move to England and once again Suffolk was given the task of heading the embassy and standing in for his sovereign at the marriage ceremony, which was held at Nancy and was followed by a week of festivities. From there she travelled to Paris and was then escorted by York to the English capital at Rouen, where she prepared for the final stage of her journey to England.

Her voyage proved to be a terrible experience. The Channel was hit by storms and her ship was beached at Portchester, on the Hampshire coast, where there was no one to meet the party and the Queen was forced to take refuge in a nearby cottage, Suffolk having been obliged to carry her ashore. Margaret had been prostrated by seasickness and it took a further two days before she was strong enough to make her way to Southampton. According to Henry, his new bride was 'yet sick of the labour and indisposition of the sea' and it was not until 23 April that she finally met her husband at the Abbey of Titchfield in the New Forest, where they were formally married by the Bishop of Salisbury. At the end of May the royal couple returned to London, where Margaret was finally crowned queen. It was a happy enough occasion but the marriage of Margaret marked the beginning of a season of severe turbulence in France, in England and in the King's mind.

What kind of a man had the sixteen-year-old French princess married? There is considerable contemporary evidence to suggest that Henry was a simple man who practised Christian virtues and took seriously his coronation oath to protect the faith and the Church: for example, in John Rous's history of the kings of England he is presented as 'a most holy man, shamefully expelled from his kingdom but little given to the world and worldly affairs'. He also seems to have had a compassionate nature and displayed a sensitivity which made many of his acts of kindness appear simple-minded or merely excessive. Other contemporary evidence suggests that in his youth he was shy of women and was probably a virgin when he married. According to the evidence of John Blacman, who served him as a chaplain and later wrote an account of the King's life, Henry was shocked to see women and men bathing naked when he visited Bath in 1449 and on another occasion angrily dismissed a Christmas pageant in which young women bared their breasts. In Blacman's opinion Henry possessed great piety which made him more of a man of God than a king capable of dealing with worldly affairs:

> He was like a second Job, a man simple and upright, altogether fearing the Lord God, and departing from evil. He was a simple man, without any crook of craft or untruth, as is plain to all. With none did he deal craftily, nor would he say an untrue word to any, but framed his speech always to speak truth.
>
> He was both upright and just, always keeping to the straight line of justice in his acts. Upon none would he wittingly inflict any injustice. To God and the Almighty he rendered most faithfully that which was His, for he took pains to pay in full the tithes and offerings due to God and the church: and this he accompanied with most sedulous devotion, so that even when decked with the kingly ornaments and crowned with the royal diadem he made it a duty to bow before the lord as deep in prayer as any young monk might have done.

This is bordering on hagiography – later commentators have questioned the concept of Henry as a royal saint – but there is other evidence besides Blacman's to suggest that Henry was a deeply pious man who took his responsibilities seriously and tried to do his best for his subjects. In no other action can Henry's goodness of heart be better seen than in his creation of Eton College at Windsor and King's College at Cambridge, which are monuments to both his piety and his interest in the advancement of learning. Eton came into being on 11 October 1440 and consisted of a provost, ten priests, four clerks, six choristers and twenty-five poor scholars. In addition to being taught grammar the scholars undertook to pray for the souls of Henry's forebears and in due course for the soul of the King himself. At the same time the King acquired land at Cambridge for the building of a university college and the foundation stone was laid six years later.

Henry's decision to found these educational centres was driven by a desire to commemorate his accession to power in a fitting way and they remain as monuments to the only entirely successful personal initiatives of his reign. During his lifetime Henry relished every opportunity to visit Eton College to talk to the boys and to enjoin them not to neglect their studies and be 'gentle and teachable'.

Unfortunately, Henry seems to have been simplistic in his approach to other matters – for example, he craved peace with France but knew not how to achieve it – and often appeared simple-minded in his dealings with the council. All too often he succumbed to the failing of agreeing with the last piece of advice given to him and then just as suddenly changing his mind. This was no way for a king of his period to behave and, given his inability to impose himself in any meaningful way, it was perhaps inevitable that he was easily swayed by those closest to him, including, in time, the woman he had just married.

Especially influential was Suffolk, who enjoyed considerable temporal power and had the King's ear. The Burgundian chronicler Georges Chastellain described him as being England's 'second king' and he had cleverly reinforced his position at court through skilful patronage of allies in key positions who endorsed his policies and prospered as a result. Here he was helped by Henry's tendency to be far too free with his largesse: the King maintained a large and lavish court and the courtiers closest to him benefited accordingly. For his work in brokering the royal marriage Suffolk had been created a duke, a signal honour usually given to a prince of the blood royal, and in addition to his post as Chamberlain he was appointed Warden of the Cinque Ports and Constable of Dover. A close friend of the recently released Duke of Orléans, Suffolk supported the Beaufort policy of entering into a peace agreement with France and his position was strengthened by Gloucester's death in 1447. He was also suspicious of York, who was replaced as the King's Lieutenant in France by Edmund Beaufort, Earl of Somerset, who had succeeded his brother John in 1444 and was part of the tightly knit Suffolk–Beaufort nexus which bolstered Henry's power and authority.

The period immediately following Henry's marriage was the apogee of Suffolk's power but already the situation at court was degenerating into a factionalism which had been kept at bay during the King's minority. France proved to be the main stumbling block.

Not only was the secret agreement over Maine and Anjou a time-bomb in that its exposure would outrage the country, but the English presence in France was becoming expensive to maintain at a time when the Exchequer was coming under strain from the increase in size of the court as a result of the royal marriage. The factionalism had been exacerbated in September 1447 by the decision to remove York from his position in France and send him to Ireland as the King's Lieutenant. Not surprisingly, the move embittered York, who made an immediate claim for payment of arrears to his salary and expenses. By then Charles VII had begun insisting that Henry should keep his promise to cede Maine and Anjou and when that became known – the date for the transfer was set for 1 November 1447 – English landowners in those provinces began demanding compensation for their lost properties.

To encourage the English to meet their commitments Charles VII had assembled an army of six thousand soldiers and laid siege to Le Mans. Open warfare was avoided only when Henry dispatched envoys instructing the city to hand itself over to the French as part of the peace settlement. Fatefully for her future reputation, Margaret of Anjou also became involved in the dealings by pressing her husband to make good his promises to the French king. As she told Charles VII, her uncle by marriage, 'in this matter we will do your pleasure as much as lies in our power, as we have always done already'.

It had not taken Margaret long to assert herself at court. On her marriage Sir John Talbot, now promoted as the Earl of Shrewsbury, had presented her with a volume of illuminated French romances so that 'after she had learnt English she might not forget her mother tongue'. It turned out to be a prescient gift. Margaret did indeed quickly learn English but it seemed to many of her enemies that she had not forgotten her native country. When the secession of Maine and Anjou became public knowledge she was blamed for the decision, which was widely regarded as a disastrous and shameful betrayal of English interests. Increasingly she was regarded as a liability to the country. Besides being expensive to maintain – another drawback in English eyes – Margaret was also too keen to involve herself in court politics. Suffolk seems from the outset to have recognised the Queen's quickening interest in him and taken full advantage of it. He certainly treated her in a courtly manner and wrote romantic verses in her honour. He was probably attracted to her too, despite the difference in their ages: a contemporary description by the chronicler Chastellain claimed that 'she was indeed a very fair lady, altogether well worth the looking at'. Suffolk was forty-eight and she was fifteen when they first met and during his embassies in France to conclude the marriage agreement they had spent much time in each other's company. Before his death Gloucester claimed that the mutual attraction had led them to become lovers but this seems unlikely. Certainly there was a close connection between them which offended contemporary sensibilities, but it is more likely to have been fuelled by the aphrodisiac of power than of sexual desire.

From the start Margaret made it clear that she would not be a passive onlooker but fully intended to be a player in court politics and things were made easier for her by her husband's quiet acquiescence and feeble grasp of affairs. In France the presence of a court party was a fact of life and having become Queen of England Margaret saw no reason not to develop a similar faction to strengthen her own position. It was not surprising that she took the initiative and allied herself with the powerful Beaufort clan and became especially close to its leading lights, Suffolk and Somerset. With Gloucester out of the way they made an apparently unbeatable team.

However, Margaret's partisan approach also made it inevitable that she would make enemies of other parties and thereby increase the tensions and rivalries at court. York perceived early on what was happening and in time he was to become an implacable and potentially dangerous enemy. It should be remembered that through his Mortimer relations he had a good claim to the throne and in his own right was a powerful and wealthy magnate. As de Waurin put it, 'envy reared its head among the princes and barons of England, and was directed at the Duke [York], who was gaining in honour and prosperity'.

Against that background Charles VII decided to make a fresh move to restore and strengthen his position. During the prevarications over Maine and Anjou the French king had patched up his quarrel with the Duke of Burgundy and had begun rebuilding his forces for an assault on Normandy. He was also helped by a piece of maladroit behaviour by Somerset. As part of the peace settlement England had always hoped that Duke Francis of Brittany would be a key ally but he was now in the Valois camp, although his brother Gilles, a childhood friend of Henry VI, remained solidly pro-English. To rectify that state of affairs, on Charles's orders Gilles was apprehended by his brother and kept prisoner in various fortresses. This provocation provided Somerset with the excuse to intervene and in March 1449 he sanctioned an attack on the important border town and fortress of Fougères by a force commanded by François de Surienne, a mercenary captain from Aragon who had been in alliance with the English since 1435. The raid was successful – Somerset made sure that he benefited from the plunder gained by de Surienne – but negotiations for Gilles's release foundered largely because Somerset refused to allow Charles VII to play any part in the proceedings on the grounds that Duke Francis was an English vassal.

This refusal to negotiate gave the French the opportunity they had been seeking and on 31 July Charles VII declared war. All of a sudden Suffolk's peace policies began to fall apart. Throughout the impasse with France he had based his tactics on securing a long-term peace through the secession of Maine and Anjou and the alliance with the House of Anjou but there were two drawbacks. First, Charles VII did not fall in with the idea that a two-year truce agreed at Tours should be translated into a long-term peace agreement and, secondly, Somerset had not bargained for the Breton equation. It was bad enough that Duke Francis had thrown in his lot with Charles, but the events involving his brother Gilles and the unjustified seizure of Fougères were the final straw. This reckless behaviour gave the French king his *casus belli* and allowed him to begin the process of pushing the English out of Normandy.

It helped the French cause that the English forces in Normandy were hopelessly dislocated. Lack of funds had reduced their capabilities and there was a serious shortage of manpower which Somerset had been unable to redress. Unlike York, he was not an experienced soldier and it showed in the disposition and direction of his defences. Somerset also found that he was facing a much stronger opponent. Instead of relying solely on soldiers raised by the nobility, Charles VII had built up royal forces who owed their loyalty to him and, as the chronicler Jacques Chartier made clear, the imposition of new taxes for military purposes helped to create a powerful new army: 'The king of France imposed such good order on the conduct of his men-at-arms that it was a fine thing. He caused all those men-at-arms to be equipped with good armour and weapons . . . And these men-at-arms were paid each month.'

By now Charles, with three armies at his disposal, was able to attack Normandy on as many fronts: his forces attacked through central Normandy to threaten Coutances, St Lô and Fougères while the Burgundians attacked from the east and the Bretons invaded the Cotentin Peninsula. However, those audacious moves left the French forces divided and overstretched and a better commander than Somerset could have taken advantage of the situation but one other factor intruded. The majority of the population no longer wanted English rule and tended to welcome the invading armies. During Bedford's time the English presence had achieved stability, the local garrisons protected trade and the soldiers added to the strength of the economy by buying goods locally and marrying into the local population.

In Normandy Henry V had envisaged the creation of a peaceful colonisation which would produce wealth and good government but his early death and the re-emergence of Valois authority in the shape of Charles VII had stirred nationalist sentiments. Perceived English weaknesses only exacerbated this disaffection and in some places the opposition was negligible and resistance quickly crumbled, with the townspeople simply opening the gates to the invading French armies. When Rouen came under threat in October the inhabitants rebelled and forced the garrison to withdraw from the inner defences where they had taken refuge. One by one the major centres fell – Verneuil, Pont de l'Arche, Lisieux, Carenan and Beauvais – largely as a result of an English failure to co-ordinate the defences but also because the inhabitants expelled the garrisons or persuaded them to leave in the face of the French advance. That they were able to do this speaks volumes for the renewed French military strength and Somerset's failure to counter it. (One reason for the Normans' desire to expel the English lay in the power of the artillery forces in the French army: any resistance would be punished by the overwhelming fire-power at Charles's disposal.)

On Christmas Day there was a telling blow with the capture of Harfleur, where the great adventure had begun three decades earlier. Slowly but surely the English were being squeezed out of their possessions and triumphs such as Agincourt were but a distant memory.

In an attempt to shore up the defences a new English field force was hurriedly put together as 1449 came to an end but Normandy was already a lost cause. Some idea of the disaffection and lack of morale can be found in an ugly incident that occurred during the first week of 1450 when Bishop Adam Moleyns, Lord Keeper of the Privy Seal, travelled to Portsmouth to pay the new army as its soldiers assembled for embarkation to France. The men were in rebellious mood and when Moleyns, a Suffolk placeman, arrived at the port he was accused of betraying Normandy and promptly hacked to death by the angry mob. With the deterioration of the situation in Normandy the only ports available to Somerset were Caen and Cherbourg and it was to secure these that the new force, commanded by Sir Thomas Kyriell, was dispatched across the Channel in the middle of March. It was to no avail.

As the English force, mainly archers, made their ponderous way down the Cotentin Peninsula, Kyriell, a relatively unknown soldier, was completely outclassed by his opposite number, the Constable of France, Arthur de Richemont. Knowing that the English were on the move, the French commander sent forward a force led by the Count de Clermont to block the advance and to prevent the English from mounting the defensive posture which had served them so well at Agincourt. There was another surprise. While the English were attempting to manoeuvre into their lines at Formigny, ten miles outside Bayeux, the French opened fire with their artillery from the flanks. As the French positions were beyond the range of the English archers the firing did dreadful damage before the English rushed the French guns and attempted to seize them. Shocked by the speed and aggression of the attack, the French lines broke and the day could have belonged to Kyriell had he pressed home his advantage. Instead he consolidated his lines only to see a new French force approaching from the south. This was led by de Richemont, a renowned Breton commander who had fought at Agincourt, and its arrival on the battlefield steadied the French lines.

Instead of pursuing a beaten enemy Kyriell was now fighting on two fronts and the English flanks were quickly and savagely breached. Over four thousand English soldiers were killed in the defeat at

Formigny, which was the biggest disaster to hit the English in many years. Within the next four months Caen surrendered, followed by Falaise and Cherbourg in August, and English rule in Normandy was at an end. All that was left of Henry V's empire was Calais and the holdings in Gascony.

This was a disaster. 'We have not now a foot of land in Normandy,' wrote the clerk James Gresham to his master John Paston, an old-established and well-connected landowner in Norfolk (the letters provide an intriguing picture of English life in this period), and the dismay was echoed elsewhere. The search was started for a scapegoat; the English people had taken a great deal of pride in Henry V's achievement in winning the Crown of France and fingers started pointing at Suffolk as the chief villain. As Bishop Moleyns lay dying in Portsmouth he had already implicated Suffolk as the architect of the decision to hand over Maine and Anjou to the French, or so the rumours insisted. Even if the report had not been true Suffolk's growing power and influence at court also spoke against him at a time when he was under suspicion of self-aggrandisement. When he announced the betrothal of his eldest son, John de la Pole, to the seven-year-old Lady Margaret Beaufort, Somerset's sister and a grand-daughter of John of Gaunt, it seemed that he was attempting to strengthen his own position if there were ever a disputed succession. Desperately he tried to cover his tracks by declaring his loyalty to the Crown and condemning the 'odious and horrid language' contained in the rumours about his role in creating the débâcle in France but it was to no avail.

On 22 January 1450 Parliament decided to act against Suffolk and although he defended himself by reminding the Commons of his past services to king and country, four days later he was indicted for treason and corrupt practices. Some of the charges were ridiculous. There is no evidence that Suffolk conspired with the French to have Henry murdered and replaced by his eldest son or that he accepted bribes from Charles for the defeat in Normandy, but there was enough truth in the rest of the indictment to damn him. As the long, rambling Bill of Impeachment makes clear, the worst offences came from Suffolk's agreement to cede Maine and Anjou and from his misuse of funds and other corrupt practices to maintain his position, all at the King's expense:

The said duke [Suffolk], the sixteenth year of your reign [1437–8], then being next and priviest of your council, and steward of your honourable household, then and many years since, for covetise of great lucre of good singularly to himself, stirred and moved your Highness, the said sixteenth year, you then being in prosperity and having great possession, to give and grant much party of your said possession, to divers persons in your said realm of England, by the which you be greatly impoverished, the expenses of your honourable Household, and the wages and fees your menial servants not paid, your Wardrobe, the reparations of your castles and manors, and your other ordinary charges were not had, satisfied nor do; and so by his subtle counsel, importunate and unprofitable labour to your most high and royal estate, the revenues of the demesnes and possessions of your crown, your Duchy of Lancaster, and other inheritances, have been so amenused and anientised [diminished and destroyed], that your commons of this your realm have been so importably charged that it is nigh to their final destruction.

These were serious charges, expressed in strict legal language and backed by seemingly solid evidence. When the bill was produced on 7 February Suffolk was sent to the Tower of London as much for his own protection as the indictment had increased tensions and 'the people were in doubt and fear of what should befall'. It also put Henry in a difficult position. He had been excluded from any culpability in the loss of Normandy – not so his wife, who was widely blamed for what had happened – but he had to decide what to do with Suffolk, his favourite and his mainstay at court. Either he could punish him by allowing the legal procedure to continue or he could declare the proceedings illegal. If he took the latter course he would cause a crisis; if he allowed Suffolk to be impeached his friend would certainly face execution. (Ironically, Richard II had faced a similar predicament in 1386 when Suffolk's grandfather had been similarly impeached and then excused.) Fresh charges about Suffolk's extortion and embezzlement were then produced but the main thrust of Parliament's anger was Suffolk's mismanagement of policy in France and his bad financial governance at home.

Faced by an impossible choice, Henry exercised his prerogative to deal with the matter himself and on 17 March, in front of an assembly of lords, Suffolk was summoned into the King's presence. Called upon to answer the charges, Suffolk denied them utterly and submitted to the King's will. Henry's response was to dismiss the charges of treason but to find him culpable of the secondary charges and to punish him by banishment for five years, the sentence to begin on 1 May. This Henry did of his own volition, without taking advice from the Lords and overruling the wishes of the Commons, who had brought the charges in the first place.

It was not a popular decision and when it was announced it roused the people of London to fury. Suffolk was lucky to get out of the capital intact, for a mob attacked him as he attempted to enter his residence at St Giles and he was forced to beat an ignominious retreat to his estates at Wingfield in Suffolk. There, in his last days in England, he wrote a pitiful letter to his son expressing his conviction that he was innocent and enjoining the young man to remain loyal to his sovereign lord the King. Together with his spirited defence of his innocence, the document shows Suffolk in a reasonably good light as the faithful servant done down by events outside his control but, ironically, the fact that he had escaped indictment and punishment sealed his fate.

On 30 April he sailed into exile from Ipswich carrying with him the King's letter of safe conduct but it was not enough to protect him. Somewhere in the Dover straits his ship was intercepted by a small flotilla which included the *Nicholas of the Tower*, a royal ship. A boarding party apprehended Suffolk, the letter of safe conduct was ignored and when the ship's master greeted him with the words, 'Welcome, traitor!' Suffolk's fate was sealed. What happened next was recorded in a letter sent to John Paston a few days after the incident:

One of the lewdest of the ship bade him lay down his head, and he should be fair ferd [fairly treated], with and die on a sword; and took a rusty sword, and smote off his head within half a dozen strokes, and took away his gown of russet, and his doublet of velvet mayled [chain mail], and laid his body upon the sands of Dover; and some say his head was set on a pole by it.

The grisly corpse lay on the beach for several days until the Sheriff of Kent ordered it to be removed and buried at Wingfield. No evidence was ever discovered about the perpetrators of the lynching, but since the *Nicholas of the Tower* was a royal ship it is inconceivable that those involved acted independently. Where then did the guilt lie? The King was an unlikely suspect: Henry's close affinity to Suffolk ruled him out of the equation. For the same reason Margaret had no reason to have one of her closest associates killed and she was prostrated by grief when the news was broken to her and kept herself in her room for three days. York is a possible suspect. He had no love for Suffolk and resented his authority as well as the decision to send him to Ireland. With his wealth and his contacts he would certainly have had the wherewithal to pay sailors to intercept Suffolk's ship and murder him. Whatever else, in the wider realm of England no grief was shown for a man who had come to be known, in a contemporary mock dirge for the dead, as a 'jackanapes':

> Pray for this duke's soul that it may come to bliss,
> And let never such another come after this!
> His interjectors blessed may they be!
> And grant them for their deed to reign with angels,
> And for Jack Nape's soul, *Placebo* and *Dirige* [the opening words
> of the funeral mass].

While Suffolk's death was a subject for mirth in an outburst of popular songs celebrating his demise, the manner of his death and the reasons for it provided evidence of a wider malaise. The loss of Normandy, the growing dissatisfaction with the weakness of the government and the country's burgeoning financial insecurity all combined to give the impression that public order was deteriorating and the King and his council could do nothing to stop the rot.

Chapter Ten

THE GATHERING STORM

The shock of Suffolk's death had scarcely died down when the south-east of England was rocked by a popular uprising led by Jack Cade, a shadowy figure who used a number of aliases, including 'John Amend-all' and, more provocatively, 'John Mortimer'. By using the Duke of York's maternal family name Cade was clearly giving his approval to any claims which York might have had on the English throne. (These were considerable as his lineage descended from Edward III through both parents: his father, Richard, Earl of Cambridge, was the son of Edward's fifth son, Edmund of Langley, 1st Duke of York, and his mother, Anne Mortimer, was the great-granddaughter of Edward's second surviving son, Lionel of Antwerp, Duke of Clarence.)

Cade's rebellion came against an atmosphere of gathering crisis. Normandy was about to be lost, the fight to save France had been massively expensive, the costs outrunning the available finance; the royal court was in debt, it cost £24,000 a year to run yet its income was only £5000; and there were strong suspicions that those close to the King had used their positions at court to better themselves financially. All those problems created a widespread feeling of unease and disaffection. As yet there was no personal criticism of Henry – he was, after all, England's anointed king – but it was apparent that he was not in control and that things were in danger of falling apart. The people of Kent understood all this. They could see the state of the soldiers returning from France as they passed through the Channel ports; most had no money or possessions and resorted to beggary or lives of crime to make good their losses.

As the rebellion followed a succession of French attacks on Kentish ports there was a growing feeling of discontent within the county and this was aggravated by an unwise comment made by James Fiennes, Lord Saye and Sele, a leading member of the council who had held several posts including Sheriff of Kent and Warden of the Cinque Ports. Already unpopular as an alleged extortionist, he was reported to have said that the people of Kent were to blame for the assassination of Suffolk and that the county should be turned into 'a wild forest' by way of reprisal. It did not take long for rumours to grow that Kent was about to be punished on the Queen's orders to avenge her murdered lover Suffolk. Soon men were looking to their weapons and making plans to resist the expected attack. Unlike the earlier Peasants' Revolt, Cade's uprising was well organised and was led by a number of respectable gentlemen, mainly from Kent but also from Essex, Surrey and Sussex, who were not prepared to go like sheep to the slaughter.

The flashpoint came during the Whitsun weekend of 1450 with a huge gathering at Ashford attended by three thousand armed men from all over the Weald of Kent. Led by Cade, they made their way to Blackheath, to the south-east of London, where they set up camp and published their grievances on 1 June. The manifesto was lengthy but its demands were summarised in five main points: namely, that the King 'has had false counsel, for his lands are lost, his merchandise is lost, his commons destroyed, the sea is lost, France is lost, himself so poor that he may not for his meat nor drink'. As had happened before, and as would happen again in England's history while the monarch remained the ultimate ruler of the country, the grievances were not directed at the King himself but at his closest circle of misguided advisers, 'the traitors that be about him' who had benefited from their positions at court and had been responsible for the loss of France. These people had to be punished, the King had to be forced to resume control of all his lands and Suffolk's supporters had to be removed from the council. There were also demands for the redress of various financial grievances and for the punishment of anyone connected to the Duke of Gloucester's death. There was nothing treasonable about these demands and under different circumstances Henry might have been able to deal with the issue in the same way that Richard II had coped with the earlier Peasants' Revolt when he was considerably younger and less experienced. Most of Cade's followers were reasonable and intelligent men who were intent on making a serious political point; they were not the unruly and unfocused mob led by Wat Tyler. But as happened all too often during his reign Henry – or, more likely, his advisers – mismanaged the crisis.

Having dissolved the Parliament which had been sitting at Leicester, Henry and a large armed retinue returned to London on 13 June, stopping in Clerkenwell, where the King agreed to send an embassy, including John Kemp, the Archbishop of York, to meet Cade. John Benet's *Chronicle* describes what happened next:

> The king sent the Archbishop of York, who was a cardinal and at that time the chancellor of England, the Archbishop of Canterbury and the Duke of Buckingham to Cade, as his emissaries. These men were instructed to treat with the captain [Cade] and to discover the reasons for the insurrection. And the captain told them of the many changes which he thought the king should make in his government of England.
>
> When the king heard of Cade's opinions, he refused to make the changes he asked. The captain with all his followers stayed at Blackheath for eight days awaiting the king's pleasure, for he meant no harm to the king, nor to England itself, and he had no wish to hurt anyone, nor to take their property. And he made an announcement to this effect.

Even at this stage all might have been well and Cade's followers could have been pacified, but Henry was persuaded by his advisers to take military action to put down the rising. The manifesto was rejected out of hand and forces were deployed to restore order at Blackheath. On 18 June the Royalist army, numbering some twenty thousand, moved on the rebel camp but they arrived only to find that Cade had already stolen a march on them by ordering his people to withdraw towards Sevenoaks, some twenty miles away. This left Henry in a quandary. He could not allow his will to be flouted by a commoner, but to pursue Cade would entail a violent confrontation with his own subjects, something which he was reluctant to do. Eventually he was persuaded that he should personally lead his army in pursuit of the rebels, the reasoning being that Cade's supporters would probably melt away at the sight of the approaching Royalist forces – if they confronted the King in the field their actions could be construed as treason. That plan might have worked. Cade was by no means certain that he would receive additional support and his followers had already made it clear that they did not want a fight with the King. A sudden move on Sevenoaks by the numerically superior Royalist army could have nipped the revolt in the bud but at the last moment the disastrous decision was taken to divide Henry's forces. The larger part was ordered to remain at Blackheath to provide protection for Henry who was thought by the Queen to be in danger, while a smaller force set off in pursuit of Cade's men.

Led by Sir Humphrey Stafford of Grafton, a kinsman of the Duke of Buckingham, the Royalists came across the rebels in wooded country between Bromley and Sevenoaks and were soon involved in fierce fighting which lasted for over two hours. Many of Cade's supporters were experienced and well-armed former soldiers who had fought in France and although some of their number were killed in the fighting they inflicted a serious defeat on the Royalist forces. Stafford was cut down and killed together with his brother William and the survivors scattered in panic. When the news of the defeat reached the King's camp Henry ordered the remainder of his army to prepare to march to avenge the setback but his order was ignored by the men who had remained with him at Blackheath. This was mutiny: far from showing any inclination to obey Henry's orders, the men shouted that they would finish Cade's work for him and demanded the arrest of 'the traitors about the king'.

Faced by this obduracy Henry panicked and retired to Greenwich where he heeded Margaret's bidding and made his way to the safety of Kenilworth Castle in Warwickshire. Before leaving London he ordered the arrest of Lord Saye and Sele who was detained in the Tower – as much for his own protection as any mark of displeasure – while Saye's son-in-law, William Crowmer, the Sheriff of Kent, was incarcerated in the Fleet Prison. Prudently the rest of the council joined Saye in the comparative safety of the Tower. Far from nipping the rebellion in the bud, as it was supposed to have done, Stafford's expedition and its defeat had destroyed any remaining belief in the

King's good intentions. It also fanned the violence which spread into East Anglia and then towards the West Country, where there was further violence and loss of life.

At the end of June William Ayscough, Bishop of Salisbury, was dragged out of Edington Church in Wiltshire and hacked to death by his congregation. Five years earlier he had officiated at Henry's marriage to Margaret but the fact that he was the King's confessor condemned him – he was held to be one of the 'traitors' who had failed to prevent the King from acting wrongly. A few days later, Cade rode back into London with his supporters who were still promising that they had sufficient 'wit and wisdom for to have guiding or put in guiding all England'. This time, though, there was none of the subservience which had accompanied his earlier ride on the capital. Cade wore a crown of blue velvet, a gilt headpiece and on his feet could be seen the gilded spurs of a knight, probably taken from Humphrey Stafford's dead body. Ahead of him strode his squire carrying a huge sword as if he were a conquering king and not the soldier of fortune that he was. However, his appearance clearly impressed the people of London who clamoured for him and his followers to be admitted and on 2 July the drawbridge on London Bridge was lowered so that Cade and his followers could enter the city in triumph.

The next day the mood turned ugly. Cade had a reputation for being able to keep his followers under control but Stafford's attack had enraged the Kentish rebels and Henry's absence from the city encouraged a mood of revenge. Their targets were Saye and Crowmer who were dragged from their prisons for hasty trials and equally rapid execution. Saye was taken to the Guildhall where he attempted to argue that he should be tried by his peers but he was promptly found guilty, taken to Cheapside and beheaded. A similar fate faced Crowmer who was removed to Mile End, where he and other followers met a similar fate. As happens so often with mob frenzy the blood-letting raised temperatures and soon Cade's followers were out of control. Several houses, including that of Philip Malpas, an alderman and one of Henry's supporters, were ransacked and looted. According to the evidence of the chronicle written by London's mayor William Gregory this was evidence that 'every ill beginning most commonly hath an ill ending'. Gregory, who had no time for Cade or his rebels, underlined the point that Malpas was a wealthy man and that he was being punished as much for that as for his royal connections:

> They [de]spoiled him and bare away much good of his, and in specially much money, both of silver and gold, the value of a notable sum, and in specially of merchandises, as of tin, woad and alum [dye and mineral salts]. With great quantity of woollen cloth and many rich jewels, with other notable stuff of feather-beds, bedding, napery and many rich cloth of arras [tapestry fabric, used for wall hangings], to the value of a notable sum.

This outrage led to a scuffle with a Royalist force from the Tower led by Captain Matthew Gough who was killed in the street-fighting which followed and which also accounted for the deaths of around two hundred innocent citizens caught up in the violence. Finally the rebels were driven out of the city by the remnants of Gough's force and order was restored, allowing the Archbishop of York to reopen negotiations with Cade inside St Margaret's Church at Southwark. In a compromise deal Cade handed over his petition and in return he and his followers received free pardons on condition that they returned peaceably to their homes. Fatally for Cade his pardon was given in the name of John Mortimer. The majority of his supporters accepted their good fortune and quit Southwark but Cade and a rump of his hard-line followers attacked Queenborough Castle on the Isle of Sheppey in an attempt to get booty to pay for their rebellion.

Retribution was not long in coming. Cade's pardon was revoked and he was hunted down in the name of 'Jack Cade' by forces led by Alexander Iden, the new Sheriff of Kent. A fortnight later, on 15 July, Cade was run to ground in a garden in Heathfield in Sussex where he fought bravely to save himself but was overwhelmed by superior numbers. Badly wounded, he was taken back to London to face inevitable execution but he died on the way. Even so, revenge was insisted upon: his body was beheaded and quartered and, according to Benet, 'afterwards his head was placed on London Bridge, although he had not appeared before a court of law and had been condemned not according to the law but according to the king's wishes'. Later in the year, eight of his followers were executed at Canterbury and a further twenty-six went to their deaths at Rochester. Showing the desire for revenge which he had originally displayed against Gloucester's family and which is strangely at odds with his piety and humility, Henry personally attended each execution.

Cade's rebellion achieved absolutely nothing. None of the points made in his manifesto and petitions was ever met, the court party was left untouched by what had happened and Henry himself seems to have been unmoved by the violent events of the summer of 1450. But, although the King was able to return to his capital, he came back to a changed situation behind the apparent normality. For a short term the governance of his kingdom had broken down and he had exacerbated the problem by leaving London to its own devices. Nothing had been done to address the main grievances raised by Cade and his followers and Henry had shown himself to be weak and indecisive when he should have used a firm but fair hand to deal with the rapidly deteriorating situation. Cade's rebels were not seeking to destroy the authority of the Crown: they wanted to strengthen it by removing the misguided advisers. Instead of negotiating with them, as Richard II had done in similar circumstances, Henry had alienated the protesters further by using extreme violence against them. Not only had this demonstrated his weakness as a king but in the longer term it was seen as a clear example of his incapacity to govern the country.

Immediately on returning to the capital Henry compounded this failing by appointing Somerset Constable of England, a curious promotion for a man who had been responsible for the run of defeats which had led to the expulsion from France. This was a doubly dangerous appointment because it heightened the existing rivalry with York and brought into the open the two men's rival claims to the throne. Five years into his marriage Henry was still childless – one reason for the Bishop of Salisbury's summary execution was the belief that he had counselled the King to pursue a celibate life – and there was no heir. As Henry's uncles were all dead and had not left heirs, there were only two contenders: York and Somerset. York had a claim through both his parents but it was weakened by the fact that he was descended from John of Gaunt's younger brother, Edmund. Somerset was descended from John of Gaunt himself but that claim had been negated by Henry IV's decision to disqualify the Beaufort family by Act of Parliament in 1407. Long disguised, that family rivalry was about to become more open and more bitter.

Throughout the Cade Rebellion there had been rumours that York was implicated in some way but it seems unlikely. Despite his dislike of the court party and his claims to the throne, he was still loyal to Henry and at that stage there was no evidence that he had ambitions to be declared heir presumptive. Even so, he had taken a proprietorial interest in what was happening. Not only was he a powerful and wealthy magnate in his own right but he possessed a sense of noblesse oblige. He would have been aware of his heritage and the part played at court by other royal princes such as Bedford and Gloucester in protecting Henry's fragile throne. In that role he had also acted as the King's Lieutenant in France and Ireland and as a member of the nobility he must have been aware of the problems that existed at court.

In September York decided to act, fearing perhaps that his own position might come under threat from Somerset, or that the court party might take pre-emptive measures against him by declaring him a traitor. He was able to make this move through a clause in his letters of appointment which permitted him to return to England in time of national emergency. Before leaving Ireland 'with great bobaunce [ostentation] and inordinate people' he made his position clear in a series of open letters addressed to the King in which he reaffirmed his loyalty to the throne and announced his intention to defend himself against any false accusation and to help punish those 'traitors' who were working against the King's best interests. When Henry instructed a deputation to intercept and arrest York and his party as traitors, Benet recorded that the alleged rebels insisted that they had a sound cause, namely the protection of the King and the destruction of his advisers:

> The duke [York] replied, commending himself to the king's good grace and saying he had never rebelled against the king and would obey him always. He asserted that his uprising had been directed against those who betrayed the king and the kingdom of England and that he was not against the king and desired nothing but the good of England. He wished to tell the king of those who were

encompassing the destruction of his two kingdoms, that is to say, of England and France. And these men were Edmund, Duke of Somerset, who had been responsible for the shameful loss of all Normandy and John Kemp, the archbishop of York, who was a cardinal and chancellor of England.

Having landed at Beaumaris in Anglesey, York made for his castle at Ludlow in the Welsh marches to gather support, and with a force of around four thousand men marched on London. Thoroughly alarmed, the council tried to have him stopped before he reached the capital but on 29 September York arrived at Westminster, where Henry had taken refuge in his apartments. Nothing daunted, York forced his way into the royal presence and having reaffirmed his loyalty told the King that he had to reform the way in which he governed England by ridding himself of his advisers and ending the corruption at court.

Henry was distressed by the treatment meted out to him and had every right to feel that way. York might have protested his loyalty but there had already been manifestations of public support for him as many people regarded him as a redeemer who would clean up the court and bring justice to the country. As we have seen, Cade had adopted the name Mortimer and there were several incidents in which people had been arrested and executed for making treasonable claims that York would make a better king. With that in mind Henry had to tread carefully. He realised that he had to appease York but he could not give in to all his demands, otherwise he would have lost what authority he already possessed. By way of compromise he agreed that there had to be changes but they would be agreed by a new council which would include York, who then withdrew to his castle at Fotheringhay to await the opening of the new Parliament on 6 November.

The session was packed with York's supporters; the Speaker, Sir William Oldhall, was a Yorkist who acted as his chamberlain and under his direction it produced a number of bills addressing the country's difficulties and pressing the need for reform. Principal among these was a petition of resumption which named those advisers whom the Commons wanted to be removed from court and provided for the return of Crown lands gifted by the King to his favourites during his reign. For the time being York was in the ascendant – he had re-entered the city accompanied by a huge armed retinue – and the mood was reflected in a letter written on 6 October 1450 to John Paston by William Wayte, who acted as clerk to William Yelverton, one of the justices in the Court of the King's Bench, the supreme court of common law, which had the power to sit anywhere in England:

> Sir, may it please you, I was in my lord of York's house and I heard many more things than those about which my master has written to you. I heard many things in Fleet Street. But sir, my lord [of York] was with the king, and he put such a front on matters that all the king's household were and are very frightened: and my lord has presented a petition to the king and asked for many things, which are much after the commons' heart. They all want justice and to put those who are indicted under arrest. Without sureties or main prise, to be tried by law as the law will have it; insomuch that on Monday Sir W. Oldhall was with the king at Westminster for more than two hours, and was well received by the king. The king asked Sir W. Oldhall to speak to his cousin York to ask him to favour John Pennycook ['esquire of the body', a member of the King's household], and to write to his tenants to allow Pennycook to go and collect his rents and revenues in the duke's lordships.

All this was happening against a tense background in London, where the retinues of the leading figures paraded through the streets, turning the capital into an armed camp. In one incident Somerset almost lost his life to an armed mob and was saved only by the intervention of Thomas Courtenay, Earl of Devon and Steward of the Duchy of Cornwall. In an attempt to protect his new favourite by getting him out of the country Henry appointed Somerset Captain of Calais, a powerful position which York coveted, but this was not enough to calm the heightened tensions. When Parliament reassembled after the Christmas recess Somerset's name headed a list of twenty-nine recalcitrant courtiers whom the Commons wanted to be removed for 'misbehaving about your Royal person and in other places'. Tellingly, many of the same people had also been named in Cade's manifesto and petitions. Forced to act, Henry suspended those named and had Somerset confined in the Tower, although he was quickly released on Queen Margaret's orders and allowed to resume his place at court.

By now York's brief period of pre-eminence was already waning. Although his moves to reform the court had been broadly welcomed and implemented by the Commons where he enjoyed the backing of Oldhall and other followers, he lacked a broad measure of support among the country's most powerful magnates. Without a solid power base his actions were always going to be circumscribed and that absence stymied the options available to him. Partly the reason for this disaffection was territorial. His lands were scattered throughout England and, unlike other great magnates such as the Earls of Northumberland and Westmorland, he lacked a single, unified region upon which he could rely implicitly. Partly it was caused by fear of civil strife – the attack on Somerset was a reminder of the enmity between these two powerful magnates which could quite easily degenerate into civil war. Partly, too, it was dynastic: the very fact that York had a submerged claim to the throne made him a potential enemy because most of the courtiers under attack owed their positions to Henry's patronage and were unlikely to support a man who wanted to change the system.

Towards the end of the parliamentary session which began early in the following year, 1451, a member of the Commons, Thomas Yonge (or Young), attempted to have York named as the heir presumptive but the move failed and for his pains its instigator was thrown into the Tower. As a result Henry promptly dissolved Parliament, which had at least won concessions on finance and the grant of lands as well as the suspension of the named favourites. However, none of this strengthened York's position, and although a programme of reforms had been agreed he was left isolated. Somerset's return to public life was a sign of continuing royal favour and with nothing to detain him in London York left for his estates at Ludlow, to go into effective internal exile. Remaining in the capital would only have reminded him and others of his lack of standing among his fellow magnates and the failure of his attempt to make a decisive inroad into court politics.

Like Cade, who had supported similar demands, York's intervention to reform the court had come to little, other than to have the grievances aired in public. He had taken considerable risks by returning from Ireland and making public his criticism of what had been taking place at court. His contempt for Somerset was also in the open but that did not help him either. Despite being suspended his rival continued to enjoy the King's support and as he was now back as the leader of the court party in succession to Suffolk it was clear to everyone that York's own position had been eroded. He had also made an enemy of the King, who had come to believe that York was not acting in the best interests of the kingdom but was merely pursuing a personal vendetta against Somerset in order to further his own ambitions. Apart from that of the Duke of Norfolk, York had received little support from the nobility and already there were moves to oust Oldhall from his leadership of the Commons. On the other side, York's enemies in the court party were united and Somerset, now firmly implanted as the Queen's favourite, had good personal reasons to want to hang on to his power and authority.

There was another difference between the two men: money. Unlike York, Somerset did not enjoy inherited wealth and needed lucrative royal patronage, including the post at Calais, to retain his public position. As a result, cupidity played a major part in fuelling his ambitions: he needed to maintain his royal connections in order to prosper. This was a powerful incentive for Somerset and helps to explain his tenacity in hanging on to power.

To a certain extent York had been hobbled by his very public declaration of allegiance to the King. Having stated that his quarrel was not with Henry but with those who surrounded him, he could hardly have accelerated his protest into a rebellion as that would have smacked of betrayal. York's one opportunity had come when he arrived in London with a large number of armed men for the opening of Parliament. Had he used force at that moment he could have pressed his claims and unseated Henry, but at that stage in his life York was not prepared to transgress into treasonable territory by usurping the Crown. It was bad enough that he was already feared and distrusted by some of his fellow nobles without giving them solid grounds for believing that he was interested only in furthering his own aspirations.

And yet York's position was not entirely hopeless. Despite being virtually exiled from court – he was unable to make any contact with the King – he had not been punished in any way, his forces had not been disarmed and he still had his wealth and authority. The King's relatively mild response meant that York remained a potent force who could bide his time for an opportunity to reassert his influence. His chance came sooner than he might have expected, in September the following year, when a row broke out between the Earl of Devon and Lord Bonville of Chewton and Shute over the disputed possession of the post of Steward of the Duchy of Cornwall. Bonville, who had served in Gascony, was close to the court party and was in alliance with James Butler, Earl of Wiltshire, while Devon was close to York for the time being. At the end of the summer the disagreement between the two men erupted into open warfare when the Earl of Devon took a substantial armed force across the county of Somerset and defeated Wiltshire's men at Lackham, near Bath. He then marched back to Taunton to besiege Bonville's forces, who were taking shelter in the castle. It was at that point that York appeared on the scene with an armed retinue of two thousand men to force Devon and Bonville to come to terms.

It was an extraordinary incident. Four private armies were in the field, one (Devon's) had inflicted a defeat on another (Wiltshire's) while York had entered the fray to prevent the conflict from spreading. The peace-broker (York) might have had the ulterior motive of forcing a confrontation with Somerset, in whose lands the affray had taken place, but the episode is a good indication of the underlying tensions which existed in England at the time. Here were private armies taking the law into their own hands with no thought for the King's authority and behaving in a way which disrupted the natural order.

In an attempt to settle the issue and to regain his position Henry summoned all the parties to Coventry, where Wiltshire and Bonville were ordered to be confined in their castles for a month. Henry was outraged by the incident, which he regarded not as an intervention to preserve law and order but as a further example of York's intransigence and ambition. The King's supremacy had been challenged but there was nothing he could do to gain any redress. When York and Devon received his summons they simply ignored it. Following the display of armed force in the West Country, this refusal to obey a royal command showed how deep was the estrangement between the King and one of the country's most powerful noblemen,

York. So weak had Henry allowed himself to become that his magnates were able to ignore royal authority and act with impunity.

Two months later the existing tensions were exacerbated when Oldhall was forced to take sanctuary in the Royal Chapel of St Martin-le-Grand to escape an indictment of high treason, a move which clearly threatened York's position. (Founded in 1068 by William the Conqueror, this collegiate church reserved the right of sanctuary, the right for an individual to be safe from arrest, which was recognised in English law until the seventeenth century.)

Faced by this development, York realised that he had to take matters into his own hands and could not allow events to overtake him. On 9 January 1452, after what seems to have been a lengthy period of deliberation, he issued a public statement of loyalty to the King in which he claimed that his good name was being traduced by 'enemies, adversaries and evil-willers' who were attempting to turn the King against him. In the same manifesto he asked the King to send three lords to Ludlow so that he could protest his loyalty on the sacrament. It was to no avail. The attempt at appeasement was ignored in London and on 3 February York announced his intention to arraign Somerset and bring him to trial, if necessary by using force, on the charges of losing France and subverting the court by abusing his own position.

To underline the seriousness of his intentions York began mobilising his men and sent out letters to the principal towns in the East Midlands, where many of his estates were situated, asking for support in the way of arms, money and manpower. A move of that kind could not be kept secret for long and so it proved: both Colchester and Oxford were loyal to the King and forwarded York's letters to the court. Henry heeded the advice given to him, notably by his wife and Somerset, and moved swiftly. Having summoned his loyal nobles to 'rebuke and chastise' York, he led his forces to Northampton on 16 February after ordering the closing of the gates of London against the rebels. At the same time, backed by Devon and Lord Cobham, who had supported him in the quarrel with Bonville, York set off to London with his army, gathering men to his cause as he progressed, and arrived at Kingston Bridge only to be refused entry to the capital. The sight of Londoners setting up defences convinced York that he could not take the city by storm and so he set off in a south-easterly direction and established a camp on Dartford Heath.

By now the King had received the intelligence that York had arrived in the London area and, having taken the advice of the principal nobility who had answered his summons for armed support, among them the Duke of Buckingham and the Earls of Salisbury and Warwick, he decided to head back to the capital. On 27 February the Royalist army crossed London and two days later halted at Blackheath, where Cade had arrived with his rebels in 1450.

The two armies were now three miles apart and a clash seemed inevitable. York had drawn up his forces in three battles, with his men in the centre and Devon's and Cobham's on either flank. He also possessed a number of modern artillery pieces and seven ships lay in the Thames to the north to provide him with food, supplies and ammunition. Contemporary reports are unclear about the exact size of the rival forces – some say that each was around twenty thousand – but given the lack of support from the nobility, who had mostly flocked to the King's side, it is probable that York's was smaller. Although some towns in East Anglia had answered his call for assistance and had demonstrated in his favour they had not been able to send many men to swell the Yorkist ranks. That absence of popular support and the failure of the nobility to side with him were blows to York's cause and, with neither side keen to fight, the way was open for a compromise.

On 2 March a royal delegation including the Bishops of Winchester and Ely and the Earls of Salisbury and Warwick arrived in York's camp to broker an agreement which would end the confrontation. York must have known that he was in a weak position. His army was not strong enough to take on the Royalists with any confidence of winning, he realised that his show of force could be construed as treason and he lacked allies, but at the same time he was determined to get something from the negotiations. When the Royalist delegation put it to him that his position was hopeless and that he had no option but to compromise York agreed to renew his loyalty to Henry provided that Somerset was arrested and punished. The deputation returned to the Royalist camp, where York's demands were discussed and accepted. Thinking that he had scored a triumph, York rode to Henry's tent on Blackheath only to find Somerset in his company. The attempt to arrest him had apparently been thwarted by the Queen's intervention and his brazen presence at the King's side showed that he was once more back in royal favour.

A furious row broke out as York reiterated his claims but there was little he could do to redress the situation. Not only was Somerset still at liberty and predominant in the King's camp but, with only forty of his retainers accompanying him on Blackheath, York was virtually a prisoner. This latter point was given added edge when he was forced to return to London with the court, riding ahead as if he were under arrest, and made to swear a solemn oath of allegiance to Henry at the high altar of St Paul's. In this he pledged that he would obey the King's commands and never again raise a body of armed men in any attempt to use violence against the King's person. Having made his vow in front of a huge congregation – another sign of obeisance – he was allowed to return to Ludlow, once more in exile from the court.

Yet again York's influence had waned and his armed intervention had achieved nothing except to alienate him even further from the source of power. The court party retained its supremacy and Somerset's position was strengthened by the promotion of key allies such as John Tiptoft, recently created Earl of Worcester, who was appointed Treasurer, and the Earl of Wiltshire, who became the King's Lieutenant in Ireland in succession to York. Nothing had changed and Henry felt so emboldened by the heady experience of being in the ascendant that he announced that he would emulate his father and take an army to France to attack and defeat the forces of Charles VII.

On 26 January 1452 the first steps were taken to raise the funds and to provide the ships 'for our crossing into our kingdom of France, which, God willing we are disposed and determined to undertake with the greatest diligence and expedition'. However, nothing came of these plans as that summer Henry was required to make a number of progressions through England in order to show the royal presence and also to mete out justice in areas where disaffection and unrest had degenerated into public demonstrations against the authorities. Some of them were violent. Amid rumours that Cade was still alive there were disturbances in Kent in the first week of May and in Shropshire a number of men declared their intention of putting York on the throne. This perambulation was one of the longest of Henry's reign. It took him as far west as Exeter and north to Coventry by way of the

Severn Valley and the Welsh marches but pointedly he did not meet York while passing through Ludlow, preferring to spend the night in the local Carmelite religious house.

That same year the English position in France was on the point of final collapse. Instead of attacking Calais, as might have been expected, the French switched their operations to Gascony, where the English had had a presence for over three hundred years. In May 1451 a French force of seven thousand soldiers had moved on to the offensive to threaten the fortresses on the Gironde Estuary. Bourg was taken, then Bordeaux on 12 June, and everywhere English interests started collapsing. Not only were the French winning battles and regaining lost territory but they had superior weapons, mainly artillery, which they used to good effect. They also had good leaders in the Count of Dunois and Jean Bureau, who acted as master of artillery, and, more importantly, they had the renewed self-confidence of those accustomed to winning. As de Waurin noted, the earlier advantage conferred by the longbow had disappeared, and during the siege of Fronsac in Guyenne the English were overawed by the power and professionalism of the French forces ranged against them:

> In spite of all this, though, after about fifteen days of siege, the English inside [Fronsac] began to see the enormous strength in numbers of noblemen and warriors before them, and realised that they did not even represent half of the king of France's forces, as less than a quarter of them were even in the region.
>
> They also saw the bombards, cannons and other pieces of artillery ranged against them, and the increasing proximity of the trenches and tunnels. Moreover they knew that in every siege begun by the French – there had already been several – the invading army had been too strong for all the forces that the English king then had in Gascony.

Gascony, the region lying between the Pyrenees and the River Garonne, had been in English hands since 1152, when Aquitaine was acquired by Henry II after his marriage to Eleanor of Aquitaine, the former wife of Louis VII of France. To great dismay the whole of the Duchy of Aquitaine fell into French hands at the end of August. Not that Charles VII was made universally welcome. The area had been in English hands for so long that the French were not always greeted as liberators but as invaders and potential oppressors; by the same token the loss was keenly felt in England as Gascony had been a home from home for several generations of Englishmen.

Attempts were made to win back Bordeaux by an army under one of England's best soldiers, the fiery Earl of Shrewsbury, who enjoyed a huge reputation in France for the speed and aggression of his attacks, but his efforts were in vain. (He was also under parole which meant that he was forbidden to take up arms against the French, a huge liability when attempting to lead an army in battle.) Despite entering Bordeaux in October 1452 Shrewsbury's expedition was doomed to failure, largely because of the accuracy and power of the French artillery, the new battlefield force-multiplier, and within a year the duchy was back in French hands.

The last engagement was the successful siege of Castillon in July 1453, when the French master gunner Jean Bureau made good use of his artillery to rout the English forces which had been sent to raise the siege. By withdrawing their cavalry, the French lured the English into a trap: Shrewsbury's forces went into the attack without the support of the English men-at-arms and their assault was halted in its tracks by sustained French artillery fire. Shrewsbury, his son Viscount Lisle and large numbers of English soldiers were killed in the resulting bombardment and the remnant of the force was forced to flee in disarray.

This defeat at Castillon virtually ended the Hundred Years War – Charles VII re-entered Bordeaux in triumph three months later – and for the time being there was to be no more serious fighting between the two sides. To the increasingly ill French king fell the task of bringing Normandy and Gascony under full control, an undertaking that was made more difficult for him by his inability to deal with his son Louis, the Dauphin, who was showing growing signs of impatience to succeed to the throne. The two men had been estranged since 1445, when Louis made an ineffective attempt to seize power and was punished by being sent to south-eastern France, where he entered an ill-advised compact with the Duke of Savoy, whose daughter Charlotte he married in 1452. For all that Charles had triumphed in Aquitaine he was never reconciled to his son.

For Henry's reign, defeat at the hands of superior French forces was another blow. Since the heroic victory at Agincourt the English had become accustomed to the idea that they were the masters in France, capable of beating the French in any battle, and the loss of their kingdom was a humiliating experience. Henry V had believed that a dual monarchy was not only possible but that it could have produced a lasting peace between the two countries. His early death put paid to that assumption but the truth about the loss of France ran deeper than personalities.

For a start, after the humbling defeats earlier in the century Charles VII had rallied France and his forces had become better disciplined than they were at the time of Agincourt. At the same time the quality and numbers of the forces available to the English garrison had deteriorated. Recruitment was a perennial problem and shortages of funds meant that garrisons fell into disrepair, encouraging growing numbers of English soldiers to resort to criminal activities to fund their existence in France. Not only was this the cause of a great deal of local disaffection but the policy reduced whole areas of the country to a state of bankruptcy which was deplored by contemporary chroniclers such as the Norman cleric Thomas Basin, Bishop of Lisieux:

> Most of the fields for long remained, over the years, not only uncultivated but without men enough to till them, except for a few odd pieces of land where it was impossible to extend the little that could be cultivated away from the cities, towns and castles owing to the frequent forays of the robbers.

This was no way to run a colonial possession and the misery was compounded when Parliament refused to vote any subsidies for those who had lost their livings in Normandy as a result of the surrender of England's possessions in France. The only piece of good news for the embattled nation was the pregnancy of the Queen, which was announced in the early summer of 1453, well before the revelation of the English setbacks in Gascony.

Chapter Eleven

YORK'S PROTECTORATE: THE FIRST BATTLE OF ST ALBANS

In the spring of 1453 the news of the Queen's pregnancy proved to be a great boost to Henry VI's fortunes. After seven years of marriage and the recent bout of internal turbulence involving York and the court party there was now a good chance that the birth of an heir would settle Henry's reign by solving the issue of the royal succession and for the first time in many years there was a renewed sense of national self-confidence. In Gascony Shrewsbury's forces had not yet been decisively defeated at Castillon and there were early optimistic indications that he would recapture the region around Bordeaux. In Parliament York's supporters, notably Speaker Oldhall, had been ousted from the body, and when it reassembled at Reading on 6 March it was more amenable to Henry than it had ever been. Additional funds were found for the court and money was made available to allow him to raise forces for his personal protection should they ever be required in the future.

There was also a subtle strengthening of Henry's personal allegiances. Early in the previous year his half-brothers, Edmund and Jasper Tudor, became members of the royal entourage and were ennobled as the Earl of Richmond and the Earl of Pembroke. As these titles had once belonged to Henry's uncles Bedford and Gloucester it was a clear sign of royal favour. To cement the relationship the brothers were given custody of Lady Margaret Beaufort, daughter of the old Duke of Somerset (the present duke, Edmund, was her brother) and previously the intended bride of Suffolk's son John de la Pole. (The intention was that Lady Margaret should now marry

Richmond and the wedding duly took place in October 1455, when she was still only twelve years of age, two years under the normal legal age for sexual intercourse. Even so, the marriage was rapidly consummated and from this union sprang the Tudor dynasty when she gave birth to her only child, Henry, fifteen months later. It was a terrible experience as she was still immature and she never conceived again. By then Henry Tudor's father, Edmund, had died of plague and the boy was brought up under the protection of the Herbert family and later his uncle Jasper Tudor. His mother seems to have had little to do with his upbringing.)

But the real prize for Henry VI was the subjugation of York, who had been condemned to the political wilderness. His armed intervention had been crushed, he had been personally humiliated and his power and authority had been diminished. As a result England was at peace and, just as importantly, Henry had demonstrated that he possessed the will to rule as a king, an important consideration given his previous vacillations. At the same time the court party was still supreme, with Somerset's position not only strengthened but seemingly impregnable. York's standing had also been weakened by the punishment of many of his lesser supporters during Henry's perambulation of England in the previous late summer and autumn.

One of the judicial sessions had been held in Ludlow, a Yorkist stronghold. According to one contemporary account, the accused, all Yorkist supporters, were ordered to appear before the King naked and with nooses tied loosely around their necks, but given Henry's well-known prudish tendencies such public nudity seems an unlikely embellishment. Nonetheless, these judicial commissions of oyer and terminer (writs for empowering the King's judges to hear cases of treason and other similar felonies) did much to stamp Henry's authority on England and reinforce his authority in the aftermath of York's attempt to intervene and influence events. The perambulations were an important element in Henry's reign. Not only did they allow the King to be seen but as the royal retinue made its way around the country dispensing justice and settling local disputes the journeying through the kingdom became an important symbol of regal authority.

Henry's perambulation in 1453 began in Greenwich in the first weeks of January and his journey took him to Windsor, Eltham,

Barking, Norwich, Thetford, Sudbury, Berkhamsted, High Wycombe and Reading. On his return to Greenwich in July he found that he had to deal with an outbreak of dissension between Warwick and Somerset, who had become involved in a dispute over the possession of matrimonial lands in south Wales. Warwick's deceased father-in-law had married for the last time Isabel Despenser, widow of Richard Beauchamp, Earl of Worcester, and on her death her lands had been divided between the Warwick and Worcester families. For reasons which are vague but proved disastrous for his reign Henry had put the Despenser lands in the custody of Somerset. As they had been held by Warwick since 1450 this was bound to cause offence and, not unnaturally, he took steps to hold on to his possessions. A strong garrison was placed in Cardiff as Warwick built up an army to protect his interests and to use force if Somerset decided to move against him. Once again rival magnates were taking the law into their own hands, and open warfare between the two factions seemed inevitable.

At that stage Henry should have recognised the danger and would have shown some common sense if he had taken steps to defuse Warwick's anger, but instead he simply fuelled the controversy. When the council met at Sheen at the end of July it ordered Warwick to comply with the King's wishes by handing over his Welsh possessions to Somerset. To compound the sense of injustice, as it seemed to Warwick, Somerset had attended the council meeting while he had not been there to present his case.

An armed struggle now seemed inevitable and the tension was increased by news from the north of an outbreak of rivalries between the Nevilles and the Percys, two of England's most powerful families. Both held lands along the border with Scotland and both had made advantageous marriages which had strengthened their own positions. Ralph Neville, the 1st Earl of Westmorland, had taken as his second wife Joan Beaufort, a daughter of John of Gaunt, and their son Richard had become Earl of Salisbury on marrying Alice Montacute, the heiress of the earldom of Salisbury (the holder of the title, Thomas Montacute, having been killed in France in 1428). Their son, also called Richard, married Anne Beauchamp, daughter of Henry VI's former tutor, and that matrimonial alliance gave him his father-in-law's title of Earl of Warwick. History would remember him as 'Warwick the Kingmaker'. The fact that his father's sister Cecily was married to York should have made him a natural Yorkist supporter but during the recent confrontation with the Crown young Warwick had remained neutral. Henry's foolhardy behaviour, especially his strong attachment to Somerset, was to change all that.

Thomas Percy, Lord Egremont and brother of the Earl of Northumberland, had a long-standing disagreement with Sir John Neville, son of the Earl of Salisbury, over land, and this had rumbled on throughout the year despite Henry's summonses to both men to appear before the council to answer for their breaches of the King's peace. In the middle of July 1453 Henry appointed a commission of oyer and terminer to settle the issue but before it started work he was forced to deal with the confrontation between Warwick and Somerset in south Wales, which at the time appeared to be much more inflammatory.

At the end of the month Henry left London for Dorset and on the way stopped at the old royal hunting lodge at Clarendon, to the east of Salisbury. There he suffered a complete mental collapse which left him, according to Benet, 'so lacking in understanding and memory and so incapable that he was neither able to walk upon his feet nor to lift up his head, nor well to move himself from the place where he was seated'. The reason for the breakdown is difficult to ascertain. There are no eyewitness accounts of the King's condition at the moment when he lost his reason but it was obvious that the onset of this psychotic illness was disastrous for Henry. What we do know is that he lapsed into a catatonic state that lasted for eighteen months, during which he was insensible to what was happening to him. To all intents and purposes he was lost to the world, suffering from a condition which John Whethamstede, Abbot of St Albans, characterised as leaving him completely impotent: 'a disease and disorder of such a sort overcame the King that he lost his wits and memory for a time, and nearly all his body was so uncoordinated and out of control that he could neither walk nor hold his head up, nor easily move from where he sat'.

The reasons for this sudden mental collapse have been much discussed but from this distance in time it is almost impossible to provide a reasonable diagnosis. It could have been genetic. His mother was a Valois and, as we have seen, her father, Charles VI of France, suffered from periodic fits of mental instability, all of which were recorded and provide hard evidence of the manias which affected him during his lifetime. But there were differences. During Henry's madness he was quiescent and withdrew from normal life; unable to communicate with those around him, he had to be looked after by his retainers and was almost childlike in his behaviour. By contrast his maternal grandfather was violent and manic during his periods of ill health; he would become extremely violent, foaming at the mouth and behaving more like a beast than a man. Henry was spared that kind of manic behaviour and although one account says that he was 'smitten with a frenzy' it adds that he simply lost his 'wit and reason'.

Contemporaneous events could also have provided the tipping point which produced this mental collapse. While Henry was at Clarendon he received the news of the disastrous defeat at Castillon and this confirmation of the final loss of his French possessions could have unmanned him and led to his breakdown. This was certainly the opinion of John Paston, who wrote that the King received a 'sudden and thoughtless fright', and it could well be that the shock was occasioned by the news from France. Never a mentally robust person and one who constantly changed his mind to the detriment of good governance, Henry was weak-willed and indecisive. Coming on top of York's 'rebellion' and the trouble caused by his quarrelsome magnates, the defeat of his armies in France could have been the final straw.

The medical treatment meted out to the King cannot have helped and perhaps even made matters worse. He was put under the general care of John Arundel, the Warden of the Hospital of St Mary of Bethlehem, who had studied mental illness and administered a variety of remedies, including laxatives, gargles, potions, poultices, bleedings and cauterisation to expel 'corrupt humours' from his body. None of these no doubt well-intentioned treatments worked, and equally fruitless was recourse to exorcism to remove evil spirits. Henry had taken leave of his senses and there was no cure, a situation which left his supporters to do the best they could to paper over his condition and find some means of running England while the King was, so to speak, absent without leave.

For the first few months of his collapse the governance of England was in the hands of the council, but they could only rule in Henry's name and lacked the ultimate authority of kingship. There was also the problem of the succession. Until Margaret gave birth there was no single accepted heir and there were lingering fears that the rivalry between York and Somerset could yet ignite a civil war. No one would have forgotten the fact that Charles VI's mental collapses had ushered in a period of internecine fighting between the factions at the French court and it was only too possible that there could be a similar outcome in England. Even when Margaret did give birth, to a boy, on 13 October 1453, the signs were still ominous. He was named Edward after his father's favourite saint, Edward the Confessor, and the news of his birth was greeted with great rejoicing throughout the land except in the one place where it mattered most: the royal palace at Windsor. As the *Paston Letters* make clear, while the rest of the country celebrated Prince Edward's birth Henry remained in a daze, unaware that a son had been born to him and betraying none of the emotions normally expected of a new father:

> At the Prince's coming to Windsor, the Duke of Buckingham took him in his arms and presented him to the King in goodly wise, beseeching the King to bless him; and the King gave no manner answer. Nevertheless the Duke abode still with the Prince by the King; and when he could no manner answer have, the Queen came in, and took the Prince in her arms and presented him in like form as the Duke had done, desiring that he should bless it; but all their labour was in vain, for they departed thence without any answer or countenance, saving only that he looked on the Prince and cast his eyes down again without any more.

There was more than the cementing of family relationships to consider in the ceremony of presenting the Prince to his father: until Henry formally acknowledged Edward as his son – a necessity before legislation could be passed to confirm the succession – the council could neither determine the succession nor take any steps to confirm the legality of the boy's position. As a result the country remained in a dangerous state of flux. The birth of Prince Edward and the King's incapacity affected both York and Somerset. Without Henry's protection the latter was now in a vulnerable position at court, while the birth of a male heir had dented the former's claims to the throne. At the Prince's christening, which followed later in the month in

Westminster Abbey, Somerset was named as a sponsor but that did little to strengthen his position as the honour sparked a malicious rumour that Edward was not Henry's son at all but the issue of an adulterous relationship between Somerset and the Queen. No one believed the gossip but it was followed by equally scandalous stories that Prince Edward was a changeling who had been smuggled into the palace so that everyone would believe that Margaret had given birth to an heir. As for the King, if he had lost his mind, what could he possibly know about it and what could he have done to prevent it?

Edward's birth and christening brought into sharp focus the need for the country to have a sound form of governance, both to protect the body politic and to end the uncertainty caused by the King's mental breakdown. Unrest was still being fomented in the north by the Nevilles and the Percys, who were unwilling to end their feud and happily ignored summonses from the council ordering them to bring their supporters to heel and settle their differences. Instead the two families continued to take the law into their own hands and by the middle of August, during the King's mental breakdown, their rivalries had degenerated into violence when a force of Percys, led by Lord Egremont, ambushed a party of Nevilles as they made their way from a family wedding back to their home at Sheriff Hutton near York. The brawl took place on Heworth Moor and quickly sprawled over the nearby countryside. No one was killed but the fact that over seven hundred Percy retainers and assorted thugs could behave in this way was a clear sign that the royal writ did not run as far as Yorkshire and the kingdom was in danger of spiralling out of control.

In an attempt to retain order the council managed to maintain a semblance of normality in its regular business meeting but there were too many rumours about the King's madness to keep up the pretence for ever. To begin with the council attempted to sideline York from its deliberations but by the beginning of November 1453 he was in London with a large retinue to protect his interests. From the outset he showed that he had no intention of making concessions or of co-operating with Somerset. His old crony and close ally Norfolk reasserted the familiar claim that Somerset was guilty of losing the territories in France and condemned him for his vainglory in presuming 'over-great authority in this realm'. It had the desired effect and on 23 November Somerset was arrested and interred in the Tower of London.

This was a direct challenge to Margaret's authority and she responded in a style that typified her robust attitude to the need to hold on to power. Towards the end of January 1454 she made a spirited attempt to affirm her son's rights and her own claim to be his regent. Her argument consisted of five articles, four of which were recorded by John Paston for posterity:

> The first is that she desireth to have the whole rule of this land; the second is that she may make the Chancellor, the Treasurer, the Privy Seal and all other officers of this land; the third is that she may give all the bishoprics of this land and all other benefices belonging to the king's gift; the fourth is that she may have sufficient live-lode [resources] assigned her for the King, the prince and herself.

It was a bold attempt to reassert herself and her position at court but the Queen had gone too far. By attempting to take full control of all state appointments and 'to have the whole rule of this land', she had overreached herself. All along she had counted on gaining the support of those magnates who still entertained suspicions about York's real motives but her arrogant bid to become regent in her husband's place caused great offence.

After Margaret's intervention power began to slip inexorably back towards the Yorkist faction and on 13 February the council agreed to nominate York as the King's Lieutenant to enable a new Parliament to be called, and to permit him to preside over it. All the while tensions were mounting in London as the various magnates sought to protect their positions by bringing in large numbers of armed retainers amid persistent rumours that Somerset was using a network of spies to attempt to influence matters and take control of the country. Once again civil war seemed inevitable. One of the largest of the private armies was under the command of Warwick, now firmly in the Yorkist camp as a result of the King's decision to lend his support to Somerset in the recent territorial dispute.

On 22 March John Kemp, the Chancellor and Archbishop of Canterbury, suddenly died and his passing meant that Henry's condition could no longer be kept secret as the Archbishop's replacement in the See of Canterbury could only be authorised by the

King. Faced by the very real danger that the Queen or Somerset, or more likely the two of them working in tandem, might seize power, the council decided to act. Once again its members made a formal visit to Henry to ascertain his mental state and, in the words of Benet's *Chronicle*, they 'perceived that if the king did not recover, England would soon be ruined under the government of the Duke of Somerset, so the noblemen of the kingdom sent for the Duke of York'. Five days after Kemp's death York was invested as the Protector and Defender of the Realm, thereby resurrecting an office similar to the one that had been occupied by Henry's uncle Gloucester during the King's minority.

As things stood York could have exploited the unexpected chance that had been presented to him to rescue himself from political oblivion. Before Henry's collapse he had been living in virtual exile yet he now occupied the most powerful position in the country, while his great rival Somerset was languishing in custody. Although the remaining members of the council were a powerful counterweight York was still in a position in which he could exert his authority over them by getting his own people into key appointments. Salisbury, his brother-in-law, was appointed Chancellor, another close relation, Thomas Bourchier (his sister's brother-in-law), became Archbishop of Canterbury and he himself took over the captaincy of Calais in place of the disgraced Somerset. (Much good it did him: Somerset's lieutenants refused to recognise his authority.) At the same time he ordered Queen Margaret to be removed to Windsor, where she was held in conditions which amounted to open arrest.

However, York confounded the fears of his enemies by emerging as a fair and conscientious protector who took his duties seriously and behaved with remarkable moderation. During the eighteen months of his rule his most notable achievement was to reduce expenditure at court and to cut back the size of the royal household. He also managed to resolve the dispute in the north of England with a show of force in the summer of 1454 but the decisive moment came when Egremont, now in alliance with the ambitious and unstable Duke of Exeter, fell into the hands of Sir Thomas Neville, Salisbury's younger son, after a skirmish between the two factions at Stamford Bridge near York in November. Arraigned for disturbing the peace, Egremont and

Exeter were fined heavily and consigned to house arrest in their respective residences. More of an armed affray than a pitched battle – fewer than two hundred men were involved on both sides – the confrontation at Stamford Bridge was all too typical of the inter-family squabbling of the period, being short, brutish and ill-tempered. To add to the complications Exeter had his own royal pretensions, being the grandson of Elizabeth of Lancaster, daughter of John of Gaunt and sister of Henry IV.

It could be said that York had little option but to rule within the conditions of the protectorate. Despite his alliance with Warwick and Salisbury many of the great nobles still distrusted him – they refused to back his demand to try Somerset for treason – and he faced a hostile Parliament. The terms of his office were also ambiguous: he was to hold it until Edward came of age, which would have given him at least fourteen years as Protector, and he was still subordinate to the person of King Henry. Given time York might have resolved those hindrances and taken advantage of his sudden and unexpected elevation, but before he could strengthen his position or benefit from it Henry recovered his senses. The amazing transformation took place on Christmas Day 1454, when the King was suddenly restored as if he were a man waking from a long and deep sleep. It soon became apparent that he had no inkling of what had happened to him during his long illness and could recall absolutely nothing about the events of the past months.

Prayers were said in St George's Chapel for the King's complete recovery but on 28 December, according to the Paston correspondence (Edmund Clere to John Paston), there came further disturbing evidence that Henry had been so severely incapacitated during his illness that he had no idea that he had a son:

Blessed be God, the king is well amended and hath been since Christmas Day; and on St John's Day commanded his almoner to ride to Canterbury with his offering, and commanded the secretary to offer at St Edward's [shrine in Westminster Abbey]. And on the Monday afternoon the Queen came to him, and brought my Lord Prince [Edward] with her. And then he asked what the Prince's name was, and the Queen told him Edward; and then he held up his hands and thanked God thereof. And he said he never knew till

that time, nor wist [knew] not where he had be whilst he hath been
sick till now. And he asked who was the godfathers, and the Queen
told him and he was well apayed [content]. And she told him that
the Cardinal [John Kemp] was dead, and he said he knew never
thereof till that time; and he said one of the wisest lords in this land
was dead.

By contrast with the first occasion, when Henry had been
presented with his son and failed to recognise him, this time his
recovery allowed him to acknowledge Prince Edward as his own and
thereby ensure the succession. (Later and mischievously, he was
reported to have concluded that Edward must have been 'the son of
the Holy Spirit' and the story gave fresh life to the rumours that the
King could not possibly have been the father and instead the child
must have been Somerset's progeny.) Inevitably, given the duration
of the King's illness, the recovery was not complete or lasting and,
according to contemporary evidence, there were numerous
occasions in the years to come when it was suggested that Henry was
not the man he had been before his mental collapse. Always
reclusive, he became increasingly content with his own company and
there are several contemporary references about his tendency to
indulge in long periods of sleep, when he was as good as dead to the
world.

However, the King had wit enough to preserve his own position.
On 30 December York presided over his last meeting of the council,
which effectively dissolved his authority, and within a month he faced
once more the political oblivion which he had occupied before the
King's madness. Henry moved swiftly to undo many of the decisions
taken during the protectorate. The Duke of Exeter was removed from
house arrest, Salisbury was dismissed as Chancellor and replaced by
Archbishop Bourchier, John Tiptoft, Earl of Worcester, was replaced
as Treasurer by the Earl of Wiltshire and, most tellingly of all,
Somerset was freed from the Tower and restored to his position as
Captain of Calais and Constable of England.

All these sudden changes told York everything he needed to know
about where the King's sympathies lay and about his own position.
Once again he had been sidelined and once again Somerset and his
allies were in the ascendant. After the council meeting in March York

left London and returned to his estates, as did his allies Salisbury and
Warwick. Within weeks of their departure, the chronicler Benet
reported, 'Somerset was plotting the destruction of York. He offered
advice to the King, saying that the Duke of York wished to depose the
King and rule England himself – which was manifestly false.'

The stage was now set for confrontation and once again Henry
bungled the situation by producing fresh provocations. Having
already humiliated York by reversing decisions taken during the
protectorate, he decided to act against him once and for all. On 21
April 1455 a meeting of the council was summoned to take place in
Leicester, an East Midlands town which sat in the Lancastrian
heartlands. Its main purpose was to discuss the safety of the King's
person but, as neither York nor Salisbury had been invited to the
meeting and had been ordered to disband their retinues on pain of
being arraigned as traitors, they took it to mean that their own
positions were under threat. Sensing a trap of the kind that had been
laid for Gloucester eight years earlier, York, Salisbury and Warwick
started making their own military preparations by raising an armed
force which would eventually number three thousand men. By now
York realised that he was a marked man and had to protect himself
against Somerset, who still enjoyed the powerful support of the
Queen. York's allies were also under renewed threat.

The release of Exeter, a key Percy confederate, convinced Warwick
that he had to take action to preserve the Nevilles' fortunes and
likewise Salisbury's abrupt dismissal was as clear an indication as any
that he had no future under Lancastrian rule. With both sides feeling
threatened – this time Henry seems to have believed the Queen's
warnings that York coveted the throne – civil war between the House
of Lancaster and the House of York suddenly became unavoidable.
On the one hand stood Richard of York and his allies Salisbury and
Warwick; on the other were the King and his party, composed of the
Dukes of Somerset and Buckingham, the Earls of Northumberland,
Wiltshire and Devon and Lords Clifford and Dudley, two prominent
soldiers, who had been recruited by the Queen to join the Lancastrian
cause.

Under the military conventions of the day there was still time to
negotiate before resorting to a war which would involve Englishmen
fighting against Englishmen, cousin against cousin, and in one case

father-in-law (Salisbury) against former son-in-law (Worcester). The Yorkists took full advantage of the custom by sending a letter in reply to the King's demands, protesting their loyalty, complaining about their omission from the council and demanding the extirpation of the traitors who surrounded the King. But time was running out. By the time the missive reached Henry he had left London with his supporters and their armed retinues, numbering some two thousand men, but at that stage he seems to have believed that York would hold to his solemn undertaking never again to take up arms against him. It was not until he received the letter from York that Henry realised the full implications of what was happening and took steps to increase the size of the forces available to him.

The King's retinue had left London for Leicester on 21 May, stopping for the night at Watford, but they were destined to get no further than St Albans. At the same time York halted at Ware, fifteen miles to the north. Once again there were last-minute attempts to reach a compromise. York sent his confessor, William Willeflete, to the King's camp at Watford bearing a second letter, in which he reaffirmed his loyalty and demanded the arrest of Somerset. A contemporary record written five days later and contained in the archives at Dijon makes it perfectly clear that neither side was prepared to yield any ground and that both felt that they were in the right:

> These [Yorkists], when they knew of the king's coming, immediately approached him and also the 22nd day of the said month very early the king sent a herald to the Duke of York to know the cause for which he had come there with so many men and that it seemed to the king something quite new that he, the duke, should be rising against him, the king. The reply made was that he was not coming against him thus, was always ready to do him obedience but he well intended in one way or another to have the traitors who were about him so that they should be punished, and that in case he could not have them with good will and fair consent, he intended in any case to have them by force. The reply that was made from the king's side to the said Duke of York was that he [Henry] was unaware that there were any traitors about him were it not for the Duke of York himself who had risen against his crown.

The failure to find any common ground made violence inevitable and the small abbey town of St Albans was destined to be the scene of the first battle of the conflict known to history as the Wars of the Roses. At dawn on the morning of 22 May both sides were in full battle order, the Yorkists in the fields to the east of St Albans, the Royalist Lancastrian forces in the town itself, having taken up position along St Peter's Street and Holywell Hill. The forces available to both sides were small. The King had between two and three thousand men, most of them untrained billmen carrying a billhook as their main weapon, but also a small royal guard of men-at-arms and archers. York had a slight advantage in numbers and his men-at-arms and archers were better trained. Both sides contained retinues loyal to the principal magnates who were mounted and well armed. In a last-minute change of plan Somerset was replaced by Buckingham as the field commander of the King's army and the vanguard was under the direction of Lord Clifford, a veteran of the recent fighting in France and a powerful northern landowner used to dealing with the Scots. Barriers had been set up around the unwalled town but these were no obstacles for the heavily armed and armoured Yorkist forces, which had been drawn up in three battles, under the command of York, Salisbury and Warwick.

Fighting commenced at around ten o'clock in the morning and lasted little more than an hour. Unusually for a battle of this period the main struggle took place in the town itself and involved some close-quarter hacking and stabbing in the confined streets which was bloody and intensive. The first attack was made along the ground occupied by the present-day Hatfield Road and Victoria Street but this assault was held off by the King's forces and it took the intervention of Warwick with his archers to break Royalist resolve.

Henry had taken up his own position in the marketplace, wearing full armour and standing below the royal standard, and he presented an easy target to the archers, who had been instructed by Warwick to concentrate on those guarding the King. The Abbot of St Albans was a horrified spectator and his chronicle describes the streets of the town being 'full of dead corpses' as Warwick's men fought their way towards the Royalist positions. As the lines began to thin under the arrow shower, heavily armoured knights and men-at-arms broke into St Peter's Square to complete the bloody execution. They knew what had to be done as they cut and slashed their way through the barricades: common foot soldiers were generally spared but those of any rank could expect no mercy.

One of the first to fall was Somerset, overwhelmed and cut down near the Castle Inn. Too late he saw the sign and remembered that a soothsayer had warned him that a castle would be the cause of his doom. It is possible that his killer was Warwick himself. Northumberland, too, was hacked down in the street, as was Clifford, and, all told, around a hundred men, mostly Royalists, died with them. Henry received an arrow wound in the neck and, bleeding profusely, was persuaded to take refuge in a nearby tanner's house. There he was eventually bearded by the Yorkist leaders, who knelt before him and pledged their allegiance to him. 'And when the king perceived this,' recorded Benet, 'he was greatly cheered.' Later he was taken to St Albans Abbey, where the leading commanders and the King spent the night before returning to London.

As a battle St Albans occupies a minor place in British military history but its effects were long-lasting. Great magnates had taken up arms against an anointed king and had created their own armies to impose their will on the country's governance. In so doing they had executed men loyal to the King – Henry was appalled by the news of Somerset's death, regarding it as an illegal act – and the resulting enmity left lasting scars. Northumberland's death deepened the existing divisions between the Nevilles and the Percys and Clifford's son vowed that his father's death would not remain unavenged. In the shocked aftermath of the battle men stood and stared at the havoc they had created in the narrow streets of the small market town, where, the Abbot reported, there were sights which law-abiding people should not have seen: 'here you saw a man with his brains dashed out, here one with a broken arm, another with his throat cut, a fourth with a pierced chest . . .'

For those who had managed to get away from the Yorkists there was escape and flight; to York's credit there was no pursuit but for some there was disgrace. Sir Philip Wentworth, the King's standard-bearer, had, according to Paston, 'cast it down and fled. My Lord Norfolk says he shall be hanged therefore, and so he is worthy.' In fact Wentworth survived to fight another day, only to be executed later in the conflict.

Viewed dispassionately as a military action, St Albans was little more than a street brawl with heavy weapons. Once the Yorkists had broken the Royalist lines and occupied the marketplace, known enemies, some of them great magnates, were singled out and dispatched with brutal ease. Others received debilitating wounds: Buckingham was struck in the neck by an arrow and Somerset's heir, Henry Beaufort, Earl of Dorset, had to be carried away in a cart, unable to walk. As the fighting died down the people of St Albans suffered the pillaging which follows any battle of this kind and the surrounding countryside was likewise subjected to violence by rampaging gangs of Yorkist troops. In this it was not very different from similar military actions of that period but there was a good deal more significance to the battle than the triumph of arms by one side. The fighting in the streets of St Albans was also a bloody coup.

As a result of the Yorkist intervention the court party had been crushed, albeit temporarily, and its principal figurehead, Somerset, had been killed. Of course, this was exactly what York wanted: his bitter rival had been permanently removed from the scene. Furthermore, the King was now under the control of the Yorkist faction and the following day he was escorted back to London. With a symbolism that could not have been misunderstood by anyone watching, Henry rode between York and Salisbury while Warwick rode ahead carrying the sword of state. The mystique of kingship remained intact but it was self-evident that the King was firmly in the hands of those who had defeated him.

On 25 May, the celebration of the Feast of Pentecost, Henry appeared in St Paul's wearing his crown as a sign to his people that he remained their anointed king, but the pageantry was all for show. The reality was rather different. Immediately after winning control the Yorkists started claiming the main offices of state. York became Constable of England, Warwick was appointed Captain of Calais and Henry Bourchier, the Chancellor's brother, was appointed Treasurer in place of Wiltshire, who had been forced into hiding, having fled the field dressed as a monk, or as Gregory unkindly put it, he had 'fought mainly with his heels for he was frightened of losing his beauty'.

At the same time Parliament was summoned and Henry was moved out of the London area to Hertford Castle, where he took up residence with the Queen. When Parliament opened on 9 July it was packed with Yorkist supporters and its business was dominated by the need to restore normality in the wake of the fighting at St Albans. Oaths of allegiance to the King were renewed and legislation was introduced to justify the actions taken by the Yorkists, who claimed that they had been forced to intervene in order to redress the 'great tyranny and injustice to the people'. Somerset and two minor associates were blamed for the disorder and pardons were issued for everyone else, as if St Albans had been an aberration and not a turning point. At the same time Gloucester's reputation was rehabilitated and an act was passed revoking most of the grants made by the King to his favourites during the first part of his reign.

York was now in full control of the governance of England and his paramount position was confirmed in November when a further meeting of Parliament appointed him once more Protector and Defender of the Realm. As the Dijon chronicle concluded its musings, 'the said Duke of York will now be without contradiction the first after the King and will have the government of all. God give him the grace to carry out his tasks well and have pity on the souls of sinners. Amen.'

The conditions of York's office were similar to those he had accepted at the end of 1453 and the reasons for the appointment were the same. His new standing was also timely. Henry had succumbed once more to a mental breakdown – probably as a result of his wound and the trauma of battle – and was deemed to be incapable of ruling his country. The King's illness gave York the upper hand but, as he had done during the first protectorate, he was careful to rule through the council and was conscious of the limitations of his position. He was right to be so circumspect. For all that he enjoyed the support of Salisbury and Warwick his power base was narrow and he was still viewed with misgiving by his fellow magnates, who could not rid themselves of the suspicion that he had ambitions to win the Crown. York also had made many enemies, not least the sons of the men who had been slaughtered at St Albans.

Then there was the Queen. Margaret of Anjou had been horrified by the death of Somerset and although exiled from London she set about strengthening the court party, which was still in existence. Henry Beaufort, Somerset's son and the new duke, pledged his allegiance to the Queen, as did his brother Edmund and Henry Percy, the new Earl of Northumberland. Other prominent supporters included the Tudor Earl of Pembroke, the Earl of Wiltshire, and Clifford's son, who gained the nickname 'Black-faced Clifford' on account of his undisguised desire to avenge his father's death. The enmity seems also to have been personal: the Queen now regarded York as a threat not just to her husband but to the future well-being of her two-year-old son, Prince Edward. Although an uneasy peace had returned to the realm there was to be no easy dissipation of the underlying tensions which had plunged England into a crisis that challenged Henry's capacity to rule.

All over England there was a sense of foreboding which was compounded by the fact that violence had broken out and that the growing disorders presaged worse times ahead. The apprehension was captured in an address to the King written by John Hardyng, the author of a contemporary verse chronicle written between 1440 and 1457 and later revised to incorporate a slant towards the House of York:

> In your realm there are no justices of the peace that dare take the responsibility to suppress the quarrellers. Such is the extent of the sickness that has taken hold that they will not recognise the rioting or the fighting so common now throughout your people.
>
> This I dread fearfully, that from these riots shall more mischief arise, and from the sores unhealed a scab will form, so large that nothing may restrain its growth. Wherefore, good lord, if you will give me leave, I would say this to your excellency: withstand misrule and violence.

Hardyng's imagery is instructive and neatly sums up the mood of apprehension which had gripped the country: the English body politic was ailing and a scab was growing that urgently needed to heal to prevent the country going into terminal decline.

Chapter Twelve

A GREAT AND STRONG-LABOURED WOMAN

Once again, within a few months of York's second protectorate, Henry VI confounded everyone by regaining his sanity and was sufficiently recovered to be able to return to the throne and reassert his authority. On 25 February 1456 he appeared in Parliament and, according to Benet, 'in front of the King the Duke [of York] resigned his office and left Parliament before the session was over'. In fact York seems to have been aware of the development and fully expected to be dismissed: two weeks earlier he had arrived back in London with Warwick, each man accompanied by a large armed retinue in a show of force designed to protect and reinforce their positions. It was a sensible precaution; otherwise, as John Paston noted at the time, the King might have ordered their arrest.

This time, though, Henry was minded to keep York on friendly terms; he remained on the council and was confirmed in the lieutenancy of Ireland while Warwick was permitted to retain the captaincy of Calais. This latter appointment had the double advantage of keeping Warwick happy and making sure that he remained out of the country. Instead of appointing a lieutenant to deputise for him, as was the usual custom, Warwick decided to take up residence in Calais, although it was not until April that he was able to come to an agreement with the local staple merchants about the payment of wages owed to the garrison. (The Company of the Staple, or Staplers, had been established in 1345 to regulate and manage the lucrative wool trade and effectively ruled Calais.)

At the same time an opportunity arose to get York out of London when King James II of Scotland broke a previous truce by sending raiding parties into the north of England. Emboldened by the new Burgundian alliance which had come about through James II's marriage to Mary, daughter of the Burgundian Duke of Gueldres, in 1449, the Scots had used the connection to re-equip their army with new-fangled siege artillery and muskets. Although these were still relatively primitive and liable to cause more trouble to those firing them than to their intended targets, the possession of great guns gave an advantage and James had already made use of them the previous year to cow his old enemies the Douglas family into submission. After the razing of key strongholds at Abercorn in Fife and Threave in Kirkcudbrightshire by the royal artillery the young Earl of Douglas (James Douglas, the 9th Earl) had fled south into England to seek shelter with York. (He had good reason to fear the Scottish king as James II had stabbed his father to death in 1452.) When requests for his return were ignored James led an army into Northumberland and to compound the insult he claimed that York was the rightful King of England and would do well to assert his rights. At first it was thought that Henry might lead an army north to deal with the threat but sending York instead was too good an opportunity to miss as it removed him from London and kept him out of further mischief.

As it turned out, York's arrival in Durham persuaded the Scots to retire and for the time being this put an end to the danger of invasion from the north. Four years later the Scottish king's enthusiasm for artillery was to be his undoing. Thinking to lay siege to Roxburgh Castle and wrest it from English hands, James led an army complete with 'cartis of war' to surround the castle and to test its walls with his new weapons. When the siege began James supervised the positioning and laying of each of the siege guns and when Mary of Gueldres arrived on 3 August 1460 he ordered a cannonade to be fired. Unfortunately one of the weapons exploded and a piece of iron smashed into the King's thigh, killing him. Undaunted, his widow ordered the siege to continue and the castle was pounded into submission.

At the time of Henry VI's return to sanity the English king made it clear that he wanted York to play a leading role on the council. From a purely pragmatic point of view this made sense. The King's capacity to govern was still in question – the mental instability could return at any time – and despite York's earlier violent behaviour in raising a rebellion he had shown a sure touch while acting as Protector. However, there was now a new and much more potent force at court in the shape of Margaret of Anjou, who emerged after Somerset's removal as the main focus of the opposition to York.

There had not always been such bitter enmity between them. Earlier the Queen had given lavish presents to York and his wife, Cecily, and they had remained on reasonable terms, in spite of the quarrel with her favourite, Somerset. The birth of the Prince of Wales changed all that and she came to regard York not just as a menace to herself and her husband but as a serious threat to her son's succession. As Benet put it, the King might have received York and Warwick graciously but the Queen 'loathed them both'. Her fears were exacerbated by York's use of force against the Crown, first at Blackheath and then, more seriously, at St Albans. Here was a man who had resorted to violence to get his way and might do so again. It had also not escaped her notice that during York's two protectorates he had attempted to limit the size of her household and reduce her finances. As Margaret could no longer count on her husband's complete support to maintain the dignity of the Crown, owing to his intermittent madness, she had to secure her position by exerting her own authority within the court. Even after York had been dismissed from his protectorate Margaret continued to regard him as an implacable enemy and in the summer of 1456 she started taking steps to ensure the safety of herself, her husband and her infant son.

In August she removed the family to her dower castle at Tutbury in Staffordshire and established the court not far away at Coventry and Kenilworth, taking with her a large number of artillery pieces from the Tower. The move from the capital was more than symbolic. From the outset Margaret had not been popular in London – she shared with Suffolk the blame for the loss of Anjou and Maine and the collapse of English power in France – and she came to regard the city as pro-Yorkist. In fact throughout the conflict the capital remained largely aloof from events and the merchant companies within the City resisted the temptation to take sides.

However, the Queen did not feel safe in London and preferred to move the court to the Midlands, where she could feel secure in the

Lancastrian heartlands. Once there she was surrounded by close allies and powerful courtiers: in Staffordshire were the Earl of Shrewsbury and the Duke of Buckingham; to the north, in Lancashire, was the Chamberlain of the Royal Household, Lord Stanley; to the east were Viscount Beauchamp in Leicestershire and Lord Welles, a key Somerset ally in Lincolnshire; and to the south-west in Gloucestershire there was Ralph Butler, Lord Sudeley, a veteran of the French wars who had served the King as both Treasurer and Chamberlain. Wales was held by Pembroke and in the West Country the Earl of Devon transferred his affections once more by allying himself with the Queen's party, joining forces with the Duke of Exeter and the Earl of Wiltshire.

At the beginning of October Margaret's position was strengthened further when the Bourchier brothers, Henry and Thomas, were dismissed as part of a move to distance her new court from Henry's previous councillors. In their place William Wayneflete, Bishop of Winchester, became Chancellor and the Earl of Shrewsbury Treasurer. Both were adherents of Margaret's court party. Small wonder that in the Paston correspondence John Bocking wrote to his master, Sir John Fastolf, that the Queen was 'a great and strong-laboured woman, for she spares no pain to sue her things to an intent and conclusion to her power'. Fastolf, an East Anglian landowner, had served as a soldier under Henry IV and Henry V and had used his time in France to create great personal wealth which he used to good effect, bequeathing funds for the foundation of Magdalen College, Oxford, and establishing his East Anglian estate at Caister Castle in Norfolk. He was later immortalised by Shakespeare as Sir John Falstaff, the depraved and cowardly knight who does his best to debauch Prince Hal, but that was the creation of the playwright's fancy. The real-life Fastolf was very different: a man of learning, a patron of education, a courageous and virtuous soldier who served with great honour and distinction as a young soldier at Agincourt.

It was a curious time for England. The country was not in a state of war but tension was never far below the surface of everyday life. There was occasional trouble in London, with riots taking place in Lombard Street against Italian merchants who were thought to be undermining the wool market in Flanders. The odium was compounded by gossip that the Italians had been given preferential treatment as a result of the patronage of the court party and were favoured by Queen Margaret. There were also persistent rumours that there had been further fighting between the King and his enemies.

In addition to the ever-present invasion threat posed by the Scots there was an outbreak of violence in Wales, where Sir Walter Devereux, a Yorkist ally, crossed the border to harry Hereford in August. Having taken the town and made the mayor prisoner, he tried and hanged a number of innocent men before taking his retinue back into Wales and seizing the castles of Carmarthen and Aberystwyth. Both were nominally possessions of the Duke of York as Constable but at the time were garrisoned by Somerset supporters who had refused to hand them over to their liege lord's sworn enemy. To complicate matters the castles had also been granted by the King to the Earl of Richmond, who suddenly found himself imprisoned by Devereux, shortly before he succumbed to plague. In his defence Devereux insisted that he was acting with parliamentary authority – the return of both castles had been demanded from Somerset earlier in the year – but he overstepped his authority by taking the castles by force. Even if he did not act with the complicity of York he was a known supporter and it was not difficult to believe that the action was part of a wider plot against the King.

Anarchy was overtaking the country and neither Henry nor his queen was capable of doing anything to retrieve the situation. In the *English Chronicle* the anonymous compiler placed the blame for the breakdown firmly in Margaret's hands:

> The queen with such as were of her affinity ruled the realm as her liked, gathering riches innumerable. The offices of the realm, and specially the Earl of Wiltshire, treasurer of England [he succeeded Shrewsbury] for to enrich herself, peled [robbed] the poor people, and disinherited rightful heirs, and did many wrongs. The queen was defamed and dislandered that he that was called Prince, was not her son, but a bastard gotten in avoutry [adultery] wherefore she dreading that he should succeed his father in the Crown of England, allied unto her all the knights and squires of Cheshire for to have their benevolence, and held open household among them; and made her son called the prince give a livery of swans to all the gentlemen of the country, and to many other throughout the land,

trusting through their strength to make her son king; making privy means to some of the lords of England for to stir the king that he should resign the crown to her son: but she could not bring her purpose about.

While the *English Chronicle* was composed with a strong Yorkist slant it shows that there was a pattern to Margaret's methods. Having removed her court from London to Coventry, where she had surrounded herself with Lancastrian supporters, she set about promoting the concept that the Prince of Wales was the rightful focus of Royalist support. Although she had no constitutional right to rule England she was able to work within the framework of royal power and, her husband being incapacitated, she used her son's name and authority to make appointments. Another chronicler, Thomas Gascoigne, was not far wrong when he complained that 'almost all the affairs of the realm were conducted according to the queen's will by fair means or foul'. Of course, it could also be argued that Margaret was simply protecting herself and safeguarding her son's inheritance from the claims of a powerful rival at a time when her husband was incapable of ruling the country and she was the only member of the royal family in a position to redress matters.

More than any other, one episode makes clear Margaret's growing pre-eminence and the sharp decline of her husband's reputation. On the Feast of the Exaltation of the Cross in September 1457 she entered Coventry, where she was greeted by a pageant featuring representations of prophets, patron saints and nine conquerors, one of whom was represented as the Queen herself in the form of St Margaret slaying a dragon.

Of the King there was no mention and the records show that increasingly he played little part in public life, leaving the *English Chronicle* to mourn that 'the realm of England was out of all governance . . . for the king was simple and led by covetous council, and owed more than he was worth'. While Henry had regained his sanity he was a changed man. Always religious-minded and devout, he now spent long hours in prayer and devotion and seemed to need more sleep than other men.

Worse followed in the summer of 1457, when a French fleet commanded by Pierre de Brézé, the Grand Seneschal of Normandy and Poitou, raided the Kent coast and set fire to the port of Sandwich. At the time Margaret had been attempting to enter into a new treaty with Charles VII for military support and had used Brézé, a former admirer, as a go-between. Hardly surprisingly, when this became known there were rumours that either she had instigated the raid or ordered Brézé to carry it out. Neither allegation was true but in the overheated atmosphere there were always those who were ready to believe the slanders. No one thought to place any blame on Warwick, who had been building up his strength in Calais and used his great wealth to create a personal fleet of ten warships which he had used to attack the French in the Channel. Lacking funds from official sources and wanting to recoup his own expenditure, he simply took matters into his own hands and encouraged his captains to engage in what amounted to acts of piracy in the Channel's shipping lanes.

Warwick's exploits endeared him to the merchants of London, who had seen their trade decline during Henry's reign, and inevitably his popularity rubbed off on the Yorkist cause. He was able to move freely between Calais and London and during this period he opened up channels of communication with both the French court and the Duke of Burgundy. Warwick's largesse, a result of his huge personal wealth, also helped – he visited London regularly and was lavish in his entertainment – and as a result he emerged as the acceptable face of the opposition to the King, becoming, in de Waurin's words, 'the prince whom they held in the highest esteem and on whom they placed the greatest faith and reliance'. That popularity came at a price. By the end of 1456 he had been more or less excluded from power and at the council meeting which was held in Coventry in the autumn he and York, alone of the members, were required to swear oaths of allegiance.

In the late summer of 1457 Henry appeared to have entered a short period of relative sanity and returned to London – these revivals were always temporary and never complete – but even then he spent most of the winter in seclusion in the abbeys at Reading, Abingdon and Chertsey. Council meetings were still held but all too often they turned into armed camps, with the Yorkists and the Queen's party bringing with them large retinues of armed men to protect them. In an attempt at reconciliation Henry demanded that York and his supporters endow a chantry (the singing of mass) at St Albans to atone for the deaths during the fighting in the town and that the families of Somerset, Northumberland and Clifford receive financial compensation for their losses at the same battle. However, the gloss was taken off this well-meant action when it became clear that Henry had agreed to it only after young Clifford had arrived in London at the head of a large armed force to demand financial compensation for the loss of his father.

This was followed by a so-called 'love-day', which was held in London on 24 March 1458, the Feast of the Annunciation, and turned into a colourful piece of political theatre. With the King walking ahead, robed and crowned, York followed hand in hand with the Queen and in their wake followed Salisbury and Somerset, while other rivals made a great show of friendship as they made their way to St Paul's. The occasion delighted Henry but it was all a sham. Behind the smiles in London the two parties were gripping their swords and preparing once again for confrontation.

The first flashpoint was provided by Warwick, who used his powerful position at Calais to flout royal authority. Not only did the port's garrison contain one of the largest English armies but Warwick continued to use his warships in piratical raids on foreign fleets. In May 1458 his captains attacked a Castilian fleet before launching an even more audacious assault on ships of the Hanse League as they passed through the Channel. This was in direct violation of a truce agreed two years earlier with this commercial entente which embraced the important north German and Baltic trading ports, and not unnaturally their representatives made a vigorous complaint to Henry about the illegality of Warwick's behaviour.

Largely at the instigation of the Queen, who saw a chance to rid herself of a troublesome opponent, the council summoned Warwick to appear before them to account for his behaviour. Nothing daunted, he crossed the Channel with an armed retinue and marched into London, where his many supporters took to the streets to demonstrate their allegiance. Unfortunately their actions turned violent and there were clashes between Warwick's supporters and forces sent into the capital by the Queen to restore order. There was further trouble in the autumn when Warwick was involved in an accident at Westminster in which a kitchen worker almost stabbed him with a spit. A fight broke out between Warwick's men and the royal guard and although order was quickly restored Warwick contended that the kitchen hand had made an attempt on his life. The Queen insisted otherwise and encouraged the council to take steps to arrest Warwick, who took the line of least resistance and hurriedly beat a retreat to Calais.

By this time neither side was interested in making any attempts at reconciliation and both began planning for an uncertain future. At the end of the year the Queen's party started hoarding arms, including the provision of five hundred pikes and a similar number of lead-coated clubs for the protection of those around the King against 'certain misruled and seditious persons'. Three new cannon were also ordered from the Master of Ordnance, John Judde, who assured the King that they would be able to break down the walls of any castle which dared to oppose him.

This was followed in May 1459 by the removal from the Tower of three thousand bows and sheaves of arrows, and at the same time the court moved back to Kenilworth and Coventry, where a meeting of the council was summoned to take place on 24 June. Fearing for their personal safety, York, Salisbury and Warwick refused to attend and were duly indicted as the Lancastrian magnates prepared their forces at Coventry 'defensibly arrayed'. The Yorkists, too, were making preparations. York, Salisbury and Warwick all had well-armed and experienced retinues but they were scattered around the country and it would take time for them to assemble at Ludlow, where York waited with his sons Edward, Earl of March, and Edmund, Earl of Rutland.

The Calais garrison, which included a force of six hundred experienced soldiers under the command of Sir Andrew Trollope, Master Porter of Calais and 'a very subtle man of war', arrived in Kent and after entering London on 21 September headed north; at the same time Salisbury's forces left Middleham in Yorkshire and marched across the Pennines towards the Yorkist heartlands. The news reached the Queen while she was recruiting in Cheshire and the decision was taken to send a force under the command of Lord Audley, a trusted Lancastrian supporter, to intercept Salisbury while the royal family took shelter in Eccleshall Castle in Staffordshire. It was a sensible move as the Yorkist forces were still fractured and the Lancastrians outnumbered them two to one.

The two forces duly collided on the barren, rolling countryside of

Blore Heath near Market Drayton in Shropshire. Finding his way blocked by the Lancastrian forces when he saw their banners and standards behind the crest of a ridge, Salisbury deployed his forces on rising ground to the east of Hempmill Brook, where his left flank was protected by woods and his right was guarded by a line of supply wagons. It was a good defensive position as Audley's foot soldiers and cavalry would have to contend with the rising ground, which had become sodden and heavy after days of rain, and they would be forced to negotiate the high sides of the strong-flowing Hempmill Brook. As the Yorkist forces got into position there was the customary attempt at negotiation but this ended when Audley refused free passage to Salisbury and the trumpets were sounded for battle.

First into action were Audley's knights and men-at-arms. They attacked across the brook, where they came under heavy fire from Salisbury's archers, who, wrote de Waurin, 'began to shoot so intensely that it was frightful, and so violently that everything in range suffered'. With the Lancastrians unable to make any progress and falling under the sustained fire of Salisbury's battle-hardened archers, many of them veterans from the wars in France, the Yorkist knights and men-at-arms counter-attacked and began slaughtering their floundering opponents. A second Lancastrian assault met the same fate and all was lost when Audley was killed leading a third charge, which, like its predecessors, was beaten back with a huge loss of life.

Realising that the battle was lost, men began fleeing for their lives and were hotly pursued by Salisbury's men, who quickly showed that they were not prepared to give any quarter. Around two thousand Lancastrians died on the battlefield, others while being pursued, and, according to local legend, the waters of Hempmill Brook ran red with blood for three days after the fighting. It was a massive victory but it was not decisive. The bulk of the Royalist army was encamped at Eccleshall, ten miles away, and Salisbury still had to get his forces to Ludlow and safety.

He was also pained by the fact that his two sons, Sir John and Sir Thomas Neville, Warwick's brothers, had been taken prisoner while pursuing the enemy and faced the possibility of instant execution. Realising that he had no option but to press on, Salisbury set out that same night – the battle had lasted the better part of the afternoon – and left some artillery pieces in the care of a friendly Augustinian friar who agreed to make use of them to give the impression that the Yorkist forces were still on Blore Heath. The ruse worked and when the Royalist forces arrived the next morning they found the area empty.

Today the main road from Market Drayton to Newcastle-under-Lyme crosses the site of the battle, which lies on private farmland. A cross, erected in 1765, is supposed to mark the spot where Audley fell and a more recent stone marks the site of the Lancastrian positions. There are other memorials. Legend has it that Queen Margaret watched the battle from the spire of St Mary's Church in nearby Mucklestone, before fleeing when she realised that Audley was being defeated. It is said that she employed a blacksmith, William Skelhorn, to reverse the shoes on her horse to disguise the route of her escape but this seems unlikely as she was probably with the rest of her forces at Eccleshall. Nevertheless, the anvil from the smithy stands in the churchyard at Mucklestone to commemorate what would have been an inspired escape.

Salisbury made good progress and arrived at Ludlow, followed shortly afterwards by Warwick and his men. All told, they had about twenty-five thousand under their command – exact numbers are impossible to compute – but they were vastly outnumbered by the Royalists, who had anything from forty thousand to sixty thousand men available. There were other differences. Whereas the Royalists had the support of a large number of leading magnates, including Buckingham, Northumberland, Shrewsbury, Devon, Wiltshire and Beaumont, the Yorkists numbered only themselves and had failed to attract any substantial aristocratic support. Slowly the Yorkists began to move south towards Worcester, hoping to swing eastwards towards London, but they found their road blocked by the larger Royalist army, drawn up in battle order with the King's standard flying.

This placed York in a quandary, for all along he had insisted that his quarrel was not with Henry but with his evil advisers, yet here was the King himself bearing his royal banner and leading his own army to crush opponents who were now regarded as traitors and rebels. To buy time York led his men back into Worcester, where he took mass in the cathedral and swore oaths of loyalty to the King which were then written on vellum and dispatched to the Royalist camp. Either these never reached Henry or were intercepted by Margaret because the gesture was ignored out of hand. The only response was the offer of a pardon to all the rebel earls bar Salisbury, presumably because he had been responsible for the bloodshed at Blore Heath.

Sensing that his position had been weakened by the strength of the Royalist army opposing him, York decided to pull back towards Ludlow and his own territory, partly to defend it against the forthcoming onslaught but mainly because he had no other realistic tactical option. So began the long retreat through Kidderminster and on through Ledbury and Leominster, with the Royalists in pursuit. On 12 October York decided to make a stand at Ludford Bridge on the River Terne south of Ludlow. The fields were fortified with carts and cannon 'set before the battles' and, according to Gregory, York's men built a 'great deep ditch fortified with guns, carts and stakes', but despite the solidity of the position and the fact that York was fighting on home territory things were already looking bad for him.

For a start morale was low. Not only was York's army numerically smaller and the men probably tired after the long retreat, but many of them were dismayed to find themselves about to take part in a battle against the King. It was one thing to fight on behalf of their liege lords in their quarrels with other magnates but it was quite another to take up arms against an anointed monarch. To engage in that kind of activity was treason; to the medieval mind it was also sacrilege, a sin which put at risk not only their lives but their mortal souls. And it was all too evident that the King was present in the opposing army: across the meadows the royal standard could be seen flying as evening gave way to nightfall. In vain the earls sent another message protesting their loyalty to the King and cataloguing 'the great and lamentable complaints of your poor, true subjects, of robberies, ravishments, extortions, oppressions, riots, unlawful assemblies, wrongful imprisonments universally throughout every part of your realm'. Henry had no need to take heed of the protestations: he held the upper hand and his supporters knew it.

Some time during the night York's position was weakened further when Trollope decided to defect to the Royalist camp, taking with him his experienced troops. He had served in France under Henry V and although he had committed himself to Warwick he could not bring himself to lead his men into action against his former commander's son and successor, the rightful King of England. Others followed suit, overawed by the size of Henry's army and the sight of his fluttering standards. York tried to halt the rot by spreading rumours that Henry had died, but the ploy came to nothing when it became all too evident that the King was still at the head of his army.

A council of war was then held to judge the situation, during which it must have become abundantly clear to all the participants that their men would not fight and that even if they did the result would be their complete annihilation at the hands of the superior Royalist army. All the rebel earls were brave and experienced men but they were also hard-headed realists who understood the weakness of their position and the crazy reality of leading a small, demoralised force against the might of Henry's host.

According to the account found in the Rolls of Parliament, 'about midnight they stole away out of the field, under colour they would have refreshed them[selves] awhile in the town of Ludlow, leaving their Standards and Banners in their battle directly against the field, fled out of the town unarmed, with few persons into Wales'. Once out in the open countryside they split into two groups: York and his son Edmund, Earl of Rutland, made their way to Ireland through Wales, while Salisbury, Warwick and March rode westwards into Devon, where they managed to hire a small ship to cross the Channel and eventually returned to Calais. When dawn broke the following day the Yorkist lines were still intact but of the leaders there was no sign.

They had chosen discretion over valour and while their move was inglorious and shameful it saved the lives of their followers, who knelt before the King the following day and received his pardon. There was, though, no respite for the people of Ludlow, who had to contend with the dreary aftermath as triumphant Royalist soldiers smashed their way through the town and ransacked every building, including the castle. People were assaulted and women were raped, Gregory noting that 'the misrule of the King's gallants at Ludlow when they had drunk enough of the wine that was in the taverns and in other places, the full ungodly smote the heads of the pipes and hogsheads of wine, that men went wet-shod in wine, and they robbed the town, and bore away bedding, cloth and other stuff and defouled many women'.

As for the Duchess of York, she was forced to surrender herself to the King – this may or may not have taken place in Ludlow: the records are unclear – and she was placed under the care of her sister the Duchess of Buckingham and, Gregory records, 'kept full straight and [suffered] many a great rebuke'.

The walkover at Ludford Bridge was regarded by the Royalists as just revenge for Blore Heath. Not only had they seen off the Yorkist forces without striking a blow but the opposition leaders had fled for their lives. True, York was in Dublin, where he enjoyed powerful local support, and Warwick and Salisbury were seemingly impregnable in Calais, where the garrison was strong, but their cause had suffered a grievous blow. Coming on top of earlier occasions when York had failed to impose himself on the King's will, the flight from his heartlands left him a lesser person and it could be said that he never fully recovered from the reverse.

Having seen off the Yorkist threat, Henry and his forces returned in triumph to Coventry, where a meeting of Parliament was summoned for 20 November. It was packed with the Queen's supporters and in time came to be known as the 'Parliament of Devils' as its main business was to deal with the Yorkist rebels and it quickly became apparent that for them there was to be no mercy. A Bill of Attainder was produced on the opening day in which York and his main associates – Salisbury, Warwick, March, Rutland, the Bourchier brothers, Oldhall and others – were declared traitors and their lands, honours and titles were sentenced to forfeiture. For men like York and Warwick it was a savage sentence: they had been stripped of all their offices, their estates and their incomes had been placed in the hands of receivers, their children had been disinherited and as a result their families had been effectively ruined. For those who supported the King it was a just outcome as they believed that those attainted were guilty of treason; but many more thought that the punishment was excessive and matched the retribution that had been handed down to the Duke of Gloucester in the previous decade.

The loss of possessions and honour was not the end of the matter. In return the spoils were spread among Lancastrian supporters and so it came about that York's fears were fully justified. His lands, name and titles had been destroyed by his enemies. Somerset was declared Captain of Calais but he could accept that appointment in name only as Warwick and his allies refused to yield possession of the town to him. At the same time Wiltshire was promoted to Lord Lieutenant of Ireland but again that was in name only as the Irish Parliament had promptly declared their support for York and supplied him with a retinue of archers. Even so, nominal decapitation and disinheritance were brutal sentences and York and his allies had paid dearly for their attempt to extricate the King from the Queen's followers at court.

From Calais they issued the usual manifesto declaring their loyalty to the King and condemning their enemies at court for their misfortune, but it was only bravado. The document was quoted in the *English Chronicle* and it provides a good flavour of the mixture of outrage and self-justification which underpinned the Yorkist cause. In their eyes they were not rebels deserving punishment but loyal subjects of the King, whose only interest was the well-being of the country:

> The Earls of Wiltshire and Shrewsbury, and the Lord Beaumont, not satisfied nor content with the king's possession and his good, stirred and excited his said highness to hold his parliament at Coventry, where an act is made by their provocation and labour against us and said Duke of York, my sons March and Rutland, and the Earls of Warwick and Salisbury, and the sons of the said Earl of Salisbury, and many other knights and esquires, of divers matters falsely and untruly imagined, as they will answer afore Almighty God in the day of Doom, the which the said Earls of Shrewsbury and Wiltshire and the Lord Beaumont provoked to be made to the intent of our destruction and of our issue and that they might have our lifelode [livelihood] and goods, as they have openly robbed and despoiled all our places and our tenements and many other true men.

At the same time voices were heard condemning the Yorkists and their violent actions. Not only had they disturbed the body politic but they had taken up arms against an anointed king and shown themselves to be traitors and rebels who deserved to be punished for their presumption. In 'A Defence of the Proscription of the Yorkists in 1459' an anonymous pamphleteer put forward the case against the Yorkists on the grounds that they had upset the peace of the realm to the detriment of everyone living in England. As such they were like an illness or a canker that had to be cured for the sake of the rest of the healthy body:

Here is a similitude for it. I have a rotten tooth in my mouth that vexeth me night and day. Is it better to pull him out and so make a gap in my mouth, the which I wot well is not good, or else to plaster him to the confusion and undoing of all the other, and at the last he will fall according to his nature and do me a shrewd turn? Forsooth if the king had no moo [more] lords in this land than they, yet were it better without comparison to give them to the hands of Sathanas [Satan] in perpetual subversion than to reconcile them, for the restoring of them were none other but a wilful submission and exposing of the king to their will, the which was never good nor never shall be, for as Saint Augustine saith, *Veternose consuetudinis vis nimis alto radices habet.* They have been inextirpable, they have been incurable.

As it proved to be impossible for Henry to lay hands on York in Dublin – before long the Irish Parliament had passed legislation stating that any attempt on the Lord Lieutenant's life would be treated as treason – he turned his attention to Warwick in Calais. Somerset was determined to take possession of the colony: it would give him considerable temporal powers – as 'Christendom's finest captaincy' it provided wealth and a large standing garrison – and in any case it had earlier belonged to his father. Trollope's desertion at Ludford Bridge also suggested that Warwick might not be as secure as he thought himself to be and there might be an opportunity to convince others to turn against him. With Margaret's support Somerset took an armed retinue across the Channel in December and demanded to be admitted into Calais so that he could take up his position. Not surprisingly, the gates were closed against him and the garrison remained loyal to its commanders, Warwick, Salisbury and March, leaving Somerset with no option but to retreat.

To underline his superiority, at the beginning of 1460 Warwick then ordered an impudent raid on Sandwich to attack his rival's forces, and the raid, led by Sir John Dynham, brought off a spectacular coup by capturing Richard Woodville, Lord Rivers. Woodville had been commissioned by the Queen to lead a relief expedition to assist Somerset but while he was asleep with his wife, Jacquetta (the widow of the Duke of Bedford whom he had married in 1436, causing a huge scandal as she came from the nobility and he was of lower rank, being a Northamptonshire squire), Dynham's men detained them and took them and their son Anthony back to Calais. Once they were safely in the town Rivers was hauled before the earls and given a sound dressing-down, not just because he supported the Queen but because, as William Paston recorded, he was a man of humble birth, who owed his nobility to his wife's position:

> And there my Lord of Salisbury [be]rated him, calling him a knave's son, that he should be so rude to call him and these other lords traitors, for they all shall be found the king's true liege men, when he should be found a traitor, etc. And my Lord of Warwick rated him, and said that his father was but a squire, and brought up with King Henry the Vth, and sithen himself made by marriage, and also made lord, and that it was not his part to have such language of lords, being of the king's blood. And my Lord of March rated him in like wise. And Sir Anthony was rated for his language of all three lords in like wise.

Along with Rivers almost three hundred Royalist troops went into captivity and the daring sortie sparked fears of an invasion from France. These were well grounded as Warwick had continued his dealings with Burgundy with a view to securing a marriage agreement between March and the Duke's niece, Katherine, daughter of the Duke of Bourbon.

Undeterred by the earls' audacity and by the continuing cross-Channel threat, Somerset raised a new army which included the professional soldiers under Trollope's command. After arriving on French soil they captured the nearby and subsidiary castle at Guînes, within the Calais Pale, which gave them a base and a means of continuing operations against the main Calais garrison. Desultory fighting continued throughout the spring of 1460 but Somerset was unable to make any progress and if anything Warwick held the whip-hand. A fresh relief expedition was mounted under John Touchet, the new Lord Audley, son of the Lancastrian leader killed at Blore Heath, but this too was a failure and young Audley was taken prisoner. Shortly afterwards he transferred his sympathies to the Yorkist cause.

Meanwhile the men inside the Calais garrison had not been idle. Building on the grievances that had been extant since Cade's rebellion ten years earlier they magnified their propaganda campaign by sending letters and manifestos to possible supporters explaining the reasons for their disaffection and listing the problems that existed at Henry's court – the influence of the Queen's party, the profligacy, the jobbery and corruption, the loss of France and the enrichment of those who had the Queen's ear. At the same time they presented themselves as reformers and the preservers of good governance, men who were prepared to defend the birthrights of all loyal and decent Englishmen. All the while they repeated the message that their loyalty to the King's person remained paramount and that their sole quarrel was with those who gave bad advice and turned Henry away from his rightful duties.

Their words fell on willing ears, for the winter of 1459–60 had been one of huge discontent throughout England. The Yorkist uprising had unsettled people and there was a strong sense of grievance against the court which was exacerbated by the decline in the economy. By taking Calais out of the financial equation Warwick had forced the council to place an embargo on the wool trade and this had made life difficult for England's traders, especially those living in London, where there was open hostility towards the court – another good reason for its continuing to sit in the Midlands. There were also fears of invasion, either by the French or by the Yorkists, or indeed both, and military preparations continued, with John Judde undertaking a nationwide survey of the state of the country's defences. It did the Master of Ordnance no good personally: while returning to London before Christmas he was murdered by Yorkist sympathisers near St Albans. New commissions of oyer and terminer were issued by the council to arrest known Yorkist supporters, heightening fears that a civil war must be in the offing.

All over England men considered their options as they took heed of the message coming out of Calais. The Yorkists might have lost the advantage at Ludford Bridge but against the odds they were slowly regaining support for their cause. In the spring the people of Kent sent a message to Warwick and his fellow earls, 'beseeching them that they would in all haste possible come and succour them from their enemies, promising that they would assist them with all their power'.

In his role as propagandist Warwick proved to be a masterful and persuasive influence and he was also a good role model for York's son

Edward of March, who had decided to throw in his lot with the Calais garrison rather than follow his father and brother to Dublin. It turned out to be a sensible and far-reaching decision. Still a young man – he was only seventeen during that first winter in Calais – Edward was free to follow his own pursuits and learn from his powerful mentors. From the staple merchants he became versed in commerce and from taking part in the skirmishes against Somerset's forces he gained his first experience of fighting. A big man, well over six feet tall, he was open and affable in personality and, according to a contemporary description, was of 'a gentle nature and cheerful aspect'.

Edward was also something of a womaniser who was not above seducing other men's wives or, as Dominic Mancini, a visiting Italian diplomat, shrewdly put it in his account of his time in London, 'he [Edward] pursued with no discrimination the married and the unmarried, the noble and the lowly'. One of the ironies of William Paston's letter describing the scolding of Lord Rivers is that four years later Edward was to be so besotted by his victim's daughter, Elizabeth Woodville, that he would end up marrying her even though she was the daughter of a man he had 'rated' for being a mere squire. By then England had been plunged into its first civil war.

Chapter Thirteen

CIVIL WAR

Some time in March 1460 a ship carrying Warwick slipped out of Calais and made its way down the Channel before heading north for Waterford in Ireland. After the disastrous rout at Ludford Bridge and the enforced exile in Ireland and Calais, Warwick and York had agreed to hold a council of war and to decide their next move. The fact that Warwick enjoyed command of the seas meant that he was able to travel unhindered and unobserved through the Channel even though by then rumours were sweeping through England that the rebels were intent on retrieving their positions.

There is no record of what took place during the meeting but as it was followed a few months later by the invasion of England the two men must have agreed to a plan which would see the Calais garrison cross over to England to occupy Kent and London before York landed in the north to rally support in his heartlands and in Wales. From Yorkist spies in England they knew the extent of the discontent in Kent and realised that they could count on the support of a county that had already suffered under Henry's rule in the wake of the Cade Rebellion ten years earlier. What was said about York's actual position with regard to the Crown is not clear, the party line seeming to be that the Yorkists wanted to take possession of Henry and to reform his court but to stop short of actually deposing him. Before the invasion took place they increased their propaganda campaign especially in Kent, where they were already assured of a warm welcome; later Edward of March recalled that when Warwick returned to Calais from Ireland he brought with him 'the greatest joy and consolation earthly'.

Their campaign was given an added fillip when the Royalist fleet under the command of the Duke of Exeter failed to intercept Warwick during his return voyage and, worse, its crews began voicing Yorkist sympathies. It was now not so much a matter of *if* an invasion would take place but *when*.

On 26 June Warwick and his supporters finally made their move, crossing the Channel and landing at Sandwich with a force of some two thousand men under the tactical command of experienced soldiers such as Dynham, Sir John Wenlock and William Neville, Lord Fauconberg, Warwick's uncle. Wenlock was one of the most intriguing personalities of the period: a Bedfordshire landowner, he had served Margaret of Anjou and had fought for Henry VI at the First Battle of St Albans but his growing friendship with Warwick encouraged him to transfer his loyalties to the Yorkists. (As we shall see, it was not the only occasion when he turned coat.) The invaders received a warm welcome, not just from the people of Sandwich but also from the inhabitants of the other Cinque Ports.

From the coast they made their way to Canterbury to receive the blessing of the Archbishop, Thomas Bourchier, who had decided to forsake the Queen's party and throw in his lot with Warwick's faction. With them rode Francesco Coppini, Bishop of Terni, the papal legate to Pius II, who had been sent to London in February 1459 in an unsuccessful attempt to elicit English support for a new crusade against the Turks. On discovering the extent of the rift between the Yorkists and the Lancastrians Coppini decided to use the situation to his own advantage by interfering in the quarrel and siding with the Duke of York. The following year the Pope asked Coppini to return to England as a mediator but the papal legate turned the opportunity to his own advantage by halting in Calais to encourage Warwick to act against Henry VI.

There was a solid if messy diplomatic reason for this interference: Coppini also represented Francesco Sforza, the Duke of Milan, who wanted to neutralise the claims being made on the throne of Naples by Margaret of Anjou's brother, John of Calabria, Duke of Lorraine and King René's eldest son. Because France supported John in his claims it was essential to have this balanced by English influence and Coppini clearly believed that with Richard of York on the throne France would not dare to continue the policy of backing John of

Calabria. During his discussions with Warwick the papal legate quickly discovered that he had little need to offer any blandishments or encouragement: he was talking to men who had clearly made up their minds to return to England to deal with the problems of Henry's misrule.

After leaving Canterbury Warwick and his retinue headed towards London by way of Rochester and Dartford and as they rode through Kent they picked up more supporters. In the capital there was an anxious debate about what should be done when Warwick arrived. Initially the authorities wanted to close the gates against the rebels and sent a message to that effect, but such was Warwick's influence among the mercantile community that the decision was overturned and on 2 July the Yorkist army entered the city in triumph.

As for the Royalist garrison, which was commanded by several eminent Lancastrians, including Lord Hungerford, whose grandfather had been an executor of Henry V's will, they wisely took refuge in the Tower under the protection of Lord Scales, an experienced veteran of the wars in France. From his secure position Scales was able to deploy his artillery but despite firing his weapons as the Yorkists entered the city he succeeded only in killing people in the streets and setting fire to their houses with wildfire, a highly combustible substance similar to napalm. The following day Warwick summoned a convocation in St Paul's at which the leaders of the revolt swore solemn oaths on the cross of Canterbury declaring their loyalty to the King and repeating their threat to end the misrule of the country and punish those responsible for it. They also insisted that they wanted the attainders against them to be lifted and to have their good reputations restored.

During the proceedings Coppini addressed the gathering and produced an open letter to Henry which summarised his understanding of the situation. (A copy survives in the Calendar of State Papers of Milan.) Considering what had taken place in Calais, this letter gave a somewhat biased and self-effacing interpretation of his own position but in general it underlined the Yorkists' message that they meant no harm to the King but were determined to reform the court:

> On coming to Calais, owing to recent events I found almost everything in turmoil, and those nobles all ready to cross to England, declaring that they would not wait any longer in the

existing state of affairs. Nevertheless, after I had conferred with them and exhorted them to peace and obedience, they gave me a written pledge that they were disposed to devotion and obedience to your Majesty, and to do all in their power for the conservation and augmentation of your honour and the good of your realm. But they desired to come to your Majesty and to be received into their former state and favour, from which they declare they have been ousted by the craft of their opponents, and begged me to cross the sea with them to interpose my efforts and prevent bloodshed, assuring me that they would do anything honourable and just that I should approve for the honour and estate of your Highness and the welfare of your realm . . .

The arrival of the Yorkists in London threw the Royalists into a quandary because they had anticipated that the invasion would come from Ireland through Wales and they were unwilling to make any move which might compromise their position in the north-west. Warwick made up their minds for them by moving the bulk of his forces north towards Coventry. On 5 July Fauconberg left London at the head of an army of some ten thousand men, followed by another force under Warwick, leaving Salisbury to lay siege to the Tower. Progress was slow because of the size of the armies and the poor weather, it being an unseasonably wet summer. To Henry's credit he did not funk the challenge facing him and refused to go into hiding at the Isle of Ely in the depths of the Fens as had been suggested by his supporters. Instead he rejected the advice and calmly donned his armour and set out at the head of his army to confront those who were challenging his royal authority.

The two armies met on 10 July in open country outside Northampton, between Delapre Abbey and the village of Hardingstone. The Royalist army had been the first to arrive and used the opportunity to dig a series of defensive ditches guarded by staked fences and several cannon. The army was drawn up in three battles with the swollen waters of the River Nene behind them, rain was falling heavily and Buckingham, the senior Lancastrian commander, was keen to get his smaller force into action as soon as possible and certainly within hours of the arrival of the Yorkist army. Warwick, on the other hand, preferred to take his time as his men had been on the march for several hours and were footsore and soaking wet.

However, before any blow could be struck the armies had to go through the formalities of parley and negotiation. This turned out to be a long-winded business as Warwick did his best to gain permission to be allowed to address the King directly. First he sent a delegation consisting of Richard Beauchamp, Bishop of Salisbury, and other clerics with a request to the King to listen to the Yorkists' complaints but this met with short shrift. Standing beside the King, Buckingham simply retorted that if Warwick came into the King's presence he would be killed, and for good measure he added that he considered that the Bishop was not a man of God but a man of war and would have to face the consequences of supporting the Yorkist cause. Further attempts were made to arrange a meeting between the King and Warwick but by early afternoon these too had failed and a battle became inevitable.

Warwick had drawn up his army in the traditional three battles, commanded by himself in the centre, Fauconberg on the left and March on the right. Before giving the order to advance he made it clear that his army was to be selective in its killing when it engaged the opposition, 'that no people should lay hand upon the king nor on the common people, but only on the lords, knights and squires'. Shortly after two o'clock in the afternoon Warwick ordered the trumpets to sound and the Yorkist army moved slowly forward to engage their well-defended opponents.

At this point in the battle, even before the men got to sword point, the Royalists were as good as beaten. Not only had the rain soaked the gunpowder and made their cannon useless but before the battle began March had received a message from his direct opponent on the King's right, Lord Grey of Ruthin, that he would change sides and allow the Yorkist left to advance into his ranks. Grey was a wealthy and rapacious landowner who had answered the Queen's call for support and had played a leading role in her party. For reasons which appear to have involved a quarrel over property – his father had engaged in similar disputes with Owen Glendower earlier in the century – he decided to switch his allegiance to the Yorkists. (Three years later he received his thanks when he was appointed Treasurer.)

To the horrified astonishment of the Royalist forces Grey's men pushed over the defences and started helping the advancing Yorkists to climb over the barricades. What had been a secure defensive position became a death-trap; once inside the trench system March's men started cutting down their opponents and as panic set in the survivors did their best to get out of the killing ground. Many were drowned in the Nene as they tried to cross it.

The combat phase of the battle lasted little more than half an hour and, as had happened at St Albans, the final stages were marked by the butchery of anyone wearing armour and the colours of the nobility. Among the estimated four hundred casualties were Buckingham, Shrewsbury and Lords Egremont and Beaumont, the latter being Constable of England. The King was quickly apprehended and led away from the battlefield to the safety of his tent, where Warwick, Fauconberg and March greeted him and asked for his forgiveness, all the while protesting their loyalty to his person.

No doubt they were sincere. All the records from the period insist that they were acting in the King's best interests as 'true liegemen', but the fact remains that they were the masters of the field and that Henry was in their hands and powerless to act. The one person capable of saving him was his wife, but she spent the day at Eccleshall Castle waiting for the outcome of the fighting, and while she was there it had quickly become apparent that her cause was hopeless. Her Royalist forces had been defeated and four of its leading commanders killed; in the wake of the battle others had made good their escape, while some, such as Grey, had switched sides and thrown in their lot with the Yorkists. Suddenly Margaret and her son Edward were in danger of being apprehended, or worse, and she had to act quickly. With a small retinue she set off for Harlech Castle in west Wales, the seat of her stepbrother-in-law Jasper Tudor, Earl of Pembroke.

The Queen's escape was not without incident. At one point one of her servants, John Cleger, tried to rob her and she only managed to escape his clutches thanks to the intervention of a young attendant who led her to the safety of Harlech. Even then she was not completely secure within the castle's walls and Pembroke took her north to Denbigh Castle in the Vale of Clwyd, deep in the heart of Lancastrian territory. There she was joined by Exeter and set about rallying support among those magnates who remained loyal to her and the King. For the rest of the year she remained in the fastnesses of north Wales, where Pembroke began recruiting reinforcements for the Royalists in the name of the infant Prince of Wales.

Meanwhile the King had been taken back to London, where Salisbury had succeeded in ending the resistance of the Tower's garrison by starving them into submission and using heavy cannon to break down the outer defences. Scales, who had expected to hold out until a Royalist army reached London, tried to escape but was recognised as he attempted to get into a boat and was murdered by an angry mob. His body was thrown into the churchyard of St Mary Overy in Southwark, a sorry end for a proud (if brutal) veteran soldier who was known by his men as 'good old Lord Scales'.

The end of the siege marked the final defeat of the extant Royalist forces and when Henry arrived in London on 10 July he was well and truly in the hands of the Yorkists. With a rapidity and decisiveness conferred by their positions as victors, the Yorkists set about making their own appointments to the principal offices of state. Warwick rewarded his brother George Neville, Bishop of Exeter, with the position of Chancellor and Thomas Bourchier was made Treasurer. Parliament was summoned with the intention of cancelling the Acts of Attainder and the Duchess of York was released from her house arrest to return to London, where she took up residence first at Sir John Fastolf's house in Southwark and then at Baynard's Castle, her husband's town house, on the other side of the Thames.

Throughout the operation York had been party to the plans of the Calais earls but his entrance into the proceedings is shrouded in some mystery. There was never any doubt that he would return to England or that he would time his journey to coincide with the reopening of Parliament in October but it is not clear if he had pretensions to seize the throne before he set out. At any rate he left Dublin in the first week of September, some two months after the Battle of Northampton, and landed at Chester on 9 September. From there he set out for London and at some stage in his leisurely progress south he had his arms emblazoned with the royal arms and trumpeters announced his progress as he made his way towards the capital.

His timing was also immaculate. Unwilling to meet his co-conspirators in advance, he arrived in London on 10 October, three days after Parliament had assembled, and from the outset he made it clear that he was a changed man. York had no intention of taking up his old position as Protector: this time he wanted the Crown and the manner of his arrival made that intention perfectly clear. Gone was any false humility and in the words of the Abbot of St Albans, who was an eyewitness, in its place was 'great pomp and splendour, and no little exaltation of spirit' as trumpets sounded and York's drawn sword of state was carried aloft before him as he made his way to Westminster:

> And there entering the palace he went straight through the great hall until he came to the usual room, where the king, with the commons, was accustomed to hold his parliament. And coming there he walked straight on until he came to the king's throne, upon the covering or cushion of laying his hand, in this very act like a man about to take possession of his right, he held it upon it for a short time. But at length withdrawing it, he turned to the people standing quietly under the canopy of Royal state, he looked eagerly for their applause.

None came. By making the symbolic gesture of laying his hand on the empty throne York was staking his claim to the Crown of England and he fully expected to receive the backing of those present. But instead of acclaim there was an embarrassed silence which York had to break by announcing that he challenged the right of Henry to rule the country and that he intended to be crowned king at the month's end. His argument carried strength – through his mother he was descended from Edward III's second surviving son and was senior to Henry, who was descended from the third son – but the claim was made in the wrong place and at the wrong time. While it is true that his supporters had won a great victory over the Royalists at Northampton and had Henry in their power, it is also true that they had predicated their success on remaining loyal to the King's person. Given the sacred nature of that sworn fealty to an anointed king they could hardly break their word without forfeiting their honour.

As a result history did not repeat itself: just over sixty years earlier, in 1399, Henry Bolingbroke had returned to England and dissimulated to his supporters before grabbing the throne in similar circumstances. Despite some objections from those who believed that he was only pursuing the return of his title and attainted estates, Bolingbroke had succeeded because he had sufficient support.

However, this time there was to be no repetition, either because the magnates did not support York wholeheartedly or because they were unwilling to unseat Henry, for all that he had shown himself a feckless ruler. Either way, having defied and challenged Henry on five earlier occasions, when the main chance of winning the throne came tantalisingly close York was unable to grasp it and was left with his dreams unfulfilled.

Thomas Bourchier, Archbishop of Canterbury, broke the spell by suggesting that York should place his claim before the King as the highest authority in the country but this only brought the angry retort, 'I do not recall that I know anyone within the kingdom whom it would not befit to come sooner to me and see me rather than I should go and visit him.' Despite those hot words York did as the Archbishop suggested and confronted Henry in his chamber. Given the circumstances the King was surprisingly calm: he refuted the claim and suggested that it should be taken to the Lords for their consideration. 'My father was king; his father was king; I have worn the crown for forty years from the cradle,' he told the assembled peers. 'You have all sworn fealty to me as your sovereign, and your fathers did the like to my fathers. How then can my right be disputed?' What followed next was like a child's game of pass-the-parcel as each section of the establishment did their best to avoid coming to any decision to respond to York's demand to succeed to the throne.

On 16 October York presented his claim in writing and handed it to the Chancellor, the Bishop of Exeter, who then passed it to the Lords. The Parliament Roll describing what took place recorded that the Lords hedged their bets by replying: 'In as much as every person high and low, suing to this high Court of Parliament, of right must be heard, and his desire and petition understand that the said writing should be read and heard, not to be answered without the King's commandment for so much as the matter is so, and of so great weight and poise . . .' Unable to find any solution, the Lords passed the claim to the King's justices but they too refused to be drawn, arguing that 'the matter was so high and touched the king's estate and regalie, which is above the law and passed their learning, whereof they durst not enter into any communication thereof . . .'

Forced to fall back on their own devices, the Lords debated the issue again, this time in closed session, and rather than reach any definitive conclusion they produced a list of objections which pointed out the impossibility of accepting York's claim. First and foremost the Lancastrian line had produced three kings since 1399, all had been anointed, with all the mystical and religious connotations surrounding the ceremony, and the nobility, including York, had sworn oaths of allegiance to all three of those monarchs. Any change to the status quo would invalidate all legislation passed in their reigns and that would cause chaos. There was also a question of interpretation: York was basing his claim on his mother's line to the Duke of Clarence, Edward III's second surviving son, and this was thought to be an innovation as previously his descent had been traced from his father's line – the Earl of Cambridge – back to Edmund of Langley, Edward III's fourth son. The result of their deliberations was a compromise: the passing of an Act of Accord which kept Henry as king but passed the succession to York and his heirs. On 8 November York was proclaimed heir to the throne and once again he became Protector of England; the lords swore allegiance to him and he swore allegiance to Henry.

Despite the fact that his claim had not been accepted and indeed had caused a great deal of dismay among his own supporters, York was in a stronger position than he could possibly have anticipated before he made his dramatic intervention earlier in the year. His enemies at court had been defeated and scattered, the attainders on him had been lifted and, even though it was highly improbable that he would sit on the English throne, that right would pass to his son Edward of March. The result helped to calm the passions that had been running high in London in the wake of York's announcement of his claim.

It also restored a degree of equanimity in his relationship with Warwick, who had not been best pleased by his co-conspirator's sudden and intemperate announcement. He had already made his displeasure felt when the two men met at Westminster shortly after York had made his initial claim, using 'hard words' to castigate his ally for his recklessness in making the bid. Warwick was in a difficult position. He could have supported York's bid and may even have hinted that he would do so when the two men had met earlier in Ireland, but at the end of the successful crushing of the Royalists at Northampton he had renewed his oaths of allegiance to Henry, as had

Salisbury and March. Since he had done so, any move against Henry would have been treasonable.

One other party was left dissatisfied with the outcome: Queen Margaret, who saw her son Edward being disinherited from what she considered to be his rightful legacy. Not being the kind of person to accept such an unwelcome turnaround without protest, she immediately started planning to confront and defeat the family which had usurped her son. As soon as she heard the news from London she began summoning her supporters and their armed retainers to create a new army, and she pointedly ignored demands from her husband to return to London. Among those she counted on were her natural supporters, Somerset, Pembroke, Northumberland, Devon and Wiltshire, and with them came a number of experienced captains, all of whom promised to bring armed retinues to the gathering place at Pontefract Castle in Yorkshire, where they would be well placed to lay waste the lands of York and Salisbury. According to Gregory, 'all these people were gathered and conveyed so privily that they were whole in number of 15,000 ere any man would believe it'.

Once again the country was hovering on the brink of a fresh round of civil strife but this time there was a subtle difference. With the passing of the Act of Accord the struggle had become dynastic. Margaret was fighting for her son's right to succeed to the throne of England and York would be forced to respond to defend his own family's claim to be the King's rightful heirs. As for Henry, he had been sidelined and his own future would depend on the outcome of the next round of internecine fighting.

Margaret had taken one other step to strengthen her position. From north Wales she had sailed to Dumfries in south-west Scotland and over New Year she was ensconced in nearby Lincluden Abbey with the Queen Dowager, Mary of Gueldres, the recently widowed queen of James II, who had been killed by the exploding cannon outside Roxburgh Castle. Together with the young heir James III, a boy of nine, the two queens spent almost a fortnight discussing ways in which Scotland could offer military support to the Lancastrian cause. Money was out of the question as Scotland was habitually poor throughout this period; it had also just emerged from a period of further civil strife between James II and the powerful Douglas family, who had sided with the Yorkists. However, for all that funds were out of the question men and arms would be made available to Margaret to enable her to reinforce the depleted Royalist army. There was a price: in return for Scottish help the strategically important east coast town and port of Berwick-upon-Tweed would be ceded to the Scots and Prince Edward would marry one of the daughters of Mary of Gueldres.

Protected by a force of Scottish soldiers led by the Earl of Angus, who had been promised that his men would be paid by way of booty gained in England, Margaret set out across the border in the middle of January 1461 to join up with her forces in Yorkshire.

No longer could the news of the Lancastrians' preparations be kept secret and shortly before Christmas York had left London for the north with Salisbury and Rutland, taking with them a force of around five thousand soldiers. After encountering some of Somerset's men near Worksop in Nottinghamshire they made for York's castle at Sandal, near Wakefield, where they spent Christmas in comfort and safety. Their plan was to sit tight while March built up his forces in the Yorkist heartlands of Staffordshire, Shropshire and Herefordshire, but for some reason York decided to do battle with the Lancastrian forces which had been building in strength ten miles away at Pontefract.

Why York took this uncharacteristically rash course of action is far from clear. Perhaps he felt that his position was sufficiently secure inside Sandal. Perhaps he had underestimated the size of the opposing forces and thought that they were smaller than they really were, for later there were suggestions of treachery and accusations that the Lancastrians had disguised some of their men as Yorkists in the colours of Warwick. Perhaps he felt under threat and needed to act to safeguard his position. During the Christmastide period a local truce had been arranged to run until the Feast of Epiphany (6 January) but this had not stopped the Lancastrians from attacking Yorkist foragers whose appearance outside the castle walls seemed to suggest that food was in short supply within Sandal and that York would be unable to hold out for very much longer. In other words the Yorkists thought that those opposing them were smaller in number than they really were while the Lancastrians knew that they held the upper hand and that the garrison inside Sandal Castle was probably having to forage for food and fuel.

Whatever the reason for York's decision it proved to be a costly mistake. On 30 December a force led by Somerset appeared outside Sandal and York and Salisbury led out their men to attack them. They were not to know that, on the advice of the professional soldier Andrew Trollope, two flanking columns led by Wiltshire and Lord Roos, a veteran of the French wars, had been concealed in nearby woodlands to wait their opportunity to join the battle. At first the Yorkists seemed to have the upper hand as they joined battle on the open ground of Wakefield Green, south of the River Calder, but too late they realised they were in a trap, when a fresh attack came in from the flanks. As Edward Hall put it so graphically in his sixteenth-century history, York's men were 'environed on every side, like a fish in a net, or a deer in a buckstall'.

What happened next on that freezing-cold and darkening winter's day was all too typical of combat of that period. Ordinary foot soldiers were spared and allowed to leave the battlefield but for the nobility there was no mercy. York was dragged from his horse and killed, as was his son Rutland, who was intercepted by Lord Clifford as he attempted to escape. Clifford's words as he dispatched the seventeen-year-old boy have the authentic ring of a civil war: 'By God's blood, thy father slew mine! So will I slay the accursed blood of York!' (The story was related in Hall's history of the century.) Others cut down included Salisbury's son Thomas Neville, a son of Lord Bourchier and many Yorkist knights. Exact numbers are difficult to compute but Benet claims that after the battle Wakefield Green was thick with corpses; many men who survived the fighting but were wounded died later in the intense cold. It was a bad defeat for the Yorkist cause.

One of those taken prisoner was Salisbury, who was led off to Pontefract Castle. Once incarcerated he attempted to bribe his jailers to free him but, according to the *English Chronicle*, the ruse failed as 'the common people of the country, which loved him not, took him out of the castle by violence and smote off his head'. It was an ugly end for one of England's most powerful magnates but once he had turned coat to support York his life was probably forfeit anyway and it left his son Warwick the most powerful man in England. Then, in an equally repulsive piece of spite, Clifford took Salisbury's head, together with the decapitated heads of York and Rutland, which had been retrieved from the battlefield, and had them placed on spikes above the Micklegate Bar in York. To add further insult a paper crown was placed on York's head to mock his pretensions to the throne of England.

John Whethamstede, Abbot of St Albans, went further in his chronicle by suggesting that both York and Salisbury were taken alive, but it is more likely that the former was killed during the fighting:

> They stood him [York] on a little anthill and placed on his head, as if a crown, a vile garland made of reeds, just as the Jews did to the Lord, and bent the knee to him, saying in jest, 'Hail King, without rule. Hail King, without ancestry. Hail leader and prince, with almost no subjects or possessions.' And having said this and various other shameful and dishonourable things to him, at last they cut off his head.

This unexpected victory at Wakefield returned the initiative to the Lancastrians. They had defeated a Yorkist force and killed two of the faction's leading personalities; they also had superior numbers at their disposal and, bolstered by their Scottish allies, were in a good position to march on London, where Warwick was nervously trying to gather reinforcements from Essex and East Anglia. At the same time March was busily building up his forces at Ludlow, in his family's home territory, where he was joined by local Yorkist landowners and supporters such as Sir William Herbert, Sir John Wenlock and Sir Walter Devereux, all tried and tested soldiers. His immediate instinct would have been to march north to avenge his father or to return to London through Gloucestershire, but when he received information of the whereabouts of a large Lancastrian army led by the Earls of Pembroke and Wiltshire which was making its way through the Midlands to link up with Queen Margaret, he decided to engage it first. It was a good decision. March's force included a large number of English and Welsh archers, they were ably led by experienced soldiers and he and his supporters would be fighting to defend their own territory. Against them the Lancastrian force was about the same size, around four thousand men, but many of them were French, Breton and Irish mercenaries whose professionalism and loyalty to the cause were dubious.

One other factor gave Edward hope. When the two armies met at Mortimer's Cross, between Ludlow and Leominster, on 2 February, Candlemas Day, they were confronted by the curious meteorological phenomenon of a perihelion ('mock sun') which appears in winter skies when light refracted through ice crystals in the atmosphere produces an apparition that suggests several suns rising through the frosty air. To the terrified Yorkist soldiers it seemed to be a terrible portent but Edward took advantage of the imposing spectacle and the awe it created by declaring: 'Beeth of good comfort, and dreadeth not. This is a good sign, for these three suns betoken the Father, the Son and the Holy Ghost, and therefore let us have a good heart, and in the name of Almighty God go we against our enemies.' At that his men sank to their knees in prayer in preparation for the ensuing battle, heartened by 'the sun in splendour', a vision so marvellous that Edward later used its imagery for one of his badges.

Edward had drawn up his army between rising ground and the nearby River Lugg, to the south of Wigmore Castle. They were arrayed in their usual three battle formations, with the archers in front, ready to meet the Lancastrian attack from the west as Pembroke's forces started advancing across the frozen ground towards the Yorkist lines. As they did so Edward's archers went into action, firing heavy volleys at the advancing foot soldiers, most of whom lacked suitable protection from the arrow storm. As the Lancastrian lines began to thin out under the onslaught, Edward ordered his right flank to charge and the shape of the battle began to change. Slowly but inevitably the Lancastrian lines began to collapse and the advancing Yorkists were able to wrap them up against the banks of the River Lugg. The end was not long in coming. In common with many other battles fought during the Wars of the Roses, the details of the fighting are scarce, but it seems that the combat phase lasted about half an hour and ended in the rout of Pembroke's forces. Soon men were running or riding for their lives, hotly pursued by the Yorkist knights, who kept up the pursuit as far as Hereford.

The battle was known as Mortimer's Cross and it produced the bloodiest fighting of the wars to date: unlike in previous battles, where the common soldiers were spared and the knights slaughtered, Edward's men did not hold back in their hour of victory. Some four thousand Lancastrians are thought to have been killed on that cold winter's day in the Yorkist heartlands. Most of them were Welshmen in Pembroke's service.

Those who managed to escape included Pembroke and Wiltshire but it was not the end of the blood-letting. Among those taken prisoner was old Owen Tudor, husband of Queen Katharine and father to Pembroke, but his royal connections and venerable age could not save him. He was stepfather to Henry VI, although he had never played any official role in the boy's upbringing, and Edward was intent on avenging his own father, who had fallen at Wakefield. Tudor was sentenced to die, along with a number of other captured Lancastrian knights, but, according to Gregory, the old man did not fully realise that he was about to meet his end until he saw the axe and his doublet was ripped off prior to his execution in the marketplace at Hereford. 'Then he said: "That head shall lie on the stock that was wont to lie on Queen Katherine's lap", and put his heart and mind wholly unto God and fully meekly took his death.' After Tudor's execution his head was stuck up on the market cross but 'a mad woman' took pity on his remains and, having carefully washed the severed head and combed its hair, she lit a hundred candles around it.

The execution of prisoners was commonplace throughout the conflict and followed a pattern which is all too familiar in civil wars. Deaths of fathers were avenged by sons and vice versa and the opposing families rarely lost an opportunity to take revenge on men who had killed their own people in earlier battles or skirmishes. As he was Pembroke's father, Tudor's life was probably forfeit but his execution was also a reprisal for the deaths and executions at Wakefield. Suddenly the war was getting more barbaric as opponents brought personal animus to the battlefield.

The conflict was also spreading and involving greater numbers of soldiers. More were killed at Mortimer's Cross than had fallen at the three earlier battles combined and across England there was growing fear about the size of the armies which were marching and counter-marching the length and breadth of the country to do battle. It has become commonplace to argue that from a purely military point of view the battles in the York–Lancaster conflict involved only small numbers of men and that they were bloodthirsty only in that large numbers of nobility were killed or executed. For the most part that assertion is true but as the wars got into their stride in the 1460s contemporary evidence shows that large numbers of ordinary people found themselves caught up in the fighting and were killed on a massive scale.

Of particular concern to many people was the creation of the huge Lancastrian field army in the north of England which contained substantial numbers of Scots and would soon be making its way south. To most Englishmen the Scots were a barbaric northern race known only for their depredations in raiding the northern English marches; they were an alien species, unknown and unknowable, violent and undisciplined, and although the English knew little about them, what they did know made them mightily afraid. Here was an army of unintelligible savages which was not fighting for a cause, the notion of which was unfamiliar to most of them, but was in the field with the sole intention of killing, robbing and plundering:

> The duke [York] being thus removed from this world, the northmen, being sensible that the only impediment was now withdrawn, and that there was no one now who would care to resist their inroads, again swept onwards like a whirlwind from the north, and in the impulse of their fury attempted to overrun the whole of England. At this period too, fancying that every thing tended to insure them freedom from molestation, paupers and beggars flocked forth from those quarters in infinite numbers, just like so many mice rushing forth from their holes, and universally devoted themselves to spoil and rapine, without regard of place or person. For, besides the vast quantities of property which they collected outside, they also irreverently rushed, in their unbridled and frantic rage, into churches and other sanctuaries of God, and most nefariously plundered them of their chalices, books and vestment, and, unutterable crime! Broke open the pixes in which were kept the body of Christ and shook out the sacred elements therefrom. When the priests and the other faithful of Christ in any way offered to make resistance, like so many abandoned wretches as they were, they cruelly slaughtered them in the very churches and churchyard. Thus did they proceed with impunity, spreading in vast multitudes

over a space of thirty miles in breadth and, covering the whole surface of the earth just like so many locusts, made their way almost to the very walls of London; all the movables which they could possibly collect in every quarter being placed on beasts of burden and carried off. With such avidity for spoil did they press on, that they dug up the precious vessels which, through fear of them, had been concealed in the earth, and with threats of death compelled the people to produce the treasures which they had hidden in remote and obscure spots.

That description appeared in a document known as the *Croyland* (or *Crowland*) *Chronicle*, which is the single most important source for the period. It exists in several parts or 'continuations' which were written between 656 and 1486 and for many years the originator was supposed to be Ingulph (or Ingulf), Abbot of the Benedictine Abbey of Croyland and secretary to William the Conqueror. He died in 1109 and the work was subsequently found to be a forgery but the Second Continuation of the *Croyland Chronicle*, covering the years 1459–86, is a reasonably reliable guide to the reigns of Edward IV and Richard III. A marginal note describes the author as a doctor of canon law and a member of the royal council who took part in an embassy to Burgundy in 1471; this was probably Bishop John Russell, who served as Lord Keeper of the Privy Seal to Edward IV and Chancellor to Richard III. Because he was a senior royal servant his eyewitness accounts of key events have an authority which makes the chronicle both absorbing and credible.

Although in this case the Croyland chronicler exaggerated the extent of the violence unleashed by the Scots he reflected the growing concerns of many people who feared that they would be caught up in the fighting. And they had good reason to feel that way. As it turned out, on this occasion Croyland Abbey was spared, but large numbers of men in Margaret's army, mainly the Scots, were not receiving any pay and as they made their way southwards through England they were counting on plunder to give them some reward for their service. Another chronicler, John Whethamstede, compared the speech of the northern horde to the sound of barking by the hounds of hell and in an angry verse described them as 'northern people, faithless people, people prompt to rob'. As happens so often in civil conflicts of this kind, even normally law-abiding sober young men turn into foul-mouthed soldiers who feel no shame in plundering, pillaging and raping and feel little guilt about what they do.

While the civil war in England during this period cannot be compared to the ravages of the English Civil War in the seventeenth century, far less to the Thirty Years War, which devastated Germany during the same period, the violence and irrationality of the fighting between the rival houses of York and Lancaster turned the world upside down for all who found themselves caught up in the path of the opposing armies. It was the beginning of a long season in hell.

Chapter Fourteen

THE BATTLE CONTINUES

Mortimer's Cross was a declaration: in battle both sides would now fight to the knife to press home their advantage and there would be little sympathy for those on the losing side. As the Lancastrian army made its way south through the East Midlands towards London it left behind a huge swath of destruction as soldiers made sure that they got food and shelter and their horses received forage and water, whatever the cost to the local population.

While Queen Margaret's army was making its southern progression Warwick had assembled his forces and on 12 February had marched north out of London to meet the opposition, taking with him the captive king. With the geography imposed by the main north–south routes in the middle of England it was perhaps unavoidable that the two rival armies would clash once again in the vicinity of the town of St Albans. There were a number of preliminary skirmishes near Luton and Dunstable, including one in which the Yorkist forces were led by a local butcher who, according to Gregory, committed suicide 'for shame of his simple guiding and loss of the men, the number of eight hundred'. By this stage the Yorkists had attracted additional numbers of the nobility to their ranks and with Warwick rode the Dukes of Norfolk and Suffolk, the Earl of Arundel and Lords Bourchier and Bonville. Warwick also had the assistance of a number of veteran soldiers from the French wars, notably Sir Thomas Kyriell, commander of the English forces at Formigny ten years earlier, as well as five hundred Burgundian mercenaries, the majority of them archers. However, a lack of urgency in the Yorkist planning meant that March's army was still slowly making its way from the west, picking up supporters as it moved through Gloucestershire.

The two armies were more or less evenly matched. Gregory claims that Warwick had 100,000 under his command but this was obviously a gross exaggeration and it is probable that he had only a tenth of that number. The Lancastrian army was under Somerset's control and those who accompanied him all owed their loyalty to the Queen and represented the flower of England's aristocracy: Exeter, Devon, Shrewsbury and Northumberland. Riding with them were Lords Clifford and Roos, both powerful Lancastrian supporters, and in addition the army had the benefit of the professional soldier Trollope, who commanded the vanguard. One of the problems faced by Somerset was the indiscipline of the Scottish contingent. As they moved further south the Scots began to worry about the distance that was growing between them and their homeland, not least because by now they were weighed down with plunder. Showing more concern for their well-being than the claims of the Lancastrian cause, they began slipping away and headed back north as the main part of the army approached St Albans. Not only did their desertions reduce the number of men available to Somerset but the stragglers held up his progress and made it impossible to compute the size of the army that would be available to him.

Problems faced Warwick, too. As he approached St Albans from the south he had little clear idea of the opposition's dispositions: instead of making towards Ware and Waltham the Lancastrian army had moved further west and was heading towards Dunstable. To counter the move Warwick decided in the first instance to deploy some of his men, mainly archers, in defensive positions inside St Albans while the main bulk of his army was spread out to the north along a four-mile stretch of road which led to Normansland Common. Having arrived earlier than the opposition army, Warwick used his time to good effect by constructing defences which included caltraps, specially constructed nets of cord with an array of sharpened points laid on the ground to deter cavalry. (They were not dissimilar to the modern 'stinger', a spiked device thrown across a road by police to halt a car by puncturing its tyres.) Warwick's army was also defended by pavises, wooden barricades with spikes, and had a limited number of artillery pieces; some of his Burgundians were equipped with primitive matchlock handguns, similar to the harquebus, which fired lead pellets and in some cases iron arrows. It was the first time weapons of this kind had been seen in England.

Warwick's tactics were guided by a number of circumstances: his lack of accurate intelligence, the composition of his army, many of whom were raw and frightened recruits, and the requirement to guard St Albans from attack. This last need was paramount in his mind as the town guarded the route to London, but by splitting his forces and deploying them over a large swath of territory he ran the risk of overstretching his army and leaving its defences spread out over uncertain ground. Not knowing the exact whereabouts of the Lancastrian forces also hindered him and, as it turned out, he was surprised by their next move. From Dunstable Somerset had taken his forces eastwards along the old Roman road, Watling Street, and this change of direction meant that they approached St Albans from the west, with the River Ver on their right flank. As they had marched by night – an unusual manoeuvre in those days – they took the Yorkist archers by surprise and in the first phase of the battle, on 17 February, were able to enter the town through the gate on Fishpool Street before pressing on over Tonman Ditch.

As dawn began to break the Yorkists quickly regrouped and unleashed heavy fire on the attacking force from their positions in the town's marketplace. The concentrated fire forced the Lancastrians to retreat across the river, where they regrouped and held a council of war to decide their next move. It was at this point in the battle that Trollope used his military experience to good effect. After discovering from his scouts that Catherine Street was unguarded he ordered a pincer movement to outflank the defenders who had grouped in St Peter's Street. This was effected by the vanguard, with one group entering Fishpool Street while another skirted Tonman Ditch along Branch Road, Verulam Road, Folly Lane and Catherine Street. Both forces then entered St Peter's Street to outflank and outnumber the Yorkists, who had no option but to begin withdrawing to the north towards the bulk of their army on Bernard's Heath. Despite encountering fierce resistance, Trollope's inspired move allowed the Lancastrians to overrun the town centre after brutal hand-to-hand fighting in the narrow streets. Both sides suffered heavy casualties.

While Trollope's vanguard was engaged with the Yorkist archers the rest of the Lancastrian force moved round the town and began attacking Warwick's scattered ranks on Bernard's Heath, where his brother Lord Montague was attempting to realign his defensive positions to meet the new threat. Eventually he got his men into a rough and ready defensive posture along the Harpenden and Sandridge road but already the battle was slipping out of his hands. The carefully positioned caltraps and pavises failed to halt the Lancastrian cavalry and as snow began swirling down from the surrounding higher ground the artillery and handguns began to malfunction. Some refused to fire because the powder had become damp while others misfired or exploded, killing the gunners.

As Montague's division came under heavy attack he sent a desperate message to his commander requesting help, but there was an unexplained delay and too late Warwick received intelligence about the attack on his brother's outnumbered forces. There was then a further delay as Warwick attempted to bring his horsemen to the rescue but this took time to arrange and time was not on the Yorkists' side. Even at that stage Warwick's intervention could have been decisive but the narrow lanes and high hedgerows hindered his progress and by the time he reached a position known as Dead Woman's Hill Montague had been captured and the survivors were beginning to stream away from the field as darkness fell.

With little option but to retreat Warwick rallied those around him and set off westwards for Chipping Norton, where he hoped to meet up with March. Around a thousand men lay dead on the field, most of them Yorkists, but, unlike in earlier battles, they were mainly archers and men-at-arms. The only nobleman of any note killed was the commander of the Lancastrian cavalry, Sir John Grey of Groby, who left a strikingly attractive widow, Elizabeth Woodville, the daughter of Lord Rivers and his wife Jacquetta. Within three years she would be destined to play a decisive role in the fortunes of the Yorkist cause.

Throughout the battle Warwick had been outwitted by Trollope, who handled his men well and grasped the advantage when it was presented to him. His pincer movement unseated the Yorkists in St Albans itself and allowed him to bring the full weight of his attack on to Montague's smaller division strung out to the north of the town.

Treachery also played a part in the Lancastrian victory. Inevitably in a civil conflict of this kind, where some loyalties will always be of the fair-weather variety, there were men who had their eyes on the main chance and were prepared to play fast and loose with their allegiances to their commanders.

One such was Henry Lovelace, steward of Warwick's household, who started the day firmly in the Yorkist camp and ended it by serving the Lancastrian cause. His story is all too typical of this kind of behaviour. Earlier in the conflict Lovelace had enjoyed Warwick's patronage and, as an experienced soldier, had been given command of the Yorkist vanguard. At Wakefield he had been taken prisoner and was on the point of being executed when Queen Margaret decided to spare him if he changed his allegiance. This he did in return for a promise that he would be made Earl of Kent and as a result of turning coat he and his men were part of the Lancastrian force which marched south. At Luton, either through treachery or as part of a grander design which only he knew, he changed sides once more to rejoin the Yorkist forces. It was not his last about-turn. As it became clear that Montague was unable to withstand Trollope's attack, Lovelace cannily crossed back to the Lancastrian side, leaving a huge hole in the Yorkist defences. As a hired hand Lovelace had no particular loyalties other than a need to better himself at the expense of the highest bidder, not unlike the earlier turncoat at Northampton, Lord Grey of Ruthin, who had used the conflict to further his own ends.

With the Lancastrians masters of the field the way was now open to march on London but first the victorious commanders had to deal with the aftermath of battle. Astonishingly, Henry was found sitting under an oak tree from where he had watched the battle and its outcome, laughing and singing all the while, according to a report to the French court. He was under the personal guard of Lord Bonville and Sir Thomas Kyriell. Both were men of honour who had been charged by Warwick with the honourable task of ensuring the King's safety during the battle and both had carried it out without demur. In the circumstances they had good reason to believe that their lives were not in jeopardy, but they too faced the rough justice of the time.

The next day, after a number of leading Lancastrian captains, including Trollope, had been knighted by the seven-year-old Prince of Wales, Bonville and Kyriell were dragged in front of the court.

Before the King could say anything – earlier he had promised to save their lives – Margaret turned to her son and asked what should be done with the two men. 'Let them have their heads taken off,' was the boy's cool reply, to which Bonville angrily responded, 'May God destroy those who taught thee this manner of speech!' Both men were taken outside and beheaded without further ado. Gregory's explanation for the Prince's decision was that Bonville had used intemperate language but the real reason for his downfall was more likely to have been the enmity of the Earl of Devon, who sought revenge for the land dispute which had brought the two families to blows twenty years earlier.

For the people of London the Lancastrian victory at St Albans was the worst possible outcome. It was from the capital that Warwick had taken his armies north and as he was a firm favourite with the merchant community they feared that Margaret would now take her revenge. Their greatest fear was that the Scots would be unleashed on London but they were not to know that after the fighting at St Albans the majority of the Scottish contingent were already making their way back home laden with loot. To offset the danger the Lord Mayor wrote an ingratiating letter to the King and Queen insisting that he remained loyal and begging them not to bring their army into the capital. By way of reply Margaret sent a delegation consisting of the Duchesses of Bedford and Buckingham to reassure the people of London that she had no intention of occupying their city and that for the time being they were safe. This opened the way for Henry and Margaret to return to their capital, a move which the Mayor and his aldermen were minded to support, even though it would be unpopular with most of the citizens. Years of misrule had put the House of Lancaster out of favour and the Queen was especially disliked on account of her open disdain for London and its people. (Her being French did not help her cause either.) At the same time Londoners were afraid of what might happen in the immediate future and certainly did not want armed troops entering their city. Some Lancastrian forces had already made their way towards London and were demanding entrance, a move which so alarmed Cicely, the Dowager Duchess of York, that she sent her younger sons to France to be put under the protection of Duke Philip of Burgundy.

All this indecision sealed the Lancastrians' fate. If they had marched on London immediately they would have had no difficulty securing the Tower, with its strategic assets, and this would have prevented Warwick from returning to a city which he regarded as a vital power base. The Queen's protracted negotiations put paid to any quick solution. While the parley was being strung out Warwick had joined up with March and their forces were rapidly advancing on London. That changed everything. Rather than force a new battle with fresh forces and at a time when their own army had been weakened by the Scottish desertions, the Lancastrians decided to pull back towards Dunstable as a preamble to returning to their main area of support in the Midlands.

While the move probably reassured the people of London it also passed the advantage back to the Yorkists. March and Warwick now had London at their mercy and when they made their move into the capital they were greeted with an acclaim which Fabyan described as a prelude to greater things to come:

And upon the Thursday [27 March 1461] following the Earls of March and Warwick with a great power of men, but few of name, entered into the City of London, the which was of the citizens joyously received, and upon the Sunday following the said earl caused to be mustered his people in St John's Field, where unto that host were proclaimed and shewed certain articles and points that King Henry had offended in, whereupon it was demanded of the said people whether the said Henry were worthy to reign as king any longer or no. Whereunto the people cried hugely and said Nay, Nay. And after it was asked of them whether they would have the Earl of March for their king and they cried with one voice, Yea, Yea. After the which admission thus by the commons assented, certain captains were assigned to bear report unto the said Earl of March then being lodged at his place called Baynard's Castle.

This time the Yorkists were taking no chances. Fabyan's chronicle makes it clear that the people of London were only too happy to accept Edward of March as their king – in stark contrast to the way they had greeted his father's claims in the previous year. Fear of the Lancastrians was one reason, a general despair after the years of misrule was another; but the main pointer was that March offered the means of changing a system of government which had fallen into disrepute and which many people wanted to be changed. In this respect Edward offered a fresh start. With the strategic situation now balanced in the Yorkists' favour they had to act decisively. At St Albans they had lost their control over Henry and had returned the advantage to his supporters; if they were to enjoy any legitimacy with the people of England they needed their own king and, with the security of his family's claims to the throne, Edward fitted the bill perfectly. It was also important that the steps taken to achieve their goal were open and above board and that precedents were followed so that the symbolism of making Edward king was understood by as many people as possible.

Behind Fabyan's terse description of the Londoners hailing Edward as king the Yorkists had in fact acted quickly, smoothly and, more importantly, according to precedent, to create the conditions whereby Edward could be crowned King of England. The whole progression was brilliantly stage-managed. The meeting referred to by Fabyan took place on Sunday 1 March at St John's Fields and was addressed by Bishop George Neville, who assured the crowd that Edward had a rightful claim to the throne. If that was what the people wanted, then it was legitimate to hail him as king. Their acclamation allowed the news to be carried to York's London residence and the following day Neville's articles were formally proclaimed. On 3 March, having ascertained that the people supported his claim, a Yorkist council met at Baynard's Castle and made the final administrative arrangements to offer the throne to Edward. Among those present were Warwick, Norfolk, the Archbishop of Canterbury, the Bishops of Salisbury and Exeter and 'many others unnamed'.

The next stage was to crown Edward of March as King Edward IV. A formal coronation would have to wait until later as Edward wanted first to defeat Henry in a decisive battle, the Croyland chronicler noting that 'he would not at present allow himself to be crowned, but immediately, like unto Gideon or another of the judges, acting faithfully in the Lord, girded himself with the sword of battle'. Even so, despite those sentiments in which the chronicler handily crossed the Bible with the sword, it was essential that Edward should be acclaimed as king in front of his people. On 4 March, after hearing mass in St Paul's, he was led to Westminster Hall, where he took his oath as King of England and, having donned a purple robe, he entered the Abbey, where he sat on the throne and, with St Edward the Confessor's sceptre in hand, asserted his right as king. Offerings were made at the high altar, the *Te Deum* was sung and, as Fabyan summed up the proceedings, 'thus took this noble prince possession of this realm of England'. In November of that year, 1461, Edward's first Parliament confirmed his legitimate inheritance of the crown in a petition which stated that he was the rightful king and Henry VI had been a Lancastrian usurper who had plunged the realm into 'unrest, inward war and trouble, unrighteousness, shedding and effusion of innocent blood, abusion of the laws, partiality, riot, extortion, murder, rape and vicious living'.

The problem was that Henry was still alive, as was his son the Prince of Wales, and the Lancastrians still had a formidable army in the field. Edward had made his claim not, in his view, as a usurper but as the rightful king by descent from Edward III and by right of the succession made legitimate by the Act of Accord, which named York and his descendants as the rightful heirs to the throne. However, the harsh reality of the situation was that Edward had become king only through the support of powerful magnates, particularly the Nevilles, and because he had contrived to seize control of London with all its wealth and assets. Before he could be really safe in his position he would have to deal with the Lancastrian succession by either killing Henry and his son or driving them into exile. Writing from Paris, Prospero di Camulio, Milan's ambassador to the French court, produced a shrewd assessment of the situation in England and concluded that amid all the rumours sweeping the capital the final outcome was almost too difficult to predict and would be decided by the strength and tenacity of the supporters of the rival kings:

> Those who support the claims of Edward and Warwick say that the chances in favour of Edward are great, both on account of the great lordship which he has in Ireland, and owing to the cruel wrongs done to him by the queen's side, as well as through Warwick and [the City of] London, which is entirely inclined to side with the new king and Warwick, and as it is very rich and the most wealthy city in Christendom, this enormously increases the chances of the

side that it favours. To these must be added the good opinion of the temper and moderation of Edward and Warwick. Some, on the other hand, say that the queen is exceedingly prudent, and by remaining on the defensive, as they say she is well content to do, she will bring them into subjection and will tear to pieces these attacks of the people, who, when they perceive that they are not on the road to peace, will easily be induced to change sides, such being the very nature of the people, especially when free, and never to let things go so far that they cannot turn.

Edward entered his putative reign with a characteristically positive outlook and firmness of purpose. Realising that he had to crush the Lancastrians, who still enjoyed the support of the majority of England's great noble houses, he issued proclamations calling on all Englishmen to accept him as king and forbidding them to offer support to Henry. Those who submitted to him would be pardoned, while prices were put on the heads of a list of Lancastrian soldiers whose lives were now forfeit. Among these were Trollope (for his desertion at Ludford) and the sons of the Duke of Exeter (thought to have executed Salisbury after Wakefield). Edward's next step was to raise additional funds to pay for the raising of a new army which would march north to take on the Royalist army. The majority of the new recruits came from the Welsh marches and East Anglia, regions where Yorkist support was strong.

A week after Edward's swearing-in the first contingents left London under Fauconberg's command, followed two days later, on 13 March, by the main force, led by the King and Norfolk. With them went a number of Burgundian mercenaries and an impressive array of artillery pieces – even though most had misfired at St Albans because of the wet conditions they were still considered to be battle-winners. The new king was in no hurry because he counted on raising additional support as his army passed through the Midlands, where Warwick was already engaged on the task of recruiting men aged between sixteen and sixty.

While the Yorkists were consolidating their power base the Lancastrian forces had been regrouping outside the city of York, where Queen Margaret began rallying support for Henry and the Prince of Wales. In Wales itself her support remained strong, with the fortresses of Carreg Cennen, Denbigh, Harlech and Pembroke for the time being still under the control of Jasper Tudor. A request sent to Mary of Gueldres resulted in the dispatch southwards of a fresh force of Scots and appeals for men locally brought in new recruits from the north. While accurate figures are impossible to assess there is general agreement that the Lancastrians had the larger army, one contemporary account claiming that it numbered thirty thousand knights and foot soldiers.

What is certain is that Henry still retained the support of the majority of the nobility, nineteen peers to Edward's eight; among them were Somerset, Exeter, Northumberland, Devon, the newly ennobled Sir Andrew Trollope and Lords FitzHugh, Hungerford, Beaumont, Dacre of Gilsland, Roos and Clifford. Their plan was to keep the royal family safe within the walls of York while they confronted the smaller Yorkist army, which had reached Pontefract by 27 March. Between them the rival armies had mustered around fifty thousand men, the largest show of force ever seen in England, and the battle they were about to fight was destined to be the bloodiest encounter of the entire civil war. It was fought on 29 March, a bitterly cold Palm Sunday with flurries of snow blowing down from the north, and the fighting itself was equally sharp and to the point.

In fact the first blows had been struck two days earlier, when a Yorkist forward detachment clashed with a Lancastrian force led by Clifford while attempting to seize a crossing over the River Aire at Ferrybridge. Finding the bridge destroyed, Lord Fitzwalter, a veteran of Mortimer's Cross, ordered his men to repair it but failed to guard the working parties, allowing Clifford to make an undetected attack. In a short and bitterly contested action the Yorkists were driven back and their commander was killed. In response Edward ordered his vanguard under Fauconberg to ford the river at Castleford, about four miles upstream.

This move allowed the Yorkists to outflank Clifford, who was felled by an arrow to the neck as his men fled northwards into Dintingdale Valley. The destruction of this holding force meant Edward's army could cross the Aire and approach their opponents, who were drawn up in a line on the ridge a hundred feet above them, with the village of Towton behind them to the north and the flooded waters of Cock Beck, a tributary of the Aire, on their right flank. As the senior commander, Somerset commanded the centre, with Northumberland and Trollope on his right and Devon and Dacre on his left.

Both armies spent a bitterly cold night in the open with fresh snow being blown in on the biting wind and although there were the usual attempts at negotiation, with Henry pleading that no battle should be fought on such a holy day, everyone on the plateau knew, when night gave way to a grey dawn, that they were about to face a hard fight. There was still some concern in the Yorkist camp that Norfolk had not yet arrived and was reported to be at least ten miles away, but Edward was determined to force the issue and fight, come what may.

During the night the wind had backed to the south and this gave the Yorkists a priceless advantage, for all that they had spent a miserable night in the cold and windy conditions. When their archers commenced firing at around ten o'clock in the morning they had the wind behind them and their arrows fell on their opponents more or less unseen amid the snow flurries which blew across the battlefield. At the same time the Lancastrian archers had to fire their weapons into the wind and the extreme weather conditions made it impossible for them to gauge distances. Stung by the ferocity of the Yorkist attack, Somerset gave the order to advance and Trollope's vanguard charged downhill into the Yorkist left flank, scattering the horse. If Northumberland had attacked the right flank simultaneously the Yorkist lines would have broken, but this failed to happen and the battle in the centre degenerated into a grim slugging match in which quarter was neither given nor expected. It was an ugly business which lasted several hours as men stabbed and hacked their opponents to death with swords, axes, halberds and assorted blades; the ferocity of the fighting left the snow blood-stained, a fact that later gave the area the name 'Bloody Meadow'.

Amid the mêlée it was impossible for either side to see if they had gained the advantage and it was not until dusk that the Lancastrian lines fell back to the west, where they found themselves trapped in the steep-sided gully of the River Cock, which was 'not very broad but of great deepness'. Those who could not cross the swollen waters were drowned or simply hacked to death where they stood. At this crucial stage, with hundreds lying dead on the battlefield, Norfolk's men arrived and their appearance put fresh heart into the Yorkists and brought dismay to the Lancastrians, who began falling away as best they could from the place of slaughter. As the Yorkist horse gave chase men were cut down as they fled towards York and the final death toll, as estimated by Edward's heralds, was twenty-eight thousand, probably an overestimate but indicative of the slaughter that had undoubtedly taken place that day.

After the battle Warwick's brother George Neville, Bishop of Exeter, wrote to Coppini deploring the loss of life in what was fast becoming an increasingly savage and wasteful civil war:

> That day there was a great conflict, which began with the rising of the sun, and lasted until the tenth hour of the night, so great was the pertinacity and boldness of the men, who never heeded the possibility of a miserable death. Of the enemy who fled, great numbers were drowned in the river near the town of Tadcaster, eight miles from York, because they themselves had broken the bridge to cut our passage that way so that none could pass, and a great part of the rest who got away who gathered in the said town and city, were slain and so many dead bodies were seen as to cover an area six miles long by three broad and about four furlongs. In this battle eleven lords of the enemy fell, including the Earl of Devon, the Earl of Northumberland, Lord Clifford and Neville with some cavaliers and from what we hear from persons worthy of confidence, some 28,000 perished on one side and the other. O miserable and luckless race and powerful people, would you have no spark of pity for our own blood, of which we have lost so much of fine quality by the civil war, even if you had no compassion for the French!
>
> If it had been fought under some capable and experienced captain against the Turks, the enemies of the Christian name, it would have been a great stroke and blow. But to tell the truth, owing to these civil discords, our riches are beginning to give out, and we are shedding our own blood copiously among ourselves.

Towton was not only the bloodiest battle fought in England up to that date; it also broke Lancastrian power north of the Trent. Devon is listed among the dead in Neville's letter but he was in fact found among the wounded in York and promptly beheaded. A similar fate befell Wiltshire, who was taken prisoner a few days later in

Cumberland and transferred to Newcastle for execution; he had managed to escape unharmed from earlier battles, but his luck had finally run out. Also among the prominent Lancastrian dead were Northumberland and Trollope, two of the best soldiers on either side, and in the shocked aftermath of the fighting a total of forty-two Lancastrian knights were put to death on the battlefield.

For Edward it was a crushing victory over his rival but it was not a complete success as there were still two kings of England: Henry, his wife and son had been able to escape from the shambles. They had spent the day in York awaiting the outcome and as the first survivors reached the city, bringing with them news of the disaster, they fled north towards Scotland, stopping briefly at Newcastle and then at Wark Castle, where they narrowly escaped falling into Yorkist hands. Only the intervention of forces loyal to Northumberland allowed the royal party to make their way to Berwick, where they waited for the necessary passes to allow them to stay in Scotland.

In fact the turnabout in the Lancastrians' fortunes was an acute embarrassment to Mary of Gueldres, who was effectively ruling Scotland during her son's minority. Although she had entered into a treaty with the Lancastrians, largely at the bidding of the influential Bishop James Kennedy of St Andrews, her uncle was the Duke of Burgundy and through his friendship with Warwick he largely supported the Yorkist claims to the English throne. If Mary provided any further military support to Henry and Margaret it would damage his attempts to forge a close relationship with Edward. However, Mary was alert to the problem and found a way out of it by offering asylum to Henry's party but declining to provide any further military assistance to them in the immediate future.

To begin with Henry was housed in a convent in Kirkcudbright while his wife and son were given apartments in the royal palace at Linlithgow, west of Edinburgh, but it was a parlous existence. Although they were joined by prominent supporters, including the Dukes of Somerset and Exeter, Lord Roos and Sir John Fortescue, the exiled court lacked funds and had to borrow money from the Scottish court, no easy matter given the country's customarily creaking finances. That did not stop Margaret from plotting to regain her position. Her son Prince Edward was betrothed to James II's sister Margaret Stewart and in return the earlier agreement to cede Berwick was made public, much to the fury of King Edward, who demanded that the Lancastrian couple and their son be returned to England 'without delay'.

The failure to capture Henry and Margaret after the victory at Towton was to prove an expensive lapse. As long as they lived Edward's position could not be totally secure, a point that was made by Prospero di Camulio in one of his regular reports to the Duke of Milan:

> Firstly, if the King and Queen of England with the other fugitives mentioned above are not taken, it seems certain that in time fresh disturbances will arise, nor are the people disinclined to these, since the storm falls equally on the heads of princes as on their own, and the less nobles there are the better they are pleased, and think that they are nearer a chance for liberty; and from what I have been told the people of London have great aspirations. If, however, they are taken, then that kingdom may be considered settled and quiet under King Edward and he Earl of Warwick.

However, all those problems lay ahead; in the days following the battle Edward was able to bask in his victory. For the first time his opponents' military power had been shattered and when he entered York in triumph on Easter Monday 1461 he was met by cheering crowds. One of his first acts was to order the removal of his father's and brother's heads and to replace them with those of his defeated enemies. Edward remained in the north of England until the beginning of May, when he returned to London, leaving Fauconberg and Montague in charge of his forces. On his arrival in London he was given a rapturous welcome and his coronation as King Edward IV followed, on 28 June, with a sonorous ceremony in Westminster Abbey.

Earlier he had created thirty-three new Knights of the Bath and rewarded those who had served him well during the campaign against Henry. Fauconberg was made Earl of Kent and his powerful brother Warwick was confirmed as Captain of Calais and created Warden of the East and West Marches, charged with guarding the border with Scotland. Other Neville relatives were also put into positions of power and authority. George Neville was reaffirmed as Chancellor and

Edward's younger brothers were ennobled, George as Duke of Clarence and Richard as Duke of Gloucester.

To the people of England the new king also had words of encouragement, promising to end Lancastrian oppression and to redress 'the very decay of merchandise wherein rested the prosperity of the subjects'. It augured well and an unknown letter writer reflected the general mood, describing the country's reaction to the coronation in ecstatic terms: 'the entire kingdom keeps holiday for the event, which seems a boon from above'.

The reality was rather different as Edward still had a number of difficulties to overcome before his position could be properly secured. In addition to the continuing presence of the rival king and his entourage on the other side of the border in Scotland, the Yorkists still had to contend with parts of his kingdom where support for the Lancastrians remained strong. These were surprisingly widespread: large swaths of the north and west, Wales and the marches. There was also the danger of interference from outside, particularly from France, where Louis XI had become king in succession to Charles VII and showed worrying signs of wanting to capitalise on England's internal problems by threatening to support Henry. For that reason Edward had to impose his authority on the country quickly and effectively because any setback, however minor, would have disastrous effects for the new regime.

To cement his position the King needed to muster support, not just among the relatively small number of nobles who had backed him during the campaign but among those who had been on the Lancastrian side and might be willing to accept the new circumstances. Factionalism had been an unsettling influence during Henry VI's reign and Edward made it clear that he represented a new beginning and a fresh opportunity to unite the kingdom. Inevitably, in those unsettled times there were those who found it prudent to change their allegiance and Edward assisted the process by explaining that he was prepared to show clemency to those who would trim their beliefs. Among those restored to royal favour was Lord Rivers, who had been closely involved with Henry's affairs and had been mercilessly 'rated' by Edward and Warwick during his period of captivity in Calais a year earlier.

There was also a necessity to restore good governance after the years of Lancastrian misrule. From the outset Edward was determined that his court should be solvent and although he was not averse to enjoying life's luxuries he managed to ensure that he paid his way, mainly by raising funds from the nobility through a system known as 'benevolences'. (Allegedly free gifts offered to the monarch through the *benevolentia*, or good will, of the donor, they were in effect forced loans and later fell into disrepute.) Edward also managed to repay debts of £97,000 which had accrued during Henry's chaotic reign and proved to be a better manager of the Crown estates by introducing realistic rents and clamping down on corrupt practices. Taxes were raised only to pay for military operations and Edward introduced a new office, the Chamber, which became the principal conduit for royal funds, thereby bypassing the Exchequer and allowing the King to have greater control over his own finances.

Other measures aimed at restoring confidence included the passing of Acts of Resumption which revoked many of the grants and awards made by Henry. Edward even considered closing Eton College. One of the first acts of his first Parliament was to revoke all grants made to it since its foundation and in 1463 he applied for a papal bull authorising the college's abolition. Four years later he relented and Eton was spared, but elsewhere in Windsor he was responsible for erecting a new chapel dedicated to St George, a magnificent Gothic building which became Edward's greatest memorial.

Some idea of the parlous nature of the early years of Edward's reign can be seen in his unquiet relationship with the north of England, which very quickly became a focus for Lancastrian disaffection. The first sign of trouble came in June 1461 when an army of Scots and Lancastrian supporters laid siege to Carlisle and had to be dislodged by forces led by the newly ennobled Earl of Kent. Another raid was mounted the following month when a party including Henry VI rode south and reached Brancepeth in south Durham before being forced to retire by local levies led by the Archbishop of York. It was not the end of Edward's problems. To all intents and purposes the whole of Northumberland answered to the Percys and key fortresses, including Alnwick and Dunstanburgh, remained in the family's hands. It was a measure of the difficulties facing Edward that he had to allow Sir Ralph Percy, Northumberland's brother, to retain power in the area even though he was hardly a natural ally: his father had been killed at

St Albans and his brother at Towton, both fighting on the Lancastrian side.

Wales was also a problem. The castles at Pembroke, Harlech and Denbigh were all in Lancastrian hands and it was not until October that a measure of control was restored, when forces led by Jasper Tudor, the Earl of Pembroke, were defeated at Twt Hill, near Caernarfon. Among those captured was Pembroke's four-year-old nephew Henry Tudor, who was placed in the hands of Sir William Herbert, Edward's principal ally in Wales. With Sir Walter Devereux, Herbert quickly set about consolidating the Yorkist position in the principality and soon made solid gains: Pembroke Castle fell in September, followed by Denbigh and Carreg Cennen the following spring. Only Harlech continued to hold out but for the present time Pembroke's defeat at Twt Hill was a setback to Queen Margaret's hopes of retaining Lancastrian support in Wales. However, old habits died hard in the principality and, as it turned out, the garrison inside Harlech managed to hold out long enough to intervene once more in support of Pembroke, who had made good his escape north to reach Margaret's exiled court in Scotland.

Chapter Fifteen

WARWICK, MAKER AND BREAKER OF KINGS

On becoming King of England Edward IV presented a noble picture to the rest of the world. Standing six feet three inches tall, he was a big and well-made man who was well aware of the effect he had on other people. Although a surviving anonymous portrait shows a beefy face with narrow eyes and small pinched mouth, Sir James Strangeways, the first speaker of his Parliament, addressed the new king in terms that were complimentary to his looks and made a point of referring to 'the beauty of personage that it hath pleased Almighty God to send you'. Lest this be taken as simple flattery, other accounts insist that Edward was not only fine-looking but, as we have seen, attractive to women, a fact he used to good advantage, and his 'licentious' behaviour was noted by several contemporary chroniclers and letter writers.

Edward dressed well, another attribute which made him a pleasing personality and added to his reputation as a genial and open soul. Sir Thomas More, who knew him, described him as 'a goodly personage and very princely to behold, of heart courageous, politic in counsel' and there is evidence to suggest that Edward was not above using his personal charm to get his own way, particularly in securing loans and gifts from wealthy merchants in London.

On the debit side, he could appear lazy and vainglorious and had a tendency to overindulge, not least as far as women were concerned, a fact noted many years later by Dominic Mancini:

Moreover, it was said that he had been most insolent to numerous women after he had seduced them, for as soon as he had satisfied his lust he abandoned the ladies much against their will, to other courtiers. He pursued with no discrimination the married and unmarried, the noble and lowly. However, he took none by force. He overcame all by money and promises, and, having conquered them, he dismissed them.

Edward was fond of saying that he always had three concubines – one the merriest, another the wiliest and the third the holiest – but the identities of most of his many mistresses remain a mystery, although his numerous affairs are well attested. Only two names are remembered: Elizabeth Lucy, the daughter of a Hampshire squire, and Elizabeth Shore (also called Jane), a goldsmith's wife in whom, according to More, Edward 'took special pleasure'. The first mistress bore the King an illegitimate son, Arthur Plantagenet, and the second remained a lifelong friend. More left a charming portrait of Mrs Shore in her youth, praising her for her beauty and pleasant behaviour: 'For a proper wit had she and could both read well and write, merry in company, ready and quick of answer, neither mute nor full of babble.'

The matter of Edward's marital status is one of the great mysteries in an otherwise transparent life. With his looks and his easy personality he was a good catch and early in his reign thought was given to entering him into a strategic marriage. One possibility was Mary of Gueldres, James II's widow, as it was thought that a Scottish marriage would be advantageous, as would the relationship through her to her kinsman Duke Philip of Burgundy, but her sudden death in 1463 put paid to that idea. Another option was the twelve-year-old Princess Isabella, the Infanta of Castile, who eventually married Ferdinand of Aragon, but Warwick favoured a French alliance and entered into negotiations with Louis XI for the hand of his sister-in-law, Bona of Savoy, who was renowned for her good looks. This would have been a useful match but when the latter proposal was being negotiated in the summer of 1464 Edward astonished everyone by suddenly announcing that he had already married in secret.

His new wife was Elizabeth Woodville (or Wydeville), the eldest daughter of Lord Rivers (from his marriage to Jacquetta of Bedford) and the widow of the Sir John Grey of Groby, a prominent Lancastrian who was killed at the Second Battle of St Albans. It was a curious match. For all that Elizabeth was considered a great beauty she was four years older than Edward, she had two sons by Grey and, more to the point, she was a commoner whose only royal connection was her having been a lady-in-waiting to Margaret of Anjou. The announcement was made by the King on 14 September at a meeting of the council and it caused a sensation. It had never been the custom for English kings to make their own matches with brides from their own people and, as de Waurin made clear, they were certainly not supposed to marry commoners. If they did they were not meant to do it in secret:

> They [members of the council] answered that she was not his [Edward's] match, that however good and fair she might be, she was not a wife for so high a prince as he; and he knew this well, for she was not the daughter of a duke or earl, but her mother had married a simple knight, so that though she was the daughter of the Duchess of Bedford, and the niece of the Count of St Pol, still she was no wife for him.

In fact Edward's new wife came from a thoroughly respectable Northamptonshire family and, as de Waurin conceded, her mother Jacquetta had been married to the Duke of Bedford, brother of Henry V. In the eyes of the nobility the Woodvilles might have been upstarts who had formed useful marriage alliances to better themselves, but in their own way they were an old-established and well-regarded family, as were the relatives of Elizabeth's first husband, who lived at Groby Castle, near Leicester.

Edward and Elizabeth married in secret on 1 May at Grafton in Buckinghamshire, near the family home at Stony Stratford, and astonishingly they managed to keep their relationship a secret for a good while. The reasons for Edward's infatuation were much pondered over at the time and gave rise to many wild theories, the most common being that Elizabeth had refused to have sexual relations with the King unless he married her. That was certainly possible. Elizabeth Woodville was a respectable widow with a reputation to maintain and she refused to be just another of the King's conquests to be bedded and discarded later. She must also have understood the strength of the King's passion for her because a ploy of demanding marriage in return for sex could have been a dangerous game. If Mancini is to be believed, Edward was used to getting his way in such matters and must have known that the match would cause a huge upset.

There were also rumours that Elizabeth had used sorcery or witchcraft to beguile Edward into marrying her. The day before their marriage was one of the witches' four Sabbaths and local tradition had it that the couple were betrothed under an oak tree, thought to be a place where witches worshipped. Her mother was also thought to be involved in the sorcery and several years later a neighbour made the astonishing accusation that Jacquetta had been implicated in a plot to have her daughter married to the King by using a black magic spell involving small leaden figures.

Whatever the reasons for the King's infatuation and his secret marriage it was considered shocking enough to be recorded in minute detail in Fabyan's diaries:

> In such pass time, in most secret manner, upon the first day of May, King Edward spoused Elizabeth, late the wife of Sir John Grey, knight, which before time was slain at Towton or York field [it was in fact at the Second Battle of St Albans], which spousals were solemnised early in the morning at a town named Grafton, near Stony Stratford; at which marriage was no persons present but the spouse, spousess, the Duchess of Bedford her mother, the priest, two gentle-women, and a young man to help the priest sing. After which spousals ended, he went to bed and tarried thereupon three or four hours, and after departed and rode again to Stony Stratford, and came in manner as though he had been on hunting, and there went to bed again.

Perhaps the best answer is supplied by Gregory, who noted simply, 'now take heed what love may do for love will not cast no fault nor peril in nothing'. As Queen Elizabeth the King's new wife was presented to the court on Michaelmas Day and was led into the abbey chapel at Reading by Clarence, her new brother-in-law, and by Warwick, the most powerful man in the kingdom. The ceremonial augured well – the chronicles of William Worcester (*Annales*) recorded that she was 'honoured as queen by the lords and all the people' – but within weeks of her arrival the new queen had started causing resentment by seeking preferment for her many relatives. Elizabeth had twelve brothers and sisters and in quick succession she started arranging advantageous marriages for them and influencing her husband to provide lucrative sinecures. This was precisely the kind of behaviour that had bedevilled Henry VI's court but Elizabeth was wildly ambitious and had her husband in such thrall that he found it impossible to refuse her requests.

Within a month of the announcement of the royal marriage her sister Margaret had been betrothed to Thomas Maltravers, the heir of the Earl of Arundel, and, according to the Worcester chronicle, there was a steady progression of matches involving Woodvilles to powerful families: her twenty-year-old brother John was married off to the elderly Duchess of Norfolk, 'a diabolical marriage' to 'a slip of a girl about eighty years old' who had already survived three marriages (she was in fact in her sixties and survived her young husband by fourteen years); another sister was paired off with the Duke of Buckingham 'to the secret displeasure of the Earl of Warwick'; while other sisters found themselves in matches with the heir of the Duke of Exeter and the heir of the Earl of Kent (now Anthony Grey of Ruthin as Fauconberg, the previous holder of the title, had died). Finally, in October the following year, Thomas Grey, the Queen's son from her first marriage, was put down to marry Lady Anne Holland, heiress of the Duke of Exeter, 'the king's niece, to the great and secret displeasure of the Earl of Warwick, for a marriage was previously bespoken between the said Lady Anne and the son of the Earl of Northumberland, the Earl of Warwick's brother [previously Montague]'. Patronage was also forthcoming: Warwick's uncle Lord Mountjoy was relieved of his post as Treasurer and replaced by Rivers, now created an earl, again 'to the secret displeasure of the Earl of Warwick and the magnates of England'.

Although the contemporary reports of Warwick's displeasure were exaggerated he had good reason to feel discomfited. Not only were these dynastic marriages disliked on account of the Woodvilles' lack of social standing, but the all-powerful Nevilles were sufficiently jealous of their closeness to Edward IV to feel threatened by the sudden emergence of a new faction at court. While there was a certain amount of snobbishness in the reaction – Mancini alleged that the Woodville family was 'detested by the nobles because they were advanced beyond those who excelled them in breeding and wisdom' – the main reason for the disapproval was power play.

Once again a rival faction was being created, this time with the intent to threaten the Nevilles. For Warwick the emergence of the Woodvilles at court was frustrating for a variety of reasons. First, it put pressure on his own position as the principal power-broker in England; secondly, it allowed the creation of a new set of alliances in a family which had been firm supporters of the Lancastrians; thirdly, the Woodvilles made it clear that they did not agree with all of Warwick's policies, especially his plan to seek an alliance with Louis in preference to Burgundy. (The revelation of the Woodville alliance had put paid to the plan to marry Edward to the Savoy princess.) All this was very galling for Warwick, who had spent the first three years of Edward's reign securing the northern border and virtually ending the Percys' power in Northumberland, all to the King's benefit.

Bringing security to the north of England was an important consideration in the early years of Edward's reign as the Scots still remained a threat, not least because of their support for the Lancastrian cause. Since moving to Scotland after Towton Henry VI had become part hostage, part pawn. But even though he was personally powerless he was still a focus for Lancastrian hopes and despite the attainder that had been passed by Edward ending his kingship he still thought of himself as the anointed King of England. Others also found him useful. The Scots harboured hopes of gaining an advantage over England but so faction-ridden was the Scottish court and so poor the country that it was impossible to imagine that they would be able to offer any substantial support by way of funds or manpower.

Finding herself isolated at the Scottish court, Margaret decided to look to France for backing and crossed over to Brittany in Easter 1462, carrying with her a promise from her husband to hand over Calais in return for armed support from her French cousin. At Touraine Louis reluctantly agreed to the terms but his help was half-hearted and consisted of a small force of eight hundred soldiers under the command of Margaret's old friend Pierre de Brézé, the former Seneschal of Normandy and Poitou. With them Margaret returned to Scotland to pick up her husband and Somerset and their forces sailed down the coast to land near Bamburgh Castle. Although the main northern fortresses of Alnwick and Bamburgh were occupied the onset of winter forced her to withdraw and most of her fleet was wrecked. She and her husband managed to get back to Berwick with de Brézé but the survivors of the shipwrecks were washed ashore near Lindisfarne, where they were set upon and massacred by Yorkist forces.

Nevertheless, the French incursion had thoroughly unsettled Edward, who moved north with a large army to meet the threat posed by the Scots. On reaching Durham the King fell ill with measles but Warwick took command and set about besieging Dunstanburgh and Bamburgh. Both castles surrendered on Christmas Eve 1462 and Alnwick followed early in the new year. This restored the strategic advantage to Edward's forces but the success was marred by an astonishing piece of bad judgement, to which the young king was always prone. An offer made by Somerset to change sides was accepted – he was created a knight of the bedchamber and given an annuity – and in a move which defies rational explanation Sir Ralph Percy was allowed to remain in charge of the strongholds provided that he swore allegiance to Edward.

While this was typical of Edward's generosity of spirit and conformed to his thinking that the kingdom had to be unified and old animosities healed, it was madness to offer an open hand to Somerset given his family's past history of support to the Lancastrian cause and his own close relationship with Margaret of Anjou. Equally, it made no sense at all to allow a Percy to control the main fortresses in Northumberland. Sir Ralph Percy had already broken an earlier agreement by opening the gates of Alnwick to a prominent Lancastrian, Sir William Tailboys, and within months he repaid the King's latest act of generosity by handing over Bamburgh, Dunstanburgh and Alnwick to a joint force of Scots and French, thus restoring most of Northumberland to the Lancastrians. Once again the Scots came over the border, this time in a full-scale invasion, and laid siege to the fortress at Norham on the River Tweed, a few miles inland from Berwick.

In response to this new threat Warwick and Montague rallied their forces and marched north. Outside York the Scottish army was repulsed and the survivors fled back into Scotland hotly pursued by the Nevilles, who took their forces over the border into Scotland to harry the southern uplands before a lack of supplies and reinforcements forced them to retire. The siege of Norham was lifted and, with support falling away from her, Margaret escaped to Berwick, where a

French ship took her and her son to Sluys, in the French fiefdom of Flanders, and exile. Once in France, she established a small court at the chateau of Koeur-la-Petite, near St Mihiel on the River Meuse close to Commercy, which belonged to Margaret's father. There Margaret and her supporters lived in what one courtier called 'great poverty', unable to act without French support and waiting for events to unfold. As for Henry, the hopelessness of his position was underlined when he was taken back to Scotland, to be placed under Bishop Kennedy's care and protection, first in Edinburgh and then St Andrews. The Lancastrian cause was dented further during the summer, when Edward concluded a tripartite truce with Louis and the Duke of Burgundy before attempting to sign a separate treaty with the Scots.

There was some respite for the Queen's party when Somerset changed sides once more. He had been treated well – the attainder against him had been lifted and he was appointed Captain of Newcastle – but he remained a Beaufort and his heart lay with the Lancastrian cause. Having raised a force which included Sir Ralph Percy and Lords Hungerford and Roos, he intercepted a force of Nevilles while it was moving north to Norham to meet the Scottish envoys, who had been given safe conducts to conclude the treaty. During the fighting on Hedgeley Moor, some nine miles north-west of Alnwick, on 21 April 1464 the Lancastrian left flank, commanded by Roos and Hungerford, was quickly broken and the affray became a one-sided business. Percy was killed – his last words were suitably enigmatic, 'I have saved the bird in my bosom' – and the remainder of the force retreated into the valley of the River Tyne, where three weeks later they were trapped in a narrow defile called the Linnels on the Devil's Water, not far from Hexham. (The battle site has been identified as lying between Linnels Bridge and Teasdale Fell.) Unable to deploy in the confines of the narrow ground, Somerset's men were crushed by the superior Yorkist forces on 15 May. Those who escaped death on the battlefield were executed: among them were Somerset, Roos and Hungerford, all of whom paid the price for being on the losing side.

The collapse of the Northumberland fortresses followed the defeat. Alnwick and Dunstanburgh surrendered without a shot being fired, but the defenders at Bamburgh under Sir Ralph Grey, another Yorkist turncoat, attempted to hold out and the castle was battered into submission by 'the great ordnance of England', heavy siege guns which were gradually coming into service at the time. Before ordering his gunners to open fire Montague sent heralds to tell the garrison what awaited them if they continued to hold out, their words being recorded in the chronicle of John Warkworth, Master of Peterhouse, Cambridge:

> The king, our most dread sovereign lord, specially desires to have this jewel whole and unbroken by artillery, particularly because it stands so close to his ancient enemies the Scots, and if you are the cause that great guns have to be fired against its walls, then it will cost you your head, and for every shot that has to be fired another head, down to the humblest person within the place.

The advice was ignored and, following a brief but heavy bombardment, Bamburgh opened its gates after Grey began negotiations for its surrender. Much good it did him: he was dragged to Doncaster and immediately beheaded. Bamburgh produced the first and only setpiece siege of the civil war and its fall was decisive: by midsummer the power of the Percys in the north of England had been crushed by the Nevilles.

All effective Lancastrian resistance in England had now come to an end and the Scots prudently entered into a fifteen-year truce with Edward. As for the hapless Henry, he had taken refuge from the fighting in nearby Bywell Castle and was forced to go on the run, being sheltered in a number of safe houses in the north of England, which remained loyal to his cause. All that was found of his presence was his crowned cap and some of his belongings, which were taken into Montague's custody after the fighting in the Tyne Valley.

It was not until the following summer that Henry was eventually discovered while dining with pro-Lancastrian gentry at Waddington Hall near Clitheroe, the seat of Sir Richard Temple. Although Henry managed to make good his escape he was captured in the nearby Clitherwoods, close to a ford over the River Ribble known today as Brungerley. Taken south, he arrived in London on 24 June and was paraded through the streets as evidence of his capture before being lodged in apartments in the Tower, where he spent the next five years under guard. Lancastrian chroniclers later alleged that he was cruelly treated during his confinement but the conditions seem to have been reasonably tolerable and true to form he spent much of the time in prayer and contemplation. The records show that he had the use of a priest for daily prayers and that he was given regular supplies of wine and velvet cloth for fresh clothes. According to Warkworth, Henry 'was kept long time by two squires and two yeomen of the crown, and their men; and every man suffered to come and speak with him by licence of the keepers'.

This turnabout strengthened Edward's position in that he now had full control over his opponent but it came at the same time as he caused dismay among this supporters by marrying Elizabeth Woodville and tolerating the rash of marriage alliances. It was especially irksome to Warwick: having pacified the north, the King's closest ally now found himself at loggerheads with Edward over the policy to be adopted towards France. Although Warwick had been close to the Duke of Burgundy during his time in Calais he favoured entering into an alliance with Louis XI, whom he knew well and had come to like. Perhaps he was flattered by the French king's interest in him; he might also have boasted about his own influence over Edward at court and during the course of several embassies during the 1460s he was a constant promoter of a treaty of friendship with France. For Louis this was an important perquisite for his own policies as he was keen to break the power of the Dukes of Burgundy and Brittany and wanted to prevent England entering into a separate treaty with the former. However, this is precisely what Edward was intent on doing.

Initially Edward seems to have kept an open mind about his foreign policy. In May 1465 he appointed Warwick to lead an embassy to confer with Louis, Duke Francis of Brittany and Charles, Count of Charolais, the eldest son of the recently incapacitated Duke Philip of Burgundy, but the outbreak of fighting among all three in the short-lived War of the Public Weal prevented Warwick from making any progress. That window of opportunity closed as the Woodville faction, notably their leading light Earl Rivers, began to exercise their influence at court. Edward now began to favour a treaty with the Burgundians, who were England's largest trading partners in the wool market. The following year Charles of Charolais, a widower, put forward a proposal for the hand of Edward's sister Margaret of York while at the same time marrying Edward's brother the Duke of Clarence to his own daughter Mary. Neither proposal suited Warwick. There is contemporary evidence to suggest that he had formed an early and deep dislike for

Charles and was opposed to the idea of the King's brother marrying into the House of Burgundy as he entertained ambitions for Clarence to marry his own daughter Isabel. Unfortunately for those dreams, Edward was opposed to such a match on the grounds of their consanguinity – Clarence and Isabel were first cousins once removed – and he banned any further marriage negotiations.

There was, of course, another reason for the King's opposition: the Duke of Clarence was his heir presumptive and at that stage in his life Edward did not want to see his brother becoming allied to the powerful Nevilles. The King's fears were not without grounds: Warwick understood the authority that would accrue to him through the match at a time when he was forced to watch the Woodvilles making their own matrimonial alliances to powerful English magnates. Undeterred, Warwick entered into secret negotiations with Rome to obtain the papal dispensation which would allow the marriage of his daughter to Clarence.

In the midst of this diplomatic activity Edward tried to keep all sides guessing about his real intentions. In the spring of 1466 he concluded a truce with Louis in which he agreed to keep out of the French king's hostilities with Brittany and Burgundy in return for a French promise not to support Margaret of Anjou. These agreements were signed but neither side had any real intention of sticking to their conditions. At the same time Edward made a private pledge of friendship with the Duke of Burgundy, who had been temporarily restored to health.

Matters came to a head in June 1467 when a jousting tournament was arranged between the Duke of Burgundy's illegitimate son Antony, Bastard of Burgundy, and Anthony Woodville, Lord Scales, son of Earl Rivers. Both men were judged to be the foremost warriors of their age and whoever won the tournament would be hailed the champion of all Europe. Although jousting was not as fashionable as it had been in the previous century the opportunity to witness a clash of arms between two leading exponents of the sport created a huge amount of excitement throughout England. Not only did it promise to be a spectacular event but the tournament seemed to be a harbinger of a new period of peace and prosperity. Henry VI was confined in the Tower, Edward was secure on his throne and had taken a wife, albeit one who was not universally popular, and that same year the King gave notice that his court was solvent and that he could finally live off his own means.

As it turned out, through no one's fault, the tournament was a damp squib. On the first day there was only one joust on horseback and the second day's session with battle-axes reached no conclusion. Events were then brought to a sudden stop when a messenger arrived from the Burgundian court announcing the death of Duke Philip and forcing the Bastard to return home immediately.

Despite the unsatisfactory conclusion, the tournament had achieved its underlying aim of continuing the diplomatic discussions between the courts of England and Burgundy. In the week before the tournament the Bastard and his retinue had enjoyed the hospitality of the court and attended the opening of Parliament. While the Bastard was being entertained he did everything possible to reinforce the idea that the proposed marriage between Charolais and Margaret of York would pave the way for a lasting alliance between England and Burgundy. The Bastard was also able to witness at first hand Edward's determination to be his own man and take steps to curb the power of the Nevilles.

One of the notable absentees from London during the Bastard's visit was George Neville, now Archbishop of York, who had announced that he had no intention of being in the capital at a time when the King was entertaining representatives from Burgundy. As he also served as Chancellor this was a snub to Edward, who probably knew that Neville was busily scheming in Rome for a cardinal's hat and, against royal wishes, was working hard to gain the necessary dispensation to allow his niece to marry Clarence. Within the week the King took his revenge. Neville was removed from his position and replaced by Robert Stillington, the ambitious and time-serving Bishop of Bath and Wells, who had risen from obscurity and had the dubious distinction of visiting his see just once during twenty-six years in office.

Not only was the removal of Neville a slap in the face for his brother Warwick, who was in France on a diplomatic mission at the time, but it was a very public humiliation conducted in person by the King. On his return to London Warwick brought with him a French delegation, who were treated politely but distantly and whose embassy achieved nothing. To add insult Edward insisted on entering into a treaty with the Duke of Brittany in which he agreed to support him in the event of attack by supplying three thousand archers. This diplomatic coup was followed up with an alliance with King Henry of Castile.

Both moves cemented the King's determination to have his own way in directing foreign policy, and the change of Chancellor was a telling snub to the Nevilles as Stillington was simply a placeman. The way was now open for the King to conclude his alliance with Charles, the new Duke of Burgundy, and although he came out of the negotiations a poorer man – he was outbid in the settlement of the dowry and found himself having to find two hundred thousand gold crowns – the wedding to Margaret of York took place on 3 July 1468 at Damme in Flanders. Contemporary accounts of the nuptials make it clear that it was a grand affair but, as the Croyland chronicler insists, not everyone was enamoured of what had happened:

> At this marriage Richard Neville, Earl of Warwick who had for some years appeared to favour the party of the French against the Burgundians, conceived great indignation. For he would greatly have preferred to have sought an alliance for the said Lady Margaret in the Kingdom of France, by means of which a favourable understanding might have arisen between the monarchs of those two kingdoms; it being much against his wish, that the views of Burgundy should in any way be promoted by means of an alliance with England. The fact is, that he pursued that man [Charles of Burgundy] with a most deadly hatred.

Against all of Warwick's wishes Edward had now completed his steps in a diplomatic dance which brought England into partnership with two duchies, Burgundy and Brittany, which were already in alliance against France. Once more the long shadow cast by the years of warfare with England's greatest enemy influenced the way an English king decided to forge his foreign policy. It was a classic manoeuvre which would have been understood by any of Edward's Plantagenet forebears: take advantage of the enmity of France's enemies, both internal and external, by entering into compacts with them and then prepare for war. Not that Edward had any serious intention of attacking France in 1468: he would only assist his new allies in the event of any offensive action, but war with England's old enemy remained a possibility in the distant future.

Such a course of action brought obvious risks: as Louis became aware of Edward's hostility the more thought he gave to supporting the Lancastrian cause. The French king's immediate response was to fund an insurrection in Wales led by Jasper Tudor, who aimed to encourage the Welsh to rise up for the Prince of Wales and make contact with the garrison in Harlech Castle, which was still in Lancastrian hands. In July he landed in west Wales and initially enjoyed some success in raising numbers of men to his colours. Some idea of the extent of Tudor's achievement is given by the fact that he arrived with only fifty men and had to rely on his name and standing to encourage others to join him. It was a gallant attempt but Tudor's luck did not last. Yorkist forces led by Lord Herbert and his brother Sir Richard Herbert marched into Wales and crushed Tudor's army near Denbigh, which had previously been burned to the ground. The defeat forced the Harlech garrison to surrender on 14 August and Tudor was fortunate to make good his escape disguised as a peasant. It was a shattering blow for a man who prided himself on the strength of his support in Wales and, to make matters worse, the title granted to him by Henry VI was lost when a grateful Edward made Lord Herbert the new Earl of Pembroke.

Once again, from his own point of view, the King had made a shrewd move. Herbert came from an old-established Welsh family and was one of the first men from his background to make an impact on the English court. He was an absolute Yorkist loyalist, known as 'the King's lock-master' for Wales, and early on had forged an alliance with the Woodvilles when his son was married to Mary, one of the Queen's sisters. Forceful and ambitious, the new earl of Pembroke came to govern Wales almost as a viceroy and quickly acquired properties in England, becoming a powerful and wealthy magnate in his own right. However, the very traits which made him attractive and useful to Edward also brought him into conflict with Warwick, who was dismayed by his rival's elevation as Earl of Pembroke. History seemed to be repeating itself with the creation of opposing factions at court: one loyal to the King and consisting of the Woodvilles, including Pembroke; the other, the Nevilles, increasingly disenchanted with a group whom they considered to be upstarts and Edward's wrong-headed and avaricious advisers.

There is no single reason why Warwick's disillusionment with

Edward led him into taking action against him. It seems to have been due to a steady accumulation of setbacks, disappointments and rebuffs which produced a dawning realisation that he was no longer supreme at court but just one of several people on whom the King relied. His influence had been challenged over the country's foreign policy and his advice about alliances and marriages had not been accepted. At court he had witnessed the inexorable rise to power of the Woodville family and had seen men such as Herbert being promoted from relative obscurity to positions of power and authority.

For Warwick this was intolerable: he was a Neville, one of the wealthiest and most influential families in England; he had devoted much of his life to supporting the Yorkist cause and had seen his father and brother killed fighting for Richard of York and his son Edward. At the same time his attempt to marry his daughters to Edward's brothers had been thwarted and his family had been further humiliated by the sacking of his brother George Neville. Warwick still appeared at court and took an active part in public life and the easy-going Edward probably came to believe that the relationship was still intact, if somewhat altered in character. At the beginning of the year Warwick had been reconciled to Edward during a meeting of council when the King kept Christmas at Coventry but that was for public consumption; during the summer and autumn of 1468 the man who is known to history as 'Warwick the Kingmaker' was clearly disaffected and thinking about how he could retrieve his position.

Fatally for all concerned, it was about this time that Warwick entered into a close relationship with the Duke of Clarence, the King's brother. Like Edward, Duke George was a strapping, well-built and good-looking young man who had inherited his family's driving ambition and sense of place in the world. At his seat at Tutbury he maintained a huge household, grander and more lavish than his brother's court, with around four hundred servants in his employment. Although he received generous funding from the public purse the adoption of such an extravagant lifestyle meant that a good marriage to a wealthy heiress had become central to his plans, hence his willingness to fall in with the idea that he should marry Warwick's daughter. By 1468 he had been made aware of the secret negotiations with the papal curia to gain a dispensation and was prepared to disobey his brother's wishes if Rome should find in Warwick's favour. The fact that he was prepared to follow that path is ample evidence of a growing dissatisfaction with his lot in life, and this was coupled with a willingness to defy Edward.

Although Clarence had been rewarded more than generously for simply being a royal duke – he was granted huge estates and received an income as Lord Lieutenant of Ireland – he felt that he had little influence at court and he became that dangerous creature, a jealous prince of the realm who had no distinctive public role yet retained ambitions to become a power in the land. All his dealings with Warwick and their plotting to defy royal authority contained the makings of a clash which could once again plunge the country into a new round of civil strife.

The emergence of the Warwick–Clarence partnership came at the same time as fresh outbreaks of pro-Lancastrian sympathies. In the early summer of 1468 there was a rash of scares about Lancastrian plots to overturn the regime and return Henry VI to the throne. Most of these involved the exposure of letters to known supporters which had been written by Margaret of Anjou. One of the most serious cases involved a shoemaker called Cornelius who, according to the Worcester chronicle, was arrested in London and after spending three days in the Tower 'was tortured by burning in the feet until he confessed many things'. Under the stress – the feet-burning was followed by the stripping off of his flesh with red-hot pincers – Cornelius accused a number of conspirators, who were themselves put to torture.

One of them was John Hawkins, a servant of Lord Wenlock, Warwick's associate in Calais, who implicated Sir Thomas Cook, a wealthy London merchant. Cook was lucky to escape with his life but was ruined financially on being forced to pay a huge fine after being found guilty of misprision of treason (being privy to treasonable activities but failing to report them). The case caused a good deal of bitterness in London when it became clear that the Woodvilles had been involved in the persecution. Earlier Cook had refused to sell a tapestry to the Dowager Duchess of Bedford at the low selling price she demanded and following his punishment Queen Elizabeth insisted on imposing the ancient right of Queen's Gold on top of his fine.

This was followed by the arrest of three suspected Lancastrian sympathisers, Henry Courtenay, brother of the attainted Earl of Devon, Thomas Hungerford, whose father had been executed after the Battle of Hexham, and John de Vere, 13th Earl of Oxford and Warwick's brother-in-law. All were accused of conspiring with Margaret of Anjou. Oxford was quickly released but Courtenay and Hungerford were arraigned before a commission of oyer and terminer headed by Gloucester and were sentenced to traitors' deaths in Salisbury the following year. (Oxford was doubly fortunate as his father, the 12th Earl, had been executed as a traitor six years earlier.)

The spy scares and the treatment of Cook all helped to fuel an atmosphere of fear and general ill will and increased the belief that trouble was brewing on a grand scale. *The Great Chronicle of London* recorded that 'many murmurous tales ran in the city atween the Earl of Warwick and the queen's blood' and Warkworth claimed that the people of England were vexed over a number of issues, namely bad governance and high taxes and as a result they were 'full glad to have a change'. In fact taxation had not been heavy during Edward's reign but the disaffection seems to have been compounded by the general unhappiness with the Woodville faction at court and the favours bestowed on them.

At the same time Royalist agents reported that whenever Warwick appeared in London the people greeted him with cries of 'Warwick! Warwick!' and the same point was made in *The Great Chronicle*. It also repeated a scurrilous story about a man called Woodhouse who managed to get into the King's presence wearing a strange outfit consisting of a short coat and thigh-length boots and carrying a long marsh pole. When Edward asked why he was dressed in that fashion Woodhouse replied, 'Upon my faith, Sir, I have passed through many countries [counties] of your realm and in places that I have passed the Rivers have been so high that I could scarcely scrape through them, but as I was fain to search the depth with this long staff.' The chronicler claimed that the King understood exactly what Woodhouse meant and made light of the reference to the power wielded by Earl Rivers, but added that the incident 'was an ill prenostication as ye shall shortly hear after'.

Chapter Sixteen

DECLINE AND FALL

When it came to pursuing his own ambitions Warwick was both a great dissembler and a hard-headed realist and it is doubtful if Edward had any inkling about the Earl's treasonable plans until they were put into practice. In the spring of 1469 Warwick acted as if the spirit of reconciliation were still alive and did nothing to stir up any suspicions at court, mainly by keeping his distance and using his immense wealth to maintain his popularity in London.

All the contemporary evidence makes it clear that Warwick was an attractive personality with an affability and openness of character which captivated those who knew him. In addition to his military talents and his boundless generosity, he seems to have been that rare beast, a man of great wealth and stature who managed to retain a common touch. At the height of his own career in the latter part of the fifteenth century he was considered to be one of the greatest men of his day and that reputation survived his death to ring down the centuries. Edward Bulwer-Lytton's novel of 1847 *The Last of the Barons* is based on contemporary evidence and contains a sympathetic portrait of Warwick as an heroic figure, a king-maker capable of changing destiny, while the contemporaneous *Great Chronicle of London* notes that Warwick continued behaving in the same expansive way that had always marked his time in the capital and won him so many admirers:

The which earl was ever had in great favour of the commons of this land, by reason of exceeding household which he daily kept in all countries [counties] wherever he sojourned or lay, and when he came to London he held such an house that six oxen were eaten at breakfast, and every tavern was full of his meat, for that had any acquaintance in that house, he should have as much sodden [boiled] and roast [meat] as he might carry on a long dagger which those days were much used as now they use murderers.

It was not just in London that Warwick was cementing his public position. In April he represented Edward at a meeting with Louis XI held at St Omer, and the following month he was present at a Garter ceremony at Windsor which conferred the order on the new Duke of Burgundy. He also accepted a fresh naval commission to prosecute operations against the Hanse League and in the middle of May he was in Sandwich overseeing the preparation of his fleet and the fitting-out of his flagship the *Trinity*; he was always single-minded and committed when it came to dealing with naval matters. Everything seemed to be so normal that in mid-June Edward saw no reason to be concerned when he was encouraged to set out on a pilgrimage to the shrine of Our Lady of Walsingham in Norfolk, taking with him Gloucester, Rivers, Scales and other members of the Woodville family. It was the worst thing the King could have done, for already trouble was brewing in the north of England and these eruptions proved to be a harbinger for a fresh round of civil conflict.

The first outbreak of trouble had occurred in Yorkshire in April, when there were a number of disturbances centred on a malcontent calling himself Robin of Redesdale or Robin Mend-All; according to Warkworth, this was the name adopted by Sir John Conyers of Hornby, a cousin by marriage of Warwick. (Robin was a catch-all name for any popular people's hero and Redesdale probably refers to the Northumberland village of Ridsdale.) At the same time there was another, quite separate flare-up in the East Riding of Yorkshire led by another mysterious figure, styled Robin of Holderness, who was probably a member of the Percy family as the main complaint voiced by him and his followers was the restoration of that family to the Northumberland earldom, currently in the hands of the Nevilles.

Robin of Holderness's true identity has been posited as Robert Hillyard of Winstead, or even his son, another Robert, but that connection has never been proved. Whoever he was, his revolt was speedily and efficiently quelled by forces led by John Neville, the new

Earl of Northumberland and Warwick's brother. Unfortunately, the same outcome was not the case with Robin of Redesdale. Although Neville managed to break up their meetings, Conyers's supporters dispersed and regrouped across the Pennines in Lancashire. From there they returned to Yorkshire in May and began moving south with a force estimated by Warkworth at twenty thousand, 'a mighty insurrection of the commons'. The number was probably significantly smaller and most of them were Nevilles or Neville retainers and tenants, among them Warwick's nephew Sir Henry FitzHugh, son of Lord FitzHugh, together with sundry distant relatives. The rest of the gathering joined Conyers for a variety of related reasons, not least dislike of taxation, lingering support for Henry VI and a general dissatisfaction with Edward's government of the country. The Croyland chronicler summed up the mood of grievance when he recorded that the northern rebellion was begun by people who were 'grievously oppressed with taxes and annual tributes by the favourites of the king and queen'.

The news of the unrest reached the King's entourage while they were staying at Croyland Abbey and Edward decided to ride in person to deal with the uprising. At the end of June he made his way to Fotheringhay Castle in Yorkshire, where he stopped and waited for his main forces to arrive. These were slow in assembling and it quickly became apparent to the King that his summonses for recruits were either being ignored or being acted upon with great reluctance. Despite calls to the main towns in the Midlands to supply men it was proving difficult to raise the necessary forces, while from the north came alarming stories of the size and strength of Robin of Redesdale's armed host.

With the situation deteriorating Edward sent his Woodville relations to the safety of East Anglia and withdrew to Nottingham to wait for Welsh reinforcements which had been promised by William Herbert, Earl of Pembroke. By this time it must have been clear to the King that Warwick was in some way implicated in the crisis as he had neither offered any military support nor made any hostile move against him. On 9 July Edward wrote to Warwick, Clarence and the Archbishop of Canterbury demanding that they give some sign of their loyalty by proving that they were not disposed to act treasonably. There was no response.

By this time, having purchased the necessary dispensation in Rome, Warwick had decided that his daughter Isabel should marry Clarence without further ado and the wedding party had crossed over to Calais on 4 July, taking with them the Archbishop of Canterbury and the Earl of Oxford. A week later the ceremony took place with some haste but little pomp. With the marriage concluded Warwick decided to show his hand: from Calais he issued a declaration which allied himself and his brother to the petitions put out by Robin of Redesdale and his supporters. It was a document which Richard II or Henry VI would have recognised and understood and as it echoed the grievances uttered by the northern rebels it is easy to see that the national unrest in 1469 had been engineered by Warwick and his supporters. Their intention was to save the King from 'the deceiving covetous rule and guiding of certain seducious persons', namely Rivers, Scales, Pembroke and Devon, who had 'caused our said sovereign lord and his realm to fall in great poverty of misery, disturbing the ministration of the laws, only intending to their own promotion and enriching'.

The document also contained an ominous reminder of the fates of other kings – Edward II, Richard II and Henry VI – who had excluded princes of the blood royal from their council and surrounded themselves with favourites whose only concern was self-advancement. To correct that imbalance Warwick promised reform at court, including the punishment of the 'seducious persons', and called on his supporters to meet with him and his army at Canterbury on 16 July. Once again a magnate was taking up arms against an anointed sovereign under the pretence that it was not the King's person that was under attack but those who had given him such bad advice.

As had become customary and as had happened before his march to London to put Edward on the throne, Warwick received a warm welcome from the local people on landing in Kent after crossing from France. The enthusiasm was repeated in Canterbury and he continued to attract recruits as he and his supporters made their way through the countryside. As they approached London the city's council found itself in a dilemma about which faction to support but Warwick's long-standing popularity in the capital ensured that the gates were opened to him and he was even given a gift of money, as much to make sure his army behaved well as to help his cause. From London

An entirely fictitious episode which neatly sums up the symbolism of the Wars of the Roses. In William Shakespeare's *King Henry VI Part One* the English nobility pluck a red or a white rose from a bush in the Temple Gardens in London to signify their support for the House of Lancaster (red) or the House of York (white). (Houses of Parliament, Westminster / Bridgeman Art Library)

An imaginative depiction of the death of William De La Pole, Duke of Suffolk, on his way to France to begin his exile. He was intercepted by sailors and beheaded. (Mary Evans Picture Library)

Known to history as 'Warwick the Kingmaker', Richard Neville, 16th Earl of Warwick, was one of the great personalities of his day. He supported Edward IV's claim to the throne before changing allegiance to the House of Lancaster.

(Mary Evans Picture Library)

Sir Thomas More knew many of the main personalities of the period and as a result his history has a personal aspect to it. A noted humanist, he survived into the reign of Henry VIII but was executed after falling foul of the king's decision to become supreme governor of the Church of England. He was canonised in 1933. The portrait is by Holbein.

(Bridgeman Art Library)

Also known as 'the prudent', King Louis XI provided France with a settled reign and did much to unite the kingdom after the depredations of the earlier civil conflicts. Through his machinations, Margaret of Anjou entered into an alliance with Warwick the Kingmaker to return the English throne to the House of Lancaster. (State Collection, France / Bridgeman Art Library)

The weak-willed James III of Scotland succeeded to the throne after his father was blown up by a cannon. Unable to control his nobles, he was held captive by them during an English invasion led by the Duke of Gloucester, later Richard III. James's reputation was sullied by many fanciful stories about his sexuality and his reliance on low-born favourites. (Bridgeman Art Library

Edward IV enjoyed the fact that his subjects took pleasure in his appearance and was not shy about making sure that he himself was seen by as many people as possible.

(NPG, London)

During most of the fighting battlefield casualties were reasonably modest but that changed at the Battle of Towton fought on Palm Sunday, 1461. No quarter was given in this Yorkist victory and the casualties could have been as high as 28,000, making it one of the bloodiest battles ever fought on English soil. The Yorkist commander was the Earl of Warwick, featured here in an idealised eighteenth-century painting by Henry Tresham.

(Manchester City Art Galleries)

E·IIII·VXOR
ELIZABETH

Now take heed what love may do.'
Edward IV astonished his friends
and family by suddenly marrying
Elizabeth Woodville (or Wydeville).
Rumours abounded that she had
used sorcery or witchcraft to
beguile the king into marrying her.

(Philip Mould Ltd, London / Bridgeman Art
Library)

Warwick's decision to turn coat
and support the claims of Queen
Margaret of Anjou led to his death
at the Battle of Barnet in 1471. A
muddle in the Lancastrian ranks
led their soldiers to believe that
they were being treacherously
attacked by the Earl of Oxford's
men whereas these were joining
battle on the Lancastrian side.

(Bridgeman Art Library)

The battle that decided the fate of the House of Lancaster: on an early summer's day in 1471 at Tewkesbury in Gloucestershire King Edward IV scored a decisive victory over forces loyal to Queen Margaret of Anjou. One of the casualties was her son Prince Edward, the only Prince of Wales to have been killed in battle. (Mary Evans Picture Library)

John Millais's Victorian painting of the 'Princes in the Tower' captures the frightened helplessness of Princes Edward and Richard, the sons of the dead King Edward IV. They were right to feel insecure: following their incarceration they were never seen again, probably murdered on the orders of their uncle King Richard III. (University of London / Bridgeman Art Library)

King Richard III had the misfortune to be remembered for physical deformities so that the last of the Yorkist kings appeared not so much as a monarch but as an Antichrist and outcast. The descriptions were largely exaggerated. (NPG, London)

One of the most influential women of the period, Lady Margaret Beaufort became a prominent figure at the court of her son Henry VII. Later in life she took a vow of chastity and lived as a nun, fasting regularly and scourging herself with a hair shirt. (Ken Welsh / Bridgeman Art Library)

The Battle of Bosworth Field brought the Wars of the Roses to an end on 22 August 1485. In a rash counter-attack envisaged in a modern painting by Graham Turner King Richard III was knocked to the ground and killed. After the battle Henry Tudor was proclaimed king as Henry VII. (Graham Turner)

'The last and most doubtful of the usurpers', Henry VII was the founder of the Tudor line, the king who united the houses of Lancaster and York and ushered in an age of promise and hope. (NPG, London)

the Warwick faction headed north to Coventry, where they hoped to meet up with the northern rebels.

While this was happening Edward did nothing except to remain at Nottingham and see how events unfolded. He did not have long to wait. On 25 July Pembroke arrived at Banbury from the west, bringing with him a powerful force of foot soldiers. With him was another force, led by Lord Humphrey Stafford of Southwick, who had been appointed Earl of Devon after the attainder of Thomas Courtenay, the 14th Earl, and the execution of his brother. However, for reasons which fail to make much sense but which seem to have had something to do with precedence in the lodging arrangements, Pembroke and Devon quarrelled and Devon led off his men to separate billets. The disagreement had dreadful consequences. All of the Royalist archers were in Devon's force and that left Pembroke in a weakened position which the approaching rebels were happy to exploit.

The next morning Robin of Redesdale's men fell on the Royalist army at Edgecote Hill, to the north-east of Banbury and close to the River Cherwell. In the early stages, as the two sides battled for possession of the river crossing, Pembroke's Welsh soldiers fought bravely enough but they were outnumbered and without archers they were easy prey to the well-armed northerners. The tipping point came when a fresh force of Warwick's supporters approached Edgecote Hill; realising that this was the vanguard of Warwick's army, most of the Royalists fled the field. For the Nevilles it was a crushing victory and they exploited it to the full. Pembroke and his brother Sir Richard Herbert were taken to Northampton, where, without trial, Warwick ordered them to be beheaded even though he had no legal or moral justification for such a barbarous act other than a simple desire for vengeance.

The news of the defeat reached Edward as he made his way from Nottingham to Northampton and while spending the night at Olney he was apprehended by the Archbishop of Canterbury. From there he was taken into custody at Warwick Castle while Warwick continued his self-appointed task of bringing the King's advisers to heel. Rivers and Sir John Woodville were soon rounded up while hiding in Somerset and both men were executed outside Coventry on 12 August, again without trial. (Woodville's death left the elderly

Dowager Duchess of Norfolk a widow once again.) A week later a similar fate awaited Humphrey Stafford after he was captured in Bridgwater and executed on the spot, the second holder of the Devon title to be killed that year.

Everywhere Warwick was triumphant. He had secured a military victory over the Royalist army, the King was in his custody and he had carried out his threat to extirpate many of the Woodvilles and the Herberts, Edward's main supporters in Wales. And yet in his hour of triumph he was painfully shackled. Like York before him, Warwick had no broad support among the magnates, many of whom suspected his motives; there was the constant fear of a Lancastrian revival and, shorn of any source of funds and authority, he was unable to extend the anticipated patronage to his followers. There was also the question of what to do with Edward, who remained the country's anointed king. Warwick dared not execute him and replace him with Clarence; that would have been treason and would lose him all support. So he attempted to rule the country through the name of a captive king, an experiment that depended on Edward complying with the fiction that he still exercised the ultimate authority.

Fortunately Edward played along with the pretence and behaved impeccably throughout his confinement even when for his own security he was sent to Middleham Castle in Yorkshire. He must have realised that time was on his side and that neither Warwick nor Clarence would be able to change the status quo without deposing him. Some of the problems facing Warwick soon became apparent. There was unrest in London and throughout the country rival families took advantage of the uncertainty to pursue private vendettas, the most blatant (because it was recorded for posterity in their letters) being an attempt by the Duke of Norfolk to evict the Pastons forcibly from their home at Caister Castle.

Caister had previously been the home of Sir John Fastolf, who had died in 1459 and left his property to Sir John Paston (I), who acted as his lawyer. The will was questioned by Norfolk, who coveted the fortified manor and suspected that the Pastons had gained the castle illegally either by changing Fastolf's will when it was drawn up in November 1459 or by using undue influence during its composition. There followed a dreary succession of legal cases interspersed with acts of violence as both families did whatever they thought necessary to gain possession of the property. Despite their attempts to invoke Warwick's support the Pastons were in no position to defend Caister from Norfolk's armed retainers and a letter written by Margaret Paston, Sir John's wife, shows the extent of the violence and lawlessness that was afoot in the country at a time when central authority was at its weakest:

They [the Paston defenders] are running out of gunpowder and arrows, and the place is much broken down by the other side's guns: so unless they have help quickly, they are likely to lose both their lives and the place, and it will be as great a dishonour to you as ever happened to any gentleman, for every man in the country us astonished that you allow them to be in such great danger for so long without help or any other remedy.

In vain did Paston (II) attempt to get a writ from the King to protect his interests. Caister fell into Norfolk's hands at the end of September and the question of ownership of the castle was not resolved until the intervention of William Wayneflete, Bishop of Winchester, the following year. (Under its terms, contrary to Fastolf's wishes, the living of Caister was used to fund Magdalen College, Oxford.) There were similar outbreaks of local trouble in Gloucestershire, Lancashire and Yorkshire but the principal danger remained the threat that Henry VI's supporters would take advantage of the unrest to mount a new campaign on the usurped king's behalf. If that was Warwick's fear he did not have long to wait for something untoward to happen. In August two northern landowners, Sir Humphrey Neville of Brancepeth and his brother Charles, raised the Lancastrian standard and appealed for support in Westmorland and Northumberland.

The threatened revolt was given little or no backing locally but Warwick was sufficiently alarmed by it to raise forces and march north to deal with the trouble. In normal circumstances people would have rallied when he summoned men to join him but these were not ordinary times and his requests were simply ignored. Many potential supporters had ridden with Robin of Redesdale and they had seen their demands made good by the summary executions of the King's favourites, but they were puzzled by Edward's captivity and the part played in it by Warwick. Their message was clear and simple: they would not march north unless they did it with the legal and moral authority of the King. With no option but to turn to Edward for help, Warwick had him released and when the King appeared in front of his people at York on 10 September he was met with acclaim. As a result Warwick got his army to put down the insurrection and they quickly dealt with the two Neville brothers, who were brought to York and executed in the King's presence at the end of September.

This dramatic change in Edward's fortunes gave him the opportunity to restore his position and he took it. From York he summoned magnates whom he knew to be loyal to him: his brother Gloucester, his brother-in-law Suffolk, and a posse of earls including Arundel, Northumberland and Essex. With them he rode back to London and entered into the capital in triumph in mid-October. Now that he was at liberty and had surrounded himself with his closest allies Edward was relatively safe and Warwick's attempt at ruling through a puppet king was over. As the Croyland chronicler recorded, a fragile peace had returned to the country:

> In the end, a great council of all the peers of the kingdom was summoned and on a certain day, which had been previously named there appeared in the great chamber of parliament, the Duke of Clarence, the Earl of Warwick, and the rest of their confederates; upon which, peace and entire oblivion of all grievances upon both sides was agreed to. Still, however, there probably remained on the one side, deeply seated in his mind the injuries he had received and the contempt which had been shown to majesty, and on the other: 'A mind too conscious of a daring deed.'

In fact Edward decided to allow the recent events to be forgotten and initially he took a mollifying approach towards Warwick and Clarence. His policy boded well for reconciliation but some things could not be forgotten and Sir John Paston (II) was probably nearer the truth of the matter when he noted: 'The King himself has good language of the Lords of Clarence and Warwick, and of my Lords of York and Oxford, saying they be his best friends; but his household men have other language, so what shall hastily fall I cannot say.' One mistake would have consequences for Edward in the not-too-distant future. In an attempt to keep the north of England quiet following the recent eruption of revolts the earldom of Northumberland was restored to the Percys, a move which meant that the current holder, John Neville, had to surrender the title. By way of compensation he was promoted as the Marquess of Montague – an earlier title of his had been Lord Montague – and his son was created Duke of Bedford with the promise of marriage to the King's eldest daughter, Elizabeth. It seemed to be a magnanimous settlement which should have pleased both families but it did not appease Neville, who claimed that he had been given 'a magpie's nest', that is, a title without the means of maintaining it. What should have been a valued promotion was seen as an insult.

Neville's brother felt even more aggrieved. Although Warwick had succeeded in getting rid of the Herberts and some of the Woodvilles, Edward was still king and his own position at court had not changed very much since the period before his rebellion. Politically, Warwick was isolated and he lacked the broad level of support needed to maintain a successful bid to curb the King's power. This weakness should have warned him against any further action against Edward but, far from hindering him, those drawbacks only persuaded him to continue scheming.

He was also helped by events. In the first quarter of 1470 there was a rash of fresh disturbances in Lincolnshire involving a territorial dispute between Sir Thomas Burgh of Gainsborough, Edward's master of horse, and his neighbour Lord Welles, a second cousin of Warwick. With his son Sir Robert and another knight, Sir Thomas Dymmock, Welles attacked Burgh's manor and destroyed much of his property in pursuit of his claims. This was a common enough occurrence in England at the time but it was also one which challenged royal authority. Fearing that he was losing ground and had to re-establish his position among the nobility – both men involved in the quarrel had connections with the court – Edward decided to intervene by riding north with an armed force. His precipitate action provided Warwick with the opportunity he had been seeking.

When Welles and Dymmock were ordered to travel to London to explain their actions the former's son, Sir Robert, raised a fresh rebellion after summoning the men of Lincolnshire to attend him fully armed at Ranby Hawe on 7 March. The summons also carried the names of Warwick and Clarence although this detail was as yet unknown to the King, who had received offers of military support from both men. As Edward moved north he received further news of fresh disturbances in Yorkshire but, buoyed by the expectation that he would soon be receiving assistance from his major allies, he continued his journey, showing a determination and sense of purpose that had been lacking in the previous year.

Five days after Sir Robert Welles had issued his summons the Royalist army fell on the rebels at Empingham, five miles to the west of Stamford. Before going into action Edward showed that he meant business when Lord Welles and Sir Thomas Dymmock were brought before the army and summarily executed despite the earlier promise of a pardon.

The battle itself was over in minutes. Edward possessed a large artillery train which he used to good effect against the poorly led and inexperienced men of Lincolnshire, who quickly fled the field when they found themselves facing heavy fire. So rapid was their flight that in their haste many cast away their clothing and as a result the battle, such as it was, gained the name Losecoat Field, by which it is still generally known. When the news of the defeat reached Yorkshire the threatened revolt failed to materialise and Edward was left master of the field.

The King's triumph also revealed the extent of Warwick's and Clarence's treachery. Contemporary accounts of the uprising show that many of Welles's men had advanced into the battle shouting the names 'Clarence!' and 'Warwick!' and from the field was recovered a casket belonging to Sir Robert Welles which, according to an anonymous contemporary chronicler, was full of 'many marvellous bills, containing matter of the great seduction, and the very subversion of the king and the common weal of all this land, with the most abominable treason that ever were seen or attempted'. This gave Edward all the evidence he needed. Welles and other leaders of the revolt were captured at Grantham and, having confessed that Warwick and Clarence were 'partners and chief provokers of all their treasons', they were promptly beheaded. The King's next move was to dispatch the Garter King of Arms to summon Warwick and Clarence to attend him or face due punishment. In reply the rebels demanded safe conduct and a pardon but, having seen his trust and friendship betrayed, Edward was in no mood to offer anything that smacked of reconciliation and condemned both men as 'rebels and traitors'.

This time the King realised that he had to take firm action to safeguard his position and he was able to act in the sure knowledge that he now enjoyed military superiority. The Dukes of Norfolk and Suffolk had ridden to his assistance, as had the Earl of Worcester, and, according to Sir John Paston (II), when Edward rode north towards Doncaster never before had England seen 'so many goodly men, and so well arrayed'.

By now Warwick and Clarence could see that their rebellion had ended in disaster and that, shorn of support, they had no option but to save their lives by leaving England as quickly as possible. Having summoned their families, including Isabel of Clarence, who was in the ninth month of pregnancy, they managed to get to Dartmouth, where they took ship for Calais. Earlier Warwick had attempted to gain possession of his warship the *Trinity* in Southampton but had been beaten off by a force led by Anthony Rivers, the new Earl Rivers, and there was further disappointment at Calais when the acting captain of the garrison, Sir John Wenlock, now ennobled as Lord Wenlock, obeyed Edward's instructions to the letter and refused to let them enter the harbour. Wenlock had always been close to Warwick but on this occasion he decided to obey the King's orders and even though Isabel went into labour he would not yield. She survived the incident but unhappily the baby was stillborn.

As the Duke of Burgundy also refused to allow Warwick to land in any port in Flanders the rebels were forced to set sail for Honfleur, which they reached in the first week of May after an inconclusive battle with Royalist ships under the command of Lord John Howard, Treasurer of the King's Household. The rebels' arrival in France changed everything. For some time Louis XI had harboured hopes of effecting an alliance between Warwick, whom he liked personally, and Margaret of Anjou, whose Lancastrian cause he supported. Warwick's unexpected appearance in France gave him the opportunity to attempt to put those hopes into practice. If he succeeded in persuading Warwick to change sides it would help him to make good his earlier promise to support Margaret and put her husband back on the throne of England; in return Henry VI, by then surely a grateful ally, would provide Louis with military assistance for an attack on the Duke of Burgundy.

From the outset the French king knew that it would not be easy to bring the two parties together. Although Warwick needed French financial and military support if he was going to return to England and confront Edward with any hope of effecting a change of regime, he was hardly going to help restore the House of Lancaster when his original plan was to place the Yorkist Clarence on the throne. Margaret, too, would be difficult to placate: Warwick was the power behind the King, who had unseated her husband, and he had also been a senior commander in the Royalist army which had forced her and her family into exile. But Louis was a master in the arts of intrigue and he played a skilful cat-and-mouse game to convince Warwick and Margaret that their best hope of achieving their ambitions lay not in acting separately but in combining in common cause.

His first step was to meet the two parties at Amboise on the Loire for proximity talks, each one meeting him separately and privately so that he could put his case to them and secure some form of common ground. On 8 June the first meeting took place with Warwick and, having no viable alternatives, the English magnate agreed to an alliance with Margaret on condition that Louis supply him with funds and a suitable force of armed soldiers. In return England would assist Louis in his planned offensive against Burgundy.

As anticipated, the meeting with Margaret was not as agreeable. She found the idea of an alliance with such a man abhorrent, for not only had Warwick driven her from the kingdom but he had 'dared to defame her reputation as a woman by diverse false and malicious slanders'. (As other Yorkists had done, Warwick had questioned the paternity of Margaret's son Prince Edward and suggested that Henry could not be the father.) These were the words of a woman scorned, but Louis persevered by bluntly telling her that Warwick was her last and best hope of retrieving the English throne for her son and that without him there could be no return to England. The French king must have made a persuasive case, for although it was reported that Margaret remained obdurate she eventually conceded that she would meet Warwick in the middle of July when the court met at Angers. This, too, proved to be a difficult occasion. Warwick showed his deference by going down on bended knee and Margaret demonstrated her haughtiness by making him stay in that position for over a quarter of an hour, but agreement was eventually reached. As summed up by a contemporary report later transcribed by the sixteenth-century antiquarian John Stow, the concord was eventually fixed on three main points:

> First, by the mean of the King of France, the said Earl of Warwick purchased a pardon of the Queen Margaret and her son. Secondly, by the said mean was treated the marriage of the said queen's son called Prince of Wales, and the Earl of Warwick's second daughter. Thirdly, there was appointed upon his [Warwick] passage over the sea into England with a puissance [armed force].

This was an astonishing change in the fortunes of all of them and gave each consenting party what they wanted, even though, according to Stow's document, 'the said queen was right difficile'. With French funds and military assistance Warwick would invade England and restore the House of Lancaster and in return his daughter Anne would marry Prince Edward, who would eventually succeed to the throne as King of England. As it was painfully obvious that Henry VI would be in no state to rule the country, the regency of England would be held by Warwick until such time as the Prince of Wales was old enough to succeed. Almost everyone appeared to have benefited from the agreement. Louis had succeeded by using his money and his persuasive skills to gain a key ally to help him in the forthcoming campaign against Burgundy, and Margaret would live to see her husband's line restored to the throne of England. Only Clarence had lost out. He had placed his faith in Warwick as the best means of winning the English throne, he had betrayed his brother – a gross crime – and now he could only look on while a rival from the House of Lancaster was promoted above him.

Ten days later Anne and Edward were betrothed in Angers Cathedral – consanguinity through descent from John of Gaunt meant that they needed a dispensation from the Pope before they could marry – and Warwick pressed ahead with his invasion plans. However, it proved to be no easy task. Although he had little trouble assembling his army it was another matter getting them across the Channel as he did not enjoy command of the sea and the French ports were under a constant blockade by English and Burgundian warships. Ironically many of these had once been under his command.

Extensive military and naval preparations of that kind could not be kept secret and Edward soon knew what was afoot on the French side of the Channel, but during the summer his attention was diverted when he received intelligence about a new Neville-inspired rebellion in the north of England led by Lord Henry FitzHugh of Ravensworth, one of Warwick's brothers-in-law. Remembering what had happened in 1469 when he had dithered, and the successful policy a year later when he had marched to crush the rebels, Edward decided to deal with the uprising himself. Placing his trust in Howard's fleet to guard the Channel while he was away from London, he gathered an army and marched north to York, where he found that FitzHugh's rebellion had fizzled out and its leader had fled to Scotland. As a result Edward set out to return to London on 7 September and stopped in the Midlands, where he expected to be supported by another army commanded by Warwick's brother Montague.

By now Warwick was also on the move. A freak late-summer storm had scattered the English and Burgundian ships and by chance had given his fleet of sixty vessels a favourable wind to cross the Channel and they were able to land in England unopposed. With him went Clarence, the Earl of Oxford and Jasper Tudor, who hoped to raise forces in Wales and reclaim his old title of Earl of Pembroke, and shortly after they arrived in the west of England they were joined by the Earl of Shrewsbury and Lord Stanley. Their message was familiar: they had come from France to end the misrule of Edward IV and to restore Henry VI to the throne as the rightful King of England.

Edward had miscalculated by leaving his southern flank exposed and that was to prove a serious misjudgement. As Warwick marched north people started flocking to his ranks and at the same time they started melting away from the King's side. Edward had never enjoyed much support in the north, where Lancastrian sympathies were always stronger, and in other parts of England there was a sudden and dramatic slump in his standing. It was also the case that Warwick was well liked and that his arrival encouraged Lancastrian magnates to renew their support for the cause by declaring their hand; as happened so often in these civil wars, the mere display of success was sufficient to encourage people to declare their allegiance or change their minds. With support quickly ebbing away Edward was hit by a major catastrophe as he awaited the arrival of Montague and his army from the north. Warkworth explains what happened next:

The Lord Marquess Montagu had gathered 6,000 men, by King Edward's commission and commandment, to the intent to have resisted the said Duke of Clarence and the Earl of Warwick. Never the latter, the said Marquess Montagu hated the king, and purposed to have taken him; and when he was within a mile of King Edward, he declared to the people that was there gathered with him, how King Edward had first given to him the earldom of Northumberland, and how he took it from him and gave it Henry Percy, whose father was slain at York field [Towton]; and how of late time had he made him Marquess of Montagu, and gave a pye's [magpie's] nest to maintain his estate with wherefore he gave knowledge to his people that he would hold with the Earl of Warwick, his brother, and take King Edward if he might, and all tho[se] that would hold with him.

Montague's defection was decisive because it placed the King between a hammer and the anvil. While Edward rode down from the north with Montague behind him, Warwick was coming up from the south and the King was caught in the middle. Realising that he lacked sufficient force to take on either army, let alone both of them, he took the line of least resistance and fled east across Lincolnshire and south into Norfolk to the port of Lynn, where he and his small band of followers managed to find two Dutch ships which took him into exile in Burgundian territory. With the King went Gloucester, Earl Rivers and Lord Hastings, a loyal courtier who had started his career in 1461 as Chamberlain of the Royal Household and played a leading role in negotiating the marriage of Edward's sister to Duke Charles of Burgundy (as Charolais had become with the death of his father).

On arrival Edward hoped that his brother-in-law would lend him assistance but Duke Charles had decided to play a waiting game to see if Warwick would keep his promise to Louis. Faced by this inaction, Edward and his small court settled in Bruges, where they received help and support from Louis, Lord of Gruthuyse, a personal friend who had acted as the Burgundian ambassador to England. For the King it was a shocking reversal: only three weeks had passed between Warwick's arrival and his own flight to the continent and in that short time his support had evaporated, just as it had done in 1469. Given his enemies' numerical superiority Edward's only choice had been to quit England as he probably realised that his fate would be very different if he fell into Warwick's hands. The king-maker had proved that clemency was not an option when it came to dealing with defeated enemies.

While Edward bided his time in the Low Countries Warwick set about making good the promises he had given to Margaret in Angers. Having sent Sir Geoffrey Gate (another Yorkist turncoat who had supported Warwick) and the Bishop of Winchester ahead of him to liberate Henry VI from his lodgings in the Tower – the imprisoned king was reported to be 'amazed' at the turn of events – Warwick rode into London on 6 October with Shrewsbury and Stanley and all greeted Henry as their lawful king. They found Henry meanly dressed – 'not worshipfully arrayed as a prince and not so cleanly kept as should seem such a prince' – and Warwick ordered that he be given a blue velvet robe before being paraded through the streets on his way to new quarters at the Bishop of London's palace near St Paul's.

Here the crown was replaced on his head but it is hard to say if Henry understood what was happening to him. Contemporary accounts refer to his listlessness and inability to respond, almost as if he were a stranger to the events that were taking place around him and not a full participant in them. The chronicler Georges Chastellain supplied a graphic description of the comatose state in which the King found himself after five years of captivity: 'a stuffed wool sack lifted by its ears, a shadow on the wall, bandied about as in a game of blind man's buff . . . submissive and mute, like a crowned calf'.

Such a man was putty in Warwick's hands and no sooner had the news of Edward's flight been made known than he issued a statement that the previous king had been deposed and Henry had been restored to the throne in a move which was known henceforth as 'his readeption to royal power'. One by one prominent Lancastrians began emerging from internal or external exile while at the same time their Yorkist opposite numbers went into hiding, adopted low profiles or sought sanctuary in religious houses. Queen Elizabeth (Woodville) was given succour in Westminster Abbey, where she was provided with lodgings by Abbot Thomas Milling and later gave birth to her first son, another Prince Edward.

Both Edward IV and his brother Gloucester were disinherited and attainted but there was no unnecessary blood-letting and the most prominent Yorkist to be executed was the reviled John Tiptoft, Earl of Worcester, brother-in-law to Warwick and a renowned Latin scholar who had entered Edward's circle early in the reign and was highly regarded at court. However, he was also a sadist who had devised new and horrible ways of putting people to death using methods which attracted to him the nickname 'the butcher of England'. During Warwick's flight to Dartmouth Worcester had captured twenty of Warwick's supporters and had ordered them to be hanged, drawn and quartered; then they were beheaded and the naked corpses were pierced by wooden spikes and the heads placed on the sharpened points, to be displayed on the beach at Southampton.

Huge crowds attended Worcester's execution and the fear of a lynching led to a brief overnight postponement during which Worcester was placed in the Fleet Prison for his own safety. The next day he was led to Tower Hill, where he met his end with calm dignity, claiming that he was simply protecting the state. He was the only prominent Yorkist supporter to be punished in this way.

On 13 October, the day before Worcester's execution, Henry was paraded through London and taken to St Paul's with the cheers of the crowd ringing in his ears. His restoration was proving to be popular and Warwick also shared in the feel-good factor which accompanied Henry's return to office. To strengthen his own position Warwick claimed the office of Great Chamberlain of England and reclaimed his position as Captain of Calais; he was also recognised as Lieutenant and Protector of the Realm, while Clarence was reappointed Lord Lieutenant of Ireland. Parliament met on 26 November to confirm Henry as King of England and to name his successor as his son Prince Edward and, failing him and his heirs, the Duke of Clarence.

At the same time Lancastrian magnates had their titles and lands restored to them. Among them was Jasper Tudor, who once more became Earl of Pembroke; one of his first actions was to ride to Hereford to release his nephew Henry Tudor from the custody of Lady Herbert. As for Warwick, despite the feeling expressed by Rous that he had 'all England at his leading', his position was still not entirely secure. Lack of money and authority made it impossible for Warwick to reward those who had supported him and there was still a feeling in Lancastrian circles that despite his recent actions he remained a dangerous enemy who might one day make a personal bid for the throne. Clarence, too, was a problem, and this would get worse as soon as Margaret and her son Edward returned to England to make the Lancastrian hold on the throne a reality. According to the contemporary chronicle known as the *Arrivall of Edward IV*, which was admittedly written from a Yorkist perspective, Clarence found himself in a precarious position 'held in great suspicion, despite, disdain, and hatred, with all the lords, noblemen and other, that were adherents and full partakers with Henry the usurper'. For all that Clarence had played a leading role in the readeption he was still the exiled king's brother and could easily change his mind and allegiance once again.

The most pressing problem facing Warwick in the short term was not so much Clarence as the need to repay Louis by preparing a force to fight in France against the Burgundians. But assembling the necessary forces meant the imposition of taxation and the need to raise loans, both vastly unpopular methods which would alienate the populace at a time when there was a need to bring some calm to the country. Warwick tried to be as good as his word by promising to raise a force of up to ten thousand archers and at the beginning of 1471 he ordered the Calais garrison to begin offensive operations against the Burgundians, who were already under attack by French forces in Picardy. Having lost patience with these tardy offerings and in a move designed to put additional pressure on Warwick, Louis had ended the truce with Burgundy and declared war in December 1470.

Perversely, the outbreak of hostilities concentrated Duke Charles's mind and helped to alter his attitude to Edward. From being an embarrassing guest in Bruges the exiled English king once more became a key player and, after a meeting at the beginning of 1471, he was promised the necessary funds to return to England and ships were prepared for his use on the island of Walcheren. Slowly and in great secrecy a small invasion fleet began to assemble at Flushing, with ships being supplied by both the Burgundians and the Hanse League in return for lucrative trading rights should Edward return to the throne of England. A propaganda war had also been started. During the winter months the exiled king had used his time well by making contact with Clarence and other potential supporters in England, notably Henry Percy, to whom he had already restored the earldom of Northumberland.

However, time was not on his side. On 13 December Henry VI's son Prince Edward had married Anne Neville at Amboise and preparations were begun for the couple and Margaret of Anjou to return to England. (There is evidence to suggest that on Margaret's orders the marriage was not consummated, to allow Edward to make a better match once he became king.) Once they were back in England they would make a formidable party who seemed to have everything on their side. Edward was seventeen and ambitious to be king, Henry would surely offer no resistance to the idea that he should abdicate in favour of his son, the Lancastrian magnates had shown their hands and the combined strength of the forces available to them would have been more substantial than anything Edward IV could raise at that time.

However, disastrously for the Lancastrian cause, Margaret delayed her departure from France. She spent Christmas in Paris and the early weeks of 1471 waiting for Warwick to come to France to accompany her and her party on their return to England. And while she fretted Warwick started prevaricating, claiming that shortage of funds prevented him from making the journey. This was probably true. Although Warwick was a wealthy man he had been forced to spend freely to maintain his position after the readeption and in the absence of any realisable finance from taxation he had even been obliged to fund the royal household. As a lifelong pragmatist he must also have been aware that the return of Margaret of Anjou and her son the Prince of Wales would weaken his own influence at court.

Even when Margaret did reach Dieppe bad weather caused further delays and it was not until the last week of March that she was able to leave Harfleur for the short Channel crossing. By now it was too late: England was about to face a fresh round of civil conflict as the two rival kings vied for the control of their country.

Chapter Seventeen

The Recovery of England

Throughout the winter of 1470–1 Edward had spent his time plotting and making preparations for a return to England but his plans were always in danger of being thwarted by the fact that Warwick's fleet controlled the Channel. True to form, the master intriguer had found the funds for keeping the ships at sea by encouraging his ship masters, under the command of his kinsman the Bastard of Fauconberg (the illegitimate son of Lord Fauconberg, hence his title), to engage in piracy against Spanish and Burgundian ships and to use the proceeds to fund their operations. To cross the Channel or to approach England's south coast Edward's small invasion fleet would need either luck or excellent seamanship to avoid their clutches. The bad weather which had hindered Margaret's preparations could have prevented him from putting to sea too, but on the contrary the uncertain conditions came to his aid.

During the February storms which kept the English and French ships in port there was a brief and unexpected lull when the gales subsided, providing a welcome window of opportunity. Edward decided to risk everything on a crossing of the North Sea to allow him to land in East Anglia, where he had powerful allies, including the Dukes of Norfolk and Suffolk. On 11 March 1471 his small invasion fleet of thirty-six vessels, led by the flagship *Antony*, put out of Flushing and after a choppy overnight crossing the King's party made landfall at Cromer, where they found scant welcome. The coast had been secured by forces led by the Earl of Oxford, and the Duke of Norfolk was nowhere to be seen as he had been taken into custody by

Warwick as a precautionary measure. Because it would have been foolhardy to attempt a landing – the Yorkist army consisted of only twelve hundred armed men – Edward decided to push further north towards the coast of Yorkshire.

Once again the weather was against him and the little fleet was scattered over a wide area but two days later, on 14 March, the *Antony* arrived at Ravenspur in the Humber Estuary and the first members of Edward's party went ashore, to be joined by the rest of the force the following day. This time the omens were better. Ravenspur had seen an earlier claimant to the English throne: Henry Bolingbroke had arrived at the same spot seventy-two years earlier on his way from France to reclaim his inheritance and to unseat Richard II.

Fortunately a detailed contemporary account of the events which followed the landfall in Yorkshire is available in the form of the *Arrivall of Edward IV*. Written by one of the royal courtiers who was present throughout the operation – identified by many as Nicholas Harpisfield, Clerk to the Signet – it is a detailed but naturally partisan summary of the events as they unfolded and provides a realistic picture of the difficulties facing the King as he took his first steps to reclaim his throne.

By landing in Yorkshire Edward might have been following, albeit unconsciously, Henry IV's successful example, but he was deep in hostile territory. Despite its name Yorkshire was Lancastrian country and there was little local support for Edward's party. Bands of armed men were rumoured to be gathering to halt his progress and when the royal party approached Hull the gates were closed firmly against them. Nearby Beverley provided a warmer welcome and Edward was allowed to enter York but only after he agreed to leave his army outside the city's walls. It also helped that he had borrowed Bolingbroke's ruse of professing that he was not seeking the Crown but only wanted to reclaim his dukedom and the rights and property that went with it. Although Edward's promise soothed local anxieties and he was able to continue to his family's castle at Sandal, the author of the *Arrivall* conceded that 'as to the folks of the country there came but right few to him, or almost none'.

Edward's one stroke of luck was that Montague failed to act against him as he passed Pontefract Castle and that the Earl of Northumberland also did nothing to intervene by impeding his progress. While Percy did not make any move to lend physical assistance to Edward – to have done so would have betrayed the Lancastrian dead of Towton, many of whom were Yorkshiremen – he 'did the king a right good and notable service' by doing nothing. For Edward and his party the decision to restore the Northumberland earldom to the Percys was now reaping a useful, if unsought, benefit. Had either Montague or Northumberland decided to arrest Edward while he moved through Yorkshire, as they might well have done, his cause would have been stopped in its tracks.

By then Warwick had received news of Edward's return and immediately sent out summonses for military support, only to find that some magnates, notably Shrewsbury and Pembroke, were waiting for Margaret to show her hand. According to the *Arrivall*, where this help was not forthcoming Warwick 'straightly charged them to come forth on pain of death', but even that grim warning was not enough to encourage people to take up arms. One potential supporter, Lord Stanley, received the summons but preferred to ignore it as he was involved in a private feud with the Harrington family over possession of their castle at Hornby in Lancashire. Nevertheless, Warwick had to act decisively if he wanted to protect his position. Leaving his brother George Neville, Archbishop of York, in charge of affairs in London, he took his army north to Coventry, where he hoped to meet up with his main supporters, Clarence and Oxford, who had already sent out summonses to their own people, in the south-west and East Anglia, respectively.

Meanwhile, finding himself unhindered in Yorkshire, Edward continued marching south towards Nottingham and Leicester and as he moved away from the Lancastrian north and passed through the Midlands his support began to grow. More importantly, his brother Clarence was weighing his options and had started taking soundings among his supporters about Edward's real intentions and Warwick's ability to counter the invasion.

By the end of March the strategic position still favoured Warwick even though there were doubts about how much support would be given to him. Edward was in Nottingham gathering his forces but to the north he faced Montague, in front of him Warwick occupied Coventry and on the flanks were the armies of Clarence and Oxford. A co-ordinated attack at this point would have had dire consequences for the outcome of his invasion but Edward was alive to the danger and was determined to act quickly to retain the initiative. Instead of waiting for more followers to rally to his cause he marched his army quickly towards Coventry, where Warwick responded by staying within the city's walls, refusing all challenges to give battle.

Even when Edward proposed a general pardon to avoid bloodshed Warwick spurned the offer and simply sat tight to await the response from the main Lancastrian magnates. It was not a good move. Far from enjoying unqualified support, he was still regarded with great suspicion on account of his decision to change sides and men with long-held family links to the Lancastrian cause such as Edmund Beaufort, the attainted Duke of Somerset and John Courtenay, the heir to the Devon dukedom, preferred to await the arrival of Queen Margaret and her son the Prince of Wales before taking up arms. Their unwillingness to act immediately made Warwick anxious about the strength of his own position and his usual robust optimism gave way to caution.

He was right to be prudent. Clarence, always a fair-weather friend, had finally decided that his best interests lay in throwing in his lot with his brother. Ever since Henry VI had been returned to the throne and the succession had been settled on his own son, Prince Edward, Clarence had been gradually sidelined and outmanoeuvred by Margaret and her ally Warwick. As the *Arrivall* makes clear, he had everything to gain and nothing to lose by changing sides once again. Supporting Warwick had only strengthened the claims to the throne of Henry's son and Clarence's own position was not only parlous but offered him nothing but the contempt of the Lancastrian court:

And in especial, he considered well, that himself was had in great suspicion, despite, distain and hatred, with all the lords, noblemen and other, that were adherents and full partakers with Henry, the Usurper, Margaret his wife, and his son Edward, called Prince; he saw also that they daily laboured among them, breaking their appointment made with him, and, of likelihood, after that, should continually more and more fervently intend, conspire and procure the destruction of him, and of all his blood, where though it appeared also, that the realm and regalie should remain to such as thereunto might not in any wise have any rightwise title.

Clarence was also under pressure from his mother and his sisters as well as from other prominent Yorkist supporters, and allied to Warwick's incapacity to act, this burden was too much for him to bear. Never a particularly stable character, Clarence had from an early age been controlled by his own ambition, hence his earlier decision to betray his brother and join Henry VI; having seen his hopes thwarted by the Lancastrians, he was equally hasty to switch allegiances again once it became apparent that there was little chance of his succeeding to the throne. Shakespeare's description – 'false, fleeting, perjur'd Clarence' – does him full justice: this was a man who could not trust himself from one day's end to the next.

When Gloucester visited Clarence on 2 April and persuaded him to change sides his mind was easily made up and the following day the three Yorkist brothers met at Edward's camp at Banbury, where they were reconciled. Edward promised to restore Clarence's estates while Clarence offered the support of his not inconsiderable army and there was 'right kind and loving language betwixt them'. Together the brothers led their army back to Coventry and offered a final challenge to Warwick, who not unnaturally refused to give battle once he saw the size of the force ranged against him. Once again he decided to wait behind the city's walls to see what would happen, for by then he knew that Margaret was about to leave France for England and that her arrival would bring in the wavering Lancastrian support.

Warwick's obfuscation left Edward in a quandary. While he wanted to defeat his powerful rival and erstwhile ally, he could not afford to mount a lengthy siege of Coventry. Not only was the town well defended while his own army was running short of supplies, but he feared being caught between Montague's and Oxford's armies. There had already been a brief skirmish between his forces and a Lancastrian army led by Exeter and Oxford. Believing that his best option lay in a bold move, Edward decided on 5 April to march on London. As the author of the *Arrivall* explained, control of the capital would give him a power base, it would also allow him to take control of Henry VI and it would prevent Warwick from exercising his influence in a place which had always supported him in the past. Despite the risks London would provide him with:

> The assistance of true lords, lovers and servants, which were there, in those parts, in great number; knowing also that his principal adversary, Henry, with many of his partakers, were at London, there usurping and using the authority Royal, which barred and letted the king of many aids and assistances, which he should and might have had, in divers parts, if he might show himself of power to break their authority.

When Edward's intentions became clear the Lord Mayor, John Stockton, was thrown into a panic as he knew about Margaret's imminent arrival and had already been contacted by Warwick, who had warned him not to support Edward. Choosing sides proved to be such an awkward task that, wisely, he decided to take to his bed until the crisis was over. Stockton's removal allowed Neville to take control of the city; the Archbishop decided to parade Henry through the streets as a means of drumming up support but instead of encouraging resistance the ploy rebounded badly on him. Far from looking like an all-powerful monarch, Henry cut a sorry figure as he rode with his retinue through the streets wearing a plain blue robe 'as though he had no more to change with'. Not for the first time in his life Henry regarded the event with a vacant expression as if he were not part of it but a mere spectator. *The Great Chronicle* noted that Neville had to lead his charge by the hand and that the King looked 'more like a play than the showing of a prince to win men's hearts, for by this means he lost many and won none or right few'.

Political realism also played a part in what happened next. The council decided not to resist Edward because they claimed that they lacked the military means ('the inhabitants were not sufficiently versed in the use of arms to withstand so large a force') and that resistance would only create unacceptable casualties; besides they were anxious to avoid the destruction of property and if possible to retrieve the loans they had made to Edward in happier times. The diplomat and writer Philippe de Commines was in London at the time; he noted the council's decision and added one more reason why Edward was being offered this unequivocal support:

As I have been since informed, there were three things especially which contributed to his reception into London. The first was, the persons who were in the sanctuaries [Yorkists], and the birth of a young prince [Edward of York], of whom the queen was there brought to bed. The next was, the great debts which he owed in the town, which obliged all the tradesmen who were his creditors to appear for him. The third was, that the ladies of quality, and rich citizens' wives with whom he had formerly intrigued, forced their husbands and relations to declare themselves on his side.

Once again Edward was being helped by actions from his past – perhaps the only time in his life when his amorous nature stood him in good stead – and he continued his advance from Coventry, arriving in the capital on 11 April in time to celebrate Good Friday. His first step was to go to St Paul's to offer thanks for his restoration and to secure the person of Henry VI, who embraced him with the words, 'My cousin of York, you are very welcome. I know that in your hands I will not be in danger.' Together with Neville and other Lancastrian supporters he was then placed in the Tower while Edward made his way to Westminster to be reunited, firstly with his crown and then with his wife Elizabeth, who presented to him their son in the Abbey's sanctuary.

The following day, Good Friday, was duly celebrated but with Warwick now approaching London from the north there was little time to tarry. Having installed his wife and family in the safety of the Tower, Edward led his army north out of the capital towards Barnet, where his advance guard collided with Warwick's forward scouts during the afternoon of 12 April and drove them out of the town. By this time night was falling and both armies had to manoeuvre in darkness, a difficult procedure given their respective sizes: Warwick's army was around fifteen thousand strong, while Edward had ten thousand men under his command.

Confronting one another's forces in darkness created other problems for the field commanders. Warwick drew up his forces in the traditional three battles on a ridge to the north of Barnet – Oxford on the right flank, Montague in the centre and Exeter on the left – but in the darkness the forces failed to get into their designated positions, with each army's right flank extending beyond their opponent's left flank. It also meant that the two lines were much closer to each other than the commanders believed. (For his part Edward was in the centre while Gloucester commanded the vanguard on the right and Hastings was on the left.) The confusion was compounded by Warwick's decision to order a night bombardment of the Yorkist lines. While this produced a great deal of sound and fury the firing was ineffective owing to the proximity of the two armies and the fact that the gunners were unable to see the opposition in order to gauge the fall of shot. On the overlapping flanks they simply overshot and caused no damage. The bombardment also produced a huge amount of smoke which combined with the early morning mist to make the battlefield impenetrable when dawn began to break.

Despite the uncertainty, showing his usual sense of purpose Edward decided to attack at first light: according to the *Arrivall,* he 'committed his cause and quarrel to Almighty God, advanced banners, did blow up trumpets, and set upon them, first with shot, and, then and soon, they joined and came to hand strokes'.

The first action was on the Yorkist left, where Hastings's men came under sustained arrow fire and started faltering. Taking his chance, Oxford ordered his men to charge – his division overlapped Hastings's force – and using the advantage of the slope they attacked the Yorkist lines, slashing and battering until their opponents started running from the field. In this kind of bitter close-quarter fighting there was very little room for delicacy of touch. Men were pressed hard up against one another and death could come from sword point or from the bludgeon of the pole-axe, a fearsome weapon which incorporated a blade for hacking, a hammer for cracking open armour and a hook for pulling knights from their horses. Once a man in armour had fallen injured to the ground he stood little chance of regaining his feet and was usually smashed to death where he lay.

Gradually the 'hand-strokes' began to tell, casualties mounted and Hastings's men started to fall back on Barnet with their opponents in hot pursuit. Only a desire to exchange slaughter for pillaging prevented a greater rout and Oxford was hard pushed to prevent his men becoming a rabble; others simply continued the pursuit south beyond Barnet as the terrified Yorkists tried to make their way back to London and safety. Luckily for Edward the fog prevented his and

Gloucester's men from witnessing the collapse and disarray of the Yorkist left flank.

Similar scenes of carnage were being enacted on the Yorkist right flank, where Gloucester had charged into Exeter's lines and was attempting to roll up his position by destroying the flanks and leaving the centre exposed to a concerted assault. The misalignment of the two positions meant that he failed to make contact in his initial charge, but the mistake allowed him to engage in a flanking attack on Warwick's position, which was already under attack from Edward's forces in the centre. As the Lancastrian line on the left buckled under the strain of the attack the position of both armies began to change and they found themselves fighting along a north–south axis in a depression, aptly known as Dead Man's Bottom. In the mist and the confusion the battle lost all coherence as men simply struck out at those closest to them.

The change of the original alignment was to have one more consequence and it decided the fate of the battle. Having rallied around eight hundred of his men in Barnet, Oxford led them back to the field but by the time they returned they found themselves facing not the remnants of Hastings's flank but Montague's men in the centre. Both were allies but Oxford's men were wearing the de Vere livery of a star with streamers, which in the bad light looked remarkably like Edward's badge of the sun in splendour. Mistaking them for the enemy, the Lancastrian troops opened fire with their guns and Oxford's men ran from the field shouting, 'Treason! Treason!' Few escaped because many of Warwick's men thought that their erstwhile allies had changed sides and rapidly dispatched them in the mistaken belief that they were now fighting for Edward.

In the midst of the mayhem Edward kept his head and launched his reserves into the mêlée in Dead Man's Bottom. That decided the issue. Montague was chopped down and killed and confusion and panic quickly overtook the Lancastrian soldiers, who started fleeing the field in a disorganised rout, ignoring Warwick's pleas to withstand one last charge. Now on foot, Warwick himself joined the fleeing soldiers and tried to make his way to Wrotham Wood, where he had tethered his horse. Although Edward had given orders that Warwick was to be taken alive this was not enough to save him. Amid the carnage he was recognised by a group of Yorkist foot soldiers, surrounded, knocked to the ground and quickly dispatched.

As news of Warwick's death spread through the ranks any remaining resistance crumbled and after three hours of intense fighting the field belonged to Edward. It was scarcely daybreak yet over one thousand Lancastrians had been killed and about half that number of Yorkists. The most prominent casualties were Warwick and Montague, whose bodies were taken to London and put on public display to prevent any rumours that the brothers had survived and would return to the fray.

Others made good their escape. Exeter was horribly wounded and left for dead but survived to spend the next four years in the Tower. Oxford managed to get away and make his way to Scotland and was followed there by Viscount Beaumont. On Edward's side the casualties were smaller but they contained some illustrious names, including Lord Saye and Sele (William Fiennes, a fellow exile in Bruges), Lord Cromwell (Humphrey Bourchier, son of Henry Bourchier, Earl of Essex and nephew of Thomas Bourchier, Archbishop of Canterbury) and Sir William Blount, the heir of Lord Mountjoy.

As happens in any civil war, there were turncoats on both sides. Also fighting in the Lancastrian army were two of the Paston brothers (confusingly, both called John, but referred to as II and III), who had switched their allegiance from the Yorkists in order to regain Caister Castle from the Duke of Norfolk. The price of getting the necessary patronage from the Earl of Oxford was their presence in the Lancastrian ranks at Barnet; now they faced ruin and perhaps the forfeiture of their lives. As John (II) aptly wrote to his mother in the aftermath of the battle, 'the world, I assure you, is right queasy'.

The Pastons' one hope was that all was not completely lost and that the arrival of Queen Margaret in the West Country on 16 April would quickly restore the balance of power. She and her retinue were at Cerne Abbey when they received the news of Warwick's defeat and death at Barnet and although she was 'right heavy and sorry' she was persuaded not to give up her cause. Somerset was given command of her forces, which included a strong contingent provided by the Earl of Devon, from Wales came intelligence that Jasper Tudor was busily raising forces and the survivors from Barnet were slowly trickling westwards to join him. The trick would be to preserve the Lancastrian field army and to avoid immediate battle with Edward until there was a reasonable chance of raising sufficient forces with which to beat him.

Accordingly, Somerset gave orders for his men to retire towards Exeter before heading north in the direction of Bristol and the Severn Valley, where they hoped to meet up with the Welsh contingent. If they managed to get further north there was a good chance that they would also receive reinforcement from Cheshire and Lancashire in the shape of much-needed archers. Despite the hangover from Barnet there was still sufficient optimism that the cause was not lost and that Edward could still be defeated, provided that there was no military engagement in the immediate future.

Edward, too, had been preparing for the next round. After the battle he retired to London, where his first task was to re-muster his army, whose soldiers, as was customary, had retired to their homes. On 23 April he celebrated the Feast of St George with a Garter ceremony at Windsor and then set off westwards, taking with him some three thousand men and a large artillery train. By then artillery pieces were becoming more effective even though they remained unwieldy and were difficult to transport: most were constructed by shrinking iron hoops around iron staves on the barrel principle. Primitive handguns were also in more widespread use although these could still be more dangerous to the user than to the target. Edward had no option but to move quickly as he needed to crush the Lancastrians before they raised additional support from the regions and were in a position to threaten London. From his intelligence network of spies he had a good understanding of his opponents' movements and from the outset could work out that they were making for the Severn Valley.

On 24 April he left Windsor and pushed on to Malmesbury, where he received information that the Lancastrian vanguard was advancing towards Chipping Sodbury on the road from Bristol and appeared to be on the point of offering battle. Edward hoped that the issue could be settled then and there but on deploying his army on Sodbury Hill he quickly understood that he had been outwitted. The vanguard was a ruse; instead the bulk of Somerset's forces was making for Gloucester and its important crossing over the Severn.

This unexpected move gave the Lancastrians a sudden advantage but the weather was against them. The beginning of May was unseasonably hot and Somerset's men had to march thirty-six miles through what the *Arrivall* described as 'foul country, all in lanes and strong ways betwixt woods without any good refreshing'. At the same time Edward's men had the benefit of the higher ground, marching along the western escarpment of the Cotswold Ridge. They were also helped by the fact that Edward had sent messages to Sir Richard Beauchamp, the Governor of Gloucester, forbidding him to open his gates to Somerset's army and ordering him to deny them the use of the bridges. Beauchamp kept his word and as a result the Lancastrians had to push north towards the nearest crossing at Tewkesbury, which they reached late in the day on 3 May after a forced march of twenty-four miles.

Meanwhile Edward had passed Cheltenham and by the same evening his army was only three miles away. His men, too, were exhausted, having marched a similar distance in the blinding heat of a long day, and rations were running low, but now that they were within sight of their enemy battle was inevitable. As night drew on they took what little rest they could and made preparations for the clash that would follow when dawn broke. If Edward wanted to prevent Margaret joining forces with Jasper Tudor he knew that battle had to be joined the following day and that he had to win it.

On Saturday 4 May it seemed that the Lancastrians held the advantages. They were drawn up to the south of Tewkesbury with the River Avon behind them and the Severn to the west and they occupied the high ground, which looked down on what the *Arrivall* described as 'evil lanes and deep dykes, so many hedges, trees and bushes, that it was hard to approach them near, and come to hand'. The army was drawn up with Somerset and Sir Edmund Beaufort on the right flank, the centre was commanded by the elderly Lord Wenlock, a veteran of the First Battle of St Albans, where he had fought on the Lancastrian side and also of Towton where he had fought on the Yorkist side, while Devon was on the left. Against them to the south Edward held the centre with Gloucester on his left and Hastings on his right.

Astutely, Edward took the precaution of deploying a small force of two hundred mounted spearmen in the woods to the left of his army. Their task was to clear the ground of any enemy who broke through the left flank or they could be used as a mobile reserve to exploit any advantage gained by the main force. Having 'committed his cause and quarrel to Almighty God, to our most blessed lady his mother, Virgin Mary, the glorious martyr Saint George and all the saints', Edward ordered his archers and gunners to open 'right-a-sharp' fire which had a devastating effect on the opposition.

Unnerved by the ferocity of the assault, Somerset ordered his men to advance towards Edward's left flank. At first they made good progress as their intentions were masked by the roughness of the terrain but as they clashed with Gloucester's lines two things happened to stall their progress. If the attack was to have any chance it depended on Wenlock's battle moving forward at the same time to engage Edward's men in the centre but for reasons which are unclear the men in the centre remained static, their banners blowing in the breeze on the 'marvellous strong ground'.

The lack of any support allowed Edward to extend his line to help stem the Lancastrian attack and at this point the two hundred hidden horsemen joined the battle from the woods on the left, riding with couched lances into the Lancastrians' exposed flanks. As a result, recorded the author of the *Arrivall*, Somerset's men were now outnumbered and outmanoeuvred: the King's remedy of planning a reserve force had paid dividends:

> The said spears of the king's party, seeing no likelihood of any bushment [ambush] in the said wood-corner, seeing also good opportunity to employ themselves well, came and brake on, all at once, upon the Duke of Somerset, and his vanguard, aside-hand, unadvised, whereof they, seeing the king gave them enough to do afore them, were greatly dismayed and abashed, and so took them to flight into the park, and into the meadow that was near, and into the lanes and dykes, whereof they best hoped to escape the danger; nevertheless, many were distressed, taken and slain.

It was not the end but it was the beginning of the end. After half an hour's fierce close-quarter combat Somerset's men were in disarray as they were pushed inexorably into narrow ground by the River Avon which later received the grim appellation, 'Bloody Meadow'. Some fled the field, riding as hard as they could to get away from the slaughter; while a handful made their way back to the centre to continue the fight. Among the latter was Somerset, whose blood was up not just on account of the fighting but because he had been badly let down by Wenlock. In the words of the Victorian antiquarian and battlefield visitor Richard Brooke, 'Lord Wenlock not having advanced to the support of the first line, but remaining stationary, contrary to the expectations of Somerset, the latter, in a rage, rode up to him, reviled him, and beat his brains out with an axe.'

The incident was recorded by Warkworth and is an apt, if extreme, demonstration of the way to deal with a divisional commander who has failed on the battlefield. Rumours abounded that Wenlock had survived the incident and that another body had been buried in his place but he was never heard of again and he remains one of an infamous band who served on both sides, having turned coat first from the Lancastrians to the Yorkists and then back to the Lancastrians.

Although the readjustment of the Lancastrian lines brought some much-needed shape to the battle the advantage had now swung to Edward's forces in the centre. The King seized the opportunity presented to him and leading by example took his men forward to engage the remains of the Lancastrian defensive lines. This was a horrible phase of the battle with men standing within reach of each other, stabbing with swords and hacking with battle-axes, until the front gave way and men started running from the field as best they could with Yorkist mounted men and foot soldiers pursuing them. Most attempted to get back into the safety of Tewkesbury or took refuge in the abbey, but others were trapped by the Severn and cut down by its banks.

With the Lancastrian field army destroyed, the slaughter began in earnest. The most prominent casualty was Prince Edward, who was recognised by his surcoat emblazoned with the arms of England, and was summarily hacked to death. Also slain in the last stages of the fighting were Devon and Somerset's brother John Beaufort.

Those who had fled to Tewkesbury Abbey for safety soon discovered that it was no sanctuary. A force led by Edward, Clarence and Gloucester arrived outside its gates, swords in hands, and demanded that the abbot hand over those who were sheltering under his roof. In vain did he plead that holy ground was being polluted; the

King and his brothers demanded the expulsion of their enemies and the abbot had to comply. Among those who became prisoners was Somerset, who was given a quick trial by Gloucester and Norfolk the next day and summarily beheaded in the marketplace in Tewkesbury. Another dozen prominent Lancastrian knights received similar treatment, largely because they had proved themselves to be obdurate supporters of Queen Margaret and had broken previous promises to keep the peace. As for the Queen, who probably watched the battle from the tower of the abbey, she was apprehended three days later in a religious house near Malvern and taken to London.

Victory at Tewkesbury left Edward in complete control of England. Henry's son and heir was dead, thereby ending the Lancastrian succession, his mother was in custody, the execution of Somerset and the death of his brother extinguished the Beaufort male line, the power of the Nevilles had already been broken at Barnet and leading Lancastrians such as Northumberland had been bullied or bought into submission.

Very few opponents remained: the melancholy figure of Henry VI in London, imprisoned and to all intents and purposes out of his mind; and the more threatening figure of Jasper Tudor, who was still at large with his young nephew, Henry of Richmond, who wisely took the opportunity to go into exile in France. His mother Margaret Beaufort had been a prominent Lancastrian but having seen her son removed from England she threw in her lot with the Yorkists by marrying Edward's steward, Lord Thomas Stanley. They were all that remained of the once mighty House of Lancaster, which had suddenly disappeared from history. 'In every part of England,' claimed the *Arrivall*, 'it appeared to every man that the said party was extinct and repressed for ever, without any hope of again quickening.'

Not that Edward's troubles had completely evaporated. There was news of trouble in the north from disaffected Lancastrian supporters but without a Neville to lead them the rebels quickly surrendered to Northumberland. More serious was a raid mounted on London by the Bastard of Fauconberg, one of Warwick's cousins who arrived in Kent from Calais and using the allure of the family name persuaded hundreds of men from that rebellious county to join him and march on London to release Henry VI.

There were several reasons for this eruption of violence. The county of Kent had always been loyal to Warwick and, along with Essex and Surrey, it had a long history of opposition to authority in London. Many of the men who joined the Bastard had been incited by the prospect of plundering wealthy London and that expectation had been heightened by the uncertainty and unrest that was prevalent throughout the country. According to *The Great Chronicle*, there was also a fair amount of resentment about the low prices paid by Londoners for their dairy produce and that umbrage resulted in a novel kind of protest:

Whereof the fame being blown into Essex, the faint husbands cast from them their sharp scythes and armed them with their wives' smocks, cheese cloths and old sheets and weaponed them with heavy and great clubs and long pitchforks and ashen staves, and so in all haste sped them toward London, making their avunt as they went that they would be revenged upon the mayor for setting of so easy pennyworths of their butter, cheese, eggs, pigs, and all other victual, and so joined them unto the Kentish men.

Thus attired and arrayed, Fauconberg's motley force arrived outside the city and demanded entry. This was promptly refused as the news of Tewkesbury had already arrived and once again the mayor knew where his best interests lay. Angered by the resistance, Fauconberg withdrew his forces to Southwark, where his Calais fleet was moored, and he ordered the ships' cannon to open fire on the Tower. The following day he tried another tack by crossing the Thames at Kingston and attacked the city from the west. When this ploy also failed he attacked London Bridge but the city levies and the retinues of Earl Rivers counter-attacked and drove the rebels towards Stepney, where many of Fauconberg's followers were slaughtered. Unwilling to surrender, Fauconberg withdrew to Blackheath, to receive news that Edward was hastening back to London with a large army. For most of Fauconberg's followers this was the final straw and they began dispersing. Fauconberg himself took ship for Sandwich, where he waited in the hope of being pardoned. His wishes were granted and he went into Gloucester's service only to be executed later in the year.

The only rebel to pay the full penalty of a traitor's death was

Fauconberg's associate Nicholas Faunt, Mayor of Canterbury, who was hanged, drawn and quartered there, his home town. Warkworth's comment on the aftermath of the rebellion was succinct and to the point: 'Lo, what mischief grows after insurrection!'

Edward's return to London on 21 May was the high-water mark of his reign and he entered his capital with all due pomp and ceremony, according to the Croyland chronicler, 'ordering his standards to be unfurled and borne before him'. In his retinue rode his brothers and the Dukes of Norfolk, Suffolk and Buckingham, 'together with other nobles, knights, esquires and a host of horsemen larger than had ever been seen before'. Those who had supported the King, notably those who had resisted Fauconberg's demands to enter London, were rewarded with knighthoods. Also present was a litter carrying Margaret of Anjou, who was subjected to the taunts and derision of an angry crowd. Her presence spelled doom for her husband.

Not only was Henry VI no longer needed but his continued presence in the capital acted as a focus for unrest; as long as he lived there would always be the possibility of civil war and so he had to die. On Edward's orders he was assassinated that very night and it is highly probable that Gloucester was involved. That was the view of Warkworth and Commines and even if the King's brother did not actually carry out the deed he was probably in the Tower when Henry met his end. No one believed the account put out by the *Arrivall* that Henry had died a natural death 'of pure displeasure and melancholy' caused by his son's death and the defeat of his cause. More realistic was the point of view voiced by the Milanese ambassador: Henry had been killed because Edward had 'chosen to crush the seed'. (When his body was exhumed in 1911 his skull was found to have been smashed, indicating sharp blows to the head.) His body was displayed in public in the streets of London so that all could see that he was indeed dead. Later he was interred at Chertsey Abbey in Surrey.

As for his wife, whose ambitions had largely been responsible for the civil wars which had marred Henry's reign, she was kept in the Tower and remained in English custody for four years until Louis XI had her ransomed and returned to France. By then, as a childless widow, she no longer presented a threat to the Yorkists and could hardly be used as a focus for disaffection from what remained of the Lancastrian cause. Little is known about the last years of her life. On her return to France she was housed first in a chateau near Angers and finally at Dampierre, near Saumur, where she died on 25 August 1482.

History was not kind to Margaret of Anjou, and because the first accounts were written by the winning side she was represented as a cold, domineering and ambitious woman whose machinations plunged the country into years of internecine conflict. While it is true that she demonstrated a hard and aggressive approach to winning power and was then able to hold on to it, especially as far as her son was concerned, she was also influenced by events. The best that can be said about her is that she found herself encumbered by a weak-willed and passive husband and to protect her own position, as well as her family's, she had to show resilience and fortitude. In that respect she was a victim of circumstances who had to be a 'great and strong-laboured woman' – the Pastons' accurate if somewhat unkind description – in order to survive.

With Henry's death and the ascendancy of Edward IV the civil wars between the rival houses of York and Lancaster were as good as over, although such had been the intensity of the quarrel that there would continue to be clashes between the two factions in the decades ahead. Everything now depended on the new order producing a period of stability and good governance after Henry VI's catastrophic reign.

By defeating the Lancastrians so heavily and so decisively, Edward had reinforced his leadership abilities and shown himself to be a worthy king. In contrast to Henry VI's weak and vacillating character, he had emerged as an energetic and courageous leader who was prepared to take risks and was happy to back his judgement with his actions. By seizing opportunities when they were presented to him, not least during Warwick's dithering behaviour at Coventry, he was able to take the war to his opponents before they could unify their larger forces. At Barnet and Tewkesbury he had exposed himself to danger in combat and had displayed a boldness in leadership which inspired his men. From a military point of view he had underscored many of the virtues of kingship and in so doing he had added greatly to his personal authority. That made him an attractive king; the next step would be to stamp his personality on the next years of his reign and to provide England with a peaceful and stable form of governance.

Chapter Eighteen

MASTER OF HIS OWN KINGDOM

As events would quickly demonstrate, the second period of Edward's kingship proved that he was in a much more secure position than he had ever been in the previous decade and his second reign began with the Crown unexpectedly strong and more settled than it had been since the early years of Henry IV's rule. Edward's hold on power had been won on the battlefield – as it had been at the beginning of his reign – and his throne was virtually unassailable once it had been recovered in the summer of 1471. He did not have to look over his shoulder to see what Warwick might be plotting, his great adversary the House of Lancaster was virtually extinct, he had destroyed his most potent enemies among the aristocracy and he was well placed to stamp his own authority on his personal rule.

Never one to deny the ostentatious and pleasure-loving side of his personality, Edward now gave free rein to his vanity by spending huge sums of money on improving his wardrobe and enriching his court so that he could look every inch the king. The royal accounts for the second period of his reign confirm that Edward was not just interested in wearing fine clothes but that he was prepared to spend a fortune on setting new fashions. At Christmastide in 1482 he appeared at court 'clad in a great variety of most costly garments, of quite a different cut to those which had usually been seen hitherto in our kingdom'. Thanks to loans from well-wishers and fines imposed on his enemies there was no shortage of cash to pay for all this luxury and the wardrobe accounts for 1480 reveal that he possessed twenty-six gowns, doublets or jackets, some of them made of cloth-of-gold, satin and velvet and edged with ermine and sable.

During the later years of his reign he accumulated a huge amount of expensive plate and jewellery and he was no shrinking violet when it came to demonstrating his personal wealth. As Dominic Mancini recalled in his memoirs, Edward enjoyed the fact that his subjects took pleasure in his appearance and was not shy about making sure that he himself was seen by as many people as possible:

Frequently he called to his side complete strangers, when he thought that they had come with the intention of addressing him or beholding him more closely. He was wont to show himself to those who wished to watch him, and he seized any opportunity that the occasion offered of revealing his fine stature more protractedly and more evidently to on-lookers. He was so genial in his greeting, that if he saw a newcomer bewildered at his appearance and Royal magnificence he would give him courage to speak by laying a kindly hand upon his shoulder.

However, for all the brilliance of his court and for all the charisma he brought to the throne, Edward still faced a number of potentially irksome domestic difficulties – for example, he had to decide how to handle the shallow and easily led Clarence. Far from being grateful that he had survived and was not being punished for his earlier treacherous behaviour, the King's wayward brother was already showing signs of resentment. Instead of leading a quiet life, as might have been expected following his dealings with Warwick and the Lancastrians, Clarence showed little desire to accept his position and was soon in open disagreement with his siblings.

However, Edward's most urgent need was to complete the pacification of the realm and to take the necessary steps to prevent any fresh outbreak of hostilities. Never a vindictive man – unlike Henry VI, who had condoned several needless executions – Edward was not interested in gaining revenge. Instead he instituted a two-pronged policy by sidelining potential enemies and offering the hand of friendship to prominent supporters of Henry VI whom he felt could be trusted. In a three-year period between 1472 and 1475 thirty attainders were lifted and offices of state were offered judiciously to men who had been in the employment of the previous regime.

There were also rewards for those who had supported him throughout the period when he lost his crown and had to fight to regain it. Edward's friend and close ally Hastings was given the task, together with Lord Howard, of settling Calais and they took with them an armed retinue to give weight to what they were prepared to offer – pardons for the captains and considerable sums of money to make sure that the garrison switched its loyalty to the new order. Many of Warwick's supporters accepted the pardons when they were offered and the funds were used to pay the Lancastrian soldiers' wages, another sensible move given the propensity of the Calais garrison for acting independently and making trouble.

Edward was less lenient in Kent and Essex, where he was determined to make an example of those who had supported the Bastard of Fauconberg and in so doing to prevent any repetition of the unrest that had almost led to a fresh outbreak of civil conflict in a part of England notorious for its troublemaking. The main punishment was the imposition of heavy fines. Canterbury had its liberties taken away and had to repurchase them and these tactics helped to swell the royal coffers. Coventry, too, had to pay for its liberties to be restored as a result of its support for Warwick. It was a rough and ready system and even though it created a good deal of animosity it avoided mass bloodshed or, as *The Great Chronicle* put it, 'such as were rich were hanged by the purse, and the other that were needy were hanged by the necks'.

Alongside the punishments there were pardons for leading Lancastrians who were willing to come into the Yorkist fold. Prominent among them were administrators who had given loyal service to Henry VI but were now prepared to trim their positions to the new order simply because there was no other option following the death of their patron and his only son. As soon as it became clear that there was going to be no viable opposition to Edward's rule a number of leading Lancastrian supporters chose pragmatism and threw in their lot with the restored court. There were exceptions, the most notable being John de Vere, Earl of Oxford, and Jasper Tudor and his nephew Henry, who all remained in exile. Exeter, too, remained in custody in the Tower, but for the most part men were happy to engage with Edward and offer him their unstinting support. In turn this allowed the King to develop royal patronage and construct a network of trusted professional retainers and bureaucrats who managed his affairs and those of the country in return for grants of money, land and influence.

Among those who benefited from royal patronage were two lawyers, John Morton and Sir John Fortescue, who typified a new breed of bureaucrat who came to the fore during the second period of Edward's reign. Once it began the two showed that they were prepared to switch loyalties to keep themselves in power and seem to have had little or no fixed allegiance to those who had given them preference early in their careers. Both men had served Queen Margaret and had suffered the privations of exile with her yet when Edward offered them positions after his restoration they were happy to accept the proposal.

Morton, the son of a Dorset squire, had been educated at Cerne Abbey and had been destined for the Church, but his secular career had progressed under the House of Lancaster. In 1459 he played a role in the 'Parliament of Devils', which attempted to break the House of York, and rose quickly in Lancastrian favour, yet by 1472 he was Master of the Rolls and reportedly enjoying Edward's 'secret trust and special favour'. In later years he became Archbishop of Canterbury and Chancellor of Oxford University, an extraordinary achievement for one who had been so close to the House of Lancaster and had made no secret of his dislike for Edward IV; in 1483 in a letter to the Duke of Buckingham he explained his ability to change sides seemingly at will:

> Surely, my lord, folly were it for me to lie, for I would swear the contrary your lordship would not, I ween, believe, but that if the world would have gone as I would have wished, King Henry's son had had the Crown and not King Edward. But after that God had ordered him to lose it, and King Edward to reign, I was never so mad that I would with a dead man strive against the quick.

The same kind of self-interest propelled Sir John Fortescue, who had been Chancellor-in-exile to Henry VI. A lawyer of Lincoln's Inn, he had previously served as a Member of Parliament and Chief Justice of the King's Bench and had followed Queen Margaret into exile in Scotland in 1461. During that time he had also written forcefully against Edward's claim to the throne, but the King was anxious to let bygones be bygones.

Fortescue was the first eminent constitutional historian and his monument is the treatise *On the Laws and Governance of England*, which analyses the political upheavals of the period and argues that the English form of government, being a *regimen politicum et regale* (a constitutional monarchy), was superior to foreign systems of monarchy such as the French absolutist model. Because taxation and legislation required the people's consent in England, the whole population was free and prosperous; people were motivated to defend the country from foreign foes and take pride in civic responsibilities, such as participating in jury service. Being prosperous free farmers, jurors could not easily be bribed, whereas in France the jury system did not work, because the downtrodden peasantry could be bought off or overawed by wealthy lords.

However, Fortescue conceded that because the English system made English kings poor – taxes could be raised only through Parliament – the solution was to strengthen the Crown by allowing the monarch to acquire land and so have an independent income. Fortescue prospered as a result of his preferment in 1471 and happily transferred his loyalties to his new liege lord, King Edward IV. His estates in Gloucestershire were restored to him and he lived out his life in comfort at Ebrington, but in his book about the governance of England he was sensible enough to admit that real power was vested not in officials such as himself but in the aristocracy: 'For the might of the land, after the might of the great lords thereof, standeth most in the king's officers.'

The most prominent member of Edward's circle of advisers was now his brother Richard, Duke of Gloucester, whose loyalty had never wavered. In contrast to Warwick and Clarence, Gloucester had cemented his allegiance to Edward through his deeds and as his most recent biographer has pointed out, the story of his career between 1468 and 1483 is one of unbroken service and fidelity to the Crown. Unlike Clarence, he did not change sides to gain any advantage and he remained a loyal and diligent servant of his brother the King even during the difficult months of exile and the uncertain return to

England, when there was still much to do to cement Edward's cause. He remained loyal to the succession: when Edward proclaimed his eldest son Prince of Wales shortly after the restoration, Gloucester was the first to pledge allegiance to his nephew.

In return he was richly rewarded, as indeed he expected to be. Gloucester might have demonstrated exemplary dependability and devotion to duty but he was also extremely acquisitive and, like many other men in his position, he wanted to be rewarded so that he could enjoy the fruits of his success. As the youngest son in the Yorkist dynasty he had no settled inheritance yet he had to support his status as a royal duke and one of the greatest men in the land. During Edward's first reign he had come to believe that he was being short-changed, one reason being that the King had little in the way of patronage to give him, but the second reign changed all that and the riches and property that came his way altered the direction of Gloucester's life by turning him into a rich and powerful magnate.

After the crushing of the Nevilles Edward decided to present the bulk of their power base in the north to his younger brother. At the end of June Gloucester was granted the key Neville strongholds of Middleham and Sheriff Hutton in Yorkshire and Penrith in Cumberland and these acquisitions were quickly followed by the award of the office of Chief Steward of the Duchy of Lancaster, a post held previously by Warwick. As Gloucester was already Warden of the West March, these new possessions gave him considerable temporal power in the north and he set about buttressing it by gaining other important posts, such as Sheriff of Cumberland, Constable of Bewcastle and Custodian of the Northern Forests, the latter post previously having been held by Northumberland.

The following year Gloucester cemented his new position of authority in the north by marrying Anne, Warwick's youngest daughter and the widow of the Lancastrian Prince Edward, who had been killed at Tewkesbury. To do this he had to risk papal displeasure as Anne was a cousin and he should have sought a dispensation on account of consanguinity, but he was determined to make the match and placed the girl and her mother in sanctuary in the Convent of St Martin-le-Grand in London while he pleaded his case before the King and council. (Astonishingly, Anne appears to have been employed as a kitchen maid at the time and may even have been secreted away in that guise by Clarence in a vain attempt to prevent the marriage.)

The match was opposed by Clarence, who rightly believed that it would eat into his own authority – he was married to Anne's sister Isabel and through her laid claim to the Beauchamp and Despenser lands – but he was powerless to stop it. As a result Gloucester became one of the Neville heirs, laying claim to the Salisbury and Neville lands, and, more importantly, through his marriage he was able to present himself as the true recipient of the loyalty and obedience which the Neville retinues normally afforded their lord. In time he came to claim the support of influential northern lords such as FitzHugh, Greystock, Scrope and Dacre, all of whom had at one time thrown their weight behind Warwick. Even Northumberland gave Gloucester his allegiance and entered into what was effectively a power-sharing agreement which allowed both men to retain their positions in the north of England. This was an important consideration as Gloucester increasingly regarded the area as his power base by developing former seats of Neville authority, whereas the Percys were already one of the most dominant families in the same part of the world.

However, Gloucester's claims on the Neville inheritance were not as cut and dried as he would have wished. As long as Warwick's widow Anne lived, the outcome of the inheritance should not have been an immediate issue. Although she was under what amounted to house arrest at Beaulieu Abbey in Hampshire she was determined to protect her rights, but her continuing presence loomed over the issue and caused a huge amount of unbrotherly ill feeling between Clarence and Gloucester.

The quarrel also produced a headache for Edward. From the outset Clarence remained obdurate about his rights and behaved in a high-handed and intemperate manner which ill became the shakiness of his position. While he had been restored to the King's favour he was still a man who had changed sides more than once and was guilty of betraying both his brother and his friend Warwick, but, like many ambitious men, he paid little attention to what had happened in the past and thought only about what he could achieve in the future. In February 1472 Edward summoned his brothers to Sheen to debate the issue, but, apart from some minor tinkering involving the partition of the Warwick estates and the granting of the title of Earl of Warwick to Clarence, little was resolved.

At the heart of the quarrel was the legal position of Warwick's widow, who was the heiress of Richard Beauchamp, Earl of Warwick, and Isabel Despenser, daughter of Thomas Despenser, Earl of Gloucester. At the same time the rightful heir to her husband's Neville lands was George Neville, Duke of Bedford, the son of John Neville, the Marquess of Montague (her husband Warwick's brother), who had been killed at Barnet. To compound the difficulty, neither Clarence nor Gloucester wanted to gain the disputed lands by royal grant as their security would not be completely guaranteed: if there were a change of policy or regime they might be attainted or forced to surrender them under an act of resumption. For that reason both men were determined that the lands in question should be given to them under the law of inheritance and neither was prepared to budge on this point.

Faced by a complicated and seemingly intractable problem, Edward chose the line of least resistance and produced a policy which suited both his brothers but it proved to be a shady and squalid piece of legal chicanery. In May 1474 Parliament passed an act which divided Warwick's inheritance between the two royal dukes and to circumvent the Countess's legal claim it was declared that the decision had been taken as if she 'were now naturally dead'. A second act followed early the next year debarring Bedford or any of Montague's male heirs from laying claim to the Neville inheritance. This was carried through on the dubious grounds that Edward had been minded to attaint Montague for his treason in supporting Warwick during his recent rebellion but had been dissuaded by his brothers. As for the dispossessed Countess of Warwick, she was left bereft and penniless and was forced to live with Gloucester at his residence at Middleham Castle in Wensleydale.

No one came out of the episode with dignity. Clarence and Gloucester had shown themselves to be rapacious and unfeeling – of the two, Clarence had the least reason to be so high-handed given his earlier shameless and unremorseful behaviour – and Edward had revealed a weak side. True, he had prevented a quarrel from spinning out of control into a potential conflict between his brothers, an important point given the country's recent turbulent history, but at the same time he had ridden roughshod over the country's legal system by introducing a judgement which had no regard whatsoever for the laws of inheritance.

The squabble over the Warwick inheritance also coincided with two episodes which briefly threatened Edward's authority and may have prompted him to seek an early and lasting solution to his brothers' quarrel. In April 1472 the King decided to act against George Neville, Archbishop of York and brother of Warwick the Kingmaker, the one member of the Warwick faction who had been permitted to remain in a position of authority. Initially Edward had had no immediate plans to punish Neville and he could not remove him from his see without the Pope's authority but this worldly, acquisitive and meddlesome priest was still a power in the land and remained a threat to the King's authority: his niece was married to Clarence and as brother-in-law to the Earl of Oxford his allegiance to the King might not have been absolute. (Oxford remained a loyal Lancastrian and had married Margaret Neville, the Archbishop's youngest sister, in 1465.) Without giving any reasons Edward had the Archbishop arrested and sent into exile at Hammes Castle in the Calais Pale. Not content with ridding himself of the threat, Edward took possession of Neville's wealth and his revenues from the See of York, his household was broken up and to add to the shame the richly jewelled archbishopric mitre was smashed into pieces to make a new crown for Edward. Few mourned Neville's passing – he died in 1476 without regaining his authority – and Warkworth noted merely that 'such goods as were gathered with sin, were lost with sorrow'.

The second threat to the peace of the realm was more serious. After a short stay in Scotland the Earl of Oxford had taken himself off to France, where he hoped to win the support of Louis XI. Having already supported Warwick and Margaret of Anjou in their plottings, the French king had ample reason to assist any action that might be taken against Edward. He was already in negotiation with James III of Scotland to create a new anti-English alliance and with Oxford's arrival he too could be brought into the plot. In May 1473 Oxford attempted an armed landing in Essex but was forced to retreat and put to sea again, committing acts of piracy in the Channel throughout the summer. Four months later, on 30 September, he changed direction and landed in Cornwall with Viscount

Beauchamp (a companion during the exile in Scotland) and seized St Michael's Mount, a rocky offshore outcrop whose fortress was easily defended but needed continuous supply and resupply. It was also convenient to besiege and to cut off its supplies, as Royalist forces proved by the end of the year. Facing starvation and tempted by the offers of pardon, the soldiers in Oxford's garrison began to defect and the episode ended with everyone, Oxford included, being offered royal pardons.

For his pains Oxford was sent back across the Channel to join his brother-in-law in Hammes Castle, where he remained for the rest of Edward's reign. His attainted lands were passed to Gloucester, leaving the Dowager Countess, Oxford's mother, penniless and homeless. Placed in confinement in a priory at Stratford-le-Bow, she was forced to hand over her property and lands to Gloucester after he had petitioned Parliament and threatened her with 'heinous menace of loss of life'. Although her son's attempt to raise a rebellion had failed to make any impression on the well-being of Edward's throne it did leave an uneasy suspicion that both Neville and Oxford might be acting in collusion with Clarence against the King's best interests. Apart from rumours mentioned in the Pastons' correspondence about the involvement of Clarence in Oxford's plans there is no firm evidence to support such a charge but as matters were soon to show it is clear that Edward had become highly suspicious of Clarence's intentions since the restoration. His unsteady and immoral brother was the only man in England who possessed sufficient authority, wealth and opportunity to effect a change of rule and Edward probably understood that.

The settlement of his brothers' quarrel over Warwick's possessions allowed Edward to turn his attention to the great matter of France and Burgundy. Despite the expulsion of English forces from the country Edward still styled himself King of France and his arms quartered the lilies of France with the leopards of England. He was also well aware of the fact that he had been born in Rouen when it was still in English possession. It was still possible that he might be able to reassert English claims to the throne or at the very least reclaim some of the lost English territories in Normandy and Aquitaine. There was also a good deal of personal animus involved as Edward resented the hostility shown to him by Louis XI, who had supported the House of Lancaster and was still a source of mischief, as demonstrated by his recent dealings with the Earl of Oxford.

However, Edward was enough of a realist to understand that a war against France had the potential to be a ruinous expense on the English Exchequer and he understood that he could hardly attempt it without allies. The obvious candidate in this latter respect was the Duke of Burgundy but Edward remembered only too well the tardy treatment he had received from Duke Charles during his exile in Bruges and he could not bring himself to rely solely on a fair-weather friend who offered his support only at the last minute and when he himself knew that he could benefit from it. A more reliable option was Duke Francis of Brittany, who, having no male heir, was forced to protect his interests by entering into foreign alliances.

To offset French attempts to attack Brittany Edward dispatched two thousand archers in April 1472 and this was followed by an embassy led by the trusted Earl Rivers. The result was the signing of the Treaty of Châteaugiron on 11 September, which allowed the English to use Brittany as a springboard for the invasion of France in return for territorial concessions and agreement over English protection of the duchy during the military operations.

For Edward the next stage was to withdraw his reservations about Burgundy and to begin negotiations with Duke Charles, whose support would be essential for any successful English invasion of France. The middleman was Louis, Lord of Gruthuyse, Edward's host in Bruges, who had been rewarded for his help by being appointed Earl of Winchester, and a series of embassies made their way in both directions across the Channel as part of a general diplomatic offensive. By now Burgundy was ready to resume hostilities against Louis XI but he exerted a high price for entering into an alliance with Edward and Duke Francis: if the operations were successful Burgundy would support Edward's claims to be crowned King of France but he expected to be rewarded with territory in Champagne and the Somme which would allow him to achieve his ambition of linking his northern and southern possessions.

Having completed the diplomacy and laid military plans, Edward then had to persuade Parliament to find the money to pay for the adventure but when the notion was discussed it soon became clear that an attack on France was not an attractive proposition. Edward countered by arguing that control of northern France would reduce expenditure on the defence of the Channel and that there were exciting possibilities for an expansion of trade. In November 1472 Parliament finally agreed to grant a special tax of one-tenth of all incomes from land to pay for the war but, as *The Great Chronicle* recorded, Edward still had to raise funds by other means and was forced into the unseemly position of having to beg or borrow contributions from his wealthier subjects, using whatever means came to hand:

> He rode into Essex, Suffolk and Norfolk and other countries of this land and entreated the people so favourably that he had more money by those means than he should have had by two-fifteens [rate of tax expressed by proportion of income]. It was reported that as he passed by a town in Suffolk and called before him among other a rich widow and frayed [asked] of her what her good will should be toward his great charge, and she liberally had granted to him £10, he thanked her and after took her till him and kissed her, the which kiss she accepted so kindly, that for that great bounty and kind deed, he should have £20 for his £10.

Not everyone was as delighted as the wealthy widow. Writing to her son John (III), Margaret Paston lamented that the indulgences had impoverished the entire country: 'the king goes so near us in this country, both to poor and rich, that I wot [know] not how we shall live if the world amend'.

However, at the very moment that Edward seemed to be succeeding in building up his war chest his allies started faltering. Both Duke Charles and Duke Francis were destined to be the last of their line and over the next four decades their dukedoms were doomed to be subsumed within France. (Duke Charles was killed fighting against the Swiss at Nancy in 1477 while attempting to add to his dukedom in Lorraine, the possession of which would have allowed him to unite his territories in Flanders and the Duchy of Burgundy. On his death without a male heir his line collapsed. Duke Francis died in 1488, also without a male heir, and Brittany's sovereignty merged with France in 1519 on the accession of Henry II, the son of Duke Francis's granddaughter Claude and Francis I. Both dukedoms remained autonomous until the French Revolution of 1789.)

Even at the time Edward was dealing with two rulers whose powers were waning, and that might help to explain the lack of resolution they demonstrated during negotiations with the English king. Before the year was out Burgundy and Brittany had gone back on their promises and entered into local truces with Louis XI. Foiled by their defections, Edward had to follow suit and signed a year-long truce with the country he had been planning to attack. The problem was exacerbated by the fact that Duke Charles's daughter Mary had been promised in marriage to the Archduke Maximilian of Austria, heir to the Hapsburg Emperor Frederick III, and this match had encouraged Burgundy to believe that he might revive the ancient title of King of Lotharingia, the area on which most of Lorraine was based. If that ever happened his dukedom would become a kingdom and that possibility of elevation was bound to rank higher than uncertain English plans to unseat the French king. As it turned out, the Emperor Frederick went back on his promise to carry out the Lotharingian coronation and Maximilian and Mary were only able to marry after Duke Charles's death.

However, those events still lay in the future and to keep all his options open Duke Charles changed tack once more and entered into a formal alliance with Edward on 25 July 1474, its terms being similar to the previous agreement, namely that Duke Charles would recognise Edward's claim to the French throne in return for substantial territorial compensation and for English military support against Louis XI. The agreement allowed Edward to start planning for an invasion in the following year and he used the intervening period to reach an agreement with the Hanse League to end a long-standing dispute over commercial privileges and to prevent the eruption of a new naval war in the Channel.

Diplomacy also kept Scotland in the English fold. Although James III had been in negotiation with Louis XI this irresolute Scottish king was not keen to pick a fight with his English neighbours and was happy enough to enter into an agreement with them. Agreed in September 1473, the treaty would see his son, also James, marry Edward's four-year-old daughter Cecily; this arrangement formed the basis of a truce which was due to last until 1519. Five years after the agreement with Edward was signed the détente was strengthened by the proposed marriage of James III's sister Margaret to Earl Rivers, Edward's brother-in-law, who had lost his wife a year earlier. As we shall see, the match never happened and by the end of the decade optimism had given way to a renewal of enmity when Scots raiders started causing trouble along the border to break the truce, no doubt with the connivance of the Scottish court.

Having brokered an agreement with Burgundy and seen off the ever-present threat posed by the Scots, Edward was now in a position to proceed with his plans to invade France. The preparations were detailed and extensive. In December 1474 steps were taken to requisition the ships that would be necessary to transport the English army and its supplies across the Channel. The majority came from English ports – the Cinque Ports alone provided fifty-seven – but such was the demand that additional ships had to be hired from the Low Countries through the good offices of the Duke of Burgundy. Orders were also given for additional bows and sheaves of arrows as well as a well-equipped artillery train. The latter force was supposed to be even larger than the one employed by Burgundy in the siege of the city of Neuss on the Rhine, which was currently taking up his attention. (This was part of an extraordinary campaign begun by Burgundy in the previous summer to gain control of Lorraine, but the move dragged in the Swiss, who were in alliance with the Hapsburgs and were receiving subsidies from Louis XI.) Thirteen of Edward's artillery pieces were huge siege guns armed with over seven hundred stone projectiles.

The army consisted of over eleven and a half thousand armed men, together with as many non-combatants in support, and if Commines is to be believed it was the largest army ever assembled for a campaign in France, although he added that when they assembled the 'men seemed very inexperienced and unused to active service'. Leading them were five dukes, including Clarence and Gloucester, three earls, one marquess and a dozen barons, a contingent that represented the flower of the English aristocracy. From the end of May the huge army began assembling in Kent and the first elements sailed to Calais on 20 June 1475.

Everything now depended on Burgundy making a move but he continued to be obsessed with the siege of Neuss and when he met

Edward at Calais the English were disconcerted to discover that their main ally was accompanied by only a small personal retinue and not the substantial army which they had expected. This placed Edward in a dreadful quandary. It was a massive risk to continue his advance into French territory without Burgundian support, yet to retire back across the Channel or to stay put in Calais would produce a huge loss of face, as well as the waste of the funds raised during the past months. He could hardly do nothing but he was also uneasily aware that his forces were both inexperienced and badly balanced: there were too many archers and too few men-at-arms. It was also proving to be a wet and cold summer and the campaign got off to the worst possible start when the English army, at Burgundy's suggestion, started to move south-eastwards towards Péronne on the Somme.

When they arrived outside St Quentin they were met with sustained cannon fire and most of the advance guard was either killed or taken prisoner. The English were now deep in French territory and Louis XI had started moving his army from their positions in Normandy, where they had expected Edward to land, towards Artois and Picardy. Far from striking any blow, the English were now in danger of being caught in a trap. It was also abundantly clear that Burgundy had no intention of helping them until he had concluded his operations in Lorraine.

Facing this impasse, Edward fell back on diplomacy. In fact he had already paved the way for a negotiated settlement by sending the Garter Herald to the French court even before what he called the 'great enterprise' began. Ostensibly the herald's task was to present Louis XI with Edward's official demand for the return of English territory and to make his claim to the French throne but, according to Commines, who was present throughout, there was also a private discussion about the possibility of a settlement without going to war, provided that the approach was made by the French. And that was the eventual outcome. Louis did not want to engage in a potentially ruinous war with an adversary who had a large if untested army and he realised that Edward also wished for an accommodation.

Accordingly, after an exchange of envoys, the French king offered the opportunity of a meeting for peace negotiations. The two sides met near Amiens – Dr John Morton was among the English delegation – and a deal was quickly produced. In return for the payment of 75,000 French crowns and an annual tribute of 50,000 crowns the English army would be withdrawn as soon as was practical. Also included in the arrangement were a number of commercial agreements to allow greater mercantile freedom and a private understanding for continuing friendship which would be cemented by the marriage of the Dauphin to Edward's daughter, Elizabeth of York.

Louis was keen to execute the plan before Burgundy could intervene once more in the process and the English demands were accepted without demur. To give the whole proceedings a dignity which was missing from what was in reality a sordid commercial transaction, the English and French armies proceeded towards Amiens in full battle array. It was all for show and so concerned was Louis to keep the peace that he produced lavish entertainment for the English soldiers, who immediately took advantage of the huge amounts of food and drink made available to them, as Commines reported:

> The king [Louis XI] had ordered two large tables to be placed on each side of the street, at the entrance of the town gate, which were covered with a variety of good dishes of all sorts of food most proper to relish their wine, of which there was great plenty, and of the richest that France could produce; and abundance of servants to wait on them, but not a drop of water was drunk. At each of the tables the king had placed five or six boon companions, persons of rank and condition, to entertain those that had a mind to take a hearty glass . . . Those English who were within sight of the gate, saw the entertainment, and there were persons appointed on purpose to take their horses by the bridles, and lead them to the tables where every man was treated handsomely as he came, in his turn, to their very great satisfaction.

Commines also noted somewhat tartly that during the three-day spree the English would be seen drunk in the streets as early as nine o'clock in the morning: then, as now, the constant flow of wine clearly being too great a temptation to men who were far away from home and enjoying free hospitality. Another account claimed that women were also made available to the English host but 'many a man was lost that fell to the lust of women, who were burnt by them [infected by venereal disease]; and their members rotted away and they died'.

Against that unedifying backdrop – drunken behaviour and sexual overindulgence by the English and a disdainful response from the French – the two kings finally met at Picquigny, some three miles downriver, on 29 August. A bridge had been built across the Somme and the French had taken the sensible precaution of including a palisade or barrier in the middle to allow discussion but keep the two sides apart. They wanted no repetition of the incident at Montereau, where Duke John of Burgundy had been killed on a bridge during similar negotiations back in 1419. Agreement was quickly reached; this had been made easier by Louis's decision to offer bribes to Edward's advisers, all of whom left France with pensions and lavish gifts of plate. According to Commines, the two kings were soon on amiable terms, with Edward addressing Louis 'in quite good French', and the agreement known as the Treaty of Picquigny was quickly sealed.

War had been averted, Edward returned from France with a healthy profit and few lives had been lost, but, far from being the 'honourable peace' claimed by the Croyland chronicler, the French expedition left a bitter memory in many minds, a belief that it was without honour and that somehow the English had been duped by getting drunk and accepting bribes. Louis, though, was well pleased with the outcome because he had avoided a costly war and had managed to uncouple Edward from Burgundy. 'I have chased the English out of France more easily than my father did,' he boasted, 'for he had to drive them out with armies, while I have seen them off with venison and good French wine.'

When Edward returned to England later in the summer he faced criticism in some quarters for failing to wage a successful war against the French and the feeling lingered that it was a dishonourable episode in the country's history, but the general sentiment was relief. From Edward's point of view the best that can be said of this sorry episode is that he came out of it with his hands clean and his reputation intact. He also brought final settlement to the problem posed by Margaret of Anjou, who was handed over to Louis XI on payment of a ransom and on condition that she renounce her claim to the English Crown and all her dower lands in England. With her removal one more vestige of Lancastrian rule was ended; she lived on for another six years but it was a pitiful existence as Louis forced her to give up all claims inherited from her father, King René of Anjou, and her mother, Isabella of Lorraine.

All things considered, Edward had emerged from the Picquigny negotiations with his reputation in credit. While the Croyland chronicler continued to voice some alarm about the King's 'unfair management of the resources of the kingdom', this was balanced by the removal of trading restrictions. Humiliating in some respects the French pensions might have been but at least the funds allowed Edward to be financially independent for the rest of his reign.

The real loser was Burgundy, who failed to help Edward because of his military commitments in Lorraine. By the end of the year he was engaged in total war against the Swiss, whose army was among the best trained and equipped of the day, especially its disciplined infantry forces. In February the following year Burgundy captured the town of Granson, a possession of the Savoyard Jacques de Romont, on the borders of Switzerland and Alsace, and hanged or drowned the entire garrison. This atrocity led to a vicious Swiss counter-attack in which the speed and aggression shown by their forces demoralised the Burgundian defenders, who fled in panic, leaving behind most of their supplies and their artillery train.

Worse followed on 22 June 1476, when a Burgundian army besieging Morat, about twenty miles from Berne, was overrun and destroyed by a smaller Swiss force. Almost ten thousand Burgundian soldiers were killed whereas the Swiss losses were negligible. At the beginning of the following year the Swiss attacked deep into Burgundian territory and crushed a new army at Nancy on 5 January. Duke Charles of Burgundy was killed during this battle and on his death his line came to an end, with his vast territorial holdings being divided between France and his daughter Mary and her husband, Archduke Maximilian. Five years later Mary of Burgundy also died, as a result of a fall from her horse, and in the same year, 1482, as a result of the Treaty of Arras, Louis XI was confirmed in possession of the duchy. The Duke's death ended Edward's hopes of an alliance to challenge France and to make any fresh claim to the French throne.

Chapter Nineteen

GLORY AND TRANQUILLITY

On his return to England Edward was at the peak of his powers. For the time being at least, he no longer had to worry about France, his finances were secure, with his main rivals killed or sidelined his kingdom was at peace and he could afford to indulge himself and his family. The commercial returns from the Treaty of Picquigny allowed English merchants to prosper once more by ending tiresome commercial restrictions and there was a welcome expansion of trading with France, especially in the cloth and wool markets, which had stagnated during the recent civil wars. Because of this the King had no need to raise parliamentary taxes and was able to live of his own, a remarkable achievement and one which helped to alleviate any lingering concern about the recent flawed operations in France.

Another innovation was Edward's decision to engage in trade himself: he became a shrewd and successful venture capitalist with several profitable import–export concerns under royal control. Much of the enterprise was in the hands of factors or business managers but, according to the Croyland chronicler, Edward was involved in trade and royal ships were used to export wool cloth, tin and other products, all to the advantage of his Exchequer. A number of leading aldermen in London received knighthoods and Edward was unusual in maintaining cordial relations with the merchant class. Coming after the profligacy and reckless expenditure of the House of Lancaster, Edward's good housekeeping and solid financial judgement helped to make the years after 1475 something of a golden age in English history, a quiet period which the Croyland chronicler was moved to describe as a time of 'glory and tranquillity'. Together with the King's French pensions and other revenues, continued the chronicler, 'all these particulars in the course of a very few years rendered him [Edward] an extremely wealthy prince'.

He was also becoming increasingly vain and sensuous in his approach to life. During the meeting on the bridge at Picquigny Commines had expressed his surprise that Edward was running to fat and had lost the youthful handsomeness which had been much admired during his earlier years with Warwick in Calais. Greed and lack of exercise were the cause. According to Mancini, one of Edward's less pleasing failings was the use of an emetic during banquets so that he could gorge and then regorge for the simple pleasure of eating and drinking as much as possible. Added to this was the continuing and well-attested interest he took in women. Writing later, Sir Thomas More complained that the King's 'greedy appetite was insatiable, and everywhere all over the realm intolerable. For no woman was there anywhere, young or old, rich or poor, whom he set his eye upon . . . but without any fear of God, or respect of his honour, murmur or grudge of the world, he would importunely pursue his appetite and have her, to the great destruction of many a good woman.' To put the observation in historical perspective, More was quoting the Duke of Buckingham in 1484 at a time when Edward's character was under attack, but even though a very young boy at the time the author was probably cognisant of the King's incontinent behaviour.

Edward's principal mistress remained Jane Shore, who finally received an annulment of her marriage on account of her husband's impotence, at the time an unusual and rarely used reason for ending a marriage. She had the happy knack of not only having captivated the King sexually but making friends with him, and it proved to be lifelong bond. More also makes the point that the King listened to her and there were occasions when she was able to intercede in his affairs: 'Where the king took displeasure, she would mitigate and appease his mind; where men were out of favour, she would bring them into his grace.' Not unnaturally, the situation did not please Queen Elizabeth, who was said to hate 'that concubine whom the king her husband most loved', and she was also resentful of the role played by Hastings, whom she thought 'secretly familiar with the king in wanton company'. But the Queen's displeasure over these antics did not prevent Edward from carrying out his marital duties: by 1480 the royal couple had ten children, two of whom, Margaret and George, died in infancy.

The one blot on this otherwise settled landscape was Clarence. With Gloucester he had accompanied his brother to France and had provided a well-armed retinue, but on his return to England his behaviour became increasingly erratic. In December 1476 his wife Isabel died in childbirth at Warwick Castle, where her husband had assumed all the rights and properties of her father, Warwick the Kingmaker, and this left Clarence free to marry again. One suggestion was Burgundy's heiress Mary, who had already been promised to the Archduke Maximilian, but such a match would have caused problems. It would have strengthened Clarence's own position as a possible claimant for his brother's throne and there was a further, though distant, Burgundian claim through Mary's grandmother Isabella, who was a granddaughter of John of Gaunt. Edward forbade the match on the grounds of consanguinity and common sense and as a result of the King's ruling the relationship between the brothers quickly deteriorated.

Clarence seems not to have learned from his previous mistakes. Instead of standing behind his brother and supporting him as Gloucester had done, he spent too much of his time attacking the King and, from the scant evidence available, involving himself in plots against him as 'each began to look upon the other with no very fraternal eyes'. The Croyland chronicler takes it further, alleging that the situation was exacerbated by 'flatterers running to and fro, from the one side to the other, and carrying backwards and forwards the words which had fallen from the two brothers, even if they had been spoke in the most secret closet'.

Two incidents combined to bring about Clarence's downfall and it is clear from both of them that he was largely the author of his own misfortunes. In April 1477 he arranged for the abduction from her house in Somerset of Ankarette Twynho, a former servant in his household, whom he suspected of poisoning his duchess Isabel by giving her 'a venomous drink of ale mixed with poison'. In a single day Twynho was taken to Warwick Castle, tried before the justices, indicted and then summarily hanged with an alleged accomplice,

John Thursby. This was a disgraceful abuse of power and it was followed by another equally serious error of judgement.

In the month following Twynho's lynching an Oxford astronomer, Dr John Stacey, was arrested for attempting to use magic against the King and under torture he implicated one Thomas Burdett, a Warwickshire landowner and a member of Clarence's household. A third man, Thomas Blake, was also arrested and all three faced trial on charges of using necromancy to kill or 'imagine the death' of the King and the Prince of Wales. (This involved creating a horoscope which predicted the life expectancy of Edward and his son; the calculations found that both would die soon.) During the trial Blake was reprieved but on 20 May Stacey and Burdett were taken to Tyburn and hanged, drawn and quartered. Clarence was already implicated in that Burdett was in his employment, but instead of staying clear of the affair and keeping silent he decided to intervene by making sure that the two condemned men's declarations of innocence were read aloud to the council. To make matters worse, Clarence arranged for the protest to be read out by John Goddard, a friar who had become notorious during the readeption by preaching on Henry VI's absolute right to the throne. This act of lèse-majesté enraged Edward, who decided that enough was enough. Clarence was arrested in June and incarcerated in the Tower of London.

He remained there until Parliament convened on 19 January 1478, its main business being to arraign him on charges of high treason, the attainder being introduced by the King. This was a staged political trial, for Clarence could not call witnesses and was only permitted to refute the charges made against him. Nor did Edward stint in listing the accusations against his wayward and foolish brother. Clarence was, he said, guilty of 'heinous treasons', he had betrayed his loyalty to the King by whispering that Edward was a bastard (it was not the first occasion that he had made the allegation), he had committed a crime by hanging Ankarette Twynho and he had presumed the innocence of Burdett, who had committed treason. In short, Clarence was 'incorrigible' and had committed 'a much higher, much more malicious, more unnatural and loathely treason than at any time heretofore had been encompassed, purposed and transpired'.

Despite their closeness as brothers and for all that the King was generally minded to forgive his enemies, in this instance Clarence had tried Edward's patience so sorely that he deserved to be punished. It was a sorry business. Clarence was doomed before the trial began and Edward was determined that on this occasion there should be no second chance. As the Croyland chronicler makes clear, the charges against Clarence were vague and unsubstantiated and when witnesses were produced they were present not to give impartial evidence but to add to the chorus of condemnation:

> The circumstances that happened in the ensuing parliament my mind quite shudders to enlarge upon, for then was to be witnessed a sad strife carried on before these two brethren of such high estate. For not a single person uttered a word against the duke, except the king; not one individual made answer to the king except the duke. Some parties were introduced, however, as to whom it was greatly doubted by many, whether they filled the office of accusers rather, or of witnesses: these two offices not being exactly suited to the same person in the same cause. The duke met all the charges made against him with a denial, and offered, if he could only obtain a hearing, to defend his cause with his own hand [by meeting his accusers in personal battle]. But why delay in using many words? Parliament, being of the opinion that the informations which they had heard were established, passed sentence upon him of condemnation, the same being pronounced by the mouth of Henry, Duke of Buckingham, who was appointed Seneschal [Constable] of England for the occasion.

Clarence was taken back to the Tower and there he lay for ten days while Buckingham delayed the imposition of the death sentence. Being newly appointed Constable of England, Buckingham was not anxious to rush the execution of a man who was, after all, the King's brother and it was not until the Speaker of the Commons intervened to demand an immediate execution that he arranged for Clarence to be dispatched on 18 February. To avoid unnecessary scandal the imprudent duke was done to death privately within the Tower and afterwards a legend grew that he escaped hanging or beheading – the normal method of execution – only to be drowned in a butt of sweet Malmsey wine. This explanation came to be accepted, although it is equally possible that Clarence was drowned while bathing in a tub, but whatever the method the act was little more than judicial fratricide.

The case against Clarence was largely trumped up and was pushed through Parliament by the King, who used the kind of language that brooked no disagreement. In terms of natural justice the treatment of Clarence was illegal and immoral, but in terms of realpolitik Edward had been pushed into a corner. His brother had already sorely tried his patience by siding with Warwick and then by switching his allegiance when it suited his ambitions. Clarence was devious, insubordinate and untrustworthy and it was highly probable that after the return from France he continued to act duplicitously with a view to push his claim on his brother's throne. Even though the execution of a brother leaves a stain on Edward's reputation the situation had reached a point where he had to act against Clarence to ensure his own survival. In that light the wonder is not that Clarence was done to death but that he managed to survive for so long: most other European kings of the period would not have been so lenient and would have dealt with the threat much sooner than Edward did.

Hardly had the furore over Clarence died down than Edward was forced to deal with a new foreign policy crisis involving France and Burgundy. The death in battle in 1477 of Duke Charles had reopened the question of where Edward's allegiances should lie. Following his détente with Louis XI, his acceptance of the French pensions and the offer of his daughter in marriage to the Dauphin, Edward was honour-bound to maintain the harmonious agreement which had been brokered at Picquigny, but the balance of power was immediately altered when French forces started moving into Picardy, Artois and Burgundy to capitalise on the Duke's death. This changed everything. Louis was now taking advantage of Burgundy's enfeeblement to add to his kingdom and, worse, the moves threatened English mercantile interests in Calais.

There was also a domestic angle: Margaret, the Dowager Duchess of Burgundy, Charles's widow, was Edward's sister and she began pressing him for support by insisting that he had to find an English husband for her daughter. Had Clarence possessed a balanced personality and acted as a loyal brother he would have fitted the bill but as he had enjoyed neither of those virtues Edward was left to solve the matter by diplomacy. On the one hand there was the traditional

English distrust of France and the tendency to favour Burgundy; on the other were the substantial benefits gained by the Treaty of Picquigny and Edward's unwillingness to surrender them. It was a tricky problem and one which alarmed Sir John Paston (II), who recorded that it seemed to him 'that all the world is quavering'.

In order to buy time Edward reinforced the Calais garrison as a signal to Louis XI to stay away from the English possession and sent an embassy to France led by Dr Morton and Sir John Donne, another trusted official who had given loyal service to the House of York. (A Welshman by birth, he had served in France and had been knighted after Tewkesbury. His links to the throne had been strengthened through his marriage to Hastings's sister Elizabeth.)

As a result of their negotiations Louis agreed to extend and strengthen the terms of Picquigny but these were little more than diplomatic niceties. At the same time a half-hearted attempt was made to marry Rivers to Mary of Burgundy but, as Commines pointedly noted, this was hardly a serious offer as 'Rivers was only a petty earl and she the greatest heiress of her time'. Eventually the problem was solved by Duchess Margaret's decision to allow the match between her daughter and the Archduke Maximilian to proceed in order to forge an alliance between Burgundy and the Hapsburgs.

The question of matches for his own progeny also occupied Edward's mind. He had eight surviving children and was determined to make suitable marriages for all of them, both to strengthen his dynasty and to give England powerful allies. First and foremost, he had to settle his son Edward, Prince of Wales. One possibility was marriage to the Infanta Isabella, the heiress of Ferdinand of Aragon, but this came to nothing when a son and heir was born to the Spanish rulers in 1478, making the match less attractive. Other names mooted were Maximilian of Austria's sister and the daughter of the Duke of Milan. Edward was keen to pursue the latter as she came from a wealthy family but, as the Milanese ambassador reported to his master the Duke, that was ample reason for denying the match. In April 1479 the ambassador wrote a candid assessment of the situation in which he spoke of the 'great quantity of money' which Edward would demand in a dowry and expressed his belief that he would do this as 'one who tends to accumulate treasure'. (Edward's avarice was known throughout Europe.)

To balance his relationship with Louis – another example, it may be considered, of the English King's greed – Edward then thought to marry Prince Edward to Anne of Brittany, the elder daughter and heiress of Duke Francis. The negotiations for this match were lengthy and complicated and involved the use of substitutes should any of the children die – Prince Richard was a first reserve for Prince Edward – but nothing came of the discussions. Later Richard would be affianced to Anne, the daughter of the Duke of Norfolk and heiress to her family's great Mowbray fortunes. The marriage took place in January 1478, when both partners were little more than six years old, but Anne died three years later. As she was still a child, under the law of inheritance her fortune should have passed back to her family but, as Edward had already demonstrated in his dealings with the Warwick family, mere laws were not a bar when it came to enriching his own family. In January 1483 an act was passed by Parliament which allowed Prince Richard and his heirs to inherit the Norfolk fortune and should he die childless the inheritance would pass to King Edward. Like the propensity for overindulgence at the dinner table, this greedy side of Edward's nature leaves a question mark over his later years, when acquisitiveness seemed to replace his earlier generous and open disposition.

Equally Machiavellian were Edward's plans for his daughters. The eldest, Elizabeth, had already been promised to Louis' son and heir Charles, the Dauphin, while Cecily, the third daughter, had been put down to marry James III of Scotland's son, the future James IV. For Mary, the second daughter, nothing had been arranged as she had to provide cover for her sisters and was not allowed her own match until 1481, when her hand was offered to the King of Denmark. For the fourth daughter, Anne, Edward wanted to take advantage of the new alliance created by Maximilian and Mary of Burgundy by betrothing her to their infant son, Philip. This was eventually agreed in August 1480 but only after another unseemly tussle over dowries.

Not unreasonably, Maximilian expected his prospective daughter-in-law to arrive with a suitable dowry – just as the English expected the Duke of Milan's daughter to be financially well endowed – but Edward argued that the price of the match should be his military support. None of the matches would take place until the children concerned came of age but Edward placed great emphasis on establishing alliances of this kind to further England's foreign policy and to cement his own position in the wider world. It was also a system of checks and balances: the marriage of his eldest daughter to the Dauphin would settle the French alliance, while the Burgundian marriage would act as a counter-weight and give support to an older and deeper friendship.

This was marriage as a tool of diplomacy and Edward proved to be skilled in the art, although, as it turned out, nothing ever came of any of the intended alliances. Neither Elizabeth nor Cecily married the princes to whom they had been betrothed and indeed Cecily found herself becoming a bargaining chip in an unseemly quarrel with the Scots in 1480. Until then there had been no sign of any unrest between the two countries, the truce of 1474 remained intact and relations remained cordial, but James III had problems of his own and these impinged on his relations with England. During his minority James had been more or less kidnapped by the powerful Boyd of Kilmarnock family, who kept him a prisoner in Edinburgh Castle, and he had not managed to regain his liberty until his marriage to Princess Margaret of Denmark in 1469, a good match which brought Scotland possession of Orkney and Shetland. He also had to deal with the threat posed by John MacDonald, Lord of the Isles, and the exiled Earl of Douglas, with whom Edward IV had entered into an agreement in 1462. Under its terms James III would have been unseated and Scotland would have been divided and partitioned, with MacDonald and Douglas ruling as English vassals.

Then there was the Auld Alliance to consider, the military and political contract with the French throne which had come into being as a Franco-Scottish bulwark against Plantagenet aggression. Over the years it had changed complexion, sometimes being a diplomatic lever, at other times a military alliance with soldiers from both countries lending assistance to the other in the perennial wars against the English. The royal families of the two countries were linked by marriage, another brick in the alliance, but by the reign of James III the Scots felt an increasing need to balance the French connection by keeping the peace with England.

Unusually in the Stewart succession, James III was actively interested in foreign affairs and during his reign there emerged a new national self-confidence. Partly out of personal inclination – a contemporary account says that James 'delighted more in singing and playing upon instruments than he did in defence of the borders' – and partly out of common sense, for the first time in many years Scotland wanted and needed a long and lasting peace with its neighbour. There had been a growth in the country's prosperity centred on the creation of new burghs, with the construction of some fine public buildings; two universities had come into being, at St Andrews and Glasgow; in 1472 St Andrews became an archbishopric; and trade was becoming increasingly important for Scottish well-being. True, James's reputation has been sullied by many fanciful stories about his sexuality and his reliance on low-born favourites, but during his reign it was possible to see the first signs of progress in a country that had always lagged behind England economically and socially. James wanted peace and quiet in relations between the two countries and at that particular moment in Scotland's history was not minded to follow the wishes of Louis XI, who hoped that the Scots would cause a military diversion which would take Edward's mind off any possible rapprochement with the Burgundians.

However, James, like Edward, was cursed by brothers whom he could not control. In his case both his siblings were imprisoned in Edinburgh Castle in 1479 on suspicion of treason and the younger of the two, John Earl of Mar, died while in captivity, probably murdered on the King's orders. His brother, the headstrong Alexander, Duke of Albany, did not wait for the same fate to befall him and escaped to France, where he attempted to ingratiate himself with Louis XI and acquired a French wife, Anne de la Tour, daughter of the Count of Boulogne and Auvergne. By then Edward had decided to act against the Scots as a punishment for a resurgence of cross-border raids and also to dissuade James from lending any assistance to the French by invading England.

Early in 1480 an embassy was sent to Scotland, taking with it a list of impossible demands. These included the return of Berwick and Roxburgh, the pardoning of Douglas and the handing over of Prince James, the eldest son and Crown Prince, to be educated in England, just as James I had been. Most humiliating of all, James would be required to pay homage to Edward as his liege lord. No king could accept those conditions and hope to survive, and James was no exception. As England started preparing for war the Scots took the initiative in August, when the Earl of Angus led a large raiding party into Northumberland and set fire to Bamburgh Castle.

This incursion led Gloucester and Northumberland to call out their own forces for a retaliatory raid but even at that late stage James was keen to pull back from all-out war. In an attempt to find common ground two heralds were sent to London in November, but they were angrily ignored as Edward and his council made preparations to invade Scotland with a land army of seven thousand soldiers and a sizeable naval force to operate off the east and west coasts. For the first time in the history of warfare between the two countries the naval element played the major role in the opening stages. In the summer of 1481 a squadron under the command of Lord Howard entered the Firth of Forth to capture eight Scottish merchantmen and sink a number of smaller craft. At the same time the small port at Blackness was torched. On the west coast a smaller force operating out of Chester kept up standing patrols to discourage Scottish shipping, but there was little movement on land. Although Edward had threatened to lead the English forces in person he failed to make any move during the summer of 1481 and all military activity was left in the hands of Gloucester, who contented himself with mounting a number of cross-border raids.

Nor were the Scots idle. In September 1481 their forces raided English territory again, to burn and loot, before withdrawing back into Scotland. At the same time Gloucester began preparations to besiege Berwick, which became the main target. The idea was to use English naval supremacy to block the seaward defences and prevent the town and its garrison from being supplied from the sea, but, largely because of the King's inaction, progress was slow. By the end of the summer Edward was still in London and when he finally did move he failed to get beyond Nottingham. There were also reports that he was ailing in mind and body, that he now preferred his bed and home comforts to the hardships of campaigning and, to compound the general air of unease, the winter of 1481–2 produced bitterly cold and wet weather. In an age when portents were often more potent than reality and when a king's ability to reign was measured by his personal capacity to impose his authority on the kingdom, these were worrying signs that things were amiss in Edward's life and that the country would suffer as a result.

A new campaign against the Scots was planned for the summer of 1482 under the command of Gloucester as Lieutenant of the North. With him he had most of his brother's most trusted adherents. Lord Stanley, Steward of the Royal Household, led a force from Lancashire and Cheshire, Northumberland was there with his northerners, the Woodville levies were under the command of the Marquess of Dorset, the Queen's eldest son from her first marriage. Other notable lieutenants included Rivers and Sir Edward Woodville, both of whom were distinguished jousters, but the surprise element in Gloucester's force was provided by the Duke of Albany in his role of Scottish Warden of the West March.

Albany shared many similarities with Clarence. Headstrong, truculent, pushy, a stranger to loyalty, he entertained ambitions to seize his brother's throne and after discovering that Louis was not inclined to offer French help he had tried his luck at Edward's court. There was no need for any persuasion. Edward's agents had already contacted him and on 11 June 1482 the unscrupulous Albany entered into an agreement at Fotheringhay which would see him crowned 'Alexander of Scotland by the Gift of the King of England'. In return he would hand back Berwick to the English as well as other places on the border, including Lochmaben, Eskdale and Annandale, the alliance with the French would be ended and Albany would acknowledge Edward as his feudal superior. To cement the new arrangement he would get rid of his French wife 'according to the laws of the Christian church' and marry Edward's daughter Cecily. Foolish and ruthless though Albany undoubtedly was, he must have realised that the agreement would never be accepted by the Scottish nobility, who would hardly allow such humiliating conditions to be imposed on them and the country. But, having betrayed his brother James, he now had nothing left to him other than to tie himself to Edward's plans.

The invasion began in earnest in July with the siege of Berwick under Lord Stanley, while Gloucester took most of the army into the Lothians towards Edinburgh. At the same time James rallied his own forces, declaring that he would 'defend the realm in honour and freedom, as his noble progenitors had done in times past'. It was at this point that legend clouds the story from the Scottish point of view, and it becomes difficult to separate fact from fiction as most of the narratives were written long after the event and are mostly inaccurate or fanciful. One of the reasons for the emergence of the surviving mythologised version is that it was underpinned by a highly satisfactory morality story which was given a wider currency in later years in Sir Walter Scott's novel of 1820 *The Abbot*.

Having assembled his army on the Burgh Muir, Edinburgh's traditional mustering point, James led it south into Lauderdale, where his nobles finally decided to end their support for him in dramatic fashion. Led by the Earl of Angus, they demanded that the King rid himself of his favourites, most notably Robert Cochrane, a commoner, who had reformed the currency and been promoted to the vacant earldom of Mar, an elevation that had angered the older and more venerable Scottish noble families. On being told that the Scottish nobles were like the mice in the fable who agreed that it was in their interests to hang a bell around the cat's neck but none was prepared to take any action, Angus is supposed to have proclaimed to his fellow conspirators, the Earls of Huntly, Lennox and Buchan, that he would 'bell the cat'. He then promptly led the way and hanged Cochrane and the other favourites over the bridge at Lauder. Having accomplished their mission, the conspirators took the King into their custody and marched back to Edinburgh.

For ever after Angus's nickname was 'Bell the Cat' and the incident passed into Scottish folklore to become an accepted historical fact. While it is likely that there was an incident at Lauder involving the King, that tale, attractive though it is, is not the whole story. The English State Papers make it clear that Gloucester invaded Scotland and quickly gained the upper hand; it is also true that Albany was treasonably implicated on the English side and James had problems with his nobles. But the reality of the events in Scotland in the summer of 1482 is more prosaic. When Gloucester reached Edinburgh James and his followers locked themselves in the impregnable castle and sat tight. To the frustration of the English there was no pitched battle and the episode ended in compromise. Backed by the citizens of Edinburgh, who agreed to repay the marriage dowry due to

Edward, James had his authority restored to him and was able to negotiate with Gloucester for a return to the status quo and the renewal of the earlier peace agreement, including the marriage of his son to Cecily. In return Berwick would be surrendered, as it was at the end of August, never to be returned to Scotland – it had changed hands fourteen times since 1296 – and a new truce between the two countries came into immediate effect.

Having concluded the business to his own satisfaction, Gloucester decided to withdraw his army and returned to England with his reputation not only intact but enhanced. Berwick had been restored – the main point of the exercise – and while there had been no outright victory England's war aims had been largely achieved, even though it had been a costly operation.

As a result of his triumph Gloucester was awarded palatinate authority in Cumberland and any Scottish territory in the West March, of which he was Warden, moves which confirmed his pre-eminence among his peers. Even his brother was well pleased with the outcome, writing to Pope Sixtus IV that Gloucester's 'success is so proven that he alone would suffice to chastise the whole kingdom of Scotland'. The other winner was Albany, who renounced his claim to the Scottish throne and was restored to his earlier position and authority within the country. Like Clarence, though, he did not know when to stop intriguing and in his feline way kept open his links to the English court with the hope of one day being able to reforge the Fotheringhay agreement.

While Gloucester had benefited from the Scottish expedition it had done little to help Edward, and the Croyland chronicler lamented the decision to pull back out of the country without inflicting a decisive blow against the Scots. As he pointed out, bar the capture of Berwick little had been gained in return for a great deal of effort and unnecessary expenditure: 'This trifling, I really know not whether to call it gain or loss – for the safe-keeping of Berwick each year swallows up ten thousand marks – at this period diminished the resources of the king and kingdom by more than a hundred thousand pounds.' As ever, it was not the end of the matter. Contemporary accounts make it clear that throughout this period of his reign Edward was determined to maintain an aggressive posture towards his northern neighbour and intended to reopen hostilities with James when the campaigning season opened in the summer of 1483.

The sudden return to England of the unstable Albany at the beginning of that year rekindled hopes that the English would be able to renew hostilities on the northern front but, as with much else in Edward's foreign policy at this stage of his reign, it is hard to avoid the impression that the King had lost his grip on affairs. The basic mistake he had made while pursuing his tripartite foreign policy was his failure to recognise that James III was unwilling to uphold the Auld Alliance by going to war against England at Louis' behest. Having entered into an agreement with the Scottish king in 1473, Edward would have been better advised to maintain friendly relations at a time when there was no threat apart from the never-ending cross-border raids, which were commonplace and could have been contained by Gloucester. Instead he seems to have harked back to his earlier policy of wanting to crush the Scots and force their king to pay allegiance to him. This notion had first become an issue in 1463 when James III's mother had offered military support to Margaret of Anjou and the House of Lancaster and when Yorkist control of the north of England was insecure. Twenty years later it still rankled with Edward that the Scots had gone unpunished. On his restoration to the throne he had vowed to raise a great army to march into Scotland and, with the support of the Earl of Angus, crush the Scots once and for all, but he was prevented from acting by lack of funds and the willingness of the Scots to conclude a truce following the collapse of Lancastrian authority.

That left the problem posed by France, where Edward was under pressure from Maximilian to support Burgundy by invading France. Until then the conflict with Scotland had provided a good excuse for keeping out of that particular quarrel but the end of 1482 had brought about a dramatic change of direction in the long-running saga of English, French and Burgundian relations. Earlier in the year Mary of Burgundy had died in a riding accident and this unexpected event led to a détente with Louis, who took advantage of the new situation by proposing a match between the Dauphin and Margaret, the infant daughter of Maximilian and Mary. This altered everything and France and Burgundy agreed to the proposal in the Treaty of Arras, which was signed shortly before Christmas.

Under its terms the match was negotiated, with Mary's dowry being found from the lands of Artois and Burgundy. As Edward no longer brought anything to French interests there was now no need to keep the terms of the Treaty of Picquigny and the pension payments were stopped forthwith.

All in all, Edward's diplomatic efforts had achieved very little. To the King's displeasure the Treaty of Arras had ended the fruitful relationship begun at Picquigny: the Croyland chronicler recorded that Edward 'thought of nothing else but taking vengeance', for not only had he lost his pension but there was no longer any chance of his daughter marrying the Dauphin. For a few wild days Edward considered the possibility of building up his forces to invade France and went so far as to promise to send a force of archers to Brittany if Duke Francis decided to support him in France but these were only the reactions of a disappointed man. Eventually he decided on compromise and sent an embassy to the French court in February 1483 to negotiate a new truce.

Unfortunately Edward's problems with the shifting alliances of France and Scotland were mirrored by a sudden and growing discordance at court. Ever since the marriage to Queen Elizabeth the Woodvilles had maintained and reinforced their pre-eminent position, much to the chagrin of the King's associates, who believed that they were being sidelined by powerful rivals who were far too close to the throne. At the beginning of 1483 the Queen's brother Earl Rivers was the master of the Prince of Wales's household, his brother Sir Edward Woodville was poised to take command of the navy and another brother, Lionel, was Bishop of Salisbury. In the next generation the Marquess of Dorset was deputy-governor of the Tower of London and enjoyed a close friendship with the King.

All this alarmed the faction centred on Hastings, the Duke of Buckingham and Lord Stanley, Steward of the Royal Household, and the result was an alarming confrontation between the rival magnates. The main clash was between Rivers and Hastings, although the latter also entertained contempt for young Dorset. Both the main protagonists were powerful men in their own right and enjoyed strong links to the throne. As Anthony Woodville, Rivers had built up an international reputation as a jouster and had fought in the Yorkist army at Barnet and Tewkesbury. Soldiering came easily to him but he was also an ascetic who wore a hair shirt and took an interest in the arts and literature. Mancini thought highly of him, claiming that 'however much he prospered, he never harmed anyone, while doing good to man', but this was an overstatement. Rivers was as cunning and ruthless as any other English magnate of the period and he was determined to crush Hastings's influence at court.

From the outset Hastings had been a committed Yorkist. His father was a retainer to Edward's father, the Duke of York, and he had risen rapidly in royal favour, becoming a wealthy and substantial landowner. He had accompanied the King into exile and was a prominent supporter when he returned; crucially he was rewarded by being granted the lieutenancy of Calais, which he received in 1471 in succession to Rivers, who had incurred the King's displeasure by planning to go on a crusade against the Moors in Portugal. At the same time Hastings built up his power and authority in England, entrusting his office in Calais to his brother Ralph, and during the 1470s in his role of Lord Chamberlain he emerged as the King's main confidant. John Paston (II) said of him that 'what my said lord chamberlain may do with the king and with all the lords of England I believe it be not unknown to you, most of any one man alive'.

There was also social animus between the factions. Although Hastings was a courtier who had made his way in life, the Woodvilles were still regarded as parvenus who owed their rise to the fact that they had married into the royal family and used their position to build up powerful alliances. That was the view taken by Mancini, who observed that 'they were certainly detested by the nobles, because they, who were ignoble and newly made men, were advanced beyond those who far excelled them in breeding and wisdom'. The enmity between Rivers and Hastings was conducted by means of a whispering campaign similar to the one which finally ruined the relationship between Edward and Clarence. Supporters spread smears which were readily believed, the most common being that at different times both Rivers and Hastings had attempted to betray Calais to Louis XI. Mancini records that the King 'loved each of them' and attempted to find a means of ending the feud, but the fact that it existed is a reminder of the clash of over-mighty magnates which fuelled much of the conflict in England during the reigns of Richard II, Henry IV, Henry V, Henry VI and Edward IV. Sadly for the people of England, this propensity was to be the country's further undoing in the years that followed.

Chapter Twenty

THE END OF INNOCENCE

In general, with the exception of his uncertain foreign policy, the second period of Edward's reign had been a felicitous time for the King and his country, but it did not have long to run. In the period before Easter 1483 Edward fell ill and his condition rapidly deteriorated. He seems to have become unwell at the end of March and he died at Westminster on 9 April, three weeks before his forty-first birthday.

There is no specific evidence to suggest the cause of his death, although there was a good deal of contemporary speculation about the reason why a man in his prime should have succumbed to a fatal illness. The Croyland chronicler contented himself with the bland thought that the King was 'neither worn out with old age nor yet seized with any known kind of malady, the cure of which would not have appeared easy in the case of a person of more humble rank'. Mancini suggested that Edward had caught a chill while fishing with his courtiers, while Commines offered two explanations, the first that the King died of apoplexy brought on by excess and the second that he fell victim to melancholia caused by the failure of his French policies and the realisation that England no longer had any influence in France. There could, of course, have been a connection: if Edward had been downcast over the Treaty of Arras he might have taken comfort in immoderate consumption of food and drink and his incontinent appetite could have hastened the onset of a stroke. Both Mancini and the Croyland chronicler left ample evidence about Edward's corpulence and his tendency to overindulge. There were also hints about poisoning and a later Tudor chronicler, Edward Hall, claimed that the illness was caused by a recurrence of malaria caught while the King was in France in 1475, the disease being prevalent in the Somme region.

Although in the greater scheme of things it matters not why Edward died – his early death was the real problem – the most likely cause was a stroke due to his excessive lifestyle. It is clear from all the contemporary accounts that Edward was overweight and increasingly self-indulgent and as a result probably took little exercise. His inability to lead the previous year's expedition into Scotland could be evidence of unfitness and general lethargy. That he lingered for a while suggests that he suffered a first stroke which left him incapacitated and then a second which was fatal.

Whatever the cause of his death, Edward's funeral rites befitted his rank and his stature. For eight days his embalmed body lay in state in St Stephen's Chapel at Westminster before being carried into the abbey on 17 April. The following day the funeral procession set out for the final resting place at Windsor. From Charing Cross the body was borne to Sion Abbey before being taken to St George's Chapel, where it remained overnight. Following the funeral masses, which were taken by the Archbishop of York and the Bishops of Lincoln and Durham, the King was delivered into the tomb which he had ordered to be constructed eight years earlier. This was followed by the solemn ceremonial of a royal interment: after the burial Edward's household threw their staves and badges of office into the grave and the leading members of the nobility made their own offerings to a king whom the Croyland chronicler eulogised as a good man:

> The prince, although in his day he was thought to have indulged his passions and desires too intemperately, was still, in religion, a most devout Catholic; a most unsparing enemy to all heretics, and a most loving encourager of wise and learned men, and of the clergy. He was also a most devout reverer of the Sacraments of the Church, and most sincerely repentant for all his sins. This is testified by those who were present on the occasion of his decease; to whom, and especially to those whom he left as executors of his last will, he declared in a distinct and catholic form, that it was his desire that, out of the chattels which he left behind him in such

great abundance, satisfaction should be made, either fully, or on a composition made voluntarily, and without extortion on their part, to all those persons to whom he was, by contract extortion, fraud or any other mode, indebted. Such was the most beseeming end of this worldly prince, a better than which could not be hoped for or conceived, after the manifestation by him of so large a share of the frailties inherent to the lot of mankind.

All this was true and, laying aside the need for the chronicler to indulge in hagiography, it was a fair assessment of the man and the life he had led. Those sentiments were repeated by writers immediately after Edward's death, historians such as Thomas More and Polydore Vergil who had access to men who had known the King or lived through his reign, but in later centuries there was a radical reassessment. Rather than the fair-minded ruler portrayed by the Croyland chronicler, Edward was frequently painted as a cruel despot whose virtues were outweighed by his greed, laziness and propensity for violence, the execution of his brother Clarence being cited as a pre-eminent example of his bloodthirsty nature.

In more recent times, however, there has been further reassessment to rebalance his reputation and to present a fairer picture of him. Although criticism of his political judgement still exists, especially in his dealings with France and Burgundy and his misreading of the situation in Scotland, Edward emerges from the latest assessments in terms that his contemporaries would have recognised. The best that can be said about him is that he rescued England from the horrors of civil war and brought a much-needed stability to society and the economy after the haphazard years of Henry VI's reign. Through his capacity to bring order and a sense of direction to his country he prepared the way for the Tudors to build on foundations which were more solid than anything that had existed previously. Also, from the evidence of those who knew him or observed his behaviour, he seems to have possessed a rounded and likeable personality, especially in his younger years before he allowed the natural hunger of youth to turn into the greed and unrestrained personal appetite of his later years.

The second half of his reign was crowned by stability and with no claimants to the throne worthy of the name he enjoyed a security that had not existed since the years of Henry V. He wanted to build on that independence by enlarging his own fortune and freeing himself from the public purse, hence his obsession with dowries, his pensions from France and his involvement in trade. That made him a wealthy man and removed the financial problems that had bedevilled Henry VI and Richard II; it meant too that his subjects were not overburdened by taxation, another reason for his personal popularity during his reign. When Edward IV died England was secure, stable and relatively prosperous, the prestige of the monarchy had been restored and he had brought peace to the country after the long years of bloody civil strife.

The one thing that was missing from the picture was a settled succession and that absence was to plunge the country into another period of blood-letting as, all too typically, the magnates with most to gain or lose struggled to gain the ascendancy during the period of uncertainty that followed the King's death. At the time of Edward's passing the rift between Hastings and the Woodvilles had not been healed and there was also the potential for bad blood between Richard of Gloucester and the Woodvilles. With the King's moderating influence gone there was bound to be a power struggle over which court party controlled the heir to the throne, the twelve-year-old Prince Edward who would rule as King Edward V.

On the face of it there seemed to be little immediate concern. There had been minorities before and the new king would soon reach his majority, the kingdom was settled and at that stage young Edward enjoyed the support of all his powerful close family relatives. Richard of Gloucester in particular was in a strong position. He was Edward IV's brother, he was rich and influential in his own right and he enjoyed massive support in the north of England. During his brother's lifetime he had sworn an oath of loyalty to his nephew as successor and, according to the Croyland chronicler, on Edward's death Gloucester summoned the northern magnates to 'hold a solemn funeral ceremony' at which they reaffirmed their loyalty to 'the king's son; he himself swore first of all'.

Gloucester also reinforced his position by writing to the Queen declaring his loyalty to her son, and wrote in similar terms to the council, adding that he was well positioned to act as his nephew's protector. As Mancini pointed out, he was astute enough to make sure that the contents of the second letter were made public:

He [Richard] had been loyal to his brother Edward, at home and abroad, in peace and war, and would be, if only permitted, equally loyal to his brother's son, and to all his brother's issue, if perchance, which God forbid, the youth should die. He would expose his life to every danger which the children might endure in their father's realm. He asked the councillors to take his deserts into consideration, when disposing of the government, to which he was titled by law, and his brother's ordinance.

Mancini added that Gloucester's appeal had a positive effect 'on the minds of the people who . . . now began to support him loudly and aloud', but the council was not ready to accept this offer. They preferred to establish a council of regency in which Gloucester would play a role but would be constrained by others. Their decision was mainly due to the influence of the Woodvilles, who were also busily protecting their own positions and had the support of influential men such as Dr Morton. While this jockeying for position was taking place Prince Edward remained in Ludlow Castle under Rivers's protection but the council wanted to take the Prince of Wales (as he was until his coronation) to London as quickly as possible so that he could be shown to the people and crowned king as early as 4 May. Rivers agreed to do this and to bring with him a retinue of two thousand armed soldiers while his brother took the fleet to sea, ostensibly for the protection of the realm but more realistically to prevent Hastings from mobilising the Calais garrison and bringing it across to England. For her part, Queen Elizabeth proposed herself as regent but this was also quickly rejected.

The one person in a position to control events was Hastings, who remained in London both to safeguard his own position and to keep the Woodville faction in check. His advice to Gloucester was that he should leave the north and return to the capital as quickly as possible with a suitable force of armed men. This would enable Gloucester to secure the Prince of Wales and take any necessary action against the Woodvilles. Having Gloucester and his men in London would also help Hastings, who had made clear his dislike of 'the entire kin of the queen' and was concerned that he might be outmanoeuvred or even murdered. His one compensation during these difficult days was a small but personal one: on Edward's death Jane Shore had moved in with him. Of this More noted tartly, 'in the king's days, albeit he [Hastings] was sore enamoured upon her, yet he forbare her, either for reverence or for a certain friendly faithfulness'.

Once again in the wake of a king's death and the absence of a mature successor, the battle lines were being drawn as the rival camps built up their strength and consolidated their positions. On the one hand were the Woodvilles, who held the trump card in that Prince Edward remained in their possession and was on his way to London under the protection of Earl Rivers, one of the most powerful men in the kingdom. Dorset caught the mood of the moment when the council suggested that no further decisions should be taken until Gloucester arrived in London. Far from agreeing with the proposal, Dorset's quick and self-important response reinforced a belief that his family was in the ascendant and now had full control of the situation: 'We are quite important enough to take decisions without the king's uncle and see that they are enforced.' Soon Dorset was styling himself 'half-brother to the king', as indeed he was, being the Queen's son from her first marriage, but it was an unnecessary indulgence which only made the situation more tense than it need have been.

There were also rumours that the Woodvilles had plundered the Royal Exchequer and were preparing to take pre-emptive action to preserve their positions. Opposed to them was the faction now led *de facto* by Gloucester and supported by Hastings as well as by Buckingham, who had no love for his Woodville in-laws; he was married to the Queen's sister but always insisted that she came from a low-born family of interlopers. With the date of the coronation fast approaching both parties had to act and both had to be able to justify their actions if they were to have any hope of gaining the upper hand.

News of Edward IV's death had reached Ludlow on 14 April but it took a few days for Rivers to muster the armed retinue which he would take with him to his nephew's coronation in London. This was not just for his own protection but a normal procedure when travelling with royalty; however, in fifteenth-century England the creation of any large armed forces was bound to be suspicious. It took longer for the news to get to Gloucester but, forewarned by Hastings, he acted more quickly and left York on 23 April with a retinue of six hundred 'gentlemen of the north' and their followers. By 29 April he had reached Northampton, where he received the news that Rivers and Prince Edward were nearby at Stony Stratford. Buckingham then came in with three hundred supporters and the entire party spent the evening together. What happened when they met is a matter for conjecture but the outcome was real enough.

Having enjoyed what was reported as a convivial evening, Rivers was arrested at first light, together with his half-brother, Richard Grey, and the head of the household, Thomas Vaughan. Ominously all three were sent under close arrest north to Pontefract, deep in Gloucester's heartlands, and Rivers's forces were ordered to return to Ludlow. Gloucester and Buckingham claimed that they had acted in self-defence to preserve themselves and Prince Edward from traitors, but understandably the news caused panic when it reached London as rumours spread that Gloucester meant to seize the Crown just as his brother had done in 1461. To a certain extent those fears were allayed by Hastings, who reminded the council that Gloucester had expressed his loyalty to the Prince of Wales and that they had nothing to fear as 'all should be well'. Only the Queen was unimpressed. She fled into sanctuary at Westminster, taking with her Prince Richard, and when she was told of Hastings's words of comfort she replied, 'Ah, woe worth him, for he is one of them that labour to destroy me and my blood.'

Initially there was still little cause for alarm; there had been no pre-emptive executions or clash of arms between the rival factions, as might have happened earlier. Gloucester continued his progress to London and when he arrived in the capital he went out of his way to treat the young prince, his nephew, with all due deference. At its next meeting on 8 May the council appointed Gloucester Lord Protector of England, the appointment to run until the King's coronation, which was fixed for 22 June. Unlike Humphrey of Gloucester in 1422, who had not received full powers in dealing with Henry VI, Richard was given the guardianship of the future king's person.

The first step was to have Prince Edward lodged in the palace of the Bishop of London and then in the safety of the Tower. Gloucester then set about strengthening his own position by sacking the Chancellor, Archbishop Rotherham, a friend of the Queen's, and replacing him with John Russell, Bishop of Lincoln and the supposed author of the Second Croyland Continuation. At the same time he began packing the council with his supporters. There were rewards for Buckingham, Northumberland, Stanley, Howard and Hastings, who became Master of the Mint. The Croyland chronicler reported that the latter was 'bursting with joy over this new world' and there is no reason to disbelieve the comment. Hastings had seen his rivals' power destroyed – Rivers was under arrest, the Queen was in sanctuary and the detested Dorset had wisely fled into exile in France, as had Sir Edward Woodville – and his friend Gloucester had achieved his wish to become Lord Protector. Considering that before Edward IV's death Gloucester had no discernible quarrel with the Woodvilles, it had all turned out very satisfactorily for Hastings and Buckingham.

Crucially Prince Edward was now in the hands of his uncle and his supporters, and government business was transacted under the name of King Edward V. On the surface there was an air of normality in London. Planning for the coronation was in progress, the Woodville faction had been sidelined and Gloucester had been confirmed in his new position, but already he was thinking in grander terms than merely acting as his nephew's adviser. Gloucester now wanted the Crown for himself. Just as no one knows when Henry Bolingbroke decided to make his bid for Richard II's crown, it is impossible to place a date on Gloucester's change of heart, but it seems unlikely that he coveted the throne when he rode into London at the beginning of May. His earlier protestations of loyalty have to be taken at face value as evidence of what he really believed at the time, and for the rest of the month he went about his business normally, attending council meetings and talking to his close associates, especially Hastings and Buckingham.

The fact that he moved Edward to the Tower cannot be held against him as a suspicious move: it was a secure royal residence and entirely suited to its purpose of providing a safe haven for a young king. True, he had to decide what to do with Rivers, Grey and Vaughan, having accused them of treachery, but in his present position he could hardly have them summarily executed, much as he might have wanted to do so. All the contemporary evidence from Croyland, Mancini and other chroniclers accepts the state of normality which existed during those unreal days, yet other actions make it clear that Gloucester had already decided that he did not want to remain as Protector but preferred to reign as king in his own right by making a bid for the vacant throne.

Towards the end of the month Gloucester attempted to persuade the Queen to leave her sanctuary and to surrender her younger son Prince Richard in advance of the coronation but the bid was rebuffed. This seemed to smack of Woodville stubbornness and Gloucester was clearly angered by the snub. After a council meeting on 9 June he wrote an anxious letter to the city of York asking for military reinforcements to protect him against 'the Queen, her blood, and their affinity which have intended and daily do intend to murder us and Our Cousin the Duke of Buckingham and the Old Royal Blood of this Realm'. Similar letters were sent to the Earls of Northumberland and Westmorland.

Obviously Gloucester was looking to protect himself from an uncertain future: he had come to London with a small force and during the journey he had neutralised Rivers's retinue, yet he was now seeking reinforcement from the north and from two of his closest regional allies. Once raised, the troops were to muster at Pontefract on 18 June. This was not the response of someone trying to stay out of trouble but of someone desperate to protect his position; and, as his letters make clear, Gloucester expected the disruption to come from Queen Elizabeth and her allies. The flashpoint came four days later at a council meeting held at the Tower, ostensibly to discuss the forthcoming coronation but in reality to allow the Lord Protector to mount an audacious *coup d'état*.

Fittingly for what happened next, 13 June fell on a Friday, the conjunction of date and day being considered unlucky from time immemorial, and there were other portents. One of those attending the meeting was Lord Howard, the Yorkist loyalist who had fought at Towton and would later become Duke of Norfolk and Earl Marshal. He called at Jane Shore's house to accompany Hastings to the meeting and while walking together along Tower Street they met a priest who fell into conversation with Hastings only for Howard to complain that they must hurry as his friend had no need of a priest yet. More, who recorded the incident and enjoyed the benefit of hindsight, added that the tone of voice suggested that Howard meant 'you shall have need of one soon'. And so it proved.

Gloucester arrived at nine o'clock in a good mood – famously he asked Dr Morton to fetch 'a mess' of strawberries from his garden in Holborn – but all that changed after he excused himself and returned at half past ten wearing 'a sour and angry countenance'. In an outburst which shocked and surprised those present he charged Hastings, his closest confidant, with conspiring with the Queen and others to commit treason. Banging his fist on the table, he shouted, 'Treason!' and at this prearranged signal armed men rushed into the room and apprehended Lord Stanley, who was struck in the face, Dr Morton and the recently sacked Chancellor, Archbishop Rotherham.

The man most affected by this unexpected turn of events was Hastings, who was taken out to the green and instantly beheaded, the one kindness shown by Gloucester being the arrival of a priest to take his confession before execution. It was an extraordinary moment. Gloucester had moved with his usual speed and efficiency to deal with an alleged threat, but in so doing he had acted like a tyrant. The wretched Hastings, without being given a trial or any opportunity to defend himself, was summarily executed on Gloucester's word.

An act of that kind required forethought; it was not done on an impulse and in any case Gloucester was not normally a reckless man. At the time he accused Hastings of making association with 'that sorceress [the Queen] and others of her counsel, as Shore's wife, with her affinity', and while the allegation has never been fully disproved there has never been any material evidence to support it. Given Hastings's contempt for the Woodville family it is most unlikely that he would have changed sides in such a dramatic and damaging way unless it was done to preserve young Edward or to improve his own position. Gloucester was the brother of the king who had made Hastings's career, and contemporary evidence shows that he welcomed his friend's appointment as Lord Protector and supported the idea of a settled succession. The only thing that could have made him reconsider his loyalty was if Gloucester had confided in him any plan to usurp the throne and needed to keep it confidential. But there is nothing to suggest that this happened.

The most likely explanation is the one given by Mancini, namely that, having taken Edward into custody and having hobbled the Woodvilles, Gloucester had to remove his brother's loyal servant Hastings if he was to have any chance of seizing the throne. As the Italian recorded: 'Thus fell Hastings, killed not by those enemies he had always feared [the Woodvilles] but by a friend whom he had never doubted.' Another consideration is the role played by William Catesby, a prominent lawyer who had served the Warwick family and was a close adviser to Hastings while acting as a double agent for Gloucester. His shadowy role is difficult to determine but he could easily have been both spy and intermediary who had his own reasons, namely cupidity, for wanting to get rid of Hastings. There seems to have been no personal animus in the quarrel and everything points to the act being a savage pre-emptive strike by Gloucester. Mancini got close to the matter when he observed that Gloucester was simply protecting his back before he made a bid for the throne:

> Having got into his power all the blood royal of the land, yet he considered that his prospects were not sufficiently secure, without the removal or imprisonment of those who had been the closest friends of his brother, and were expected to be loyal to his brother's offspring. In this class he thought to include Hastings, the king's chamberlain; Thomas Rotherham, whom shortly he had relieved of his office; and the Bishop of Ely [Dr Morton]. Now Hastings had been from an early age a loyal companion of Edward, and an active soldier; while Thomas, though of humble origin, had become, thanks to his talent, a man of note with King Edward and had worked for many years in the Chancery. As for the Bishop of Ely, he was of great resource and daring, for he had been trained since King Henry's time; and being taken into Edward's favour after the annihilation of King Henry's party, he enjoyed great influence.

After the execution Hastings's wife, Katherine, daughter of Richard Neville, Earl of Salisbury, was permitted to keep her husband's fortune and the victim was buried in the place he had requested in his will, alongside Edward IV in St George's Chapel at Windsor. The other 'conspirators' were eventually released and two of them, Stanley and Morton, were to be heard of again.

In the aftermath of the coup Gloucester quickly set about consolidating his position. Following a show of armed force the Queen agreed to surrender Prince Richard, first to Archbishop Bourchier and then into Gloucester's care at the Tower, where he joined his brother Edward. At the same time Gloucester made arrangements for Clarence's son, the young Earl of Warwick, to be brought to London, where he was kept in similar confinement. (As an attainted son he posed no immediate threat, but Gloucester knew that attainders could be reversed and that the young man had a distant claim to the throne through his Neville and Beaufort ancestry.)

To put a stop to the Woodvilles' influence orders were given for the immediate execution of Rivers, Grey and Vaughan, and this was carried out by the Earl of Northumberland, who received his orders in a letter carried north by Sir Richard Ratcliffe of Derwentwater, one of Gloucester's loyal lieutenants. These steps were necessary to protect his position, but Gloucester also needed to convince others that his actions were justified as punishment for treasonable activities. In the hours following Hastings's execution a herald read a proclamation which stated that one of the key players in the alleged treasonable plot had been Jane Shore, 'with whom he [Hastings] lay nightly, and namely the night past before his death'. As punishment she was taken into custody and the following month was forced to do penance, walking through the streets of London with the traditional lighted taper as a symbol of her willingness to embrace God's light of forgiveness. As a punishment it was a mixed success: Shore looked 'so fair and lovely' that the watching crowds, mainly men, were 'more amorous of her body than curious of her soul'.

More successful in Gloucester's propaganda campaign was the besmirching of his brother's reputation. Shore's punishment had been part of the process – she was arraigned as a 'common harlot' and not as the former king's mistress – but there was also a more substantial attack, this time on the probity of the succession. On Sunday 22 June Dr Ralph Shaw (or Shaa), brother of the Mayor of London, preached and published a sermon at St Paul's Cross, next to the cathedral, claiming that Edward IV's marriage to Elizabeth Woodville was invalid because he had already been betrothed to Lady Eleanor Butler, a daughter of the Earl of Shrewsbury. Although she had died in 1468 she had been alive at the time of the Woodville marriage and the 'pre-contract' was still in existence, thereby making the later match illegal. If that were true the Woodville marriage was invalid and young Edward and Richard were bastards and could not succeed to the throne as their father and mother had lived together 'sinfully and damnably in adultery, against the law of God and his Church'. The message was clear: if Edward had been adulterously married to Elizabeth Woodville only Gloucester had the right to succeed to the throne. Two days later Buckingham repeated the allegation and on

25 June, according to *The Great Chronicle*, he led a delegation of noblemen and aldermen to Baynard's Castle to ask Gloucester to accept the Crown on the grounds that he was the rightful heir because Edward's marriage was

> made of great presumption, without the knowing and assent of the lords of this country and also by sorcery and witchcraft, committed by the said Elizabeth [Woodville] and her mother Jacquetta Duchess of Bedford, as the common opinion of the people, and the public voice, and the same through all this land . . . It was made privily and secretly, without reading of banns, in a private chamber, a profane place, and not openly in the face of the Church, after the Law of God's church, but contrary thereunto and against the laudable customs of the church of England.

For good measure Shaw also claimed – quite wrongly – that both Edward and his brother Clarence had been born illegitimate and only Gloucester within wedlock. Once again it is difficult to ascertain the veracity of Shaw's sermonising and Buckingham's use of it before making the offer to Gloucester. The allegation of Edward's illegitimacy had been used before and enjoyed a wide currency. However, the facts were incorporated in *Titulus Regius*, the document which was produced to affirm Gloucester's right to the throne. The story of the marriage to Lady Eleanor Butler was also given credence by Robert Stillington, Bishop of Bath and Wells, a curious character who had risen from obscurity to become Edward's chancellor before being sacked in 1473 and sent to the Tower. He claimed to have married Edward and Lady Eleanor and if this is true it could explain why he received so much royal patronage. Given the fact that Edward kept his marriage to Elizabeth Woodville a secret for so long it was not impossible that he had entered into an earlier marriage compact with another woman and then needed to remove himself from it. It is probable that people did not believe the story at the time or did not know what to believe, but the rumour's importance lies not in its veracity or otherwise but in the fact that it provided Buckingham with the chance to offer Gloucester the throne. It also gave Gloucester the opportunity to accept the proposal, albeit after much theatrical prevarication.

That same day, 25 June, Rivers, Grey and Vaughan were executed at Pontefract and their bodies thrown into a common grave. The coup was complete and the following day Gloucester rode from Baynard's Castle to Westminster Hall, where he sat for the first time on the King's Bench and in the presence of the judiciary consented to execute justice according to the laws of the land as King of England in place of his nephew. He would reign as King Richard III, ironically being presented with the opportunity to do what his father, the Duke of York, another Richard, had failed to achieve in the same place in 1460.

The coronation took place on 6 July and was a suitably grand occasion. Richard was dressed in a blue and gold doublet and a purple gown trimmed with ermine. His wife, Queen Anne, was carried in a sumptuous litter with five ladies-in-waiting, the chief one being Lady Margaret Beaufort, whose husband, Lord Stanley, had been restored to royal favour and would shortly become Constable of England. The coronation procession left the Tower and proceeded to the Palace of Westminster accompanied by a huge retinue which included Buckingham, Norfolk (as Lord Howard had become) and Northumberland, together with a representative selection of the aristocracy, knights and gentlemen. Stripped to the waist, both the new king and his queen were anointed with holy oil before the crowns were placed on their heads by a clearly reluctant Archbishop Bourchier. There followed a coronation banquet and everyone agreed that it had been a grand occasion, as well it might have been, the arrangements having already been made, albeit for the coronation of a different king.

It was significant that neither Prince Edward nor Prince Richard was present at the coronation. As the King's nephews they were expected to attend, despite being exposed as the illegitimate sons of Edward IV. Being a 'bastard' was not a crime in the Middle Ages, when many kings and princes fathered children out of wedlock and made sure that they were cared for; and 'Bastard' was used throughout Europe as a title and term of respect. On grounds of protocol, therefore, there was no reason why they should not have been present at Westminster during their uncle's coronation service. It would have been wiser had they been there because they had not been seen in public since their removal to the Tower and already there were rumours about their well-being.

Mancini reported that his friend and colleague Dr Argentine, the royal physician, had been in attendance on the Princes and that Edward had taken to daily confession and repentance 'because he believed that death was facing him'. After the removal of Hastings, the one man who might have been in a position to save them, they were moved into the inner apartments of the Tower and were never seen again in public. Together with their uncle's usurpation of the throne, the fate of the 'Princes in the Tower' is one of the great mysteries of Gloucester's life. There is little doubt that they were done to death or that they were killed on Richard III's orders, but the exact timing and reasoning behind the act are open to question. (We need not concern ourselves with wild theories that the two boys survived Richard's reign only to be killed by his successor, Henry Tudor, or with other speculation that their uncle was not to blame. Only Richard stood to gain by their execution for as long as they lived his hold on the throne was not totally secure.)

The problem of the Princes' fate is exacerbated by the reputation which Richard III has left to history. Through William Shakespeare he has been represented as a malign hunchback and wicked schemer who murdered his way to the throne and let nothing stand in the way of his ambitions. A man of that kidney was certainly capable of committing that most heinous of sins, the murder of two young boys who were related to him and whom he should have protected. So rooted in fact has Shakespeare's representation become that Richard exists only as a man 'determined to prove a villain' for whom no crime would be too extreme. According to this version, Richard III murders the saintly Henry VI and his son Edward, seduces Lady Anne to acquire the Neville inheritance, arranges the death of his brother Clarence and then disposes of the two Princes.

While there have been more recent attempts to rescue Richard's reputation by proving that he was a fair-minded king who was not physically deformed and was more sinned against than sinning, by and large Shakespeare's version is still widely accepted as historical fact. As a result Richard is regarded as the only man capable of committing such a dreadful crime and, to be equally fair to those who accept Shakespeare's version and those who dispute it, that view of him – as an infanticide – is very much the truth of the matter.

The most detailed version about 'the dolorous end of those babes' is recounted in More's history, and while there are inconsistencies in his account it remains the most credible description of what might have happened, if it is accepted that Richard was ultimately responsible for the murders. He certainly had the motive. Shortly after his coronation Richard took off on a peregrination around his new kingdom, a journey which took him through Reading and Oxford to Gloucester and thence on to Leicester and north to York. It is all too possible that during his journey he decided that while the Princes lived they posed a threat to his succession and that he could never be totally secure. Fearing that his enemies might hatch a plot to rescue the two boys and use them as figureheads in a move to unseat him, he saw no option but to get rid of them.

According to More's version, a message was sent to Sir Robert Brackenbury, Constable of the Tower, ordering him to carry out the killing but to his credit this honest man refused to oblige the new king. When the response reached Richard he was at Warwick and while there he gave the commission to Sir James Tyrell, a reliable retainer who had been knighted for his services at Tewkesbury and could be trusted implicitly. Armed with the King's orders, Tyrell rode to London and ordered Brackenbury to give him the keys so that the murders could be carried out. This was left in the hands of Miles Forest, one of the Princes' servants and 'a fellow fleshed out in murder before-time', and John Dighton, 'his own horse-keeper, a big broad, square, strong knave'. More continues the story:

> Then, all the others being removed from them, this Miles Forest and John Dighton, about midnight (the silly [innocent] children lying in their beds) came into the chamber and suddenly lapped them up among their clothes, so bewrapped them and entangled them, keeping down by force the feather bed and pillows hard unto their mouths, that within a while, smothered and stifled, their breath failing, they gave up to God their innocent souls into the joys of heaven, leaving to the tormentors their bodies dead in the bed.

Tyrell was then summoned to view the scene and the bodies were hastily buried 'at the stair foot, meetly deep in the ground, under a great heap of stones'. Much of what More recounted was based on second-hand and frequently dubious accounts, but one salient fact backs up his story. Two hundred years later, in 1674, workmen demolishing a stone staircase in the White Tower came across a wooden chest containing the bones of two male children: these were undoubtedly the remains of Princes Edward and Richard, done to death by smothering on the orders of their uncle. In introducing his account More makes much of the fact that his version is based on what he had heard 'by such men and such means as me thinketh it were hard but it should be true', but despite that drawback it remains the only evidence from that period.

It also seems highly probable. After his coronation Richard decided that to remain safe he had to kill his nephews, who were taken from public view after Hastings's execution and never again seen alive. While the killing of innocent children is considered to be especially repugnant Richard was no stranger to violent execution and behind him lay the examples of Henry IV, who had been implicated in Richard II's death, and Edward IV, who had connived at the execution of Henry VI. During this troubled period violence was a fact of life and sometimes quite arbitrary. Richard had already usurped the throne, first killing his friend Hastings; so it is likely that similar violent and self-seeking impulses guided him when he arranged for the summary execution of his nephews in the late summer of 1483.

The truth will never be known. All that can be stated is that the two Princes disappeared from public view and were never seen again. It is possible that they died by other means – Buckingham has been accused of their murders, as have others, such as Henry Tudor and Lady Margaret Beaufort – and it has also been mooted that they died of natural causes, either from illness or during a rescue bid. Those who support Richard's innocence argue that it was not in the King's nature to murder the children of a brother to whom he had promised his loyalty and that he had no need to eliminate them as they presented no immediate threat to the succession. Under the terms of *Titulus Regius* Edward IV's marriage to Elizabeth Woodville was illegitimate and if that were accepted then the two sons were bastards and could not succeed to the throne. If Richard had wanted to prove his own innocence he could have displayed the boys in public but, because he chose not to do so, by the autumn rumours were rife that they were dead, leading the writer of *The Great Chronicle* to lament that Richard was the author of his own misfortunes, that 'had he continued still

Protector and suffered the childer to have prospered according to his allegiance and fidelity, he should have been honourably lauded over all, whereas now his fame is dirtied and dishonoured'. The best that can be said in Richard's defence is that while it is impossible to prove his guilt, his own innocence is 'not proven', the verdict handed down in Scots law when neither guilt nor innocence can be proved beyond a shadow of reasonable doubt.

Besides, the facts surrounding the Princes' deaths do not alter what happened next. By the time they disappeared from public view Richard was also facing the very threat that he feared most – a challenge to his authority mounted by possible contenders to the throne, in this case Buckingham, one of the most powerful magnates in England, and Henry Tudor, who could claim an ancestry back to Edward III. Many of those who supported their rebellions had come to believe that the Princes were dead and that Richard had given the order for them to be killed. That gave them an opportunity: if Richard had hoped to seal his hold on the Crown by getting rid of his brother's children, he had simply opened the way to other claimants, and Henry Tudor was the one man living who could mount a credible challenge to his authority with any hope of succeeding to the throne of England.

Chapter Twenty-One

THE FINAL RECKONING

After going into exile with his uncle Jasper Tudor in 1471, Henry Tudor had led a chequered existence. Initially the pair travelled from Tenby in Pembrokeshire to Brittany, where they were made welcome by Duke Francis II, but under pressure from Edward IV the hospitality turned into an existence that amounted to little more than house arrest. The two refugees were separated, Henry being kept a virtual prisoner at Largoët under the jurisdiction of Jean de Rieux, Marshal of Brittany, while his uncle was kept in separate custody at Vannes and in other locations.

On one occasion, in 1476, Edward managed to persuade Francis to hand over Henry Tudor to him in return for a cash payment, but the move was foiled when Lady Margaret Beaufort managed to warn her son of the danger facing him. When the transfer was due to take place at St Malo Henry Tudor feigned illness and was able to escape into sanctuary and Edward's agents were unable to pursue him. Edward then encouraged Louis XI to secure custody of the two men and extradite them to England but that bid also failed. This was the nadir of the relationship between Henry and the English king, but from that point onwards there was a steady improvement.

Henry and his uncle lived under Francis's protection at Vannes and legal steps were taken by his mother to protect his English inheritance. Now back at court as the wife of Lord Stanley, Lady Margaret Beaufort used the last years of Edward's reign to rehabilitate her son and to attempt to bring him back to England, not as a potential enemy of the Crown but as the King's son-in-law. In June 1482 a deed was drawn up which would have seen Henry Tudor pardoned and permitted to return to England to inherit his mother's estates and to succeed his father as Earl of Richmond. The same settlement would have paved the way for a marriage between him and Edward's eldest daughter, Princess Elizabeth of York. Had this match taken place before Edward's death it would have changed everything by bringing into the open Henry Tudor's own claims to the throne through his Beaufort ancestors. As it was, Richard seems to have been unaware of the proposals and on becoming king he did nothing to deter Lady Margaret Beaufort from pursuing her attempts to bring her son back to England.

In the first weeks of Richard's reign she had been minded to support the new king – as Steward of the Royal Household her husband enjoyed considerable influence at court and she had attended Queen Anne during Richard III's coronation – but she was unsettled by the continued detention of the Princes and by the growing rumours that they had been murdered. She may even have been implicated in an unsuccessful plot to free the two boys in July. According to *The Great Chronicle*, four men organised the rescue attempt in connivance with Jasper and Henry Tudor and if that were so the incident could have been the trigger for Richard to order the boys' execution.

Lady Margaret's concern for the Princes' welfare also encouraged her to enter into a treasonable relationship with others who were plotting the new king's downfall. Among those involved was her kinsman Buckingham (she was first cousin to his mother and widow of his uncle Sir Henry Stafford), who had become disenchanted, suddenly and dramatically, with his erstwhile friend Richard III and may even have coveted the throne himself. As a Beaufort and a great-grandson of Thomas of Woodstock, Edward III's youngest son, Buckingham possessed a distant claim and he also enjoyed the wealth, lands and prestige with which to back any bid. However, against that, he had no immediate motive to move against Richard, whom he had besides recently helped to put on the throne. He had supported him against the interests of his own relatives by marriage, the Woodvilles, and he had been amply rewarded, becoming the new king's principal adviser and a key member of his inner circle. What did he hope to gain by attacking his erstwhile ally and what were the impulses that led him to be involved with a wider rebellion against the Crown so soon after Richard's usurpation?

The answer lies in a number of factors which came together during the summer of 1483. While Richard III was making his perambulation around England there was an outbreak of discontent in the southern counties, with rumours of plots and counter-plots involving disgruntled Lancastrians, former members of Edward IV's household, associates of the Woodvilles and those who simply disliked the new king. Much of the upheaval was caused by the unknown fate of the Princes and a growing belief that they had been murdered by their uncle. There was also lingering disapproval of the way in which Richard had seized the throne and this was fanned by his brother's supporters, who would have preferred the succession to pass to Prince Edward.

Although Buckingham, at his castle in Brecon on the Welsh border, was based outside London and the south of England, he would have been aware of the mood of the country and as a powerful magnate in his own right he was in a position to take steps to decide what was best for his own interests. If anything were to happen to Richard and if he were to be toppled from the throne – by no means an impossibility in that uncertain age – Buckingham's own position as the King's closest ally could become untenable. It is possible that Buckingham decided to act because he wanted to protect himself and to strike a pre-emptive blow for those who were plotting to unseat the new king. He may even have believed that he had a legal claim to the throne – Sir Thomas More certainly thought so – but in view of what happened next this seems unlikely.

While Buckingham was based at Brecon he had the company of Dr Morton, Bishop of Ely, who had been released from arrest in the Tower and transferred into his care. It was a fateful conjunction. Morton was a persuasive and perspicacious politician, wise in the ways of the world, cunning at heart and, according to More, 'a man of great natural wit, very well learned and honourable in behaviour, lacking no wise ways to win favour'. He had given loyal service to the House of Lancaster and had served Edward IV equally well. A natural bureaucrat, he was also an elder statesman who was able to judge what was best for the country and, just as importantly, to decide where his best interests lay.

During his stay with Buckingham Morton was able to work on the younger and impressionable man and gradually convinced him to change his allegiance. To begin with Buckingham swore his support for his friend King Richard but Morton countered this with a potent argument. He put the case that in the natural scheme of things Henry VI's son should have become king but as he was dead Morton had decided to transfer his loyalty to Edward and 'glad would have been if his son had succeeded him'. He also reminded Buckingham that his own family had been solid Lancastrian supporters – his father and grandfather had given their lives to the cause – and this argument led on to the fact that the surviving member of that family was Buckingham's cousin Henry Tudor. If this man, a near relative, were to marry Elizabeth of York, Edward's daughter, as his mother Lady Margaret Beaufort had already proposed, the resultant match would achieve the kind of unity and peace the country so badly needed.

Morton's intervention was wise on two counts. First, it removed any obligation on Buckingham's part to make a personal bid for the throne which might not have won widespread support; and, second, it put him in the role of king-maker. Having won over Buckingham, Morton sent a message to Lady Margaret Beaufort, who had already been in secret contact with Edward IV's widow Queen Elizabeth to gain her support for the plan to put Henry Tudor on the throne on condition that he marry the Princess Elizabeth. On receiving word from Morton she wrote to her son in Brittany to persuade him to raise a rebellion which would be led by Buckingham and supported by a confederation of old Lancastrian backers, Woodvilles and others in the south and west of England who were disenchanted by the way in which Richard had seized the throne. That outline of what happened is confirmed by both More, who heard the story from Morton, and the Croyland chronicler, who added his own personal belief that Edward IV had probably 'died a violent death':

Accordingly, all those who had set on foot this insurrection, seeing that if they could find no one to take the lead in their designs, the ruin of all would speedily ensue, turned their thoughts to Henry, Earl of Richmond, who had been for many years living in exile in Brittany. To him a message was, accordingly, sent, by the Duke of Buckingham, by advice of the Lord Bishop of Ely, who was then his prisoner at Breaknock [Brecon], requesting him to hasten over to England as soon as he possibly could, for the purpose of marrying Elizabeth, the eldest daughter of the late king, and, at the same time, together with her, taking possession of the throne.

It is possible that Henry Tudor was not contacted immediately and might not have been apprised of the plans until later in the year; the dating in all the near-contemporary accounts is sketchy. But the fact remains that Buckingham was involved in a revolt against Richard in the autumn of 1483 and that Henry Tudor made an effort to launch an invasion in the south-west of England early in November in an attempt to claim the throne of England. What is surprising about this uprising is that it enjoyed widespread support across the south of England and that it happened so soon after Richard's accession to the throne. It was not just Lancastrians and Woodvilles who were involved, and many of those who joined the rebellion had everything to lose if it failed: establishment figures such as justices of the peace, sheriffs, minor landowners and other well-established types who would normally have relied on Richard's patronage. That they should have rebelled against an anointed king in the first months after his coronation shows how deeply Richard was loathed by a large and influential section of his subjects. The rebels' feelings may have been enflamed by the fact that Richard had built up his power base in the north of England and was regarded as a powerful northern magnate who had little interest in the needs of those living in the south. The Croyland chronicler underlines the fact that the murmurs were especially loud in 'the vicinity of the City of London [and] throughout the counties of Kent, Essex, Sussex, Hampshire, Dorset, Devonshire, Somerset, Wiltshire and Berkshire'.

However, the very disparate nature of the revolt and the lack of a strong central leadership proved to be its undoing. The only co-ordination was a vague plan to begin the uprising on 18 October (St Luke's Day) but the rebels in Kent, always anxious to strike the first blow, took the initiative a week earlier than expected and marched on London only to be repulsed by forces led by the Duke of Norfolk. This alerted Richard that trouble was brewing and he was also helped by a lack of any sustainable command and control within the rebel camp.

On the day itself the south of England experienced a number of uprisings in the main county towns, as planned, but everything hinged on Buckingham being able to get his Welsh forces through the

Forest of Dean to meet up with his followers coming from the West Country. Almost immediately the weather turned foul and it rained incessantly for over a week, the Severn and Wye broke their banks, the surrounding countryside was flooded and the hard going made it impossible for Buckingham to make any progress. He soon found that his Welsh soldiers were unwilling followers and that any enthusiasm they might have felt for the operation quickly melted away in the atrocious weather. By the end of the month his army had more or less disintegrated and Buckingham was forced to flee in disguise into north Shropshire. His luck did not hold. Although he sought refuge at Wem with one of his retainers, one Ralph Banastre (or Bannister), there was a reward on his head and it could not be resisted.

The news of Buckingham's revolt had deeply shocked Richard, who wrote to his Chancellor, Bishop Russell, describing his erstwhile friend as 'the most untrue creature living, whom with God's grace we shall not be long till we will be in that part and subdue his malice'. Lured by the promised bounty Banastre promptly betrayed Buckingham, who was taken to Salisbury and beheaded in the marketplace on 2 November, All Souls' Day. In vain did he try to seek an audience with the King. Richard had no intention of making any exchanges with such an ungrateful wretch and, as happened so often during this violent period, Buckingham was savagely dispatched without further ado. In the weeks that followed his execution many other supporters were rounded up and executed, among them Sir Thomas St Leger, the husband of Richard's sister Anne, whose pleas for clemency fell on deaf ears. His was a betrayal which reveals the extent of the animus against Richard. Not only was he a royal brother-in-law and a trusted courtier but in 1471 Edward IV had permitted Anne to divorce her husband, the Duke of Exeter, in order to allow her to marry St Leger, who was her lover.

Another casualty of the rebellion was Henry Tudor, who had left Brittany with high hopes and a sizeable force, only to be caught up in the storms which scuppered Buckingham's uprising. Although he made landfall first at Poole and then at Plymouth, the disastrous news of Buckingham's failed revolt and Richard's gathering strength in the West Country forced him to sail back across the Channel and return to winter quarters in Brittany. Also on the run were the Marquess of Dorset, whom Richard denounced as a seducer who had 'many and sundry maids, widows and wives damnably and without shame devoured, deflowered and defiled', and Dr Morton, who managed to escape to his diocese in Ely and then crossed the Channel to go into exile in Flanders. From there he made contact again with Henry Tudor, who was slowly rebuilding his strength at Rennes and it was there, in the cathedral on Christmas Day, that his followers knelt before him as a king-in-waiting.

Although Buckingham's revolt had not succeeded in its aims it had brought Henry Tudor's claim into the open. From being a penniless and insignificant member of the House of Lancaster who was unknown to most English magnates (Buckingham was an exception), he now emerged as the main contender to end Richard's reign and claim the throne for himself and Elizabeth of York. All this was now known to Richard, who suddenly had to accept the fact that he faced a serious challenger and that his own life and hold on the throne had suddenly become extremely insecure. Owing to good intelligence and the plotters' incompetence he had been able to put down the first revolt without any difficulty and most of its leaders had been punished or forced into exile but even in that respect he caused further offence. Under attainders the defeated rebels' property was confiscated and the Croyland chronicler had difficulty restraining his annoyance that the main beneficiaries were Richard's 'northern adherents, whom he planted in every spot throughout his dominions, to the disgrace and loudly expressed sorrow of all people in the south who daily longed more and more for the return of their ancient rulers, rather than the tyranny of these people'.

Richard kept Christmas in sumptuous style at Westminster but despite his ostentatious wealth and his hold on the throne he was by now a worried man. As More makes clear the strain was beginning to show:

He never had quiet in his mind, he never thought himself sure. Where he went abroad, his eyes whirled about, his body secretly armoured, his hand ever on his dagger, his countenance and manner like one always ready to strike back. He took ill rest an-nights; lay long waking and musing, sore wearied with care and watch; rather slumbered than slept, troubled with fearful dreams – suddenly started up, leapt out of his bed and ran about his chamber.

While there is an element of poetic licence or being wise after the event in More's description, Richard entered 1484 with many troubles on his mind. He had been badly shaken by the attempted revolt, not least by Buckingham's treachery, and by the sudden emergence of Henry Tudor as a rival to his authority. The former had betrayed him while the latter had emerged from the shadows to threaten his hold on royal power. Soon Richard had to contend with the terrible blow of his son's early death. Aged only ten, young Edward of Middleham died at the beginning of April, leaving the King without any direct male heir, and it soon became apparent that Anne was incapable of bearing further children. With few other close associates Richard turned increasingly to Stanley, who had played no part in the rebellion even though his wife, Lady Margaret Beaufort, had been implicated in it behind the scenes. Her standing and credibility had been damaged by her suspected involvement but she escaped being attainted on condition that her possessions were made over to her husband, who was also made responsible for her custody and future good behaviour. For his loyalty and steadfastness in such difficult times Stanley was appointed Constable of England in succession to Buckingham.

Richard's first act of the new year was to hold a meeting of Parliament, which had been postponed from November 1483. It was the only Parliament of his reign and its main business was to reinforce his claim to the throne and to chastise those who had opposed it. Over a hundred attainders were issued to punish those who had supported the recent rebellion and, more importantly, the statute *Titulus Regius* was enacted by Parliament to underline the right of Richard's hold on the throne. Central to its argument was the invalidity of Edward IV's marriage to Elizabeth Woodville and the consequent bastardisation of their children, especially the Prince of Wales. The document was an important element in strengthening Richard's legitimacy as king: it presented him as the natural successor to a monarch whose reign had been blighted by his connection to the Woodville faction, who were opposed to the common good of the country and its people. As part of this move to prove himself the natural successor and a superior being to his brother, Richard also agreed to end the unpopular practice of seeking benevolences and there were reforms in the land tenure system and, in the criminal justice system, of the right to bail.

A College of Arms also came into being to regulate the granting of heraldic arms and during the sitting of Parliament steps were taken to find a rapprochement with the Woodvilles by inducing Queen Elizabeth and her daughters to come out of sanctuary in return for the 'surety of their lives' and a promise that 'they shall not suffer any hurt'. Astonishingly, in spite of everything that had taken place, she accepted. Not only had Richard usurped her son's right to the throne and probably had him and his brother murdered but the *Titulus Regius* document had effectively destroyed her husband's reputation. Yet despite the collapse of all her family's hopes she took Richard at his word and placed herself and her daughters under the King's protection.

In another attempt at atonement, in the summer of 1484 Richard arranged for the reburial at Windsor of the body of Henry VI, whom he was popularly supposed to have murdered. A cult had grown up around the dead king at his resting place at Chertsey Abbey; this was said to be the scene of several miracles, which helped to reinforce the idea that the murdered king was a saint. Understandably, as Richard was uneasy about the sanctification of an earlier Lancastrian king and his own role in his demise, he arranged for the body to be removed to the more dignified ambience of St George's Chapel in Windsor, where it was interred to the south of the high altar.

Other attempts at penitence included the expenditure of substantial sums of money on chantries and chapels in which masses would be sung for the souls of the dead. One grandiose plan foresaw the creation of a huge chantry with six altars at York Minster where a hundred priests would sing mass in perpetuity around the clock; another grant was given to the Grey Friars at Richmond to sing one thousand masses for the soul of the King's dead brother Edward. The Croyland chronicler complained that these 'splendid and highly expensive feasts and entertainments' were arranged to 'attract himself to the affection of the people' and there is much to support that conceit: Richard was clearly concerned to use these religious obligations to reinforce his right to the throne and to place himself in the best possible light.

Alas for all those fond hopes, 1484 was not a good year for the King. In April he had endured the misery of his son's untimely death and as the year progressed there were signs that his tenure of the

English throne was becoming increasingly unpopular. It was now almost impossible to halt the growing rumours about the fate of the Princes in the Tower and it was taken for granted that in all probability they had been murdered on Richard's orders. By the standards of the day Richard was not a particularly bloodthirsty man. His executions of Hastings and Buckingham were no worse than many other judicial murders carried out by his predecessors and in the latter's case he had the excuse that he was only punishing a previously loyal friend who had acted treasonably against him. Nonetheless, the question of the fate of the Princes left a stain on his character and only served to increase the feelings of disquiet within the realm. Not only were they innocent children but Richard was supposed to be their protector and his hands were sullied by the blood of two young nephews who were under his care and protection, a heinous crime.

For all that Richard attempted to salve his reputation through his grants and his benefices, his high-minded patronage failed to win over his subjects and by the end of the year his reputation was in tatters. Matters came to a head during the summer when William Collingbourne, a Wiltshire gentleman in Edward IV's household, published a famously derisive couplet attacking Richard and his principal officers at court, namely William Catesby, Richard Ratcliffe and Viscount Lovell:

> The Catte, the Ratte, and Lovell our dogg,
> Ruleth all England under an Hogge.

Their names are suggested by the animals listed in the first line and the reference to a hog evokes the white boar which appeared on Richard's badge. The message was obvious: Richard was surrounded by favourites, ridiculed as lowly animals, who had an undue influence over the King and encouraged him in his bestial behaviour. In itself the couplet was little more than a lampoon which in other circumstances could have been safely ignored or written off as a display of pique by Collingbourne, who had been dismissed as Sheriff of Somerset, but there was more to it than name-calling. The author had been in contact with Henry Tudor and when that 'treasonable correspondence' became known his fate was sealed. Before the year was out Collingbourne was sentenced to the traitor's death of being hanged, drawn and quartered. The execution was described vividly by *The Great Chronicle*:

> He was drawn unto the Tower Hill and there cruelly put to death, at first hanged and straight cut down and ripped [disembowelled], and his bowels cast into a fire. The which torment was so speedily done that when the butcher pulled out his heart he spake and said JHESUS, JHESUS. This man was greatly monyd [admired] of the people for his goodly personage and favour of visage.

As the year drew to a close England was inundated with various proclamations and manifestos, many of them expressed in a similar vein to Collingbourne's couplet and all of them attacking Richard in one way or another. Very few of these documents have survived but that they did exist is made clear from Richard's own musings on the subject. Not only did he instruct the authorities at York to take steps against anyone slandering him but he made it clear that he himself was greatly concerned by the sudden outbreak of propaganda activity which was aimed at him by 'seditious and evil disposed persons' who had been found to 'sow seed of noise and slander against our person'. In themselves an outpouring of slanderous rhymes and angry accusations was not enough to threaten Richard's hold on the throne but they were symptomatic of a wider malaise within the kingdom and a growing belief that he was not worthy of his crown.

Those feelings were quickened by the death of Edward of Middleham and by the realisation that Anne was unable to bear him further children. Although Richard attempted to settle the succession by passing it to Clarence's son Edward (at the time still a prisoner in the Tower) and then to John de la Pole, the youthful Earl of Lincoln, son of his sister Elizabeth and the Duke of Suffolk, there was no denying the reality that he possessed no direct heir of the blood royal. This weakened him considerably. He needed a son but his wife was incapable of giving him one; inevitably his thoughts turned to finding a substitute who came from the right background and would be suitably fecund. His choice fell on his niece Elizabeth of York. During the Christmas celebrations at Westminster Richard cast caution aside and made it clear to his entire court that he meant to make the match even though his wife was still alive and Elizabeth was a blood relative. His behaviour could not be ignored and it outraged the Croyland chronicler:

> Oh God! Why should we any longer dwell on this subject, multiplying our recital of things so distasteful, so numerous that they can hardly be reckoned, and so pernicious in their example, that we ought not as much suggest them to the minds of the perfidious. So too, with many other things which are not written in this book, and of which I grieve to speak; although the fact ought not to be concealed that, during this feast of the Nativity, far too much attention was given to dancing and gaiety, and vain changes of apparel given to Queen Anne and the Lady Elizabeth, the eldest daughter of the late king, being of similar colour and shape; a thing that caused the people to murmur and the nobles and prelates greatly to wonder thereat; while it was said by many that the king was bent, either on the anticipated death of the queen taking place, or else, by means of a divorce, for which he supposed he had quite sufficient grounds, on contracting a marriage with the said Elizabeth. For it appeared that in no other way could his kingly power be established, or the hopes of his rival be put an end to.

It was a high-risk policy but Richard seems to have been sufficiently besotted by the idea to make no attempt to conceal his ambitions. Elizabeth was dressed as a queen – she seems to have been a willing accomplice – and even allowing for the Croyland chronicler's outrage it is clear that Richard was willing to go to great lengths to find a way to remedy the absence of an heir. Three months later the issue was again tested when Anne died, leaving Richard free to marry his niece. This time there were substantial objections, spurred by rumours that Richard had simply murdered his wife to facilitate the new match. His northern supporters disliked the idea of an alliance with a Woodville, arguing that it would restore the prominence the family had lost at the time of Edward IV's death, and there were religious objections to the marriage of an uncle to his niece. As a result Richard was forced into making a public declaration repudiating his intentions. Not that his disavowal did him any good: the King entered 1485 without a wife and amid suspicions about his right to the throne and his capacity to hold on to it. He was also short of funds as Edward IV had left an empty treasury and in February he was forced to seek loans from Parliament. While these were not the same as the benevolences he had previously outlawed, the request was unpopular and added to a belief that Richard had squandered his brother's inheritance.

While this was happening in England Henry Tudor was slowly reinforcing his power base in Brittany. His position had been strengthened by the escape from Hammes Castle in the Calais Pale of the Earl of Oxford and by the arrival of several influential magnates, including Jasper Tudor, the Earl of Devon, Richard Lord Rivers (brother of the recently executed earl) and prelates such as the Bishop of Exeter and Richard Fox, who later became Bishop of Winchester. By the summer of 1484 his court in exile at Vannes consisted of some five hundred supporters and he entertained high hopes of reattempting an invasion of England before the year was out. There was a scare for him during the summer while Duke Francis was suffering a periodic fit of insanity. During the Duke's incapacity Richard took the opportunity of attempting to bribe Brittany's corrupt Treasurer, Pierre Landais, to surrender Henry Tudor, but the plot was foiled by the intervention from Flanders of Dr Morton. Having gone into exile in the wake of Buckingham's revolt, Henry Tudor maintained contact with those opposed to Richard and it is likely that he received notice of the King's intentions from Lady Margaret Beaufort, who, in turn, probably heard it from her husband, Lord Stanley.

The intervention was decisive. Morton passed on the warning through a trusted priest, Christopher Urswick, who acted as Margaret's chaplain, and Henry Tudor was able to leave Vannes and cross over the border into France in September. By then Louis XI had died and under the regency for his son Charles VIII there was an inclination to oppose Richard III, who was seen as a potential enemy intent on reclaiming English interests in France. In this respect Charles's elder sister Anne de Beaujeu was particularly influential and once Henry Tudor and his supporters had arrived in Rouen she agreed to provide the necessary financial and military support for a fresh invasion of England. Backed by that support and encouraged by the arrival of the Earl of Oxford, Henry Tudor spent the rest of the year writing to potential supporters in England, condemning Richard as a 'homicide and unabated tyrant' and in a telling move he signed those letters 'H.R.': Henricus Rex.

Nor was Richard idle. As it became clear that his succession could not be guaranteed he turned his attention to the man who was most likely to make a challenge, his distant cousin in France. In June he issued a proclamation against 'divers rebels and traitors' and called on Commissioners of Array to provide the necessary forces for the defence of his kingdom. In raising an army he was heavily reliant on three great allies – Lord Stanley, the Duke of Norfolk and the Earl of Northumberland – and during the summer he moved his power base north to Nottingham. Later the historian Polydore Vergil claimed that Richard was 'overwhelmed by pinching cares on every hand' but even though the King knew that he faced a challenge from Henry Tudor and supporters who were threatening 'to do the most cruel murders, slaughters and robberies and disherisons that were ever seen in any Christian realm', he still believed that he had the military capacity to counter any challenge to his position. For a start he had numerical superiority over any forces that Henry Tudor would be able to muster and despite the uncertain times he still commanded obedience in his realm. It is possible that Richard mistrusted Lord Stanley, who was busily mustering troops on the King's behalf, but to prevent any possibility of recidivism he ordered Stanley's son, Lord Strange, to take his father's place at court.

Even when news arrived that Henry Tudor and his supporters had arrived at Milford Haven in south-west Wales on 7 August, the Croyland chronicler reported that Richard remained supremely confident that he could protect himself and his crown:

> On hearing of their arrival, the king rejoiced, or at least seemed to rejoice, writing to his adherents in every quarter that now the long wished-for day had arrived, for him to triumph with ease over so contemptible a faction, and thenceforth benefit his subjects with the blessings of uninterrupted tranquillity. In the meantime, in manifold letters he dispatched orders of the greatest severity, commanding that no men, of the number of those at least who had been born to the inheritance of any property in the kingdom, should shun taking part in the approaching warfare; threatening that whoever should be found in any part of the kingdom after the victory should have been gained, to have omitted appearing in his presence on the field, was to expect no

other fate than the loss of all his goods and possessions, as well as his life.

His warnings were to no avail. By the beginning of the summer Henry Tudor had managed to raise an army of some three thousand men, including fifteen hundred French troops under the command of Philippe de Crèvecoeur and a number of Scottish mercenaries commanded by Bernard Stuart (or Stewart), 3rd Seigneur d'Aubigny, the captain of the Scots guard of the French kings. (Later, between 1494 and 1503, Stuart won undying fame by commanding the French forces in Italy whose actions resulted in Charles VIII's capture of Lombardy.) On 1 August the invasion fleet left the Seine and a week later arrived in south-west Wales, where Henry had been promised the support of a number of landowners, mainly from Pembrokeshire, where his uncle still retained some influence. Support was slow in coming and it was not until Henry reached the English towns on the Welsh marches, Stafford, Litchfield and Tamworth, that his numbers began to swell.

Everything hung on the Stanleys, who enjoyed considerable support in north Wales, but as yet they were not prepared to show their hand. Summoned to join Richard at Nottingham, Lord Stanley prevaricated by pleading illness, while his brother, Sir William Stanley, sent forces into the western marches without actually joining up with the invaders. Lord Stanley's son insisted that his father would remain loyal to Richard but all the while the family played a waiting game, biding their time to see what would befall the King. They were in a difficult position: all the evidence points to their wanting to support Henry Tudor, Stanley's stepson, but at the same time they had to tread carefully as Lord Strange was a hostage in Richard's camp and it was by no means certain that the Tudor challenge would succeed. Astutely, Stanley took his force of six thousand men towards Atherstone, to the south-west of Leicester, so that he could claim he was going to join Richard while also being in a position to throw in his lot with the invaders.

Although it was taking undue time for Northumberland and Norfolk to rally their forces behind the King's cause, Richard had high hopes that his army would eventually number twelve thousand soldiers and that they would all be in place by the third week of August. Against them, Henry Tudor had some five thousand men. By the night of 21 August both armies, and Stanley's shadowing forces, were in the

English Midlands and a battle was imminent. Richard's army was camped near Sutton Cheney, while Henry's smaller force spent the night to the west at Whitemoors, both close to the market town of Market Bosworth in Leicestershire. As the contemporary accounts are sparse and in some cases contradictory it has proved difficult to piece together the precise course of the battle and the disposition of the two forces, so much so that, until recently, there was no commonly agreed narrative about what in fact happened or indeed where the fighting took place. Over the years, other sites have also been mooted and the exact position was the subject of heated debate. It was not until February 2010 that the true position of this decisive battle was finally revealed. Following years of intensive archaeological research and study of contemporary documents, the actual battlefield was shown to be in fields two miles to the south-west of the commonly accepted site and modern visitors' centre on Ambion Hill. The discovery of pistol bullets and cannon balls also demonstrated that firepower played a greater part in the battle than had generally been supposed.

What seems to have happened is this. In the early morning of 22 August Richard moved his army on to the high ground near Ambion Hill (or Ambien, at 417 feet no great height but still a commanding presence in the generally flat landscape) and facing west, they took up position with the Duke of Norfolk's men spread out in a defensive column with artillery on both flanks. Behind them was Richard's main guard and covering them was Northumberland's force ready to protect the flanks. For the Lancastrian army advancing from the west it must have been a daunting sight. Not only were they outnumbered but their opponents enjoyed a superior position.

To face them, Oxford took up position with Sir Gilbert Talbot on the right southern flank and Sir John Savage to the left, with Henry taking command of a small mounted force to the rear. One other army was in the vicinity and it would play a decisive role: the Stanleys, under the operational command of Sir William Stanley, were also close by, probably to the north of Dadlington covering the wet and marshy ground to the south-west. Known as 'Redemore', it means 'the place of the reedy marsh', and this is an alternative name for the battle. One thing is now for certain: the battle was not fought on Ambion Hill, the traditional site, but on a featureless solid Leicestershire farming land close to the present-day Fenn Lane Farm.

On the face of it Henry Tudor's cause was not particularly hopeful. While he had an experienced subordinate field commander in the Earl of Oxford, he himself was untested in battle and the odds were stacked against him. To gain any advantage he needed the support of the Stanleys but even though the two parties had been in touch before the battle Sir William had sent a dusty reply that he would not make any precipitate move but would join battle at the appropriate moment. In the meantime Henry and Oxford should put their forces in order and make the first move. They had little option but to follow that course of action. (When it became clear that the Stanleys were not going to intervene on the Yorkist side Richard gave the order for Strange's immediate beheading but in the confusion the execution was not carried out.)

The battle then began in earnest, with Norfolk's archers firing on Oxford's lines, followed by a general advance down the slopes of Ambion Hill. To protect himself Oxford shortened his line and as a result Norfolk's advancing men slammed into a concentrated mass of men on the lower slopes. This was a hard, pounding slugging match with men engaged in fierce hand-to-hand combat as the two lines reeled under the shock of the first collision. Some of the impetus of Norfolk's charge had been countered by the cohesion of Oxford's concentrated defensive positions, but as the Yorkists pulled back to regroup for a further onslaught they still held the initiative. Sensing the seriousness of their predicament, Henry Tudor made a move, not by joining battle but by riding with his retinue towards the Stanleys' lines to beg them to intervene on his side by attacking the Yorkist flanks. This proved to be the decisive moment of the battle.

Richard noticed the move and recognised that he had a sudden chance to defeat his rival by charging and engaging Henry Tudor's smaller band of horsemen. The tactics were risky as it was an all-or-nothing attack, but Richard had seen a gap opening up on Oxford's right flank between Talbot's position and the marshy ground. If this could be exploited and he could engage Henry Tudor and kill him, the day would be his. With his mounted knights in support the King rode down the slope towards the opposition – recent research suggests along the old Roman road from Atherstone – and in the first stage the impetus of the charge seemed to work in the Yorkists' favour. Henry Tudor's standard-bearer, Sir William Brandon, was cut down and the fighting degenerated into a succession of individual battles with Richard to the fore, cutting and hacking in his desperation to reach his rival and deliver a mortal blow. He was the more experienced soldier and had he been able to engage Henry Tudor in combat the day would have turned out very differently.

At that point though, the Stanleys decided to intervene. Knowing that they would never be forgiven by Richard for not joining him and realising that their own position would be in jeopardy if they were on the losing side, they decided to throw in their lot with Henry Tudor and gave their men the order to charge into Richard's flanks. The weight of their unexpected assault altered the balance of the battle and placed Richard and his followers in great danger.

As the battle lines began to break up Richard was driven back towards the marshy ground where he was unseated from his horse and quickly struck down by Welsh foot soldiers. Although he carried on fighting to the last, death came to him at the hands of anonymous billmen who hacked him down, ripped off his crown – a circlet above his helmet – and dumped the blood-spattered body in the mire which was identified in the 2010 research. Later his body was stripped of its armour and it was taken on horseback to Newark, where it was put on display for two days to prove that the tyrant king was dead. To Richard III falls the melancholy distinction of being the only King of England to die in battle since the Norman conquest.

The battle ended with the rout of the Yorkist army. Norfolk had been killed, as had many others in Richard's retinue, and Northumberland simply melted away with his men once the fighting was over, having decided to take no part in the battle from his position as the rearguard. According to Polydore Vergil, who left the only near-contemporary account of the battle (based on the evidence of those who had witnessed it), the winning side hailed Henry as their new king and Lord Stanley cemented the moment by crowning his stepson with Richard's crown circlet, 'which was found among the spoil in the field'.

There was little of the usual blood-letting in the wake of the battle. Most of Richard's retinue had been killed in combat, among them Lord Devereux and Richard Ratcliffe, who had been denounced as 'the Rat'. His friend and colleague Sir William Catesby ('the Cat') escaped from the field but was hunted down and beheaded. Viscount Lovell escaped, as did Norfolk's son the Earl of Surrey, and, according to Vergil, most of the Yorkist foot soldiers saved their lives by promptly surrendering: 'when king Richard was killed, all men forthwith threw away weapon, and freely submitted to Henry's obeisance, whereof the most part would have done the same at the beginning'. After two hours of heavy and frequently confused pounding the Battle of Bosworth Field was over. It had not so much been won by Henry Tudor as lost by Richard III, who was undone both by his impetuosity in leading the fateful cavalry charge and by the treasonable behaviour of the Stanleys.

Of the mistake – or misjudgement – in deciding to attack Henry Tudor's retinue it can be said that Richard gambled on an all-or-nothing opportunity. He knew that his forces outnumbered the opposition and realised that he had been presented with an unexpected opportunity to close on Henry Tudor and kill him. Not only was he the superior soldier but he was well supported and he sensed a chance to settle the battle in one swift and decisive move. If Henry Tudor had been killed or even disabled it would have given victory to Richard. The Stanleys acted equally impulsively; if they had felt that the battle was swinging Richard's way there is no doubt that they would have supported him, as would have Northumberland. Perhaps Richard, too, sensed that and believed that one successful cast of the dice would see him triumph by bringing in those who were wavering.

However, by that stage Richard was also suffering from his failure to construct a series of unflinching alliances among his potential supporters. At Bosworth Field he finally came face to face with the harsh reality that he was king in name only and was about to pay the penalty of fighting without a sufficient number of trustworthy allies. 'I will die King of England,' he is supposed to have said in a last utterance. 'I will not budge a foot.' Those were brave words spoken by a man who did not lack courage or fortitude but Richard was on his own when he was unhorsed and turned to face Henry Tudor's avenging foot soldiers. He had forced his way to his brother's throne by executing his main opponents (Rivers, Grey, Vaughan, Hastings and Buckingham) and he now found himself on the losing side. In that respect he was probably no different from many of his Plantagenet predecessors and in the circumstances it was probably neither more nor less than he deserved.

Richard III lost his crown and his life at Bosworth Field but it was not the end of his story. Far from it: it was only the beginning. Because he was the main loser and because Henry Tudor continued to be regarded by many Yorkists as a usurper king, Tudor writers had a vested interest in reinforcing the legitimacy of the latter's rule. Through their efforts a picture gradually began to emerge of Henry VII as England's saviour, the King who had settled the long years of bloodshed and disharmony and who had righted the wrongs of that past tumultuous age. In turn this revisionism meant that the memory of Richard III had to be effectively besmirched. In John Rous's *History of the Kings of England*, which appeared in 1491, the last of the Yorkist kings appeared not so much as a monarch but as an Antichrist and outcast. Not only was Richard III painted as a wicked man but his physical appearance suggested a monster and so came into focus the familiar picture of Richard as a pinched little hunchback who was more than capable of committing an act of gross infanticide and other frightful acts of murder:

> He was small of stature, with a short face and unequal shoulders, the right higher and the left lower. He received his lord King Edward V blandly with embraces and kisses, and within about three months or a little more he killed him together with his brother. And Lady Anne, his queen, daughter of the Earl of Warwick, he poisoned . . . And what was most detestable to God and all Englishmen, and indeed to all nations to whom it became known, he caused others to kill the holy man King Henry VI or, as many think, did so by his own hands.

Not only did Rous claim that Richard III was a misshapen villain but he took the opportunity to sanctify the hapless Henry VI, who was the author of so many of England's misfortunes during the internecine wars and whose weak character was the cause of so many disasters. The theme was followed by other chroniclers of the period, such as Richard Fabyan, and was then taken up and enhanced by Vergil and Sir Thomas More. In the latter's history Richard III is a mirror image of the portrait produced by Rous: 'little of stature, ill-featured of limbs, his left shoulder much higher than the right . . . malicious, wrathful, envious and, from before his birth, ever forward'. Winners always get the right to construct their own versions of what happened and the Tudor account of events passed into English historiography as the solid truth. As a result Richard was quickly transmogrified from man into monster and the version coined by Rous and More was swallowed wholesale by Shakespeare to create an unforgettable dramatic character.

As Richard III's most recent biographers argue, Shakespeare had to follow that interpretation because at the time there were no other sources and he had to rely on what was available to him. From More he borrowed the conceit that Richard's grotesque personality sprang from an unnatural birth and a deformed body; in his opening soliloquy in *Richard III* Richard makes much of this misfortune, presenting himself as:

> I, that am rudely stamped, and want love's majesty
> To strut before a wanton ambling nymph:
> I, that am curtailed of this fair proportion,
> Cheated of feature by dissembling nature,
> Deformed, unfinished, sent before my time
> Into this breathing world scarce half made up,
> And that so lamely and unfashionable
> That dogs bark at me as I halt by them –
> Why, I, in this weak piping time of peace,
> Have no delight to pass away the time,
> Unless to see my shadow on the sun
> And descant on mine own deformity.

Some idea of Shakespeare's hostility towards the character can be seen in the fact that he introduces Richard in *Henry VI, Part Two* as the man who murdered the Duke of Somerset after the Battle of St Albans, even though this could not have happened as Richard of Gloucester was only three years old at the time. But for the needs of the stage that mattered not: as seen by Shakespeare, this is indeed a man who can 'smile and murder as I smile' and is 'determined to prove a villain'. It makes for good drama but as Richard's later apologists have proved there is a world of difference between the stage version of Richard III and the man who ruled over England for little more than two years and had earlier given nothing but loyalty to his brother while he was on the throne. In Shakespeare's rendering of events audiences have to believe implicitly in Richard's inherent wickedness to understand why he dragged the kingdom down with him but, of course, that necessary dramatic licence cannot be the last word on the man.

It does not help Richard III's reputation that he spent so little time on the throne, a mere twenty-six months, or that his claim to it was so shaky. He also lacked that prerequisite of any king during the period – an heir and a spare capable of surviving who would be able to follow in his place should he die or be deposed, and he never made good that defect following the death of his only son. Those drawbacks left him exposed and left his reputation open to attack. Add on the suspicion that he was a murderer who had arranged the deaths of family members close to him and it is not difficult to see why posterity has treated him badly.

He also had the misfortune to be on the losing side at Bosworth, where his failure to be protected by close allies and the treachery of the Stanleys were his undoing. That was his real failing. Given time he could have built up allegiances, especially outside the north, where he was already liked and respected as Edward IV's lieutenant and enjoyed a strong following. As a royal duke he was a loyal subordinate and perhaps this was the role that suited him best. When his brother died, Richard, after a short period of prevarication, was presented with the opportunity of claiming the throne and he took it, choosing to reign as king and disdaining to be a mere protector. Clearly he did not want to repeat the experience of Henry VI's uncle Bedford, who was little more than a caretaker, and he would have remembered, too, the example of his father and namesake Richard of York, who touched the throne but failed to claim it or hold on to it. Being a protector was not sufficient for a man like Richard III: for him it had to be all or nothing.

Unfortunately, taking that route led him into wrongdoing – the peremptory execution of Hastings and Rivers and his alleged complicity in the deaths of his nephews – and that revelation of ice in his heart lost him support. It was no worse than Henry IV's role in the disposal of Richard II, but that earlier usurper had the time to reconstruct his reputation that was denied to Richard III. Therefore this last of the Plantagenet kings remains an enigma and given the outcome of the wars which ended with his death this is perhaps predictable.

In most respects Richard III conformed to the class from which he sprang, he exploited the hereditary principle to get what he wanted and then acted ruthlessly in his own interests and in building up his territorial power, but, shorn of valid support as he was, his violence of mind and action meant that when he fell he fell mightily. There is no more telling image to delineate his downfall than the account left by Polydore Vergil of the different fates awaiting the rival kings after Bosworth Field. For Henry VII there is the ceremony and deference due to the victor; for Richard III there is only the bile and disgrace of defeat:

> Henry, after victory obtained, gave thanks unto Almighty God and for the same; then after, replenished with joy incredible, he got himself unto the next hill, where after he had commended his soldiers, and commanded to cure the wounded, and to bury them that were slain, he gave unto the nobility and gentlemen immortal thanks, promising that he would be mindful of their benefits, all which mean while the soldiers cried God save King Henry, God save King Henry! And with heart and hand uttered all the shew of joy that might be; which when Thomas Stanley did see, he set upon Richard's crown, which was found among the spoil in the field upon his head, as though it had been already by commandment of the people proclaimed king after the manner of his ancestors, and that was the first sign of prosperity. After that, commanding to pack up all bag and baggage, Henry with his victorious army proceeded in the evening to Leicester, where, for refreshing of his soldiers from their travail and pains, and to prepare for going to London, he tarried two days. In the meantime the body of King Richard naked of all clothing, and laid upon an horse back with the arms and legs hanging down on both sides, was brought to the abbey of monks Franciscans at Leicester, a miserable spectacle in good sooth, but not unworthy for the man's life, and there was buried two days after without any pomp or solemn funeral.

It was perhaps a fitting end for a war which had done so much damage and had dominated English life for almost a century: the panoply of kingship reduced to the crown being retrieved from a bush and placed on the victor's head on a battlefield whose exact location is not known to this day.

Chapter Twenty-Two

THE LAST AND MOST DOUBTFUL
OF THE USURPERS

By a grim process of terminal elimination and the passing of the years the least likely candidate of all of Edward III's lineage succeeded to the throne of England as King Henry VII, the founding father of the Tudor dynasty. By any standards Henry Tudor, Earl of Richmond, was a rank outsider and it was a combination of luck and circumstance which gave him his crown or at least allowed it to be placed on his head by his supporters in the wake of his fortuitous victory at Bosworth. His claim, if remote, was real enough: he owed it to his Beaufort ancestors, his mother, Margaret Beaufort, being the great-great-granddaughter of King Edward III and only daughter of John Beaufort, Duke of Somerset, a grandson of John of Gaunt, Duke of Lancaster, through his relationship with Katherine Swynford.

On the other hand, Henry Tudor was still something of an outsider and very few people of any rank in England had actually met him. His father, Edmund Tudor, was born a commoner and died before Henry was born, his childhood was interrupted by the fall-out from the civil conflict and he spent much of his time with guardians or in exile with his uncle Jasper Tudor. If Edward IV had not died so unseasonably and his eldest son had been allowed to succeed him, Henry Tudor might have lived out his life as one of the lesser-known male members of the House of Lancaster, either in exile in France or in reduced circumstances in England. As the Yorkist line had been strengthened by Edward IV's control of the throne and the elimination of most of the possible rivals, it could have survived and English history perhaps would have turned out very differently. If

Edward had lived longer or if his sons had not disappeared there is no reason to suppose that the House of York would not have maintained the royal line for many years to come; within the country they certainly had the support to do so.

Instead Henry Tudor was crowned king and he proceeded to honour the plans that he should marry Elizabeth of York, sister of the murdered princes. By that marriage alliance he reconciled the rival claims of the houses of York and Lancaster and in so doing initiated the process of healing the dynastic wounds that had scarred previous generations. The coronation of King Henry VII took place at Westminster on 30 October 1485 amid much solemnity and general rejoicing – Lady Margaret Beaufort 'wept marvellously' (not least in foreboding, according to her confessor John Fisher, Bishop of Rochester, for she trembled at the precariousness of her son's position and remembered the privations of the past) – and the following year he carried out his intention to marry Elizabeth of York. There was a brief moment of uncertainty before the wedding as both bride and groom shared a common ancestry, being descended from John of Gaunt, but the necessary papal consent for the match was secured through the good offices of the ubiquitous Dr Morton, now serving his third king and shortly to become Archbishop of Canterbury.

Not having many family alliances in England, Henry VII had to create his inner circle from former Lancastrian supporters and erstwhile members of the court of Edward IV. There were rewards for those who had supported him while he was in exile and during his brief military campaign against Richard III. Jasper Tudor was created Duke of Bedford and appointed Lieutenant of Calais. Later he would become Lord Lieutenant of Ireland and Earl Marshal of England; in 1491, four years before his death, he was married to Catherine Woodville, the widow of the executed Duke of Buckingham, although there were no children from the match. (Later, after Jasper Tudor's death, she married Sir Richard Wingfield of Kimbolton.)

There was also promotion for Henry VII's stepfather, Lord Stanley, who was created Earl of Derby and continued as Constable of England in return for his family's timely intervention at Bosworth. His wife, the new king's mother, Lady Margaret Beaufort, became very influential indeed, being entrusted with, among other things, the safe custody of the ten-year-old Earl of Warwick, Clarence's eldest son and a possible claimant to the throne. Later, and perhaps ominously, the boy was moved into the Tower of London for safer keeping. Throughout her son's reign Margaret Beaufort was to be a prominent figure at court, as both mother of the King and one of his principal advisers and confidantes, in time becoming so powerful that she signed herself 'Margaret R' and adopted the title 'My Lady the King's mother'. She also dressed in a manner which befitted her rank and person, causing some comment during the Christmas celebrations in 1487 by appearing at court wearing a coronet and robes similar to those worn by her daughter-in-law.

Oxford, too, emerged as a leading and trusted figure at court, becoming Henry's Great Chamberlain and High Admiral. His attainted estates were restored to him and he was installed as a Knight of the Garter. Another beneficiary of royal patronage was Sir John Paston (III), who became Sheriff of Norfolk and Suffolk and later enjoyed a close relationship with Henry, being described in one of the letters from the King as 'my right trusty and well beloved counsellor'. Others who had helped Henry during his exile were also suitably rewarded: Dr Morton was eventually appointed a cardinal and Christopher Urswick became Dean of Windsor, an apt reward for his earlier good work in ensuring Henry's safety during the years of exile in Brittany.

Conversely, with the exception of Catesby, there was little blood-letting among Richard's supporters and associates for the good reason that none of them represented a tangible threat and some of them could be useful to the new regime. Northumberland spent some time in confinement, hardly the reward he might have expected had he really offered Henry wholesome support at Bosworth. This lack of recompense to one England's greatest magnates raises the intriguing possibility that Northumberland had either not been willing to engage his forces on the King's behalf or that Richard's precipitate charge took him by surprise and he was unable to intervene because of a lack of communication on the battlefield. Whatever his motives, he paid for his inaction with his life, being murdered four years later, in April 1489, during a tax revolt in York. The unrest had been created by Parliament's need to raise funds for a possible English military intervention in Brittany but Northumberland's murder was also ascribed to northern anger over his failure to support Richard III:

there were several of the former king's followers in the crowd that lynched him. On the other hand, an equally prominent Ricardian and battlefield commander at Bosworth, Norfolk's son, the Earl of Surrey, prospered and rose in royal favour, in time becoming Lieutenant of the North.

Not surprisingly, given the dynastic turmoil of the earlier years, Henry was anxious to reinforce his claim to the throne not just through right of conquest but by descent. One of the earliest tasks undertaken by his first Parliament was to delete Richard III's *Titulus Regius* from the statute books and thereby to end the taint of his wife's illegitimacy. As for his new mother-in-law, Elizabeth Woodville, widow of Edward IV, she was not punished for her miscalculation in throwing in her lot with Richard III in the closing period of his reign. Initially she was well treated and awarded a pension, but in 1487 these gifts were cancelled and she was lodged in modest apartments in Bermondsey Abbey, where she died in 1492. It is highly probable that the change in her fortunes was caused by Lady Margaret Beaufort, who could not afford to have the matriarch of the House of York as a rival at court.

The birth of a son, Prince Arthur, to the new royal couple in September 1486 seemed to cement the Tudor succession and gave hope for the future, but Henry VII's reign was to be shaken by a number of serious challenges which showed that factional fighting and support for the Yorkist cause were not things of the past. The first incident took place the year after Henry's accession and involved Viscount Lovell, former Chamberlain of the Royal Household to Richard III, and Sir Humphrey Stafford of Grafton, who proclaimed John de la Pole, Earl of Lincoln, the rightful heir to the throne, being the son and heir presumptive of Richard III's sister Anne. The plot failed – Stafford was executed and Lovell, along with Lincoln, managed to escape into exile in Burgundy – but it provided the impetus for another attempt to challenge Henry the following year, in the spring of 1487.

This lamentable affair involved the use of a dupe called Lambert Simnel, who had been coached by a priest, Richard Simonds, to impersonate the young Earl of Warwick, Clarence's eldest son. It was doomed from the outset. Simnel was the son of an Oxford carpenter and organ-builder and there was never any likelihood that he would be taken as Clarence's son for long. Even so, he received a considerable weight of support from Yorkist loyalists. Lovell and Lincoln both backed his claim and he was hailed as a genuine candidate by the Irish Chancellor, Sir Thomas FitzGerald of Lackagh, a brother of the influential Earl of Kildare.

Another powerful supporter of Simnel was Edward IV's sister Margaret of Burgundy, who, according to Vergil, 'pursued Henry with insatiable hatred and with fiery wrath never desisted from employing every scheme which might harm him as a representative of the hostile faction'. Vergil added the thought that in all probability Margaret did not believe that Simnel was the young Earl of Warwick but the opportunity to strike a blow against the Tudor succession was too good to be missed: 'Consequently, when she learnt of the new party which had recently risen against Henry, although she considered the basis of it to be false (as indeed it was), she not only promised assistance to the envoys, but took it upon herself to ally certain other English nobles to those already active in the new conspiracy. Furthermore, Francis Lord Lovell, who had crossed over to Flanders at this time, encouraged the woman to undertake more ambitious plans . . .'

To give some momentum and authority to his cause Simons took the young man to Dublin, which remained a centre of Yorkist support and intrigue under Kildare's governorship of the country. After the demise of the Earl of Desmond, who had been executed by the detested Earl of Worcester in 1468, Kildare had become the dominant figure in Ireland, mainly by stabilising the Pale and forging links with leading Anglo-Irish and Gaelic families, including the O'Neills of Tyrone. Seeing in the person of Simnel an opportunity to restore Yorkist fortunes while increasing his own standing, Kildare lent his support to the coronation of the young man, who was crowned and anointed as Edward VI by the Archbishop of Dublin in Christchurch Cathedral on Whit Sunday, 24 May.

This was followed by the arrival of Lovell and Lincoln, together with an armed force of two thousand Swiss and German mercenaries supplied by Margaret of Burgundy and under the command of Colonel Martin Schwarz, an adventurer from Augsburg who brought with him a motley collection of *landsknecht* mercenaries: violent north German freebooters whose main interests were plunder and rape.

Together with their Irish allies led by FitzGerald of Lackagh they crossed over to England, landing at the Piel of Foudray on the Furness Peninsula in north Lancashire on 4 June and then moving quickly inland.

In an attempt to forestall the rebellion, Henry VII had ordered the real Earl of Warwick to be paraded in public in London, but there was never any likelihood that Simnel would gather much support. All that his main backers could hope for was that known Yorkist sympathisers would throw in their lot with them if Lincoln and Lovell managed to win an early victory with their mercenary army. In the event, the anticipated backing in Yorkshire failed to materialise and the only support came from small and insignificant retinues led by two influential northern landowners who were also cousins: Lord Scrope of Bolton and Lord Scrope of Masham, whose great-grandfather had been involved in the plot to unseat Henry V in 1415. Their forces besieged York but lack of support meant that they were forced to give up the attempt. Neither cousin was punished although both were admonished and Scrope of Bolton was forced to live within twenty-two miles of London to keep him apart from his northern supporters.

The Royalist military response to the invasion was led by the Earl of Oxford and strongly supported by the new Earl of Derby and his son Lord Strange. Northumberland, too, became involved by seizing York and securing it against any possibility that its pro-Yorkist inhabitants would support the rebellion. By mid-June Lincoln's force had made its way down the Fosse Way and had reached Newark, where Oxford was waiting for them to the east of the River Trent, close to the village of East Stoke. As with the events at Bosworth, little is known about the actual fighting and its exact location but it seems that Lincoln opened the battle early in the morning of 16 June with a determined attack on Oxford's forces, attempting to unsettle them before they had fully deployed. It was Lincoln's best chance of winning as not only was he outnumbered but his troops were less reliable than those ranged against him. Although the Irish knights and Schwarz's *landsknecht* mercenaries fought bravely enough most of the foot soldiers were poorly armed Irish peasants and were quickly slaughtered by Oxford's archers and men-at-arms.

Such as it was, the battle was over well before the main force, led by Henry VII, arrived on the field. During the fighting Lincoln and

FitzGerald of Lackagh were killed, but once again Lovell made good his escape, being last sighted swimming his horse across the Trent. He was never seen again although a seated skeleton discovered two centuries later within the walls of his house at Minster Lovell in the Cotswolds could well have been his remains. Most of the mercenaries fought to the bitter end – as hired hands that was their lot – but Simnel was taken prisoner. Instead of being executed as might have been expected, he was saved by his youth and lack of guile. Later he was trained as a falconer but ended his days working as a scullion in the royal kitchens, dying in 1525.

The Battle of Stoke, as it came to be known, was the last pitched battle of the civil wars involving the houses of York and Lancaster, but it did not still the undercurrent of rumour, bad feeling and incipient rebellion that had underpinned English public life since the reign of Richard II. As a result Henry VII could never relax his guard, for throughout his reign the threat of a Yorkist backlash, especially in the north, remained a real possibility. Even after Richard's death and allowing for impostors like Simnel, there were still members of the House of York who could lay claim to the throne of England and were, if so minded, more than capable of rallying support for their cause. Among them were Clarence's son Warwick and the brothers Edmund and Richard de la Pole, both of whom had a tenuous claim to the throne through Richard III's naming of their brother, the late Earl of Lincoln, as his heir apparent. The two surviving de la Pole brothers lived into the following century and the reign of Henry VIII. Edmund was eventually executed in 1513 and Richard, known throughout Europe as the 'White Rose', was killed fighting in Italy twelve years later. By then the young Earl of Warwick had also been done to death as a result of his involvement in a fresh plot centred on another impostor, named Perkin Warbeck, who emerged from obscurity in 1491 and who may have been a bastard son of Edward IV.

For the next six years Warbeck managed to keep up the pretence that he was of the royal blood and had a rightful claim to the English throne, in this instance by pretending to be Prince Richard, the younger son of Edward IV, one of the Princes in the Tower. Once again the dupe was supported by Margaret of Burgundy, who believed, or allowed herself to believe, that this son of a Tournai merchant was none other than her long-dead nephew. And once again there was some support in Ireland when the young, well-dressed man suddenly turned up in Cork after travelling around Europe. On this occasion, though, Kildare had made his peace with King Henry and was not prepared to support another Yorkist claim on the English throne. Various attempts were made to effect a landing in England and to raise Yorkist military support behind Warbeck but nothing came of them. The most serious challenge came in 1495 but the plan was betrayed and Warbeck's English supporters were rounded up and executed.

Among the plotters was Sir William Stanley, whose charge at Bosworth had changed the course of the battle in Henry Tudor's favour. In an attempt to save his life he made a full confession, probably expecting leniency, but Henry could not afford to pardon someone who had acted treasonably against him and despite his family's standing Stanley was executed. The reasons for Stanley's ill-judged change of heart are unclear but probably centred on personal dissatisfaction with the rewards he had received from the new king – he had entertained ambitions to be created Earl of Chester – but the family also had a long history of scheming and dissimulation. In 1459 he had been attainted for supporting the Yorkists at Blore Heath, while his brother Lord Stanley had kept his forces out of the battle and was subsequently pardoned by Queen Margaret.

Warbeck also tried his luck at the court of King James IV of Scotland, who acknowledged his claim and married him off to a cousin, Katherine Gordon, daughter of the Earl of Huntly. The Scots also mounted a number of raids into Northumberland in 1495, unprovoked acts of aggression which broke a truce signed two years earlier, but after the diplomatic intercession of Spain James sensibly withdrew his support for Warbeck, whom he had styled 'King Richard'. This about-turn suited Henry VII, who wanted to keep his northern border secure, and in January 1502 there came into being a treaty of perpetual peace which was concluded with the betrothal of James IV to the English king's daughter Margaret.

The following year saw the wedding of 'the Thistle with the Rose' in the Abbey Church of Holyrood in Edinburgh, an alliance which should have ensured (but did not) the end of fighting between the two countries. Shorn of Scots support, Warbeck returned to Ireland before landing in Cornwall in September 1497. Although he got as far as Taunton Henry VII had forces waiting for him and the impostor surrendered on being promised that he would not be punished. Imprisoned in the Tower of London, Warbeck came into contact with the real Earl of Warwick and a plot was alleged to have been concocted between them to act in mutual support to overthrow the King. When this was uncovered both were executed within days of each other. Warbeck was little more than a deluded, if clever, dupe who allowed the machinations of others to get the better of him while Warwick was judicially killed for no other reason than he represented, as his father had done, a threat to the royal succession at a time when Prince Arthur was about to marry Catherine of Aragon. With Warwick's death – he was beheaded on Tower Hill at the end of November 1499 – the last direct male heir in the Yorkist line disappeared and there was to be no further serious or credible challenge to the rule of Henry VII.

After the young man's execution the Spanish ambassador claimed that there 'remained not a drop of doubtful Royal blood' in England but, of course, given the tenor of the times it was not the end of the carnage. Warwick's sister Margaret, Countess of Salisbury, married Sir Richard Pole, whose mother was the half-sister of Lady Margaret Beaufort, and with him she bore five children, one of whom, Reginald, became Archbishop of Canterbury. After her husband's death in 1505 she survived into the reign of Henry VIII, who called her 'the saintliest woman in England', but the good relationship did not last. In 1538 another son, Henry Pole, Lord Montague, was involved in a plot against Henry VIII and sentenced to death. With him was executed Henry Courtenay, the Marquess of Exeter and a grandson, through his mother Catherine of York, of Edward IV.

Three years later Henry VIII lost patience with the remaining Plantagenets and had the old Countess of Salisbury executed at the Tower. It was a shocking affair: almost in her seventies, Margaret tried to run away after the executioner struck her back instead of her neck and had to be held down while her head was chopped from her body. With her death disappeared the last member of the direct blood-line of the Plantagenets – her father was the murdered Duke of Clarence.

What of the others who survived Bosworth and became part of the Tudor inheritance? Most of those surrounding Henry VII had past allegiances to both York and Lancaster which had to be trimmed to match the new order. The fate awaiting some of them we already know. Death in a York scrimmage for Northumberland, whose true allegiance was a mystery known only to himself; death in bed for old Jasper Tudor, a good uncle who had remained true to his nephew throughout their wanderings in Europe. The Earl of Surrey changed sides and succeeded his father as Duke of Norfolk in 1514; as Earl Marshal to Henry VIII he became one the most important men in the kingdom and one of the most successful military commanders of his generation. Lincoln decided to pursue his own ends and paid for it with his life at Stoke. Having chosen the winning side at Bosworth, Sir William Stanley made the wrong move when he backed Perkin Warbeck and forfeited his life, but his brother the Earl of Derby survived until 1504 and on his death left a family which prospered to become one of England's great aristocratic lines. In time it came to be said of them: 'The Stanleys do not marry; they create alliances.'

The Earl of Derby's wife, the King's mother, also flourished and in turn became one of the country's major patrons of the arts and an important source of power at court. Although much of Lady Margaret Beaufort's life had been spent apart from her son after his difficult birth when she was little more than a girl, his accession to the throne introduced a new closeness, almost as if they had to make up for those lost years. Not only did she lavish affection on her 'good and precious prince, king and only son' but she was installed as one of his principal lieutenants. Her official residence at Collyweston in Northamptonshire was transformed into a palace and became the seat of her power and authority. In 1499 she took a vow of chastity and lived as a nun, fasting regularly, scourging herself with a hair shirt and tending to paupers in Collyweston's almshouse.

There were other aspects to Margaret in addition to her spirituality and political influence. At Cambridge she became a great benefactor of the university, creating Christ's College in 1506 and founding St John's College three years later. Dr John Fisher, one of her protégés and her personal chaplain, was appointed Chancellor and her dean of chapel, Henry Hornby, served as Master of Peterhouse. The arts, too, benefited from her involvement and her readiness to spend money on their development. She became the principal patron of William Caxton, who had set up a printing press at Westminster in 1476; twelve years later she commissioned a translation of the thirteenth-century French romance *Blanchardin and Eglantine* and later in her life she arranged for the publication of her own translation from the French of *The Mirror of Gold for the Sinful Soul* and the fourth book of Thomas à Kempis's *The Imitation of Christ*. Sadly, she had the misfortune to outlive her son, if only by a few months, dying on 29 June 1509, and was buried in Westminster Abbey. She had been one of the great figures of her age, a survivor in an uncertain world and one of the first influential female figures in English history.

The other great female character from the period, Jane Shore, also lived into old age. In 1483 this beautiful former mistress of Edward IV remarried for the last time, this time to Thomas Lynom, King's Solicitor to Richard III, and she lived into the reign of Henry VIII, making a final and pathetic appearance in More's history as 'lean, withered and dried up, nothing left but ravelled skin and hard bone'.

Henry VII's daughter Margaret had a different fate. Her husband, James IV, was perhaps the most attractive of all the Stewart kings and during his reign Scotland enjoyed something of a golden age. Having succeeded to the throne after his father's death in a fight with his nobility at Sauchieburn in 1488, James IV oversaw a period of relative calm, prosperity and cultural advancement. Under his patronage King's College in Aberdeen was founded in 1495 and the Royal College of Surgeons came into being in 1506. The royal residence of Holyroodhouse in Edinburgh was begun and he encouraged the new art of printing by awarding patents to the city's burgesses Walter Chapman and Andrew Myllar to 'bring hame ane prent [printing machine]' for producing books of Scottish interest. Poetry also flourished, notably the work of William Dunbar and Gavin Douglas, both of whom benefited from the King's patronage.

In domestic affairs James IV broke up the confederacy of the Lordship of the Isles and he proved himself to be a true Renaissance prince by developing his country's military power, especially its navy, causing the *Great Michael*, the largest warship of its day, to be built. This leviathan was 240 feet long and its crew numbered 300 sailors, with space for 120 gunners and 1000 soldiers. However, the King's dabbling in military matters attracted a high price. In 1491 he had renewed the Auld Alliance with France but this was effectively cancelled by his marriage to Margaret Tudor in 1503 and the resultant truce with England.

The treaties were mutually incompatible should England and France ever go to war and it was unfortunate that Henry VIII proved to be a bellicose king, anxious to pursue an aggressive foreign policy in Europe. In November 1511 he joined Pope Julius II's Holy League, which combined the Papacy, Venice, Spain and England in an alliance aimed at stifling French territorial ambitions in Italy, a move that put him on a collision course with the Scots. James delayed taking any action until the summer of 1513 but when he did it proved to be a disastrous move.

The fleet, including the *Great Michael*, was loaned to the French and an extended raid was made into England to force English soldiers to return home from France. James's popularity created a sizeable force but it lacked gunners, the best being at sea with the fleet. Having crossed the border, his army was outmanoeuvred by an English force led by the Earl of Surrey, one of the great survivors of the earlier civil strife in England, and was heavily defeated at the Battle of Flodden on 9 September. During the fighting James was killed, together with a large number of nobles and members of his household; for the English it was a relatively tame victory but for Scotland it was a disaster which affected the whole nation.

In the aftermath Margaret threw herself into an unwise marriage with Archibald Douglas, Earl of Angus, and the country was soon caught up in an internecine conflict to win control of the child-king, the future James V. Margaret died in 1541 but not before she had tired of Angus and married Henry Stewart, Lord Methven. In common with her brother Henry VIII she did not enjoy a particularly happy matrimonial history.

In many respects Wales should have done well out of the new order. The coming of Henry Tudor to the throne seemed to fulfil the vaticination of the bards who had prophesied that a Welshman would one day secure the Crown of Britain and that there would be a new age of freedom for the country. The birth of Prince Arthur and the choice of his name increased the sense of expectation – the legend of King Arthur is central to early Welsh poems such as *Y Gododdin* and *Marwnad Cynddylan*, in which he is portrayed as a paragon – but the boy's early death at the age of sixteen was deeply mourned as a disaster for those great hopes.

There was some progress in the principality – during the reign of

Henry VII there was greater migration between Wales and England, with grants of land for those who had supported the Tudor cause – but this was balanced by an intensive incorporation of Wales into the English representative system, with twelve counties and eleven boroughs each returning one member to the English Parliament. This suited the centralising tendencies of Henry VIII, but the Welsh did not gain as much from the Tudor connection as the Scots were later to get from the Stewart nexus.

Ireland was also transformed, under successive Tudor monarchs it benefited from the control of a central government and emerged as an integrated country under an English king. This Tudor conquest of Ireland turned the sixteenth century into a time of great violence marked by a number of related internecine wars as the English pushed out the boundaries of the Pale to achieve full sovereignty throughout Ireland. During the years of fighting, which began in 1547 and did not end until 1603, the country was brutally colonised and its Gaelic Irish aristocracy was either defeated or forced into negotiated settlements with the new English overlords.

Despite the many threats to the new king's succession, Henry VII was able to hold on to his crown and lived until 1509, when he was succeeded by his son, who reigned as Henry VIII. Although the direct Tudor line eventually came to an end in 1603 with the death of the childless Elizabeth I, the succession continued through Henry VII's daughter Margaret, who had been married off to James IV of Scotland. That same year, 1603, their great-grandson James VI of Scotland was crowned James I of England, thus beginning the process of uniting Scotland and England and forging the kingdom of Great Britain. (James VI had Tudor blood on both sides of his family. He was the son of Mary Queen of Scots from her marriage to Henry, Lord Darnley, the son of Matthew Stewart, Earl of Lennox and Lady Margaret Douglas, who was the daughter of Margaret Tudor from her marriage to Archibald Douglas, 6th Earl of Angus.)

Although the Stewarts retained the Crown only until 1689, when James's grandson, James II of England and VII of Scotland, went into exile, the latter's daughter Mary went on to rule jointly with her husband, William of Orange. They died childless and the succession passed to Queen Anne, Mary's sister, and then to Sophia, Electress of Hanover, a granddaughter of James I. Through the Act of Succession her son succeeded to the throne in 1714 as

King George I, thus retaining the Tudor blood-line. It was not a bad outcome for a man described (unfairly) as 'the last and most doubtful of the usurpers', a Welsh adventurer who invaded England to win a throne – albeit from a usurping king – and had been fortunate to triumph at Bosworth, where, to begin with, all the odds had been stacked against him.

The conclusion of almost 350 years of Plantagenet rule and the arrival of the Tudor dynasty in 1485 was an important punctuation mark in British history, for the civil wars in England had also affected events in Ireland, Scotland and Wales as well as the wider world of European affairs. With the end of the dynastic conflict and the turmoil caused by the clash of rival magnates a new age did eventually dawn; the Tudors proved to be businesslike, efficient and capable rulers. It helped that they were solvent and, thanks to the income from the lands they inherited, successive kings and queens of the line were spared the financial indignities of their fifteenth-century predecessors. Henry VII began the process by ruthlessly acquiring land and money, mainly by fining the nobility and increasing rents. Not only did his acquisition of wealth make him the richest king since the Norman conquest but his methods weakened the power of the nobility; no bad thing, it might be thought, even though the fines were often bribes to escape worse punishment.

The Tudors also created a strong and centralised state which was governed not just by all-powerful magnates but largely by capable professional men from middling backgrounds. Building on the foundations created by Edward IV, the Tudors were able to marry peace with prosperity and in so doing to transform late-medieval doctrine into modern forms of ruling the country; it is hardly surprising that they have been credited with building a stable order in England, so different from the reckless turmoil of the immediate past.

By now much else was changing in the world and horizons were expanding. As the century ended the Renaissance was given new impetus by the advent of printing and by the expansion overseas of European commercial and territorial interests, notably Spanish and Portuguese, to create the first of the great modern trading empires. In 1493 the two innovations went hand in hand to symbolise the dawning of the new age as the world became a bigger place. When the

Genoese adventurer Christopher Columbus returned from his voyage to the Americas to announce his feat of sailing as far as Cuba and Hispaniola the news was produced in a printed letter. Not only did this document propagate the story of his voyage and spark huge excitement but Columbus's words encouraged volunteers to join his next expedition. New lands and new means of communicating the news: overnight, accepted theories about world geography had to be rethought and this transformation also encouraged the belief that a new age was dawning as other navigators, such as Magellan and Vespucci, joined the search.

Seen in this wider perspective, the civil wars fought between the Lancastrians and the Yorkists seem to belong to an older and darker age and the dynastic union ushered in by Henry VII brought fresh promise and new hope. It was both a beginning and an end.

Epilogue

AN END OF NAMES AND DIGNITIES

Historical periods do not always have neat beginnings and endings and only rarely do they give birth to unexpected or dramatic innovations which are capable of standing the test of time. We can look back over the centuries and identify periods such as the waning of the Middle Ages but at the time of gradual or even sudden evolution the changes are usually indiscernible or unremarkable. Kings die and new dynasties emerge but at the same time economic, social and cultural life operates according to its own dynamics.

While it is true that the future direction of England changed dramatically as a result of the events at Bosworth Field there was no sudden dawning of a new age and no lightning strike of revelation. At the time Henry VII was accepted as king just as his predecessors had been and it would take time for Tudor hegemony to get into its stride. Not until nearly halfway through the following century was there any seismic activity and that was when Henry VIII took on the Catholic Church and brought papal power and the wealth of the monasteries into royal hands. Most change is gradual and often goes unnoticed; there are too many overlaps and too much continuity. Nevertheless, the reverberations at the time are not to be despised or ignored and their echoes sometimes carry resonance.

Perhaps the most eloquent panegyric on the passing of the Plantagenets came not at the end of the fifteenth century at the time of their demise but over a hundred years later, when they had passed into history. Appropriately it involved the name of the de Veres, the

Earls of Oxford, who had played such a signal role in the Wars of the Roses. They had been there from the very beginning. The unstable 9th Earl had served Richard II until his defeat at Radcot Bridge, the 12th Earl had suffered the traitor's death of being hanged, drawn and quartered for treason, while, like his father, the 13th Earl remained true to the House of Lancaster throughout the conflict and went on to serve Henry VII with great loyalty and distinction. In so doing he strengthened the claims of his line to be one of the great English families.

Originally Norman from Bayeux, the de Veres had settled in Essex at the time of the Norman conquest and Robert, the 3rd Earl, was one of the executors of Magna Carta. When the 18th Earl died in 1625 without an heir the succession to the title was disputed in the House of Lords by Robert, 11th Lord Willoughby de Eresby, a rich and influential peer, as heir general, and by Robert de Vere, a lowly captain in the army of the United Provinces, as heir male. If the latter lost the case, the ancient name of de Vere would be separated from the title of Earl of Oxford and, without the means to support a family, the impecunious soldier would be the end of the line.

In their search for guidance on this dispute, the House of Lords called on the advice of Sir Randolph Crewe, a former Speaker of the House of Commons who had recently been appointed Chief Justice of the King's Bench. As a result of Crewe's findings the House of Lords found on the side of Captain de Vere, but the judgement did him little good: he was killed while fighting at the siege of Maastricht in 1632, a few years after succeeding to the title. His only son, Aubrey, turned out to be the last of the de Vere senior line, dying without an heir in 1703. And so ended a family name which had its beginnings in the Middle Ages and whose members had played prominent roles in the turbulent period of civil conflict which was brought about by the failure of kings to control their over-mighty magnates and by the ambitions of powerful men to take advantage of any weakness displayed by the monarchy. It is fitting therefore that the most poignant and most memorable comment on that long-lost age should have been delivered by Crewe in supporting the claims of a family whose antecedents stretched back to the reign of the Plantagenets:

I have laboured to make a covenant with myself that affection may not press upon judgement, for I suppose there is no man that hath any apprehension of gentry or nobleness, but his affections stands to the continuance of so noble a name and house, and would take hold of a twig or a twine thread to uphold it. And yet time has his revolutions; there must be a period and an end to all temporal things, *finis rerum*, an end of names and dignities and whatsoever is of worth. Where is Bohun, where's Mowbray, where's Mortimer. Nay, which is more and most of all, where is Plantagenet? They are entombed in the urns and sepulchres of mortality.

The Main Characters

During the Wars of the Roses the names of the nobility and other great families appear, disappear and frequently reappear with bewildering regularity. If a nobleman were attainted or died without a male heir the title could become extinct and then later be resurrected by the monarch to reward another family for loyal service. (Attainted titles reverted to the Crown and were frequently used in this way.) When that happened the title would remain constant but the family name would differ. Below are listed the principal titles in England, Ireland and Scotland and the names of the people who held them. Also included are the names and identities of many of the leading players in the story.

Albany

(i) Robert Stewart, Earl of Fife and Menteith, Duke of Albany (1339–1420). Third son of King Robert II of Scotland. Ruled as Governor of Scotland while King James I was in English captivity. Succeeded by his son Murdoch (c.1362–1425). Another son, John (c.1380–1424), through his second wife, Muriella Keith, became Earl of Buchan and with 4th Earl of Douglas led the Scottish forces in France. Both men were killed at the Battle of Verneuil in 1424.

(ii) Alexander Stewart, Duke of Albany (c.1456–85). Younger son of King James II and brother of King James III, recognised by King Edward IV as King of Scotland by the Treaty of Fotheringhay in 1482. Died in exile three years later.

Angus

(i) George Douglas, 1st Earl of Angus (1380–1403). Brother of James, 2nd Earl of Douglas, and married to Mary Stewart, daughter of

Robert III. Died of plague in England after being taken prisoner at Battle of Homildon Hill.

(ii) William Douglas, 2nd Earl of Angus (c.1389–1437). Son of above, Scottish Warden of the Middle March.

(iii) Archibald Douglas, 5th Earl of Angus (c.1449–1513), known as 'Bell the Cat'. Grandson of above. Opponent of King James III and supporter of the Albany faction. His son and heir, the Master of Angus (1469–1513), was killed at the Battle of Flodden and his grandson Archibald Douglas, 6th Earl of Angus (c.1489–1557), married Margaret Tudor, widow of King James IV.

ARUNDEL

(i) Richard FitzAlan, 4th Earl of Arundel (1346–97). Naval commander and member of King Richard II's council. One of the five Lords Appellant who defeated Robert de Vere's forces at Radcot Bridge. Found guilty of treason and executed in 1397.

(ii) Thomas FitzAlan, Archbishop of Canterbury (1353–1414). Brother of above. Created Chancellor in 1386 but his association with the Lords Appellant led to his downfall when he was exiled in 1397. On the accession of Henry IV he was recalled and served three terms as Chancellor.

(iii) Thomas, 5th Earl of Arundel (1381–1415). Son of 4th Earl, died of dysentery during siege of Harfleur in 1415 without leaving an heir.

AUDLEY

(i) John Tuchet, 6th Lord Audley (d.1490). Originally a Lancastrian supporter but transferred his allegiance to Edward IV. Lord Treasurer in 1484.

(ii) James Tuchet, 7th Lord Audley (c.1463–97). Second son of above. Yorkist supporter, raised rebellion in the West Country against Henry VII in 1497 and executed as a traitor.

BEAUCHAMP: SEE WARWICK

BEAUFORT: SEE ALSO EXETER AND SOMERSET

(i) Lady Joan Beaufort (1376–1440). Daughter of John of Gaunt and Katherine Swynford. Married secondly to Earl of Westmorland, by whom she had twelve children who survived.

(ii) Cardinal Henry Beaufort (c.1375–1447). Second son of John of Gaunt and Katherine Swynford. Appointed Bishop of Winchester and later cardinal, he was one of the wealthiest men in England and a close associate of Henry V.

(iii) Lady Margaret Beaufort (1443–1509). Daughter of John Beaufort, Duke of Somerset, and Margaret Beauchamp of Bledsoe. Betrothed to John de la Pole, she eventually married Edmund Tudor in 1455 and from the union came Henry Tudor, who later reigned as Henry VII. Latterly married Lord Stanley.

BEAUMONT

Lord William Beaumont (d.1508). Son of the Lancastrian Lord Beaumont, killed at the Battle of Northampton in 1460. Fought at the Battles of Towton and Barnet and with the Earl of Oxford captured St Michael's Mount in 1473. On the accession of Henry Tudor his lands were restored but he subsequently went mad and lived out his life as a guest of the Earl of Oxford, who married his widow, Elizabeth Scrope.

BEDFORD

(i) John, Duke of Bedford (1359–1435). Third son of Henry IV. Guardian of England during Henry V's expedition to France and subsequently regent of France during the minority of Henry VI. He was married first to Anne of Burgundy, Duke Philip's sister and then to Jacquetta of Luxembourg (1416–72), daughter of Peter of Luxembourg, Count of Pol, who later married 1st Earl Rivers.

(ii) Sir George Neville (d.1483). Son of John Neville, the Marquess of Montague. A supporter of Edward IV in 1470, he married the King's eldest daughter, Elizabeth, and was elevated to the dukedom of Bedford. This was stripped from him in 1478 on the grounds that he could not support the estate.

BOLINGBROKE: SEE LANCASTER

BONVILLE

William Bonville, 1st Lord Bonville (1392–1461). West Country Lancastrian supporter who changed sides when his great rival the Earl of Devon switched his support from the Yorkists to the Lancastrians. Executed after the Second Battle of St Albans.

BOURCHIER: SEE ALSO ESSEX

Cardinal Thomas Bourchier, Archbishop of Canterbury and Lord Chancellor (c.1411–86). Brother of Henry Bourchier, Earl of Essex. A leading prelate, he officiated at the coronations of Edward IV, Richard III and Henry VII.

BUCHAN: SEE ALBANY

BUCKINGHAM

(i) Humphrey Stafford, 1st Duke of Buckingham (1402–60). Captain of Calais and Constable of England, he commanded the Lancastrian forces at the First Battle of St Albans in 1455 and was killed at the Battle of Northampton.

(ii) Henry Stafford, 2nd Duke of Buckingham (1455–83). Grandson of above and married to Katherine Woodville, sister of Queen Elizabeth. Originally supported Richard III's claim to the throne but rose against him and was executed in 1483.

BUTLER: SEE ORMOND, WILTSHIRE

CAMBRIDGE

Richard of Conisbrough, Earl of Cambridge (c.1375–1415). Younger son of Edmund, Duke of York, and Isabella of Castile, thereby cousin to Henry V. Through his marriage to Anne Mortimer, sister to the English Earl of March, his heir was Richard, the future Duke of York. Executed in 1415 after a plot to unseat Henry V.

CATESBY

Sir William Catesby (1450–85). Member of Richard III's council and Speaker of the 1484 Parliament. Executed after the Battle of Bosworth.

CHICHELE

Henry Chichele, Archbishop of Canterbury and founder of All Souls, Oxford (c.1362–1443). A member of the council in 1410, he accompanied Henry V's expedition to France and was involved in the diplomatic negotiations with Emperor Sigismund in 1416.

CLARENCE

(i) Thomas, Earl of Aumale and Duke of Clarence (1388–1421). Second son of Henry IV, he served as a soldier in France and was present at siege of Harfleur. Killed while leading the English army in a rash attack on the French at Baugé in 1421.

(ii) George Plantagenet, 3rd Duke of Clarence and Earl of Warwick through his marriage to Warwick the Kingmaker's daughter Isabel Neville (1449–78). Younger brother of Edward IV, his father was Richard Duke of York and his mother was Cecily Neville, daughter of 1st Earl of Westmorland. Rebelled against his brother in 1469 and 1470, involved in treasonable activities in 1473 and 1477 and finally judicially murdered on his brother's orders, probably in a butt of Malmsey wine.

CLIFFORD

(i) Thomas Clifford, 8th Baron Clifford (1414–55). Lancastrian field commander, killed at the First Battle of St Albans.

(ii) John Clifford, 9th Baron Clifford (1435–61). Son of above and nicknamed 'the Butcher'. According to legend, he killed York's second son, the Earl of Rutland, after the Battle of Wakefield. Killed at the Battle of Towton.

COURTENAY: SEE DEVON

DACRE

(i) Humphrey Dacre, 1st Baron Dacre of Gilsland (d.1485). Warden of the West March and Yorkist supporter.

(ii) Thomas Dacre, 2nd Baron Dacre of Gilsland (1467–1525). Son of above. Supported Richard III but transferred loyalty to Henry VII.

DERBY: SEE ALSO BOLINGBROKE

(i) Earl of Derby, one of the titles of Henry Bolingbroke, Duke of Hereford and later Henry IV.

(ii) Thomas Stanley, 2nd Lord Stanle (1435–1504). Brother of Sir William Stanley, whose intervention at Bosworth won the day for Henry Tudor. The husband of Margaret Beaufort, he was created Earl of Derby in 1485.

DESMOND

Thomas Fitzgerald, 7th Earl of Desmond (c.1426–68). Yorkist supporter, appointed deputy in Ireland by King Edward IV in 1463. Attainted by his successor, the Earl of Worcester, and executed at Drogheda five years later.

DESPENSER

(i) Henry Despenser, soldier and Bishop of Norwich (1341–1406). Grandson of Hugh Despenser, who was executed with his father the Earl of Winchester after a coup mounted by Queen Isabella and Roger Mortimer in 1326.

(ii) Thomas Despenser, Earl of Gloucester (1373–1400). Great-grandson of Hugh Despenser. Married Constance, daughter of Edmund Langley, Duke of York. Supporter of Richard II and lynched by a mob after unsuccessful coup against Henry IV.

DEVEREUX

(i) Sir Walter Devereux (1411–59). Prominent Herefordshire landowner, soldier and retainer of Richard Duke of York. Together with William Herbert, Earl of Pembroke, led a force into Wales to enforce York's authority.

(ii) Walter Devereux, 1st Baron Ferrers of Chartley (c.1432–85). Son of above and brother-in-law of Pembroke. Member of Edward IV's inner circle of advisers.

DEVON

(i) Thomas Courtenay, 13th Earl of Devon (1414–58). Supported the claims of Richard Duke of York in 1452 but switched allegiance to Queen Margaret of Anjou.

(ii) Thomas Courtenay, 14th Earl of Devon (1432–61). Son of above. Captured after Towton and executed.

(iii) Henry Courtenay (d.1469). Brother of above. The Devon lands were restored to him after Towton but he was executed after plotting against Edward IV.

(iv) John Courtenay, styled Earl of Devon (d.1471). Son of 14th Earl, commanded the rearguard of Queen Margaret's army at Tewkesbury and was killed during the withdrawal.

(v) Edward Courtenay, 1st Earl of Devon, Third Creation (d.1509). Heir male to above. Attainted in 1484 and fled to join Henry Tudor in Brittany.

(vi) Henry Courtenay, Marquess of Exeter (c.1498–1538). Grandson of above and created marquess in 1525. Executed for treason against Henry VIII.

DORSET

(i) Thomas Grey, Marquess of Dorset (c.1455–1501). Son of Queen Elizabeth Woodville by her first marriage to Sir John Grey of Groby, he fought for his stepfather, Edward IV, at Tewkesbury but later went into exile when Richard III assumed power.

(ii) Thomas Grey, 2nd Marquess of Dorset (1477–1530). Third son of above. Like his father, never entirely trusted by Henry VII and imprisoned in the Tower of London. Rehabilitated by Henry VIII.

DOUGLAS

(i) James, 2nd Earl of Douglas (c.1358–88). Married Isabel, daughter of King Robert II of Scotland. Killed at the Battle of Otterburn in 1388, leaving no heir.

(ii) Archibald, Lord of Galloway and 3rd Earl of Douglas, known as 'the Grim', bastard of 1st Earl of Douglas (c.1328–1400). Warden of the Scottish West March.

(iii) Archibald, 4th Earl of Douglas and Duke of Touraine (c.1369–1424). Known as 'Tineman', or loser. Married Margaret, daughter of King Robert III. Fought in France and was killed at the Battle of Verneuil in 1424.

(iv) Archibald, 5th Earl of Douglas (c.1391–1439). In French service in the 1420s and Lieutenant of the Realm during the minority of King James II.

(v) James, 9th Earl of Douglas (1426–91). Yorkist supporter, involved in the plans put forward by King Edward IV to crown Duke of Albany as King Alexander of Scotland. An invasion of Scotland failed in 1484 and after being captured Douglas spent the rest of his life in captivity at Lindores Abbey.

DUDLEY

John Sutton, 1st Baron Dudley (1400–87). Lancastrian commander and Lord Lieutenant of Ireland 1428–30. After Henry VI's defeat at Northampton joined the Yorkist side and was appointed Constable of the Tower. Later supported both Richard III and Henry VII.

EGREMONT

Thomas Percy, 1st Baron Egremont (1422–60). Son of 2nd Earl of Northumberland and involved in Percy–Neville land disputes in 1453. Killed at Northampton.

ERPINGHAM

Sir Thomas Erpingham (1357–1428). Served the households of John of Gaunt and Henry Bolingbroke. Commanded the English archers at Agincourt in 1415.

ESSEX

Henry Bourchier, 1st Earl of Essex (c.1408–83). Brother of Cardinal Bourchier. Married to Duke of York's sister Isabel, he served under his brother-in-law in France and was appointed Treasurer by Henry VI in 1455. Fought on the Yorkist side at Northampton and served as Edward IV's treasurer between 1473 and 1483.

EXETER

(i) Sir John Holland, Earl of Huntingdon and Duke of Exeter (c.1352–1400). Half-brother to Richard II through the marriage of his mother Joan of Kent, the widow of the Black Prince, to Thomas Holland, Earl of Kent (c.1315–60). One of the conspirators against Henry IV in January 1400, he was arrested and executed.
(ii) John Holland, 1st Duke of Exeter (1395–1447). Son of above, one of Henry V's ablest commanders, he distinguished himself at Agincourt in 1415 and as a naval commander at Pontoise in 1419. Appointed Governor of Aquitaine, he was recognised for his services by the restoration of the dukedom.
(iii) Henry Holland, 2nd Duke of Exeter (1430–75). Son of above and prominent Lancastrian supporter. Married to Edward IV's sister Anne, who divorced him in 1471 to marry her lover Sir Thomas St Leger.

FASTOLF

Sir John Fastolf (d.1459). English soldier and field commander in France, present at Harfleur and Agincourt. Later served under Bedford and was present at the Battle of Verneuil. Retired from active service in 1435 to live in Caister Castle in Norfolk. His legal representatives came from the Paston family.

FAUCONBERG

William Neville, Lord Fauconberg and later Earl of Kent (d.1463). A younger son of Earl of Westmorland and brother of Earl of Salisbury, he commanded the Yorkist vanguard at Northampton and Towton and died in 1463. His illegitimate son Thomas Neville (d.1471) was the Bastard of Fauconberg, a noted naval commander who raised a rebellion against Edward IV in 1471 and was executed for treason.

FIFE: SEE ALBANY

FITZALAN: SEE ARUNDEL

FITZGERALD: SEE ALSO DESMOND AND KILDARE

Sir Thomas FitzGerald of Lackagh (d.1487). Younger brother of Earl of Kildare and Lord Deputy of Ireland. Killed at the Battle of Stoke during the Lambert Simnel rebellion.

FITZWALTER

(i) Walter Fitzwalter, 5th Baron Fitzwalter (1400–31). Yorkist supporter and field commander in France.
(ii) John Ratcliffe, 6th Baron Fitzwalter (1452–96). Grandson-in-law of above. Yorkist supporter.

FORTESCUE

Sir John Fortescue (c.1394–1479). Lord Chief Justice of the King's Bench and Lancastrian supporter. Pardoned by Edward IV and member of his council. Author of *De Laudibus Legum Angliae* and *On the Governance of England.*

GLOUCESTER

(i) Humphrey, Duke of Gloucester (1390–1447). Fourth son of
Henry IV and brother of Dukes of Clarence and Bedford. Married
first Jacqueline of Hainault and then Eleanor Cobham.

(ii) Richard, Duke of Gloucester and King of England (1452–85).
Younger brother of Edward IV, whose son Prince Edward he
succeeded in 1483. Married to Anne Neville, daughter of Warwick the
Kingmaker.

GREY OF RUTHIN: SEE ALSO KENT

Reginald, 3rd Lord Grey of Ruthin (c.1362–1440). Landowner on the
Welsh marches in contention with Owen Glendower.

HASTINGS

(i) Lord William Hastings (c.1430–83). Yorkist supporter, married
Katherine Neville, sister of Warwick the Kingmaker. Opponent of
Woodville faction and close associate of Edward IV. Charged with
treason and executed on orders of Richard III.

(ii) Sir Ralph Hastings (1440–95). Younger brother of above. Served
Edward IV, Richard III and Henry VII.

HERBERT: SEE PEMBROKE

HEREFORD: SEE BOLINGBROKE

HOLLAND: SEE EXETER

HOWARD: SEE NORFOLK

HUNGERFORD

(i) Walter Hungerford, 1st Baron Hungerford (d.1449). Speaker of the
House of Commons in 1414 and Steward of Royal Household to
Henry V.

(ii) Robert Hungerford, 3rd Baron Hungerford (1428–64). Grandson
of above. Lancastrian supporter and soldier, executed after the Battle
of Hexham. His son, also Robert (1450–69), was executed with Henry
Courtenay in January 1469.

Huntingdon: see Exeter

Kent: see also Fauconberg

(i) Edmund Grey, Earl of Kent (1416–90). Son of Lord Grey of Ruthin and Catherine Percy, daughter of 2nd Earl of Northumberland. Lord Treasurer 1463–4.

(ii) Anthony Grey (d.1480). Son of above, married to Eleanor Woodville, sister of Queen Elizabeth.

(iii) George Grey, 2nd Earl of Kent (d.1503). Younger brother of above and supporter of Richard III. Married first Anne Woodville, daughter of Earl Rivers, and then Catherine Herbert, daughter of Earl of Pembroke.

Kildare

(i) Thomas Fitzgerald, 7th Earl of Kildare (d.1478). Yorkist supporter and founder of the Kildares' ascendancy in Irish politics.

(ii) Gerald Fitzgerald, 8th Earl of Kildare, known as Gearóid Mór (1456–1513). Governor of Ireland, he served five English kings and supported the claims of Lambert Simnel in 1487.

Lancaster

(i) John of Gaunt, Duke of Lancaster (1340–99). Third son of Edward III. Married first Blanche of Lancaster, second Constanza of Castile and third his mistress Katherine Swynford. From the latter match came the Beaufort line.

(ii) Henry Bolingbroke, Earl of Derby and Duke of Hereford (1367–1413). Eldest son of above and heir to the duchy of Lancaster. One of the Lords Appellant, he was exiled by Richard II but returned in 1399 and claimed the throne as Henry IV.

(iii) Henry V, King of England (1387–1422). Eldest son of above. Married Katherine Valois of France.

(iv) Henry VI, King of England (1421–71). Son of above. Married Margaret of Anjou.

(v) Edward of Lancaster, Prince of Wales (1452–71). Son of above. Married Anne Neville, daughter of Warwick the Kingmaker. Killed at the Battle of Tewkesbury.

LINCOLN: SEE SUFFOLK (V)

LOVELL

Francis Lovell, 9th Baron and 1st Viscount Lovell (d. after 1487). Member of Richard III's council and Lord Chamberlain. Fought at Bosworth, escaped and supported Lambert Simnel's claims to the throne. Disappeared after the Battle of Stoke.

MARCH (ENGLAND)

(i) Edmund Mortimer, 3rd Earl of March (d.1381). Married Philippa, daughter of Lionel Duke of Clarence, second son of Edward III.
(ii) Roger Mortimer, 4th Earl of March and 7th Earl of Ulster (1373–98). Son of above. His brother Edmund married the daughter of Owen Glendower and his sister Elizabeth was married to Sir Henry Percy, also known as 'Hotspur'. Heir presumptive to Richard II. Killed in Ireland at the Second Battle of Kells.
(iii) Edmund Mortimer, 5th Earl of March (1391–1425). Son of above. Fought under Henry V in France and appointed Lord Lieutenant of Ireland in 1421. Died childless and title and estates passed to Richard, Duke of York.

MARCH (SCOTLAND)

George Dunbar, 3rd Earl of March (d.1420). Succeeded to title in 1371 and fought at Otterburn (Chevy Chase) in 1388. Defected to English side in 1400 when Duke of Rothesay refused to marry his daughter Elizabeth, preferring to marry into Douglas family.

MONTAGUE: SEE ALSO NEVILLE, SALISBURY

Henry Pole, Lord Montague (1492–1539). Son of Countess of Salisbury, executed for treason with Henry Courtenay, Marquess of Exeter.

MORTIMER: SEE MARCH (ENGLISH)

MORTON

John Morton, Bishop of Ely and Archbishop of Canterbury (1425–1500). Prominent churchman who served Henry VI and Edward IV. Lord Chancellor under Henry VII.

MOWBRAY: SEE NORFOLK

NEVILLE: SEE ALSO FAUCONBERG, NORTHUMBERLAND, SALISBURY, WARWICK, WESTMORLAND

(i) Robert Neville, Bishop of Salisbury and Bishop of Durham (1404–57). Younger son of Earl of Westmorland and Joan Beaufort and brother of Earl of Salisbury.

(ii) George Neville, Archbishop of York (1432–76). Son of Earl of Salisbury and brother of Warwick the Kingmaker. Created Chancellor in 1460.

(iii) John Neville, Marquess of Montague (c.1431–71). Third son of 5th Earl of Salisbury, he received title of Earl of Northumberland in 1464 after the forfeiture of the Percy earldom and estates. Forced to relinquish title in 1470 and created Marquess of Montague. Changed sides and fought against Edward IV; killed at the Battle of Barnet.

(iv) Cecily Neville, Duchess of York (1415–95). Daughter of Earl of Westmorland from his marriage to Joan Beaufort. Wife of Richard of York and mother of Edward IV.

(v) Anne Neville (1456–85). Queen of England. Younger daughter of Warwick the Kingmaker and wife of Duke of Gloucester, later Richard III.

NORFOLK

(i) Thomas Mowbray, Earl of Nottingham and 1st Duke of Norfolk (1366–99). One of the supporters of the Lords Appellant who defeated de Vere at Radcot Bridge, he was appointed Captain of Calais. On Richard II's orders he arrested Gloucester and was probably responsible for his murder on the King's orders. He was banished for life when he and Bolingbroke accused each other of treason in 1398. His son Thomas Mowbray was Earl Marshal, executed for treason against Henry IV in 1405.

(ii) John Mowbray, 2nd Duke of Norfolk (1392–1432). Second surviving son of above. His service to Henry IV in France led to the restoration of the dukedom and estates in 1425.

(iii) John Mowbray, 3rd Duke of Norfolk (1415–61). Son of above and a nephew of Duke of York. His army arrived at a critical time to secure Edward IV's victory at Towton.

(iv) John Howard, Duke of Norfolk (c.1430–85). Served in France and fought at Towton. Created Duke of Norfolk and Earl Marshal in 1483. Killed fighting for Richard III at Bosworth and attainted.

(v) Thomas Howard, Earl of Surrey and Duke of Norfolk (1443–1524). Son of above and supporter of Richard III. Entered service of Henry VII and emerged as a leading soldier. Led English army at the Battle of Flodden in 1513. Created Duke of Norfolk in 1514.

NORTHUMBERLAND

(i) Henry Percy, 1st Earl of Northumberland (1341–1408). Married to Margaret Neville; their son was Sir Henry Percy (1364–1403), also known as 'Hotspur', who was married to Elizabeth Mortimer, daughter of 3rd Earl of March (English).

(ii) Henry Percy, 2nd Earl of Northumberland (1394–1455). Son of Hotspur, married to Eleanor Neville, younger daughter of Earl of Westmorland and brother of Earl of Salisbury.

(iii) Henry Percy, 3rd Earl of Northumberland (1421–61). Son of above. Lancastrian commander, killed at Towton.

(iv) Henry Percy, 4th Earl of Northumberland (c.1446–89). Son of above, supported Richard of Gloucester when he succeeded to the throne but played no part at the Battle of Bosworth. Lynched in York in 1489.

NOTTINGHAM: SEE NORFOLK

ORMOND

(i) James Butler, 4th Earl of Ormond (1390–1452). Lancastrian Lord Lieutenant of Ireland. Maintained a thirty-year feud with John Talbot, Earl of Shrewsbury.

(ii) James Butler, 1st Earl of Wiltshire and 5th Earl of Ormond (1420–61). Son of above, created Earl of Wiltshire in 1449. Appointed Lord Lieutenant of Ireland and served in Pembroke's army which was defeated at Mortimer's Cross in 1461. Executed for treason.

OXFORD

(i) Robert de Vere, 9th Earl of Oxford (1362–92). Close associate and friend of Richard II. His appointment as Duke of Ireland in 1386 created a good deal of jealousy. In 1387 he raised an army on the King's behalf but was defeated by the Lords Appellant at Radcot Bridge and fled into exile.

(ii) John de Vere, 12th Earl of Oxford (1408–62). Prominent Lancastrian supporter, executed with his son Aubrey for treason after his attempts to make contact with Margaret of Anjou's exiled court in Scotland.

(iii) John de Vere, 13th Earl of Oxford (1442–1513). Second son of above. Prominent Lancastrian supporter, escaped to France after the Battle of Barnet in 1471. On the accession of Henry VII he received the post of Great Chamberlain and was responsible for defeating a Yorkist revolt at the Battle of Stoke in 1487. Married first to Margaret Neville, sister of Warwick the Kingmaker, and then to Elizabeth Scrope, widow of Lord Beaumont.

PASTON

East Anglian family whose correspondence is one of the main primary sources for the period: John I (1421–66), married to Margaret Mautby; John II (1442–79), son of above, married to a daughter of Sir John Fastolf; John III (1444–1502), brother of above, Sheriff of Norfolk and Suffolk.

PEMBROKE

(i) Jasper Tudor, Earl of Pembroke and Duke of Bedford (1431–95). Second son of Owen Tudor and Queen Katherine, Henry V's widow. Lancastrian field commander who fought at the First Battle of St Albans and Mortimer's Cross. Supported his nephew Henry Tudor's claim to the throne and married Catherine Woodville, widow of Duke of Buckingham.

(ii) William Herbert, Earl of Pembroke (1423–69). Yorkist supporter and commander at Mortimer's Cross. Defeated and executed by Warwick the Kingmaker after the Battle of Banbury.

PERCY: SEE NORTHUMBERLAND

PLANTAGENET: SEE CLARENCE, MARCH, RUTLAND, YORK

POLE, DE LA: SEE SUFFOLK

RICHMOND

Edmund Tudor, Earl of Richmond (1430–56). Son of Owen Tudor and Queen Katherine, widow of Henry V. Married to Lady Margaret Beaufort and father of Henry Tudor.

RIVERS

(i) Richard Woodville (or Wydeville), 1st Earl Rivers (d.1469). Made his name and his fortune by marrying Jacquetta, the widow of Duke of Bedford and rose rapidly at court, becoming Treasurer. Taken prisoner at the Battle of Edgecote in 1469, he was executed on Warwick's orders. His daughter Elizabeth married secondly Edward IV. (ii) Anthony Woodville, Lord Scales and 2nd Earl Rivers (1442–83). Eldest son of above and married to Elizabeth, daughter of Lord Scales. A veteran of Towton and Barnet, he served as Captain of Calais and on Edward IV's death was appointed guardian of future Edward V. Seized on orders of Richard of Gloucester and executed.

ROOS

Thomas, 9th Lord Roos (1427–64). Married to sister of John Tiptoft, Earl of Worcester. Lancastrian supporter, executed after the Battle of Hexham. His daughter Eleanor married Robert Manners (d.1495), a Yorkist supporter, who succeeded to the title.

ROTHESAY

David Stewart, Duke of Rothesay (1378–1402). Eldest son of King Robert III of Scotland and nephew of Duke of Albany. Betrothed to daughter of Scottish Earl of March, he married Marjory, daughter of 3rd Earl of Douglas in 1400; the decision prompted March to side with King Henry IV.

RUTLAND: SEE YORK

SALISBURY

(i) John Montague (or Montacute), 3rd Earl of Salisbury (c.1350–1400). One of the members of the plot to assassinate Henry IV in 1400. Executed as a traitor.
(ii) Thomas Montague (or Montacute), 4th Earl of Salisbury

(1388–1428). Son of above and leading field commander in France (victor at Cravant in 1423). Killed during the siege of Orléans.

(iii) Richard Neville, 5th Earl of Salisbury (1400–60). Son of Earl of Westmorland from his second marriage to Joan Beaufort and son-in-law of above (he married 4th Earl's daughter Alice in 1421). Father of Warwick the Kingmaker. Executed after the Battle of Wakefield.

(iv) Margaret, Countess of Salisbury (1473–1541). Daughter of Duke of Clarence and Isabel Neville. Married to Sir Richard Pole (no relation of de la Pole family). Her son Henry was executed for treason against Henry VIII in 1538 and she followed him to the block in 1541.

SAYE AND SELE

James Fiennes, 1st Lord Saye and Sele (c.1400–50). Variously Sheriff of Kent, Surrey and Sussex; later became Warden of the Cinque Ports and appointed Treasurer to Henry IV. Lynched by a mob during the Cade Rebellion. His son William Fiennes, 2nd Baron (c.1428–71), was killed at Barnet.

SCALES

Lord Thomas Scales (c.1399–1460). Soldier who served in France under Bedford and Fauconberg. Held the Tower of London for Henry VI in 1460 and after surrendering was murdered by boatmen while on his way to sanctuary. His title passed to 2nd Earl Rivers after his marriage to Scales's daughter Elizabeth.

SCROPE OF BOLTON: SEE ALSO WILTSHIRE

John Scrope, 5th Lord Scrope of Bolton (1435–98). Fought with Richard III at Bosworth and took part in the Lambert Simnel plot to unseat Henry VII.

SCROPE OF MASHAM

(i) Richard Scrope, Archbishop of York (c.1350–1405). Third son of 1st Lord Scrope of Masham. Executed for supporting Northumberland's rebellion against Henry IV in 1405.

(ii) Henry Scrope, 3rd Lord Scrope of Masham (c.1376–1415). Married secondly to Joan Holland, widow of 2nd Duke of York, and served

Henry IV as Treasurer. Executed in 1415 after failure of plot with Earl of Cambridge to assassinate Henry V.

(iii) Henry Scrope, 6th Lord Scrope of Masham (1459–93). Great-grandson of above and cousin of 5th Lord Scrope of Bolton. Took part in Lambert Simnel plot to unseat Henry IV.

SHREWSBURY

(i) John Talbot, 1st Earl of Shrewsbury (c.1387–1453). Lancastrian field commander in France and three times Lord Lieutenant of Ireland. Killed at the Battle of Castillon.

(ii) John Talbot, 2nd Earl of Shrewsbury (c.1413–60). Son of above. Commanded centre of Lancastrian army at Northampton and was killed there.

(iii) John Talbot, 3rd Earl of Shrewsbury (d.1461). Cousin of above. Served with Lancastrian army and was killed at Towton.

(iv) John Talbot, 4th Earl of Shrewsbury (d.1473). Son of above. Joined Warwick the Kingmaker's rebellion against Edward IV in 1470 but transferred his allegiance to the Yorkists. Fought at Barnet and Tewkesbury.

SOMERSET

(i) John Beaufort, Duke of Somerset (1404–44). Son of John Beaufort, elder grandson of John of Gaunt. Served in French wars as captain-general. Married to Margaret Beauchamp; their only child was Lady Margaret Beaufort, mother of King Henry VII.

(ii) Edmund Beaufort, 1st Duke of Somerset (c.1406–55). Brother of above and favourite of King Henry VI. Killed at the First Battle of St Albans.

(iii) Henry Beaufort, 2nd Duke of Somerset (1436–64). Eldest son of above and favourite of Queen Margaret of Anjou. Fought on Lancastrian side in all the major battles and was attainted in 1461. Killed at the Battle of Hexham.

(iv) Edmund Beaufort, 3rd Duke of Somerset (1438–71). Younger brother of 1st Duke and commander of army of Queen Margaret of Anjou. Defeated at Tewkesbury and executed next day; his brother John was killed during the same battle.

STAFFORD: SEE BUCKINGHAM

STANLEY: SEE ALSO DERBY

Sir William Stanley (c.1435–95). Younger brother of Lord Stanley, Earl of Derby, whose change of side at Bosworth gave victory to Henry Tudor. Attainted and executed in 1495 for involvement in the Perkin Warbeck plot.

SUFFOLK

(i) Michael de la Pole, 1st Earl of Suffolk (c.1330–89). Chancellor to Richard II. Impeached and died in exile in Paris.

(ii) Michael de la Pole, 2nd Earl of Suffolk (c.1367–1415). Son of above, title restored by Henry IV. Died at siege of Harfleur.

(iii) Michael de la Pole, 3rd Earl of Suffolk (c.1395–1415). Son of above, killed at Agincourt.

(iv) William de la Pole, 4th Earl and 1st Duke of Suffolk (1396–1450). Brother of above and leading member of Henry VI's council. Impeached and banished but executed by sailors on way to Burgundy.

(v) John de la Pole, 2nd Duke of Suffolk (1442–91). Son of above. Married Elizabeth, sister of Edward IV; their son, John de la Pole, Earl of Lincoln (c.1460–87), was named heir presumptive to Richard III but died at Stoke leading a rebellion against Henry VII.

SURREY

Thomas Holland, 6th Earl of Kent and Duke of Surrey (c.1374–1400). Son of Thomas Holland, 5th Earl of Kent. Half-brother of Richard II and leading supporter in struggle with Lords Appellant. Lynched by a mob after unsuccessful revolt against Henry IV.

TALBOT: SEE ALSO SHREWSBURY

Richard Talbot, Archbishop of Dublin (d.1449). Brother of Earl of Shrewsbury and prominent in governance of Ireland as Deputy Lieutenant on three occasions.

TROLLOPE

Sir Andrew Trollope (d.1461). Lancastrian soldier and Master Porter of Calais. Defected to Margaret of Anjou's camp before the Battle of Ludford Bridge. Killed at Towton.

TUDOR: SEE PEMBROKE, RICHMOND

ULSTER: SEE MARCH (ENGLISH)

VERE, DE: SEE OXFORD

WARWICK

(i) Thomas Beauchamp, 12th Earl of Warwick (1337–1401). Appointed governor to young King Richard II in 1379. Joined Lords Appellant and present at the Battle of Radcot Bridge. Arrested in 1397 but escaped death penalty and imprisoned on Isle of Man.

(ii) Richard Beauchamp, 13th Earl of Warwick (1382–1439). Son of above. Although a godson of Richard II he supported the claims of Henry IV, for whom he fought at Shrewsbury in 1403. In later life appointed Lieutenant of Normandy and France and died in Rouen in 1439.

(iii) Richard Neville, 16th Earl of Warwick (1428–71), known as 'the Kingmaker'. Son of Richard Neville, 5th Earl of Salisbury and brother of John Neville, Marquess of Montague. Marriage to Anne Beauchamp, daughter of 13th Earl of Warwick, brought him great wealth and the Warwick title as well as making him one of England's most powerful magnates. One daughter, Isabel, married Duke of Clarence and the other, Anne, Richard, Duke of Gloucester.

(iv) Edward Neville, 17th Earl of Warwick (1475–99). Son of Duke of Clarence and grandson of above. Executed for treason.

WELLES

(i) Lionel, 6th Baron Welles (c.1406–61). Lincolnshire landowner and Lancastrian commander. Through third marriage to Margaret Beauchamp became brother-in-law of Edmund Beaufort, Duke of Somerset. Killed at Towton.

(ii) Richard, 7th Baron Welles (1428–70). Son of above and member of Salisbury family through marriage to Elizabeth Montague, niece of 5th Earl. Executed with son Robert after Lincolnshire rebellion against Edward IV in 1470.

WENLOCK

John Wenlock, Baron Wenlock (d.1471). Diplomat and soldier and one of several prominent turncoats. Started in the Lancastrian camp but fought for Yorkist cause at Mortimer's Cross and Towton. Joined Warwick in supporting Margaret of Anjou and was killed at Tewkesbury.

WESTMORLAND

(i) Ralph Neville, 1st Earl of Westmorland (1365–1425). Married first Katherine Stafford and then Joan Beaufort, daughter of John of Gaunt and Katherine Swynford. The two marriages produced twenty-four children. Eldest son of second marriage became Earl of Salisbury.
(ii) Ralph Neville, 2nd Earl of Westmorland (c.1407–84). Eldest son of above and Katherine Stafford. Most of the Neville lands passed to his stepbrother Salisbury.

WILTSHIRE: SEE ALSO ORMOND

William Scrope, Earl of Wiltshire (c.1351–99). Eldest son of 1st Lord Scrope of Bolton and favourite of Richard II. Executed by Bolingbroke and died without issue.

WORCESTER

John Tiptoft, 4th Earl of Worcester (1427–70). Constable of England and Deputy Lieutenant of Ireland under Edward IV and also known as the 'Butcher of England'. Executed on Henry VI's readeption.

WOODVILLE (OR WYDEVILLE): SEE ALSO RIVERS

Elizabeth Woodville (1437–92). Queen of England. Daughter of Sir Richard Woodville, later 1st Earl Rivers, and Jacquetta of Luxembourg. Widow of Sir John Grey of Groby, killed at the Second Battle of St Albans in 1461. Married Edward IV in 1464.

YORK

(i) Edmund of Langley, Earl of Cambridge and 1st Duke of York (1341–1402). Fourth surviving son of John of Gaunt. Married Isabella, daughter of Pedro the Cruel of Castile.
(ii) Edward, Earl of Rutland and 2nd Duke of York (c.1373–1415). Son

of above. Commanded vanguard of Henry V's army at Harfleur and was killed at Agincourt.

(iii) Richard, 3rd Duke of York (1411–60). Son of Earl of Cambridge, executed in 1415, and nephew of above. Served in France and Protector of the Realm 1454–6. Married to Cecily Neville, sister of Earl of Salisbury. Killed at the Battle of Wakefield.

(iv) Edward, Earl of March (1442–83). First son of above. Reigned as King Edward IV. Married to Elizabeth Woodville. Younger brother Edmund was Earl of Rutland (1442–60).

Select Bibliography

The period has produced one of the biggest bibliographies in British history and the following suggestions for further reading can only give a brief general introduction to the literature of the late-medieval period in England, Wales, Scotland and Ireland. It is by no means exhaustive and does not list essays and articles published in learned journals.

THE CHRONICLES, PRINTED SOURCES

The main chronicles of the late-fourteenth and fifteenth centuries are all available in modern English translations. They have provided the core for the historical narrative, although all should be read with care as far as their accuracy is concerned.

Adam of Usk, *Chronicon Adae de Usk 1377–1421*, ed. and trans. E. M. Thompson, London, 1904

Adam of Usk, *The Chronicle of Adam of Usk 1377–1421*, ed. and trans. C. Given-Wilson, Oxford, 1997

Basin, Thomas, *The History of the Reigns of Charles VII and Louis XI*, ed. Mark Spenser, Nieuwkoop, 1997

Benet, John, *Chronicle*, ed. G. M. Harriss and M. A. Harriss, Camden Society, 4th series, London, 1972

Blacman, John, *Memoir of Henry VI*, ed. M. R. James, Cambridge, 1919

Bower, Walter, *The Scotichronicon*, 9 vols., gen. ed. D. E. R. Watt, Aberdeen, 1987–98

The Brut, or Chronicles of England, ed. F. W. D. Brie, 2 vols., Early English Text Society, old series 136, London, 1906–8

Calendar of State Papers and Manuscripts Existing in the Archives and Collections of Milan, vol. I, ed. and trans. A. B. Hinds, London, 1912

Capgrave, John, *The Chronicle of England*, ed. F. C. Hingeston, Rolls Series 1, London, 1858

Castries, Duc de, *The Lives of the Kings and Queens of France* (*Rois et Reines de France*), trans. Anne Dobell, London, 1979

The Cely Letters, ed. Alison Hanham, London, 1975

Chastellain, Georges, *Chronicles of the Duke of Burgundy*, vols. IV and V, ed. Kervyn de Lettenhove, Académie Royale de Belgique, Brussels, 1863–6

Chronicles of London, ed. C. L. Kingsford, Oxford, 1905

The Chronicles of the White Rose of York, ed. J. A. Giles, London, 1845

Commines, Philippe de, *The Memoirs for the Reign of Louis XI 1461–1483*, trans. Michael Jones, Harmondsworth, 1972

The Crowland Chronicle Continuations, 1459–1486, ed. Nicholas Pronay and John Cox, Richard III and Yorkist History Trust, 1986

English Chronicle of the Reigns of Richard II, Henry IV, Henry V and Henry VI, ed. J. S. Davies, Camden Society, London, 1856

English Historical Documents 1327–1485, ed. A. R. Myers, London, 1969

Eulogium Historiarium Sive Temporis, 3 vols., ed. F. S. Haydon, Rolls Series 9, London, 1858

Fabyan, Robert, *New Chronicles of England and of France*, ed. Henry Ellis, London, 1811

Fordoun, John of, *Chronicle of the Scottish Nation (Chronica Gentis Scotorum)*, 2 vols., ed. W. F. Skene, Edinburgh, 1871

Fortescue, Sir John, *The Governance of England*, ed. Charles Plummer, Oxford, 1885; ed. Shelley Lockwood, Cambridge, 1997

Froissart, Jean, *Chronicles*, ed. and trans. Geoffrey Brereton, London, 1968

Gesta Henrici Quinti, The Deeds of Henry V, ed. and trans. Frank Taylor and J. S. Roskell, Oxford, 1975

The Great Chronicle of London, ed. A. H. Thomas and I. D. Thornley, London, 1938

Gregory, William, 'Gregory's Chronicle 1189–1469', *Historical Collections of a Citizen of London*, ed. James Gairdner, Camden Society, London, 1876

Hall, Edward, *Chronicle*, ed. Henry Ellis, London, 1809

Hardyng, John, *Chronicle*, ed. Henry Ellis, London, 1812

Historie of the Arrival of Edward IV in England, ed. John Bruce, Camden Society 1, London, 1839

Ingulph's Chronicle of the Abbey of Croyland, with the Continuation by Peter of Blois, ed. and trans. Henry T. Riley, London, 1854

Mancini, Dominic, *The Usurpation of Richard the Third: Dominicus Mancinus ad Angelum Catonem de occupatione regni Anglie per Ricardum tercium libellus*, ed. and trans. C. A. J. Armstrong, 2nd edn., Oxford, 1969

Monstrelet, Enguerrand de, *Chroniques*, ed. and trans. Thomas Johnes, London, 1840

More, Sir Thomas, *The History of King Richard the Third*, ed. R. S. Sylvester, Yale, 1963

More, Sir Thomas, *The Complete Works*, vol. II, Yale, 1963

A Parisian Journal, 1405–1449 (Journal d'un Bourgeois de Paris 1405–1449), trans. Janet Shirley, Oxford, 1968

The Paston Letters, ed. James Gairdner, London, 1904

The Paston Letters and Papers of the Fifteenth Century, 2 vols., ed. Norman Davis, Oxford, 1971–6

Rous, John, *Historia Regum Angliae*, ed. Thomas Hearne, Oxford, 1745

Rous, John, *The Rous Roll*, ed. Charles Ross, Stroud, 1980

The St Albans Chronicle, Volume I, 1376–1394: The Chronica Maiora of Thomas Walsingham, ed. John Taylor, Wendy R. Childs and Leslie Watkiss, Oxford, 2003

Titi Livii Foro-Juliensis, Vita Henrici Quinti Regis Angliae, ed. Thomas Hearne, Oxford, 1716

Vergil, Polydore, *The Anglica Historia of Polydore Vergil*, ed. Denys Hay, London, 1950

Warkworth, John, *A Chronicle of the First Thirteen Years of Edward IV*, ed. J. O. Halliwell, Camden Society 10, London, 1839

Waurin, Jean de, *Chroniques*, ed. W. Hardy and E. Hardy, Rolls Series, 5 vols., London, 1864–91

The Westminster Chronicle 1381–1394, ed. L. C. Hector and B. F. Harvey, Oxford, 1982

Whethamstede, John, Abbot of St Albans, *Register of Abbot Whethamstede*, ed. H. T. Riley, Rolls Series, 2 vols., London, 1872–3

Worcester, William, *Itineraries*, ed. J. Havey, Oxford, 1969

Wyntoun, Andrew, *The Orygynale Cronikyl of Scotland*, ed. David Laing, 3 vols., Edinburgh, 1872–9

THE HISTORICAL BACKGROUND, SECONDARY SOURCES

Baldwin, J. F., *The King's Council during the Middle Ages*, Oxford, 1913

Boardman, A. W., *The Medieval Soldier in the Wars of the Roses*, Stroud, 1998

Carter, Christine, *The Wars of the Roses and the Constitution of England c.1437–1509*, Cambridge, 1997

Castor, Helen, *Blood and Roses: The Paston Family in the Fifteenth Century*, London, 2004

Chrimes, S. B., *Lancastrians, Yorkists and Henry VII*, London, 1964

Cole, Hubert, *The Wars of the Roses*, London, 1973

Cook, D. R., *Lancastrians and Yorkists: The Wars of the Roses*, London, 1984

Gillingham, John, *The Wars of the Roses: Peace and Conflict in Fifteenth Century England*, London, 1981

Goodman, A. E., *The Wars of the Roses: Military Activity and English Society 1452–1497*, London, 1981

Goodman, Anthony, *John of Gaunt: The Exercise of Princely Power in Fourteenth Century Europe*, London, 1992

Griffiths, R. A., *The Wars of the Roses*, Stroud, 1998

Haigh, Peter A., *The Military Campaigns of the Wars of the Roses*, London, 1995

Haigh, Peter A., *The Battle of Wakefield*, London, 1996

Hallam, Elizabeth, *The Chronicles of the Wars of the Roses*, London, 1988

Harriss, Gerald, *Shaping the Nation: England 1360–1461*, Oxford, 2005

Hicks, Michael, *Bastard Feudalism*, London, 1995

Horrox, R. E., *Fifteenth Century Attitudes*, Cambridge, 1994

Jacob, E. F., *The Fifteenth Century 1399–1485*, Oxford, 1961

Keen, M. H., *England in the Late Middle Ages*, London, 1973

Kendall, P. M., *The Yorkist Age: Daily Life during the Wars of the Roses*, London, 1962

Lander, J. R. *The Wars of the Roses*, London, 1965

Lander, J. R., *Crown and Nobility 1450–1509*, London, 1976

Laynesmith, J. L., *The Last Medieval Queens: English Queenship 1445–1503*, Oxford, 2004

Macfarlane, K. B., *England in the Fifteenth Century*, London, 1981

McKisack, May, *The Fourteenth Century 1307–1399*, Oxford, 1959

Myers, A. R., *England in the Late Middle Ages 1307–1536*, London, 1936

Neillands, Robin, *The Wars of the Roses*, London, 1992

Pollard, A. J., *The Wars of the Roses*, London, 1988

Reid, Peter, *By Fire and Sword: The Rise and Fall of English Supremacy at Arms 1314–1485*, London, 2007

Richardson, Geoffrey, *The Hollow Crowns: History of the Battles of the Wars of the Roses*, London, 1996

Ross, Charles, *The Wars of the Roses*, London, 1976

Ross, Charles (ed.), *Patronage, Pedigree and Power in Late Medieval England*, Stroud, 1979

Rowse, A. L., *Bosworth Field and the Wars of the Roses*, London, 1966

Rubin, Miri, *The Hollow Crown: A History of Britain in the Late Middle Ages*, London, 2005

Seward, Desmond, *The Wars of the Roses and the Lives of Five Men and Women in the Fifteenth Century*, London, 1995

Strohm, Paul, *England's Empty Throne: Usurpation and the Language of Legitimation, 1399–1422*, London, 2006

Vickers, K. H., *England in the Later Middle Ages*, London, 1937

Warren, John, *The Wars of the Roses and the Yorkist Kings*, London, 1995

Weir, Alison, *Lancaster and York: The Wars of the Roses*, London, 1995

THE REIGN OF RICHARD II

Bevan, Bryan, *King Richard II*, London, 1990

Dobson, R. B. (ed.), *The Peasants' Revolt of 1381*, London, 1983

Du Boulay, F. R. H., and Barron, C. M. (eds.), *The Reign of Richard II: Essays in Honour of May McKisack*, London, 1971

Given-Wilson, Chris, *The Royal Household and the King's Affinity: Service, Politics and Finance in England, 1360–1413*, New Haven and London, 1986

Goodman, Anthony, *The Loyal Conspiracy: The Lords Appellant under Richard II*, London, 1971

Goodman, Anthony, and Gillespie, James L. (eds.), *Richard II: The Art of Kingship*, Oxford, 1999

Hutchison, H. F., *The Hollow Crown: A Life of Richard II*, London, 1961

Mathew, Gervase, *The Court of Richard II*, London, 1968

Saul, Nigel, *Richard II*, London, 1997

Tuck, J. A., *Richard II and the English Nobility*, London, 1973

THE REIGN OF HENRY IV

Bevan, Bryan, *Henry IV*, London, 1994

Castor, Helen, *The King, the Crown and the Duchy of Lancaster: Public Authority and Private Power 1399–1461*, London, 2000

Dodds, Gwilym, and Biggs, Douglas, *Henry IV: The Establishment of the Regime 1399–1446*, York, 2003

Kirby, J. L., *Henry IV of England*, London, 1970

Mortimer, Ian, *The Fears of Henry IV: The Life of England's Self-Made King*, London, 2007

Wylie, J. H., *History of England under Henry the Fourth*, 4 vols., London, 1884–98

THE REIGN OF HENRY V

Allmand, Christopher, *Henry V*, rev. edn., London, 1997
Earle, Peter, *The Life and Times of Henry V*, London, 1972
Harriss, G. L., *Cardinal Beaufort: A Study of Lancastrian Ascendancy and Decline*, Oxford, 1988
Harriss, G. L. (ed.), *Henry V: The Practice of Kingship*, Oxford, 1985
Hibbert, Christopher, *Agincourt*, London, 1964
Jacob, E. F., *Henry V and the Invasion of France*, London, 1947
Kingsford, C. L., *Henry V: The Typical Medieval Hero*, London, 1923
Labarge, M. W., *Henry V: The Cautious Conqueror*, London, 1975
Seward, Desmond, *Henry V as Warlord*, London, 1987
Wylie, J. H., and Waugh, W. T. (eds.), *The Reign of Henry V*, 3 vols., London, 1914–29

THE REIGN OF HENRY VI

Bagley, J. J., *Margaret of Anjou*, London, 1948
Christie, M. E., *Henry VI*, London, 1922
Dockray, Keith, *Henry VI, Margaret of Anjou and the Wars of the Roses*, Stroud, 2000
Griffiths, R. A., *The Reign of Henry VI: The Exercise of Royal Authority 1422–1461*, London, 1981
Johnson, P. A., *Duke Richard of York 1411–1460*, Oxford, 1988
Maurer, H. E., *Margaret of Anjou: Queenship and Power in Late Medieval England*, Woodbridge, 2003
Watts, J. L., *Henry VI and the Politics of Kingship*, Cambridge, 1996
Wolffe, B. P., *Henry VI*, London, 1981

THE REIGN OF EDWARD IV

Baldwin, David, *Elizabeth Woodville: Mother of the Princes in the Tower*, Stroud, 2002
Hicks, Michael, *Warwick the Kingmaker*, Stroud, 1998
Hicks, Michael, *Edward V: The Prince in the Tower*, London, 2003
Hicks, Michael, *Edward IV*, Stroud, 2004
Kendall, P. M., *Warwick the Kingmaker*, London, 1957
Macgibbon, David, *Elizabeth Woodville (1437–1492)*, London, 1938
Myers, A. R., *The Household of Edward IV*, Manchester, 1959
Okerlund, Arlene, *Elizabeth Wydeville: England's Slandered Queen*, London, 2005
Ross, C. D., *Edward IV*, rev. edn., London, 1997
Scofield, C. L., *The Life and Reign of Edward the Fourth*, 2 vols., London, 1923
Simons, E. N., *The Reign of Edward the Fourth*, London, 1966

THE REIGN OF RICHARD III

Gairdner, James, *History of the Life and Reign of Richard III*, Cambridge, 1898
Gillingham, John (ed.), *Richard III: A Medieval Kingship*, London, 1992
Hammond, P. W. (ed.), *Richard III: Loyalty, Lordship and Law*, London, 1986

Hammond, P. W., and Sutton, A. F., *Richard III: The Road to the Throne*, London, 1985

Hanham, A., *Richard III and his Earlier Historians*, London, 1975

Hicks, Michael, *False, Fleeting, Perjur'd Clarence: George, Duke of Clarence 1449–1478*, Gloucester, 1980

Hicks, Michael, *Richard III and his Rivals: Magnates and their Motives during the Wars of the Roses*, London, 1991

Hicks, Michael, *Richard III*, rev. edn., Stroud, 2003

Hicks, Michael, *Anne Neville: Queen to Richard III*, London, 2006

Horrox, R. E., *Richard III: A Study of Service*, Cambridge, 1989

Kendall, P. M., *Richard III*, London, 1955

Pollard, A. J., *Richard III and the Princes in the Tower*, Stroud, 1991

Pollard, A. J. (ed.), *The North of England in the Reign of Richard III*, Stroud, 1999

Ross, C. D., *Richard III*, rev. edn., London, 1999

Storey, R. L., *The End of the House of Lancaster*, London, 1966

Tudor-Craig, Pamela, *Richard III*, Woodbridge, 1977

Weir, Alison, *The Princes in the Tower*, London, 1993

THE TUDOR SUCCESSION

Bindoff, S. T., *Tudor England*, London, 1950

Elton, G. R., *England under the Tudors*, Oxford, 1955

Griffiths, R. A., and Thomas, R. S., *The Making of the Tudor Dynasty*, Stroud, 1999

Gunn, S. J., *Early Tudor Government 1485–1558*, Basingstoke, 1995

Mackie, J. D., *The Earlier Tudors 1485–1558*, London, 1952

Pendress, Colin, *Henry VII and the Wars of the Roses*, London, 2003

Rees, David, *The Son of Prophecy: Henry Tudor's Road to Bosworth*, London, 1985

WALES

Davies, R. R., *The Age of Conquest: Wales 1063–1415*, Oxford, 1987

Davies, R. R., *The Revolt of Owain Glyn Dwr*, Oxford, 1995

Evans, H. T., *Wales in the Wars of the Roses*, Cambridge, 1915

Griffiths, R. A., *King and Country: England and Wales in the Fifteenth Century*, London, 1991

Lloyd, J. E., *Owen Glendower*, Oxford, 1931

Pugh, T. B., *The Marcher Lordships of South Wales 1415–1536*, Cardiff, 1963

Walker, David, *Medieval Wales*, Cambridge, 1990

SCOTLAND

Brown, J. M. (ed.), *Scottish Society in the Fifteenth Century*, London, 1977

Dickinson, W. C., and Duncan, A. A. M., *Scotland from the Earliest Times to 1603*, Oxford, 1977

Donaldson, Gordon, *The Auld Alliance: The Franco-Scottish Connection*, Edinburgh, 1985

Duncan, A. A. M., *Scotland: The Making of the Kingdom*, Edinburgh, 1975

Frame, Robin, *The Political Development of the British Isles 1100–1400*, Oxford, 1994

Grant, Alexander, *Independence and Nationhood: Scotland 1306–1469*, London, 1984

Laidlaw, James (ed.), *The Auld Alliance: France and Scotland over 700 Years*, Edinburgh, 1999

Lesley, John, *History of Scotland from the Death of King James I in the Year 1436 to 1561*, Edinburgh, 1830

Macdougall, Norman, *James III: A Political Study*, Edinburgh, 1982

Neville, C. J., *Violence, Custom and Law*, Edinburgh, 1998

Nicolson, Ranald, *Scotland: The Later Middle Ages*, Edinburgh, 1974

Sadler, John, *Border Fury: England and Scotland at War 1296–1568*, London, 2005

Whyte, I. D., *Scotland before the Industrial Revolution: An Economic and Social History c.1050–c.1750*, London, 1995

IRELAND

Cosgrove, Art, *Late Medieval Ireland 1350–1541*, Dublin, 1981

Cosgrove, Art (ed.), *A New History of Ireland, Volume II: Medieval Ireland 1169–1534*, Oxford, 1993

Curtis, Edmund, *History of Medieval Ireland 1110–1513*, Dublin, 1923

Lydon, J. F., *The Lordship of Ireland in the Middle Ages*, Dublin, 1972

Otway-Ruthven, A. J., *A History of Medieval Ireland*, Dublin, 1968

FRANCE

Allmand, Christopher, *The Hundred Years War: England and France at War c.1300–1450*, Cambridge, 1988

Allmand, Christopher (ed.), *Society at War: The Experience of England and France during the Hundred Years War*, Edinburgh, 1973

Bates, David, and Curry, Anne (eds.), *England and Normandy in the Middle Ages*, London, 1994

Burne, A. H., *The Agincourt War: A Military History of the Latter Part of the Hundred Years War 1369–1453*, London, 1956

Cleugh, James, *Chant Royal, the Life of King Louis XI of France 1423–1483*, New York, 1970

Curry, Anne, *The Hundred Years War*, New York, 1993

De Vries, K. R., *Joan of Arc: A Military Leader*, Stroud, 1999

Fowler, K. A., *The Age of Plantagenet and Valois: The Struggle for Supremacy 1328–1498*, London, 1967

Fowler, K. A. (ed.), *The Hundred Years War*, London, 1971

Gies, Frances, *Joan of Arc: The Legend and the Reality*, New York, 1981

Kendall, P. M., *Louis XI*, London, 1971

Labarge, M. W., *Gascony: England's First Colony 1204–1453*, London, 1976

Macleod, E., *Charles of Orleans: Prince and Poet*, London, 1969

Newhall, R. A., *The English Conquest of Normandy 1416–1424: A Study in XVth Century Warfare*, London, 1924

Palmer, J. J. N., *England, France and Christendom, 1377–99*, London, 1972

Perroy, E., *The Hundred Years War (La Guerre de Cent Ans)*, trans. W. B. Wells, London, 1951

Seward, Desmond, *The Hundred Years War: The English in France 1337–1453*, London, 1978

Sumption, Jonathan, *The Hundred Years War*, 2 vols.: *Trial by Battle*, London, 1990; *Trial by Fire*, London, 1999

Thompson, G. L., *Paris and its People under English Rule: The Anglo-Burgundian Occupation 1420–1436*, Oxford, 1991

Vale, M. G. A., *English Gascony 1399–1453: A Study of War, Government and Politics during the Later Stages of the Hundred Years War*, Oxford, 1970

Vale, M. G. A., *Charles VII*, Oxford, 1974

Vaughan, Richard, *Philip the Bold*, London, 1962

Vaughan, Richard, *John the Fearless*, London, 1966

Vaughan, Richard, *Philip the Good*, London, 1970

Vaughan, Richard, *Charles the Bold*, London, 1973

SHAKESPEARE AND THE WARS OF THE ROSES

Bates, Jonathan, and Rasmussen, Eric, *The RSC Shakespeare: The Complete Works*, London, 2007

Dockray, Keith, *William Shakespeare, the Wars of the Roses and the Historians*, Stroud, 2002

Horsley, Richard (ed.), *Shakespeare's Holinshed: An Edition of Holinshed's Chronicles*, New York, 1968

Kelly, H. A., *Divine Providence in the England of Shakespeare's History Plays*, Harvard, 1970

Norwich, John Julius, *Shakespeare's Kings*, London, 1999

Tillyard, E. M. W., *Shakespeare's History Plays*, London, 1944

ART AND LITERATURE

Bennett, H. S., *Chaucer and the Fifteenth Century*, Oxford, 1947

Brown, R. Allen, Colvin, H. M., and Taylor, A. J., *The History of the King's Works: The Middle Ages*, 2 vols., London, 1963

Chaucer, Geoffrey, *Works*, ed. F. N. Robinson, London, 1957

Green, R. F., *Poets and Princepleasers: Literature and the English Court in the Late Middle Ages*, Toronto, 1980

Harrison, F. L., *Music in Medieval Britain*, London, 1958

Kingsford, C. L., *English Historical Literature in the Fifteenth Century*, Oxford, 1913

Macaulay, G. C., *John Gower's English Works*, 4 vols., Early English Text Society Extra Series 81, London, 1900

Malory, Sir Thomas, *Works*, ed. Eugene Vinaver, Oxford, 1954

Quiller-Couch, Arthur (ed.), *The Oxford Book of Ballads*, London, 1910

Robbins, R. H., *Secular Lyrics of the XIVth and XVth Centuries*, rev. edn., Oxford, 1961

Scattergood, V. T., *Politics and Poetry in the Fifteenth Century*, London, 1971

Sisam, Kenneth, *Fourteenth Century Verse and Prose*, rev. edn., Oxford, 1962

Skeat, W. W. (ed.), *The Kingis Quair*, rev. edn., Scottish Text Society, 2nd series, Edinburgh, 1911

Index